AQA Physics A

Exclusively endorsed by AQA

AS

Jim Breithaupt

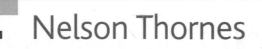 Nelson Thornes

Published in 2008 by:
Nelson Thornes Ltd
Delta Place
27 Bath Road
CHELTENHAM
GL53 7TH
United Kingdom

09 10 11 12 / 10 9 8 7 6

A catalogue record for this book is available from the British Library

ISBN 978 0 7487 8282 6

Cover photograph by Image Source RF (NT)

Illustrations include artwork drawn by GreenGate Publishing, Kent

Page make-up by GreenGate Publishing, Kent

Printed and bound in China by 1010 Printing International Ltd.

Contents

Contents

AQA introduction

Nelson Thornes has worked in partnership with AQA to ensure this book and the accompanying online resources offer you the best support for your A level course.

All resources have been approved by senior AQA examiners so you can feel assured that they closely match the specification for this subject and provide you with everything you need to prepare successfully for your exams.

These print and online resources together **unlock blended learning**; this means that the links between the activities in the book and the activities online blend together to maximise your understanding of a topic and help you achieve your potential.

These online resources are available on kerboodle! which can be accessed via the internet at http://www.kerboodle.com/live, anytime, anywhere. If your school or college subscribes to this service you will be provided with your own personal login details. Once logged in, access your course and locate the required activity.

For more information and help visit http://www.kerboodle.com

Icons in this book indicate where there is material online related to that topic. The following icons are used:

Learning activity

These resources include a variety of interactive and non-interactive activities to support your learning:

- Animations ■ Simulations ■ Maths skills
- Key diagrams ■ Glossary

Progress tracking

These resources include a variety of tests that you can use to check your knowledge on particular topics (Test yourself) and a range of resources that enable you to analyse and understand examination questions (On your marks...). You will also find the answers to examination-style questions online.

Research support

These resources include WebQuests, in which you are assigned a task and provided with a range of web links to use as source material for research.

These are designed as Extension resources to stretch you and broaden your learning, in order for you to attain the highest possible marks in your exams.

Web links

Our online resources feature a list of recommended weblinks, split by chapter. This will give you a head start, helping you to navigate to the best websites that will aid your learning and understanding of the topics in your course.

How science works

These resources are a mixture of interactive and non-interactive activities to help you learn the skills required for success in this new area of the specification.

Practical

This icon signals where there is a relevant practical activity to be undertaken, and support is provided online.

How to use this book

This book covers the specification for your course and is arranged in a sequence approved by AQA.

The book content is divided into three units. Unit 1 (Particles, quantum phenomena and electricity) and Unit 2 (Mechanics, materials and waves) match the two theory units of the AQA Physics A AS specification. Unit 3 includes information and advice about practical assessment and is followed by Chapter 16 which provides advice on essential maths skills. Units are then further divided into chapters, and then topics, making the content clear and easy to use.

Unit openers for the theory units give you a summary of the content you will be covering, and a recap of ideas from GCSE that you will need.

The features in this book include:

Learning objectives

At the beginning of each section you will find a list of learning objectives that contain targets linked to the requirements of the specification. The relevant specification reference is also provided.

Key terms

Terms that you will need to be able to define and understand are highlighted in bold blue type within the text, e.g. **antimatter**. You can look up these terms in the Glossary (page 247).

Hint

Hints to aid your understanding of the content.

How science works

'How science works' is a key part of the new A Level Physics specifications. As with the specification, 'How science works' is integrated throughout the content of the book. This feature highlights 'How science works' as it occurs within topics, so that it is always relevant to what you are studying. You will not be examined on the exact information provided in this book with relation to 'How science works'. The ideas provided in these features are intended to teach you the skills you will need to tackle this part of the course, and give you experience when dealing with applying your knowledge to different contexts. See the 'How science works' spread on page viii for more detail.

Summary questions

Short questions that test your understanding of the subject and allow you to apply the knowledge and skills you have acquired to different scenarios. Answers are supplied at the back of the book (page 251).

AQA Examiner's tip

Hints from AQA examiners to help you with your studies and to prepare you for your exam.

AQA Examination-style questions

Questions in the style that you can expect in your exam, including the new 'How science works' strand. These occur at the end of each chapter to give practice in examination-style questions for a particular topic. They also occur at the end of each unit; the questions here may cover any of the content of the unit.

When you answer the examination-style questions in this book, remember that quality of written communication (QWC) will be assessed in any question or part-question in the papers for Units 1 and 2 at AS (Units 4 and 5 at A2) where extended descriptive anwers are required. So make sure your answers to such questions are of good quality in terms of QWC as well as in terms of physics.

The answers to these questions are supplied online.

AQA examination questions are reproduced by permission of the Assessment and Qualifications Alliance.

Nelson Thornes is responsible for the solution(s) given and they may not constitute the only possible solution(s).

Web links in the book

As Nelson Thornes is not responsible for third party content online, there may be some changes to this material that are beyond our control. In order for us to ensure that the links referred to in the book are as up-to-date and stable as possible, the websites provided are usually homepages with supporting instructions on how to reach the relevant pages if necessary.

Please let us know at **kerboodle@nelsonthornes.com** if you find a link that doesn't work and we will do our best to correct this at reprint, or to list an alternative site.

Studying AS Physics

Studying AS Physics

This book is written for AS Physics students who are following AQA Physics (Specification A). It provides the entire content of all three Units in the AS course including information and advice about practical assessment. In addition, essential maths skills are provided. Guidance on how to bridge the gap between Physics at GCSE and at AS Level is given below.

About AS Physics

Welcome to Physics at AS level, the subject that helps us to understand nature from the smallest possible scale deep inside the atom to the largest conceivable distance, stretching across the entire Universe. Physics is about making predictions, testing them through observations and measurements and devising theories and laws to make more predictions. On your course, you will cover the key ideas of the subject and you will learn about topics such as particle physics, quantum physics, mechanics, materials, electricity and waves. You will learn the skills of making observations and measurements, and how to use your mathematical skills to make sense of experiments. You will also learn how to communicate your knowledge and understanding of the subject effectively. You will discover that physics is a very creative subject that calls for imagination and inventiveness. Don't be afraid to ask your teacher when something doesn't seem clear. Einstein developed a reputation for asking awkward questions and it made him into the most famous physicist ever! Even a century after he discovered the famous equation $E = mc^2$, we still don't have a clear understanding of how this equation works.

You are about to set off on a course that will further develop your knowledge, understanding and skills of the subject. At this stage, your GCSE course will have provided you with solid foundations to build on as you progress through the course. To help you make a smooth transition from GCSE to AS Physics, the key mathematical and practical skills you need to get started on your course are summarised in the online resources. Further support on practical skills, their assessment, and mathematical methods and skills is given in Chapters 14 to 16. There are also resources online that will support and develop your skills further in these areas. This book is written for the AS Physics course for AQA Specification A. It covers every topic needed for the specification, which comprises three units. The main chapters of the book, Chapters 1–13, are written in sequence to follow the content of Units 1 and 2. These are the units that are examined through written examinations offered in January or June. Practical skills are assessed internally in Unit 3 and you will be given plenty of opportunities to develop these skills as you progress through the topics in Units 1 and 2. The practical skills chapters (Chapters 14–15) provide advice on all aspects of Unit 3 including the Investigative Skills Assessment (ISA) and the Practical Skills Assessment (PSA). At the end of the book, there is a reference section consisting of useful data, a glossary, answers to numerical questions, and a comprehensive index. In addition, a full list of the formula you will be provided with in your AS examination papers is given at the end of the book. Practical experiments and animations are provided as part of the online resources.

AS course structure (% weighting of each unit shown in brackets):

Unit 1 Particles, quantum phenomena and electricity (40%) Chapters 1–6

Unit 2 Mechanics, materials and waves (40%) Chapters 7–13

Unit 3 Investigative and practical skills in AS Physics (20%) Chapters 14–15

This book is written to help you pass the AS examination so make sure you use it fully, particularly the final 'skills' chapters and the final reference section. It is also written to provide you with a firm foundation for your A2 course using the companion book *A2 Physics A for AQA*. Using this AS book will help you to pass your AS exam then to move on successfully to A2 Physics. More importantly, I hope it will give you a lasting interest in physics and on-going enthusiasm for this exciting subject!

How science works

You will already have gained some skills through the 'How science works' component of your GCSE course. As you progress through your AS Physics course, you will develop your scientific skills further and learn about important new ideas and applications through the 'How science works' component of your A level course. These skills are a key part of how every scientist works. Scientists use them to probe and test new theories and applications in whatever field of work they are working in. Now you will develop them further and gain new skills as you progress through the course.

'How science works' at A Level (and at GCSE) has several different strands (summarised in Table 1) and these are brought out in your course as appropriate in different topics. These strands include practical and investigative skills in science. They also consider the implications of scientific work in terms of how science is used not just by scientists and engineers but also by society at large. Science is often in the headlines, not only as a result of 'good news' such as major new discoveries but also through issues that concern us all, for example 'climate change' and 'energy resources'.

Most of the strands, such as those relating to practical work and the ability to communicate scientific ideas have always been part of science courses and contributed to the total course mark. Science courses have always included the aspects of 'How science works' that deal with major scientific discoveries too, for example the discovery of the atomic nucleus by Ernest Rutherford.

The strands relating to the implications of science are new at A level. They are important because what scientists do affects us all, and ethical issues are often associated with their work. For example:

■ Should children be banned from using mobile phones because of concerns about the effects of mobile phone radiation?

■ Should scientists working on the use of radiation to treat cancer use patients to test the effectiveness of new treatments?

These strands are part of all GCSE science courses and now they are in all A level science courses and can be examined. So you need to be able to discuss in depth a scientific issue by considering the benefits and the risks or the advantages and disadvantages. You will develop the necessary skills for these strands as you progress through your course and meet topics that touch on issues that show how and why science affects us all.

'How science works' is developed in this book through relevant features in the main content of the book and are highlighted accordingly. All the 'How science works' strands of AQA's A Level science specifications are the same. The 'How science works' features in this book will help you to develop the relevant 'How science works' skills necessary for examination purposes but more importantly these features should give you a thorough grasp of how scientists work and what they do, as well as a deeper awareness of how science is used to improve the quality life for everyone.

Table 1 *How science works specification summary*

Strands	Skills
A Theories, models and ideas are used to develop and modify scientific explanations.	Scientists make progress when validated evidence is found that supports a new theory or model.
B Predictions from a hypothesis (i.e. untested idea) or a theory need to be tested by experiment. If a reliable experiment does not support a hypothesis or theory, the hypothesis or theory must be changed.	Scientists use their knowledge and understanding in forming a hypothesis and when questioning the explanations of themselves or of other scientists.
C Appropriate methodology, including ICT, is used to make observations and measurements. Experiments are the key links between the 'real world' and the abstract ideas of science.	When scientists plan and carry out investigations, they need to: • identify the dependent and independent variables in the investigation and the control variables, • select appropriate apparatus and methods, including ICT, • choose measuring instruments according to their sensitivity and precision and carry out reliable measurements.

continued

Table 1 (*continued*)

Strands	Skills
D The range of experimental skills needed to carry out scientific investigations include manual and data skills (tabulation, graphical skills, etc.).	Scientists have to follow appropriate experimental procedures in a sensible order, use appropriate apparatus and methods to make accurate and reliable measurements, identify and minimise significant sources of experimental error and identify and take account of risks in carrying out practical work.
E Data must be analysed and interpreted to provide evidence, recognising correlations and causal relationships. When experimental data confirm predictions from a theoretical model, scientists become more confident in the theory.	Scientists look for patterns and trends in data as a first step in providing explanations of phenomena. They need to know how to: • process measurement data, • use equations and carry out appropriate calculations, • plot and use appropriate graphs to establish or verify relationships between variables, • relate the gradient and the intercepts of straight line graphs to appropriate linear equations.
F The methodology used, evidence and data must be evaluated and conflicting evidence resolved. The validity of new evidence is a stimulus for further scientific investigation, which involves refinements of experimental technique or development of new hypotheses.	Scientists need to be able to distinguish between systematic and random errors, make reasonable estimates of the errors in all measurements, use data, graphs and other evidence from experiments to draw conclusions and to use the most significant error estimates to assess the reliability of conclusions drawn.
G The tentative nature of scientific knowledge needs to be considered. Scientific knowledge changes when new experimental evidence provides a better explanation of scientific observations.	Scientists need to know that if evidence that is reliable and reproducible does not support a theory, the theory must be modified or replaced with a different theory.
H Research findings need to be communicated to the scientific community to see if it can be replicated, thus either confirming new explanations or refuting them.	Scientists need to provide explanations using correct scientific terms, and support arguments with equations, diagrams and clear sketch graphs when appropriate.
I The applications and implications of science and their associated benefits and risks need to be considered.	Scientists apply their scientific knowledge to develop technologies that improve our lives. We all need to appreciate that the technologies themselves may pose significant risks that have to be balanced against the benefits.
J The ethical issues associated with scientific developments need to be considered.	Scientists have a duty to consider ethical issues associated with their findings. Scientists provide solutions to problems but the solutions often require society to form judgements as to whether the solution is acceptable in view of moral issues that result. Issues such as the effects on the planet, and the economic and physical well being of the living things on it should be considered.
K The scientific community itself validates new knowledge and ensures integrity.	Scientists need a common set of values and responsibilities. They should know that scientists undertake a peer-review of the work of others. They should know that scientists work with a common aim to progress scientific knowledge and understanding in a valid way and that accurate reporting of findings takes precedence over recognition of success of an individual.
L Decision makers are influenced in many ways, including their prior beliefs, their vested interests, special interest groups, public opinion and the media, as well as by expert scientific evidence.	Scientific evidence should be considered as a whole. Media and pressure groups often select parts of scientific evidence that supports a particular viewpoint and that this can influence public opinion which in turn may influences decision makers. Consequently, decision makers may make socially and politically acceptable decisions based on incomplete evidence.

Particles, quantum phenomena and electricity

■ Introduction

This unit consists of two contrasting topic areas: particle physics and electricity. Particle physics is at the frontiers of physics, as it is about the fundamental properties of matter, radiation and energy. Electricity is a well-established topic area and has many important applications. In addition to learning about these two topic areas in depth, you should gain awareness of the on-going development of new ideas in physics and of the application of in-depth knowledge to well-established topics.

Particle physics

Experiments in particle physics have led to the conclusions that protons and neutrons consist of smaller particles called **quarks**. Electrons are fundamental particles that belong to a small family of particles called **leptons**. Thus quarks and leptons are the building blocks of matter. Experiments on the effect of light on metals led to the conclusion that light consists of wave packets of electromagnetic radiation called **photons**. The photon is the quantum or 'least amount' of electromagnetic radiation.

The theory that energy is in 'lumps' (i.e. quanta) rather than being 'evenly spread' is part of the **quantum theory**, which takes us into **energy levels** in the atom, **light spectra** and **wave particle duality**.

In this unit, we will be looking at all these topics and the experimental evidence that led to the ideas and theories in them. We will also be learning about matter and **antimatter**, and their comparative properties. This includes **annihilation** where matter and antimatter interact and turn into radiation energy, and **pair production** in which the opposite happens. We will be studying how physicists detected uncharged leptons called **neutrinos**. These are so elusive that they pass through us in their billions every second. We will consider some of the many questions that have arisen as a result of the on-going research work by physicists throughout the world. For example, exactly what is the mechanism that turns mass into radiation energy in annihilation?

Electricity

We need our electricity supplies to maintain our standard of living. About 200 years ago scientists, such as Michael Faraday, discovered how to generate and use electricity. They established the principles and laws of electricity, which engineers use to design the circuits in every electrical device. We will study these principles in this unit. We will also look at how electricity is used and measured, as well as considering important new applications such as **superconductivity**. Michael Faraday would have been truly astonished at just how important electricity has become.

What you already know:

From your GCSE studies on radioactivity, you should know that:

- Every atom has a positively-charged nucleus at its centre that is surrounded by negatively charged particles called electrons.

- The nucleus of the atom is composed of protons and neutrons which have approximately equal mass.

- Protons and electrons have fixed equal and opposite amounts of charge, and neutrons are uncharged.

- An uncharged atom has equal numbers of electrons and protons.

- Radioactive substances emit radiation because the nuclei of the atoms are unstable.

- The radiation from radioactive substances ionises substances it passes through.

- There are three types of radiation from radioactive substances

  - alpha radiation which is stopped by paper and is strongly ionising

  - beta radiation which is stopped by 2–3 mm thickness of metal and is less ionising than alpha radiation

  - gamma radiation which is very penetrating and is weakly ionising.

- The half-life of a radioactive substance is the time it takes for the number of atoms of the substance to decrease by half.

From your GCSE studies on electricity, you should know that:

- An electric current is a flow of charge round a circuit due to the movement of electrons.

- Electric current is measured in amperes (A) using an ammeter.

- Electric potential difference or voltage is measured in volts (V) using a voltmeter.

- For components in series, the current is the same in each component and the sum of the voltages across the components is equal to the total voltage.

- For components in parallel, the voltage is the same across each component and the sum of the currents through the components is equal to the total current.

- For resistors in series, the total resistance is equal to the sum of the individual resistances.

- For resistors in parallel, the current is greatest through the resistor with least resistance.

1.1   Inside the atom

Learning objectives:

- What is inside an atom?

- What are isotopes?

- How do we represent different atoms?

Specification reference: 3.1.1

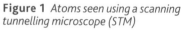

AQA   Examiner's tip

Don't mix up 'n' words – nucleus, neutron, nucleon, nuclide!

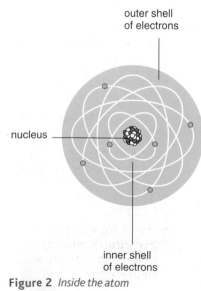

Figure 1 *Atoms seen using a scanning tunnelling microscope (STM)*

outer shell of electrons

nucleus

inner shell of electrons

Figure 2 *Inside the atom*

The structure of the atom

Atoms are so small (less than a millionth of a millimetre in diameter) that we need to use an electron microscope to see images of them. Although we cannot see inside them, we know, from Rutherford's alpha-scattering investigations, that every atom contains

- a positively charged nucleus composed of protons and neutrons
- electrons that surround the nucleus.

We use the word **nucleon** for a proton or a neutron in the nucleus.

Each electron has a negative charge. Because the nucleus is positively charged, the electrons are held in the atom by the electrostatic force of attraction between them and the nucleus. Rutherford's investigations showed that the nucleus contains most of the mass of the atom and its diameter is of the order of 0.000 01 times the diameter of a typical atom.

Table 1 shows the charge and the mass of the proton, the neutron and the electron in SI units (coulombs for charge and kilograms for mass) and relative to the charge and mass of the proton. Notice that:

1   The electron has a much smaller mass than the proton or the neutron.
2   The proton and the neutron have almost equal mass.
3   The electron has equal and opposite charge to the proton. The neutron is uncharged.

Table 1 *Inside the atom*

	charge		mass	
	/ C	/ charge of the proton	/ kg	/ mass of proton
proton	$+1.60 \times 10^{-19}$	1	1.67×10^{-27}	1
neutron	0	0	1.67×10^{-27}	1
electron	-1.60×10^{-19}	-1	9.11×10^{-31}	0.0005

Isotopes

Every atom of a given element has the same number of protons as any other atom of the same element. The proton number is usually called the **atomic number** (symbol Z) of the element. For example:

- $Z = 6$ for carbon because every carbon atom has six protons in its nucleus.
- $Z = 92$ for uranium because every uranium atom has 92 protons in its nucleus.

The atoms of an element can have different numbers of neutrons. Atoms of the same element with different numbers of neutrons are called **isotopes**.

For example, the most abundant isotope of natural uranium contains 146 neutrons and the next most abundant contains 143 neutrons.

Isotopes are atoms with the same number of protons and different numbers of neutrons.

The total number of protons and neutrons in an atom is called the **nucleon number** (symbol A) or sometimes the **mass number** of the atom. This is because it is almost numerically equal to the mass of the atom in relative units (where the mass of a proton or neutron is approximately 1). A **nucleon** is a neutron or a proton in the nucleus.

We label the isotopes of an element according to their atomic number Z, their mass number A and the chemical symbol of the element. Figure 3 shows how we do this. Notice that:

- Z is at the bottom left of the element symbol and gives the number of protons in the nucleus.
- A is at the top left of the element symbol and gives the number of protons and neutrons in the nucleus.
- The number of neutrons in the nucleus = $A - Z$.

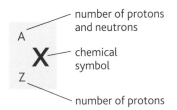

Example: the symbol for the uranium isotope with 92 protons and 146 neutrons is

$$^{238}_{92}\text{U} \quad \text{(or sometimes U-238)}$$

Figure 3 *Isotope notation*

Each type of nucleus is called a **nuclide** and is labelled using the isotope notation. For example, a nuclide of the carbon isotope $^{12}_{6}\text{C}$ has two fewer neutrons and two fewer protons than a nuclide of the oxygen isotope $^{16}_{8}\text{O}$.

■ Specific charge

The **specific charge** of a charged particle is defined as its charge divided by its mass. We can calculate the specific charge of a charged particle if we know the charge and the mass of the particle. For example:

A nucleus of $^{1}_{1}\text{H}$ has a charge of $1.60 \times 10^{-19}\,\text{C}$ and a mass of $1.67 \times 10^{-27}\,\text{kg}$. Its specific charge is therefore $9.58 \times 10^{7}\,\text{C}\,\text{kg}^{-1}$.

The electron has a charge of $-1.60 \times 10^{-19}\,\text{C}$ and a mass of $9.11 \times 10^{-31}\,\text{kg}$. Its specific charge is therefore $1.76 \times 10^{11}\,\text{C}\,\text{kg}^{-1}$. Note that the electron has the largest specific charge of any particle.

An ion of the magnesium isotope $^{24}_{12}\text{Mg}$ has a charge of $+3.2 \times 10^{-19}\,\text{C}$ and a mass of $3.98 \times 10^{-26}\,\text{kg}$. Its specific charge is therefore $8.04 \times 10^{6}\,\text{C}\,\text{kg}^{-1}$.

Summary questions

You will need to use data from the data sheet on pages 245–246 to answer some of the questions below.

1 a State the number of protons and the number of neutrons in a nucleus of

   i $^{12}_{6}\text{C}$ ii $^{16}_{8}\text{O}$

   iii $^{235}_{92}\text{U}$ iv $^{24}_{11}\text{Na}$

   v $^{63}_{29}\text{Cu}$

  b Which of the above nuclei has

   i the smallest specific charge?

   ii the largest specific charge?

2 Name the part of an atom which

  a has zero charge,

  b has the largest specific charge,

  c when removed, leaves a different isotope of the element.

3 A $^{63}_{29}\text{Cu}$ atom loses two electrons. For the ion formed,

  a calculate its charge in C,

  b state the number of nucleons it contains,

  c calculate its specific charge in $\text{C}\,\text{kg}^{-1}$.

4 a Calculate the mass of an ion that has a specific charge of $1.20 \times 10^{7}\,\text{C}\,\text{kg}^{-1}$ and a negative charge of $3.2 \times 10^{-19}\,\text{C}$.

  b The ion has 8 protons in its nucleus. How many neutrons and how many electrons does it have?

1.2   Stable and unstable nuclei

Learning objectives:

- What keeps the protons and neutrons in a nucleus together?

- Why are some nuclei stable and others unstable?

- What happens when an unstable nucleus emits an alpha particle or a beta minus particle?

Specification reference: 3.1.1

How science works

Measuring background radiation

Use a Geiger tube and a counter to detect and measure background radioactivity.

The strong nuclear force

A stable isotope has nuclei that do not disintegrate, so there must be a force holding them together. We call this force the **strong nuclear force** because it overcomes the electrostatic force of repulsion between the protons in the nucleus and (except in unstable nuclei) keeps the protons and neutrons together.

Some further important points about the strong nuclear force are:

- Its range is no more than about 3–4 femtometres (fm), where $1\,fm = 10^{-15}\,m = 0.000\,000\,000\,000\,001\,m$. This range is about the same as the diameter of a small nucleus. In comparison, the electrostatic force between two charged particles has an infinite range (although it decreases as the range increases).

- It has the same effect between two protons as it does between two neutrons or a proton and a neutron.

- It is an attractive force from 3–4 fm down to about 0.5 fm. At separations smaller than this, it is a repulsive force that acts to prevent neutrons and protons being pushed into each other.

Figure 1 shows how the strong nuclear force varies with separation between two protons or neutrons. Notice that the equilibrium separation is where the force curve crosses the x-axis.

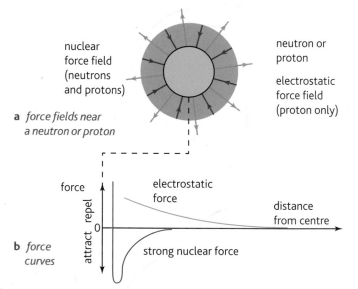

Figure 1 *The strong nuclear force*

Radioactive decay

Naturally-occurring radioactive isotopes release three types of radiation.

1   **Alpha radiation** consists of alpha particles which each comprise two protons and two neutrons. The symbol for an alpha particle is $^{4}_{2}\alpha$ because its proton number is 2 and its mass number is 4.

Figure 2 shows what happens to an unstable nucleus of an element X when it emits an alpha particle. Its nucleon number A decreases by 4

AQA Examiner's tip

Remember what the numbers stand for in the decay equations on the next page.

Figure 2 *Alpha particle emission (not to scale)*

Figure 3 *Beta particle emission (not to scale)*

and its atomic number Z decreases by 2. As a result of the change, the product nucleus belongs to a different element Y.

We can represent this change by means of the equation below:

$$^A_Z X \longrightarrow \,^{A-4}_{Z-2} Y + \,^4_2 \alpha$$

2 **Beta radiation** consists of fast-moving electrons. The symbol for an electron as a beta particle is $^0_{-1}\beta$ (or β^-) because its charge is equal and opposite to that of the proton and its mass is much smaller than the proton's mass.

Figure 3 shows what happens to an unstable nucleus of an element X when it emits a β^- particle. This happens as a result of a neutron in the nucleus changing into a proton. The beta particle is created when the change happens and is emitted instantly. In addition, an antiparticle with no charge, called an **antineutrino** (symbol $\bar{\nu}$), is emitted. You will learn more about antiparticles in Topic 1.4. Because a neutron changes into a proton in the nucleus, the atomic number increases by 1 but the nucleon number stays the same. As a result of the change, the product nucleus belongs to a different element Y. This type of change happens to nuclei that have too many neutrons.

We can represent this change by means of the equation below:

$$^A_Z X \longrightarrow \,^A_{Z+1} Y + \,^0_{-1}\beta + \bar{\nu}$$

3 **Gamma radiation** (symbol γ) is electromagnetic radiation emitted by an unstable nucleus. It can pass through thick metal plates. It has no mass and no charge. It is emitted by a nucleus with too much energy, following an alpha or beta emission.

How science works

A very elusive particle!

When the energy spectrum of beta particles was first measured, it was found that beta particles were released with kinetic energies up to a maximum that depended on the isotope. The scientists at the time were puzzled why the energy of the beta particles varied up to a maximum, when each unstable nucleus lost a certain amount of energy in the process. Either energy was not conserved in the change or some of it was carried away by mystery particles, which they called **neutrinos** and **antineutrinos**. This hypothesis was unproven for over 20 years until antineutrinos were detected. Antineutrinos were detected as a result of their interaction with cadmium nuclei in a large tank of water. This was installed next to a nuclear reactor as a controllable source of these very elusive particles. Now we know that billions of these elusive particles from the Sun sweep through our bodies every second without interacting!

Summary questions

1 Which force, the strong nuclear force or the electrostatic force,

 a does not affect a neutron?

 b has a limited range?

 c holds the nucleons in a nucleus?

 d tends to make a nucleus unstable?

2 Complete the following radioactive decay equations:

 a $^{229}_{90}$Th $\longrightarrow$ Ra + α

 b $^{65}_{28}$Ni $\longrightarrow$ Cu + β + $\bar{\nu}$

3 A nucleus of the radioactive isotope of bismuth $^{213}_{83}$Bi emits a beta particle then an alpha particle then another beta particle before it becomes stable.

 a Show that the stable nucleus that is formed is a bismuth isotope.

 b i Determine the nucleon number of this stable isotope.

 ii How many protons and how many neutrons are in the nucleus immediately after it emits the alpha particle?

4 The neutrino hypothesis was put forward to explain beta decay.

 a Explain what is meant by a hypothesis.

 b i State one property of the neutrino.

 ii Name two objects that produce neutrinos.

1.3 Photons

Learning objectives:

- What is a photon?

- What is the energy of a photon?

- How many photons does a light source emit every second?

Specification reference: 3.1.1

Electromagnetic waves

Light is just a small part of the spectrum of electromagnetic waves. Our eyes cannot detect the other parts. The world would appear very different to us if they could. For example, all objects emit infrared radiation. Infrared cameras enable objects to be observed in darkness.

In a vacuum, all electromagnetic waves travel at the speed of light, c, which is $3.0 \times 10^8 \, \text{m s}^{-1}$. As you know from GCSE, the wavelength λ of electromagnetic radiation of frequency f in a vacuum is given by the equation

$$\lambda = \frac{c}{f}$$

Note that we often express light wavelengths in nanometres (nm), where $1 \, \text{nm} = 0.000000001 \, \text{m} = 10^{-9} \, \text{m}$.

The main parts of the electromagnetic spectrum are listed in Table 1.

Table 1 *The main parts of the electromagnetic spectrum*

type	radio	microwave	infrared	visible	ultraviolet	X-rays	gamma rays
wavelength range	> 0.1 m	0.1 m to 1 mm	1 mm to 700 nm	700 nm to 400 nm	400 nm to 1 nm	< 1 nm	< 1 nm

As shown in Figure 1, an electromagnetic wave consists of an electric wave and a magnetic wave which travel together and vibrate:

- at right angles to each other and to the direction in which they are travelling,

- in phase with each other. As you can see the two waves reach a peak together so they are in step. When waves do this we say they are 'in phase'.

Photons

Electromagnetic waves are emitted by a charged particle when it loses energy. This can happen when:

- a fast-moving electron is stopped (for example, in an X-ray tube) or slows down or changes direction,

- an electron in a shell of an atom moves to a different shell of lower energy.

Electromagnetic waves are emitted as short 'bursts' of waves, each burst leaving the source in a different direction. Each burst is a packet of electromagnetic waves and is referred to as a **photon**. The photon theory was established by Einstein in 1905, when he used his ideas to explain **photoelectricity**. This is the emission of electrons from a metal surface when light is directed at the surface. We will consider photoelectricity and the photon theory in more detail in Topic 3.1.

Figure 1 *Electromagnetic waves*

Einstein imagined photons to be like 'flying needles' and he assumed that the energy E of a photon depends on its frequency f in accordance with the equation:

$$\text{photon energy } E = hf$$

where h is a constant referred to as the Planck constant. The value of h is $6.63 \times 10^{-34}\,\text{J s}$.

Figure 2 *Emitting photons*

Worked example:

Calculate the frequency and the energy of a photon of wavelength 590 nm.

$h = 6.63 \times 10^{-34}\,\text{J s}, c = 3.00 \times 10^8\,\text{m s}^{-1}$

Solution

To calculate the frequency, use $f = \dfrac{c}{\lambda} = \dfrac{3.00 \times 10^8}{590 \times 10^{-9}} = 5.08 \times 10^{14}\,\text{Hz}$

To calculate the energy of a photon of this wavelength, we use $E = hf$

$E = hf = 6.63 \times 10^{-34} \times 5.08 \times 10^{14} = 3.37 \times 10^{-19}\,\text{J}$

Laser power

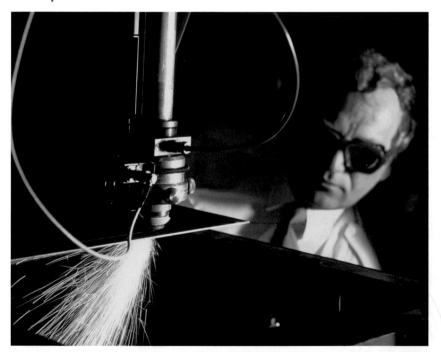

Figure 3 *A laser at work*

A laser beam consists of photons of the same frequency. The power of a laser beam is the energy per second transferred by the photons. For a beam consisting of photons of frequency f,

$$\text{the power of the beam } = nhf$$

where n is the number of photons in the beam passing a fixed point each second. This is because each photon has energy hf. Therefore, if n photons pass a fixed point each second, the energy per second (or power) is nhf.

Summary questions

$c = 3.00 \times 10^8\,\text{m s}^{-1}$
$h = 6.63 \times 10^{-34}\,\text{J s}$

1 a List the main parts of the electromagnetic spectrum in order of increasing wavelength.

 b Calculate the frequency of **i** light of wavelength 590 nm, **ii** radio waves of wavelength 200 m.

2 With the aid of a suitable diagram, explain what is meant by an electromagnetic wave.

3 Light from a certain light source has a wavelength of 430 nm. Calculate:

 a the frequency of light of this wavelength,

 b the energy of a photon of this wavelength.

4 a Calculate the frequency and energy of a photon of wavelength 635 nm.

 b A laser emits light of wavelength 635 nm in a beam of power 1.5 mW. Calculate the number of photons emitted by the laser each second.

1.4 Particles and antiparticles

Learning objectives:

■ What is antimatter?

■ What happens when a particle and antiparticle meet?

■ Are anti-atoms possible?

Specification reference: 3.1.1

How science works

Brain imaging

PET scanners are used in hospitals for brain imaging of, for example, stroke patients. The T stands for 'tomography' which is the name for the electronic and mechanical system used to perform the scan.

Figure 2 *Dirac and antiDirac!*

■ Antimatter

Fact is stranger than fiction with antimatter. When they meet, antimatter and matter particles (that is, the particles that make up everything in our universe) destroy each other and radiation is released. We make use of this effect in a PET hospital scanner. The P in PET stands for the **positron**, which is the antiparticle of the electron. When a PET scanner is used for a brain scan, a positron-emitting isotope is administered to the patient and some of it reaches the brain via the blood system. Each positron emitted travels no further than a few millimetres before it meets an electron and they **annihilate** each other. Two gamma photons, produced as a result, are sensed by detectors linked to computers. Gradually, an image is built up from the detector signals of where the positron-emitting nuclei are inside the brain.

Positron emission takes place when a proton changes into a neutron in an unstable nucleus with too many protons. The positron (symbol $^{0}_{+1}\beta$ or β^{+}) is the antiparticle of the electron, so it carries a positive charge. In addition, a neutrino (symbol ν), which is uncharged, is emitted.

$$^{A}_{Z}X \longrightarrow \, ^{A}_{Z-1}Y + \, ^{0}_{+1}\beta + \nu$$

Positron-emitting isotopes do not occur naturally. They are manufactured by placing a stable isotope, in liquid or solid form, in the path of a beam of protons. Some of the nuclei in the substance absorb extra protons and become unstable positron-emitters.

Antimatter was predicted in 1928 by the English physicist Paul Dirac, before the first antiparticle, the positron, was discovered. More than 20 years earlier, Einstein had shown that the mass of a particle increases, the faster it travels, and that his famous equation $E = mc^2$ related the energy supplied to the particle to its increase in mass. More significantly, Einstein said that the mass of a particle when it is stationary, its rest mass (m_0), corresponds to **rest energy** m_0c^2 locked up as mass. He showed that rest energy must be included in the conservation of energy. Dirac predicted the existence of antimatter particles (or **antiparticles**) that would unlock rest energy, whenever a particle and a corresponding antiparticle meet and annihilate each other.

Dirac's theory of antiparticles predicted that, for every type of particle, there is a corresponding antiparticle that:

■ annihilates the particle and itself if they meet, converting their total mass into photons,

■ has exactly the same rest mass as the particle,

■ has exactly opposite charge to the particle if the particle has a charge.

In addition to the annihilation process described above, Dirac predicted the opposite process of **pair production**. In this process, a photon with sufficient energy could suddenly change into a particle-antiparticle pair, which would then separate from each other. Figure 3 shows both of these processes.

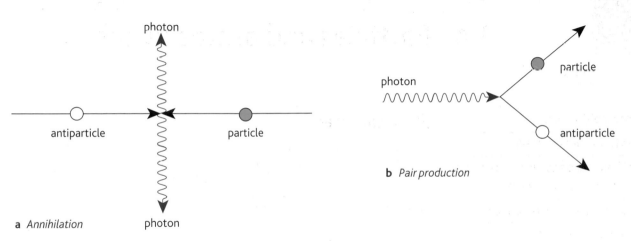

Figure 3 *Particles and antiparticles*

Particles, antiparticles and $E = mc^2$

The energy of a particle or antiparticle is often expressed in millions of electron volts (MeV), where **1 MeV = 1.60×10^{-13} J**. One electron volt is defined as the energy transferred when an electron is moved through a potential difference of 1 volt. Given the rest mass of a particle or antiparticle, its rest energy in MeV can be calculated using $E = mc^2$. But you won't need to do this type of calculation in this topic, as the rest energies of different particles are listed in the AQA data booklet and on p245 of this book.

Annihilation occurs when a particle and a corresponding antiparticle meet and their mass is converted into radiation energy. Two photons are produced in this process (as a single photon only would take away momentum which isn't allowed, as no outside forces act). Therefore, the minimum energy of each photon, hf_{min} is given by equating the energy of the two photons, $2\,hf_{min}$, to the rest energy of the positron and of the electron (i.e. $2hf_{min} = 2E_0$, where E_0 is the rest energy of the electron.)

Minimum energy of each photon produced, $hf_{min} = E_0$

In **pair production**, a photon creates a particle and a corresponding antiparticle, and vanishes in the process. For a particle and antiparticle, each of rest energy E_0, we can calculate the minimum energy and minimum frequency f_{min} that the photon must have to produce this particle–antiparticle pair. Remember, c is the speed of light in a vacuum ($3.0 \times 10^8\,\text{m s}^{-1}$).

Minimum energy of photon needed = $hf_{min} = 2E_0$

For example, the electron has a rest energy of 0.511 MeV. Therefore, for pair production of an electron and a positron from a photon:

The minimum energy of a photon = $2 \times 0.511\,\text{MeV} = 1.022\,\text{MeV}$
$$= 1.64 \times 10^{-13}\,\text{J}$$

A photon with less energy could not therefore create a positron and an electron.

The discovery of the positron

We can see the path of alpha and beta particles using a cloud chamber. This is a small transparent container containing air saturated with vapour and made very cold. The same conditions exist high in the atmosphere. Ionising particles leave a visible trail of liquid droplets when they pass through the air – just like a jet plane does when it passes high overhead on a clear day. In 1932, the American physicist Carl Anderson was using a cloud chamber and a camera to photograph trails produced by cosmic rays. He decided to see if the particles could pass through a lead plate in the chamber. With a magnetic field applied to the chamber, he knew the trail of a charged particle would bend in the field.

■ A positive particle would be deflected by the magnetic field in the opposite direction to a negative particle travelling in the same direction.

■ The slower it went, the more it would bend.

If a particle went through the plate, he thought it would be slowed down so its trail would bend more afterwards. Imagine his surprise when he discovered a beta particle that slowed down but bent in the opposite direction to all the other beta trails he had photographed. He had made a momentous discovery – a positron, the first antiparticle to be detected (Figure 4).

Figure 4 *The discovery of the positron*

Summary questions

1 **a** The rest energy of a proton is 1.501×10^{-10} J. Calculate its rest energy in MeV.

   b Show that a photon must have a minimum energy of 1876 MeV to create a proton–antiproton pair.

2 Explain why a photon of energy 2 MeV could produce an electron–positron pair but not a proton–antiproton pair.

3 The rest energy of an electron is 0.511 MeV.

   a State the minimum energy of each photon created when a positron and an electron annihilate each other.

   b A positron created in a cloud chamber in an experiment has 0.158 MeV of kinetic energy. It collides with an electron at rest, creating two photons of equal energies as a result of annihilation.

      i Calculate the total energy of the positron and the electron.

      ii Show that the energy of each photon is 0.590 MeV.

4 A positron can be produced by pair production or by positron emission from a proton-rich nucleus.

   a Describe the changes that take place in a proton-rich nucleus when it emits a positron.

   b State two ways in which pair production of a positron and an electron differs from positron emission.

Learning objectives:

■ What is an interaction?

■ What types of interaction are there?

■ What makes charged particles attract or repel each other?

■ What is an exchange particle?

Specification reference: 3.1.1

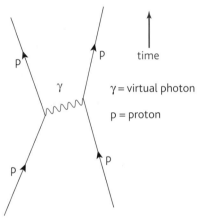

Figure 1 *The Feynman diagram for the electromagnetic force between two protons*

💡 The electromagnetic force

What is a force? We can measure forces using newtonmeters and force sensors. We know that when a single force acts on an object, it changes the momentum of the object. The **momentum** of an object is its mass multiplied by its velocity.

When two objects interact, they exert equal and opposite forces on each other. Momentum is transferred between the objects by these forces, if no other forces act on them. For example, if two protons approach each other, they repel each other and move away from each other. The American physicist, Richard Feynman, worked out in detail how this happens. He said the electromagnetic force between two charged objects is due to the exchange of **virtual photons**. He described them as virtual because we can't detect them directly. If we intercepted them, for example, by using a detector, we would stop the force acting. The interaction is represented by the diagram shown in Figure 1. This is known as a **Feynman diagram**. Note that the lines do not represent the paths of the particles. The virtual photon exchanged between the two protons is represented by a wave.

An interaction model

Imagine two people on skateboards facing each other and one of them throws a ball to the other. The thrower recoils when the ball leaves his or her hands; the other person recoils when he or she catches the ball. Figure 2 shows the idea. The ball transfers momentum from the thrower to the catcher so they repel each other. The exchange of a virtual photon between two like-charged particles has the same effect – except we can't detect the virtual photon. But the ball analogy won't work for two oppositely charged particles – it would need to be changed for a boomerang, so the thrower and the catcher attract each other!

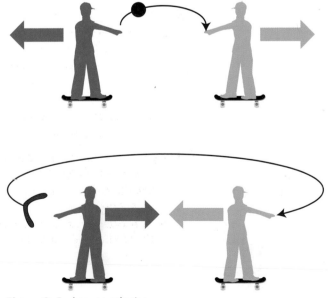

Figure 2 *Exchange analogies*

■ The weak nuclear force

The strong nuclear force holds the neutrons and protons in a nucleus together. But it doesn't cause a neutron to change into a proton in β⁻ decay, or a proton to change into a neutron in β⁺ decay. These changes can't be due to the electromagnetic force, as the neutron is uncharged. There must be a different force at work in the nucleus causing these changes. It must be weaker than the strong nuclear force, otherwise it would affect stable nuclei; hence we refer to it as the **weak nuclear force**.

In both β⁻ decay and β⁺ decay, a new particle and a new antiparticle are created in each type of decay – but they're not a corresponding particle-antiparticle pair, as one is an electron or a positron and the other is a neutrino or an antineutrino.

Neutrinos and antineutrinos hardly interact with other particles, but such interactions do sometimes happen. For example:

■ A neutrino can interact with a neutron and make it change into a proton. A β⁻ particle (an electron) is created and emitted as a result of the change.

■ An antineutrino can interact with a proton and make it change into a neutron. A β⁺ particle (a positron) is created and emitted as a result of the change.

These interactions are due to the exchange of particles referred to as **W bosons**. Unlike photons, these exchange particles:

■ have a non-zero rest mass,

■ have a very short range of no more than about 0.001 fm,

■ are positively charged (the W⁺ boson) or negatively charged (the W⁻ boson).

The Feynman diagram for each of these changes is shown in Figure 3. Notice that the total charge at the end is the same as at the start (that is, charge is conserved).

a *A neutron–neutrino interaction*

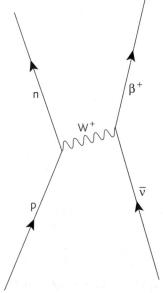

b *A proton–antineutrino interaction*

Figure 3 *The weak interaction*

🔋 Back to beta decay

So what role does a W boson play in beta decay? You can see from Figure 3 that the W boson in each case meets a neutrino or antineutrino, changing them into a β⁻ particle (an electron) or a β⁺ particle (a positron) respectively. But if no neutrino or antineutrino is present:

■ the W⁻ boson decays into a β⁻ particle and an antineutrino,
■ the W⁺ boson decays into a β⁺ particle and a neutrino.

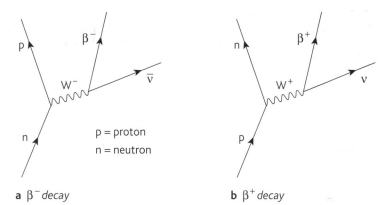

p = proton
n = neutron

a β⁻ *decay*   **b** β⁺ *decay*

💡 *Figure 4 W bosons in beta decay*

Figure 4 shows the Feynman diagram for each of these decay processes. Notice that charge is conserved in both processes.

■ Electron capture

Sometimes a proton in a proton-rich nucleus turns into a neutron as a result of interacting through the weak interaction with an 'inner-shell' electron from outside the nucleus. Figure 5 shows the Feynman diagram for this process. Notice that the W⁺ boson changes the electron into a neutrino.

The same change can happen when a proton and an electron collide at very high speed. In addition, for an electron with sufficient energy, the overall change could also occur as a W⁻ exchange from the electron to the proton.

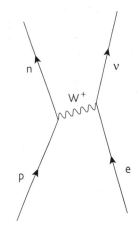

Figure 5 *Electron capture*

Summary questions

$c = 3.00 \times 10^8 \, \text{m s}^{-1}$

1 Sketch the Feynman diagram for the electromagnetic force between **a** two protons, **b** a proton and an electron, **c** two electrons.

2 Sketch the Feynman diagram for **a** β⁺ decay, **b** β⁻ decay.

3 **a** Sketch the Feynman diagram for the interaction between **i** a neutron and a neutrino, **ii** a proton and an antineutrino.

   b State the approximate range of the W boson and estimate its lifetime, given it cannot travel faster than the speed of light.

4 **a** State three differences between a W boson and a virtual photon.

   b In both Figure 4b) and Figure 5, a proton changes into a neutron. Describe how these two processes differ.

1 (a) Copy and complete the table below: *(3 marks)*

	particle or antiparticle	$\dfrac{\text{charge}}{\text{proton charge}}$
antiproton	antiparticle	
neutrino		
neutron		0
positron		

(b) The tracks of a positron and an electron created by pair production in a magnetic field curve in opposite directions as shown above.

    (i) Why do they curve in opposite directions?

    (ii) Both particles spiral inwards. What can you deduce from this observation about their kinetic energy?

    (iii) In **Figure 4** of Topic 1.4, the track is a typical beta track. Explain how Carl Anderson deduced from the photograph that the track was created by a positron rather than an electron travelling in the opposite direction. *(5 marks)*

2 (a) $^{229}_{90}\text{Th}$ is a neutral atom of thorium. How many protons, neutrons and electrons does it contain? *(2 marks)*

(b) $^{Y}_{X}\text{Th}$ is a neutral atom of a different isotope of thorium which contains Z electrons. Give possible values for X, Y and Z. *(3 marks)*

AQA, 2001

3 An atom of argon $^{37}_{18}\text{Ar}$ is ionised by the removal of two orbiting electrons.

(a) How many protons and neutrons are there in this ion? *(2 marks)*

(b) What is the charge, in C, of this ion? *(2 marks)*

(c) Which constituent particle of this ion has

    (i) a zero charge per unit mass ratio?

    (ii) the largest charge per unit mass ratio? *(2 marks)*

(d) Calculate the percentage of the total mass of this ion that is accounted for by the mass of its electrons. *(3 marks)*

AQA, 2002

4 (a) A stable atom contains 28 nucleons.

Write down a possible number of protons, neutrons and electrons contained in the atom. *(2 marks)*

(b) An unstable isotope of uranium may split into a caesium nucleus, a rubidium nucleus and four neutrons in the following process.

$$^{236}_{92}\text{U} \longrightarrow {}^{137}_{55}\text{Cs} + {}^{X}_{37}\text{Rb} + 4{}^{1}_{0}\text{n}$$

    (i) Explain what is meant by isotopes.

    (ii) How many neutrons are there in the $^{137}_{55}\text{Cs}$ nucleus?

    (iii) Calculate the ratio $\dfrac{\text{charge}}{\text{mass}}$, in C kg^{-1}, for the $^{236}_{92}\text{U}$ nucleus.

    (iv) Determine the value of X for the rubidium nucleus. *(4 marks)*

AQA, 2003

5 An α particle is the same as a nucleus of helium, $^{4}_{2}\text{He}$.

The equation $^{229}_{90}\text{Th} \longrightarrow {}^{X}_{Y}\text{Ra} + \alpha$

represents the decay of a thorium isotope by the emission of an α particle.

Determine:
(a) the values of X and Y, shown in the equation, *(2 marks)*

(b) the ratio $\dfrac{\text{mass of } {}^{X}_{Y}\text{Ra nucleus}}{\text{mass of } \alpha \text{ particle}}$ *(1 mark)*

AQA, 2005

6 (a) (i) Describe an α particle and state its properties.
     (ii) ${}^{215}_{85}\text{At}$ is an isotope of the element astatine (At) which decays into an isotope of bismuth (Bi) by emitting an α particle. Write down the equation to represent this reaction. *(5 marks)*

  (b) (i) State what happens when an unstable nucleus decays by emitting a β^- particle.
     (ii) Write down and complete the following equation, showing how an isotope of molybdenum decays into an isotope of technetium.
$$^{...}_{42}\text{Mo} \longrightarrow {}^{99}_{...}\text{Tc} + \beta- + ...$$ *(5 marks)*

7 In a radioactive decay of a nucleus, a β^+ particle is emitted followed by a γ photon of wavelength 8.30×10^{-13} m.
  (a) (i) State the rest mass, in kg, of the β^+ particle.
     (ii) Calculate the energy of the γ photon.
     (iii) Determine the energy of the γ photon in MeV. *(6 marks)*
  (b) Name the fundamental interaction or force responsible for β^+ decay. *(1 mark)*
  (c) β^+ decay may be represented by the Feynman diagram.
    Name the particles represented by A, B and C. *(3 marks)*

AQA, 2004

8 (a) (i) State the name of the antiparticle of a positron.
     (ii) Describe what happens when a positron and its antiparticle meet. *(3 marks)*
  (b) Calculate the minimum amount of energy, in J, released as radiation energy when a particle of rest energy 0.51 MeV meets its corresponding antiparticle. *(2 marks)*

AQA, 2005

9 In a particle accelerator a proton and an antiproton, travelling at the same speed, undergo a head-on collision and produce subatomic particles.
  (a) The total kinetic energy of the two particles just before the collision is 3.2×10^{-10} J.
    (i) What happens to the proton and antiproton during the collision?
    (ii) State why the total energy after the collision is more than 3.2×10^{-10} J. *(2 marks)*
  (b) In a second experiment the total kinetic energy of the colliding proton and antiproton is greater than 3.2×10^{-10} J.
    State **two** possible differences this could make to the subatomic particles produced. *(2 marks)*

AQA, 2001

10 An electron may interact with a proton in the following way
$$e^- + p \longrightarrow n + v_e.$$
  (a) Name the fundamental force responsible for this interaction. *(1 mark)*
  (b) Complete the Feynman diagram for this interaction and label all the particles involved. *(2 marks)*

AQA, 2003

11 (a) Give an example of an exchange particle other than a W^+ or W^- particle, and state the fundamental force involved when it is produced. *(2 marks)*
  (b) State what roles exchange particles can play in an interaction. *(2 marks)*

AQA, 2006

12 Describe what happens in pair production and give **one** example of this process. *(3 marks)*

AQA, 2005

2 Quarks and leptons

2.1 The particle zoo

Learning objectives:

- How can we find new particles?
- Can we predict new particles?
- What are strange particles?

Specification reference: 3.1.1

Space invaders

Cosmic rays are high-energy particles that travel through space from the stars, including the Sun. When a cosmic particle enters the Earth's atmosphere, it creates new short-lived particles and antiparticles, as well as photons. Most physicists thought, when cosmic rays were first discovered, that they were from terrestrial radioactive substances. This theory was disproved when the physicist and amateur balloonist, Victor Hess, found the ionising effect of the rays was significantly greater at 5000 m than at ground level.

Further investigations showed that most cosmic rays were fast-moving protons or small nuclei. They collide with gas atoms in the atmosphere, creating showers of particles and antiparticles that can be detected at ground level. By using cloud chambers and other detectors, new types of short-lived particles and antiparticles were discovered, including:

- the **muon** or 'heavy electron' (symbol μ) a negatively charged particle with a rest mass over 200 times the rest mass of the electron,
- the **pion** or 'π meson', a particle which can be positively charged (π^+), negatively charged (π^-) or neutral (π^0) and has a rest mass greater than a muon but less than a proton,
- the **kaon** or 'K meson', which also can be positively charged (K^+), negatively charged (K^-) or neutral (K^0) and has a rest mass greater than a pion but still less than a proton.

How science works

An unusual prediction

Before the above particles were first detected, the Japanese physicist Hidekei Yukawa predicted the existence of exchange particles for the strong nuclear force between nucleons. He thought they would have a range of no more than about 10^{-15} m and he calculated that their mass would be between the electron and the proton mass. He called them **mesons**, because the predicted mass was somewhere in the middle between the electron mass and the proton mass.

A year later, a cloud chamber photograph obtained by Carl Anderson showed an unusual track that could have been produced by such a particle. However, the track length of 40 mm indicated that it lasted much longer than a strongly-interacting particle should. Further investigations showed this unexpected particle to be a heavy electron, now referred to as a **muon** but not classed as a meson. It decays through the weak interaction.

Yukawa's meson was discovered some years later by the British physicist Cecil Powell from tiny microscopic tracks found in photographic emulsion exposed to cosmic rays at high altitude. Powell called these particles **π mesons** or pions – Yukawa's prediction was correct!

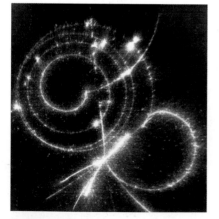

Figure 1 Creation and decay of a π meson. The short spiral track is a π^+ meson created when an antiproton from the bottom edge annihilates a proton. The π^+ meson decays into an antimuon that spirals and decays into a positron.

A strange puzzle

Less than a year after Powell's discovery, further cloud chamber photographs revealed the existence of short-lived particles we now refer to as **K mesons** or kaons. Like π mesons, they are produced through the strong interaction, when protons moving at high speed crash into nuclei and they each travel far beyond the nucleus in which they originate before they decay – in other words, they decay through the weak interaction, even though they were created through the strong interaction. However, their decay products include π mesons. These and other properties of K mesons led to them being called **strange particles**. We will return to their strangeness in Topic 2.4.

All the new particles listed above can also be created using accelerators in which protons collide head-on with other protons at high speed. The kinetic energy of the protons is converted into mass in the creation of these new particles. So these new particles could be studied under controlled conditions using accelerators to create them.

The rest masses, charge (if they were charged) and lifetimes of the new particles were measured. Their antiparticles, including the **antimuon**, were detected. Their decay modes were worked out:

- K mesons decay into π mesons, muons and antineutrinos, and antimuons and neutrinos.
- Charged π mesons decay into muons and antineutrinos, or antimuons and neutrinos. The π^0 meson decays into high energy photons.
- Muons and antimuons decay into electrons and antineutrinos, or positrons and neutrinos.
- The decays always obey the conservation rules for energy (and momentum) and for charge. We will see in Topic 2.5 that there are some further rules that tell us which interactions and decays are allowed.

🔾 About accelerators

A TV tube is an accelerator because it accelerates electrons inside the tube through a potential difference of about 5000 V. The electrons form a beam that hits the inside of the TV screen. Magnetic fields produced by electromagnets deflect the beam so it scans the screen to create an image. LCD (liquid crystal display) TVs work on a different principle.

- The longest accelerator in the world is the Stanford linear accelerator in California. It accelerates electrons over a distance of 3 km through a potential difference of 50 000 million volts. The energy of an electron accelerated through this pd is 50 000 MeV (= 50 GeV). When the electrons collide with a target, they can create lots of particle–antiparticle pairs.
- The biggest accelerator in the world, the Large Hadron Collider at CERN near Geneva, is designed to accelerate charged particles to energies of more than 7000 GeV. Unlike a linear accelerator, this accelerator is a 27 km circumference ring constructed in a circular tunnel below the ground. It will be used by physicists from many countries to find out more about the fundamental nature of matter and radiation. Protons, neutrons, π mesons and K mesons are all examples of particles that we call **hadrons** because they experience the strong interaction. We will learn more about hadrons in the next topic.

a *A TV tube*

b *The Stanford linear collider*

Figure 2 *Accelerators*

Summary questions

1 **a** List the following particles in order of increasing rest mass:

the electron, the K^0 meson, the muon, the neutron, the π^+ meson, the proton.

  b Which of the above particles are uncharged?

2 State whether the strong or the weak interaction acts when

  a a muon decays

  b a K meson decays

  c π mesons are produced.

3 **a** Which creates the longer trail in a cloud chamber, a muon or a π^+ meson?

  b In terms of their properties, state one similarity and one difference between a muon and a π meson.

4 A high-energy collision between two protons creates π mesons and K mesons which then decay.

  a What happens to i the K mesons? ii the π mesons?

  b What particles are ultimately formed by the above decays?

2.2 Particle sorting

Learning objectives:

■ How can we classify particles?

■ What are hadrons?

■ What are leptons?

Specification reference: 3.1.1

Classifying particles and antiparticles

The new particle discoveries raised the important question – how do all these new particles and antiparticles fit in with each other and with protons, neutrons and electrons? They are created through high-energy interactions and, apart from the neutrino, they decay into other particles and antiparticles. Also, charged π mesons were often produced in pairs – leading to the conclusion that the π^+ meson and the π^- meson are a particle-antiparticle pair. The same conclusion was reached for charged K-mesons. So is there an underlying pattern?

All the particles we have discussed so far are listed in Table 1 together with some of their properties. Can you see any links between the different particles?

Table 1 *Particles and properties*

particle and symbol	charge / proton charge	antiparticle and symbol	charge / proton charge	rest energy / MeV	interaction
proton p	+1	antiproton $\bar{p}$	–1	938	strong, weak decay electromagnetic
neutron n	0	antineutron $\bar{n}$	0	939	strong, weak decay
electron e^-	–1	positron e^+	+1	0.511	weak, electromagnetic,
neutrino ν	0	antineutrino $\bar{\nu}$	0	0	weak
muon μ^-	–1	antimuon μ^+	+1	106	weak, electromagnetic
π meson π^+, π^0, π^-	+1, 0, –1	π^+ for a π^- π^- for a π^+ π^0 for a π^0	–1, 0, +1	140; 135; 140	strong, electromagnetic (π^+, π^-)
K meson K^+, K^0, K^-	+1, 0, –1	See Topic 2.4	–1, 0,+1	494; 498; 494	strong electromagnetic (K^+, K^-)

Notice the symbol for an antiproton, antineutron and antineutrino is the particle symbol with a bar above it, except for the positron and the antimuon.

How would you classify them? In fact, we can divide them into two groups, called **hadrons** and **leptons**, according to whether or not they interact through the strong interaction.

■ Hadrons are particles and antiparticles that can interact through the strong interaction (e.g. protons, neutrons, π mesons, K mesons).

■ Leptons are particles and antiparticles that do not interact through the strong interaction (e.g. electrons, muons, neutrinos).

1 **Leptons interact through the weak interaction and through the electromagnetic interaction if charged.**

2 **Hadrons interact through the strong interaction and through the electromagnetic interaction if charged. Apart from the proton, which is stable, hadrons decay through the weak interaction.**

AQA Examiner's tip

■ lepton – light and weak

■ hadron – strong and heavy

Energy matters

The Large Hadron Collider is a ring-shaped accelerator that boosts the kinetic energy of the charged particles in the ring at several places round it. Fixed magnets all the way round the ring bend the path of the particles to keep them in the ring. When they collide with other particles:

■ The total energy of the particles and antiparticles before the collision = their rest energy + their kinetic energy.

■ The total energy of the new particles and antiparticles after the collision = their rest energy + their kinetic energy

Using conservation of energy,

$$\text{the rest energy of the products} = \text{total energy before} - \text{the kinetic energy of the products}$$

For example, if a proton and an antiproton each with kinetic energy of 2 GeV collide, their total energy before the collision is 6 GeV (as each particle has 2 GeV of kinetic energy and approximately 1 GeV of rest energy – see Table 1). The result could be a range of products, as long as their total energy does not exceed 6 GeV, provided the conservation rules (e.g. charge) are obeyed.

Note:

$1\,\text{GeV} = 1000\,\text{MeV}$

Baryons and mesons

When K mesons are created, short-lived particles with greater rest masses than protons may also be produced. These particles are created through the strong interaction, so they are hadrons. However, in comparison with K mesons, they decay into protons as well as into π mesons (whereas protons are never among the decay products of K mesons). Consequently, we can divide hadrons into two groups:

1 **Baryons** are protons and all other hadrons (including neutrons) that decay into protons, either directly or indirectly.

2 **Mesons** are hadrons that do **not** include protons in their decay products. In other words, K mesons and π mesons are not baryons.

We shall see in Topic 2.4 that baryons and mesons are composed of smaller particles called **quarks** and **antiquarks**.

Figure 1 *The Large Hadron Collider*

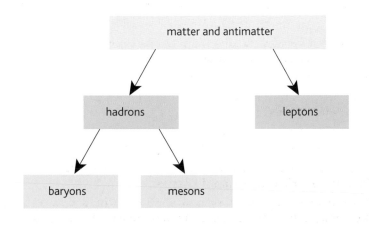

Figure 2 *Particle sorts*

2.3 Leptons at work

Learning objectives:

- Are leptons elementary?
- Are neutrinos all the same?
- Why are lepton numbers important?

Specification reference: 3.1.1

Lepton collisions

The universe would be very dull if all its particles were leptons. Neutrinos interact very little, muons are very short-lived and the electrons would repel each other. However, leptons and antileptons can interact to produce hadrons. For example, a head-on collision at high energy between an electron and a positron can produce baryons, antibaryons and mesons. Figure 1 shows two jets of hadrons produced from a single electron–positron annihilation event. The event itself produces a **quark** and a corresponding **antiquark**, which move away in opposite directions, producing a shower of hadrons in each direction.

Neutrino types

They travel almost as fast as light, billions of them sweeping through the Earth from space every second with almost no interaction. They are produced in much smaller numbers when particles in accelerators collide. A nuclear reactor produces many more neutrinos per second than an accelerator, but still far less than sweep through us from space. Recall from Topic 1.2 that the neutrino was discovered in an experiment sited next to a nuclear reactor – switching the reactor on or off affected the experiment in a way that could only be explained by changes in the neutrino 'flow' from the reactor.

In fact, further research on neutrinos showed that the neutrinos and antineutrinos produced in beta decays were different from those produced by muon decays. In effect, neutrinos and antineutrinos from muon and antimuon decays create only muons and no electrons when they interact with protons and neutrons. If there were only one type of neutrino and antineutrino, equal numbers of electrons and muons would be produced. We use the symbol ν_μ for the **muon neutrino** and ν_e for the **electron neutrino** (and similar for the two types of antineutrinos).

Figure 1 *A two jet event after an electron–positron collision*

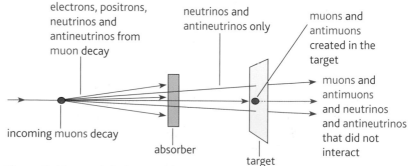

electrons, positrons, neutrinos and antineutrinos from muon decay

neutrinos and antineutrinos only

muons and antimuons created in the target

incoming muons decay

absorber

target

muons and antimuons and neutrinos and antineutrinos that did not interact

Figure 2 *Muon and electron neutrinos*

Lepton rules

Leptons can change into other leptons through the weak interaction and can be produced or annihilated in particle–antiparticle interactions. But all the experiments on them indicate that they don't break down into non-leptons. They appear to be fundamental elements of matter – in other words, elementary!

1 **In an interaction between a lepton and a hadron**, a neutrino or antineutrino can change into or from a corresponding charged lepton.

For example, as explained on page 14, an electron neutrino can interact with a neutron to produce a proton and an electron.

$$\nu_e + n \longrightarrow p + e^-$$

However, an electron neutrino and a neutron could not change into an antiproton and a positron.

$$\nu_e + n \not\longrightarrow \bar{p} + e^+$$

By assigning +1 to a lepton and −1 to an antilepton and 0 for any non-lepton, we can see that the total lepton number is unchanged in the permitted change above.

The first equation has a lepton number of +1 before the change and a lepton number of +1 after the change. So this equation is permitted.

The second equation has a lepton number of +1 before the change and a lepton number of −1 after the change. So this change is not permitted.

2 **In muon decay**, the muon changes into a muon neutrino. In addition, an electron and an electron antineutrino are created to conserve charge.

$$\mu^- \longrightarrow e^- + \bar{\nu}_e + \nu_\mu$$

However, a muon cannot decay into a muon antineutrino, an electron and an electron antineutrino even though charge is conserved.

$$\mu^- \not\longrightarrow e^- + \bar{\nu}_e + \bar{\nu}_\mu$$

The first equation has a lepton number of +1 before the change and a lepton number of +1 (= +1 −1 + 1) after the change. So this equation is permitted.

The second equation has a lepton number of +1 before the change and a lepton number of -1 (= +1 −1 −1) after the change. So this change is not permitted.

In any change, the total lepton number before the change is equal to the total lepton number after the change. In other words, **the lepton number is conserved in any change**.

A weak puzzle

Consider the following possible change for a muon decay.

$$\mu^- \overset{?}{\longrightarrow} e^- + \nu_e + \bar{\nu}_\mu$$

It obeys the lepton conservation law and conservation of charge but it is never seen. The reason is that the muon can only change into a muon neutrino. The above decay can't happen because a muon can't change into a muon antineutrino and an electron can only be created with an electron antineutrino. So we need to apply the rule above separately to each branch of leptons, namely:

■ the electron branch consisting of electrons, electron neutrinos and their antiparticles

■ the muon branch consisting of muons, muon neutrinos and their antiparticles.

■ The lepton number is +1 for any lepton, −1 for any antilepton and 0 for any non-lepton.

■ Leptons are in two branches, the electron branch and the muon branch.

■ The lepton number for each branch is conserved in any change.

1 State one similarity and one difference between

a an electron and a muon,

b an electron neutrino and a muon neutrino.

2 a What type of interaction occurs when

   i two protons collide and create π mesons?

   ii a beta particle is emitted from an unstable nucleus?

   iii a muon decays?

b The muon decays into an electron, a neutrino and an antineutrino.

   i Complete the equation below representing this decay:

   $$\mu^- \longrightarrow e^+ + \quad + \quad$$

   ii Use the rest energy values in Table 1 on page 20 to calculate how much energy, in MeV, is removed by the neutrino and the antineutrino, if the muon and the electron have no kinetic energy.

3 a What is the charge of i a muon neutrino, ii an antimuon, iii a positron, iv an electron antineutrino?

b What is the lepton number of each of the above leptons?

4 State whether or not each of the following reactions is permitted, giving a reason if it is not permitted.

a $\nu_e + p \longrightarrow n + e^-$

b $\bar{\nu}_e + p \longrightarrow n + e^+$

c $\nu_e + p \longrightarrow n + e^+$

d $\bar{\nu}_e + p \longrightarrow n + \mu^+$

2.4 Quarks and antiquarks

Learning objectives:

- What are strange particles ?
- What are quarks and how do we know they exist?
- What quark changes happen in beta decay?
- Why are there no antimesons?

Specification reference: 3.1.1

How science works

Accelerators were used to create these other particles and to study their properties. The results showed that some reactions that were predicted were never observed. For example,

1 $\pi^- + p \rightarrow K^+ + \Sigma^-$ was observed

2 $\pi^+ + n \rightarrow K^+ + \Sigma^0$ was observed

3 $\pi^- + n \rightarrow K^0 + \Sigma^-$ was observed

4 $\pi^- + n \rightarrow K^- + \Sigma^0$ was **not** observed

How science works

Evidence for quarks

Experimental evidence for the 3-quark model was first obtained using the Stanford linear accelerator to make electrons collide at high speed with protons. The results showed that the electrons were scattered by three scattering centres in each proton.

Strangeness

When K mesons were discovered, they were first called V particles because the cloud chamber photographs often showed V-shaped tracks. They were called 'strange' particles after investigations showed that the V tracks decay into π mesons only, or into π mesons and protons. Although these strange particles all decay through the weak interaction:

1 those that decay into π mesons only were referred to as K mesons

2 the others, such as the sigma particle in Figure 1, were found to:

- have different rest masses which were always greater than the proton's rest mass
- decay either in sequence or directly into protons and π mesons.

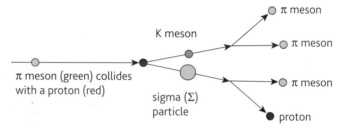

Figure 1 *Strange particles*

All the observed reactions conserve charge. To explain why certain reactions were not observed, a **strangeness number** S was introduced for each particle and antiparticle (starting with +1 for the K$^+$ meson) so that strangeness is always conserved in strong interactions. Non-strange particles (i.e. the proton, the neutron, π mesons, leptons) were assigned zero strangeness.

The strangeness numbers for the other strange particles and antiparticles can then be deduced from the observed reactions.

In reaction 1 above, S = −1 for Σ$^-$ so that the total strangeness is zero before and after the reaction.

In reaction 2, S = −1 for Σ^0 so that the total strangeness is zero before and after the reaction.

In reaction 3, S = +1 for K^0 so that the total strangeness is zero before and after the reaction.

But reaction 4 is not observed so the K$^-$ meson does not have $S = +1$.

The above interactions are all strong interactions. Observations that strangeness is not conserved when strange particles decay leads to the conclusion that strangeness is not conserved in a weak interaction.

Strangeness is always conserved in a strong interaction.

The quark model

The properties of the hadrons, such as charge, strangeness and rest mass can be explained by assuming they are composed of smaller particles known as quarks and antiquarks. Three different types of quarks and their corresponding antiquarks are necessary. These three types are referred to as 'up', 'down' and 'strange' quarks, and are denoted by the symbols u, d and s, respectively. The properties of these three quarks are shown in Table 1.

Table 1 *Quark properties*

	quarks			antiquarks		
	up u	down d	strange s	up $\bar{u}$	down $\bar{d}$	strange $\bar{s}$
charge Q	$+\frac{2}{3}$	$-\frac{1}{3}$	$-\frac{1}{3}$	$-\frac{2}{3}$	$+\frac{1}{3}$	$+\frac{1}{3}$
strangeness S	0	0	−1	0	0	+1

Quark combinations

The rules for combining quarks to form baryons and mesons are astonishingly simple:

Mesons are hadrons, each consisting of a quark and an antiquark. Figure 2 shows all nine different quark–antiquark combinations and the meson in each case. Notice that:

■ A π^0 meson can be any quark-corresponding antiquark combination.

■ Each pair of charged mesons is a particle–antiparticle pair.

■ There are two uncharged K mesons, the K^0 meson and the $\bar{K}^0$ meson.

■ The antiparticle of any meson is a quark–antiquark pair and therefore another meson.

Baryons and **antibaryons** are hadrons that consist of three quarks for a baryon or three antiquarks for an antibaryon.

■ A proton is the uud combination.

■ A neutron is the udd combination.

■ An antiproton is the $\bar{u}\bar{u}\bar{d}$ combination.

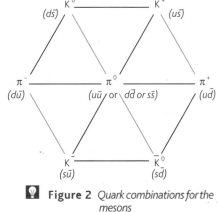

Figure 2 *Quark combinations for the mesons*

Quarks and beta decay

In β^- decay, a neutron in a neutron-rich nucleus changes into a proton, releasing an electron and an electron antineutrino. In quark terms, a down quark changes to an up quark. The Feynman diagram for this change is shown in Figure 3a).

In β^+ decay, a proton in a proton-rich nucleus changes into a neutron, releasing a positron and an electron neutrino. In quark terms, an up quark changes to a down quark. The Feynman diagram for this change is shown in Figure 3b).

a β^- *decay*   **b** β^+ *decay*

Figure 3 *Quark changes in beta decay*

Summary questions

1 **a** How does the quark composition of a meson compare with the quark composition of a baryon?

   b State the quark composition of **i** a proton, **ii** a neutron.

2 Determine the quark composition of each of the following hadrons, given its strangeness.

   a a π^0 meson ($S = 0$)

   b an antiproton ($S = 0$)

   c a K^- meson ($S = -1$)

   d a Σ^0 baryon ($S = -1$)

3 In β^+ decay, a positron and an electron neutrino are emitted when a proton in the nucleus changes into a neutron.

   a In terms of quarks, draw a Feynman diagram to represent this change.

   b Describe the changes that are represented in the diagram.

4 **a** A Σ^- particle has a strangeness of −1. Show that it is composed of a strange quark and two down quarks.

   b A K^+ meson is composed of a strange antiquark and an up quark. A Σ^- baryon is composed of a strange quark and two down quarks. They can be created in the reaction shown below:

   $$\pi^- + p \longrightarrow K^+ + \Sigma^-$$

   Describe this reaction in terms of quark and antiquarks.

2.5 Conservation rules

Learning objectives:

■ What is always conserved in a particle interaction?

■ What is sometimes conserved?

■ What is never conserved?

Specification reference: 3.1.1

Particles and properties

Particles and antiparticles possess energy; they may be charged or uncharged, they may have non-zero strangeness, and they may not be stable. They obey certain conservation rules when they interact. Some rules apply to all interactions and decays and some do not.

1 **Conservation of energy and conservation of charge** apply to all changes in science, not just to all particle and antiparticle interactions and decays. Remember conservation of energy includes the 'rest energy' of the particles. See Topic 2.2 if necessary.

2 **Conservation rules used only for particle and antiparticle interactions and decays** are essentially particle-counting rules, based on what reactions are observed and what are not observed. So far, we have used the following conservation rules (in addition to energy and charge):

a) **Conservation of lepton numbers.** In any change, the total lepton number for each lepton branch before the change is equal to the total lepton number for that branch after the change.

For example, when an antimuon decays, it changes into a positron, an electron neutrino and a muon antineutrino, as shown below.

$$\mu^+ \longrightarrow e^+ + \bar{\nu}_\mu + \nu_e$$

The properties of each particle or antiparticle in this change are shown in Table 1. We can see from this table that the lepton numbers for each type of lepton are conserved, as in all changes involving leptons.

b) **Conservation of strangeness.** In any strong interaction, strangeness is always conserved.

For example, a K^0 meson and a strange baryon called the neutral lambda particle (symbol Λ^0) are produced when a π^- meson collides with a proton, as shown below.

$$\pi^- + p \longrightarrow K^0 + \Lambda^0$$

The properties of each particle involved in this change are shown in Table 2. We can see from this table that strangeness is conserved, just as in all changes involving the strong interaction.

Table 1 The decay of the antimuon (interaction is weak)

	μ^+	e^+	ν_e	$\bar{\nu}_\mu$
charge	+1	+1	0	0
muon lepton number	−1	0	0	−1
electron lepton number	0	−1	+1	0

Note:

It is not conserved when the weak interaction is involved.

Table 2 A proton – π– meson collision (interaction is strong)

	π^-	p	K^0	Λ^0
charge	−1	+1	0	0
strangeness	0	0	+1	−1

Are baryons and mesons conserved?

Here are some reactions that are observed and some that are not observed. They all obey the above conservation laws so why are some not observed?

$p + \bar{p} \longrightarrow \pi^+ + \pi^-$	Observed
$p + \bar{p} \longrightarrow p + \pi^-$	Not observed
$p + p \longrightarrow p + p + p + \bar{p}$	Observed
$p + \bar{p} \longrightarrow \bar{p} + \pi^+$	Not observed

Let's consider the first reaction in terms of quarks:

$$u u d + \overline{u}\,\overline{u}\,\overline{d} \longrightarrow u\overline{d} + \overline{u}d$$

We can see an up quark and an up antiquark annihilate each other and the other quarks and antiquarks rearrange to form mesons.

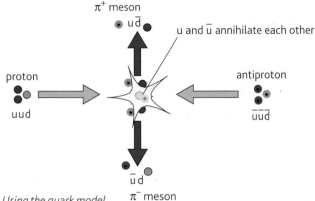

Figure 1 *Using the quark model*

This reaction shows that we can keep track of the baryons and antibaryons, if we assign a **baryon number** of:

- +1 to any baryon and −1 to any antibaryon
- 0 to any meson or lepton.

In effect, the above rules amount to assigning a baryon number of +⅓ to any quark, −⅓ to any antiquark and 0 to any lepton.

So in the first reaction, the baryon number is 0 (= +1 −1) for the left-hand side and 0 for the right-hand side. In other words, the baryon number is conserved. Prove for yourself that this rule applies to the third reaction but not to the second or fourth reactions.

In any reaction, the total baryon number is conserved.

How science works

Big questions

Is there a deeper structure of matter that is still to be discovered? Radiation released in the Big Bang produced quarks and leptons in equal numbers to their antiparticles. So why haven't they all annihilated to turn back into radiation and why is the universe made of matter, not antimatter?

The study of particle physics raises lots of interesting questions! Scientists now know there are six different quarks and six different leptons. The properties and behaviour of matter on the smallest possible scale affects what happens on the largest scale (i.e. the universe). Perhaps the Large Hadron Collider at CERN will provide some of the answers.

Summary questions

1 The following reaction was observed when two protons collided head-on at high speed:

$$p + p \longrightarrow p + n + \pi^+$$

a i Show that charge is conserved in this reaction.

ii What other quantity is conserved in this reaction?

b Use the rest energy values in Table 1 on p20 to show that the two protons must have at least 141 MeV of kinetic energy to create the π^+ meson.

c i State the quark composition of a proton and of a neutron.

ii The π^+ meson has a quark composition of $u\overline{d}$. Describe the above reaction in terms of quarks.

2 a State the baryon number of **i** an up quark, **ii** an antiproton, **iii** a muon.

b State the lepton number of **i** a neutrino, **ii** an antimuon, **iii** a neutron.

3 The omega minus (Ω^-) is a baryon with a strangeness of −3 and a charge of −1.

a Determine its quark composition.

b It decays into a π^- meson and a baryon X composed of two strange quarks and an up quark.

i Determine the charge and the strangeness of X from its quark composition.

ii What type of interaction occurs in this change?

iii Describe the quark changes that take place.

4 A K⁻ meson is found to decay into three charged π mesons.

a i What type of interaction takes place in this decay?

ii Is strangeness conserved in this decay?

b i In terms of conservation of charge, explain why two of the π mesons are negative and the other is positive.

ii Write down the equation for this decay.

c A K⁺ meson was found to decay into a charged π meson and a $\pi°$ meson.

i Write down the equation for this decay.

ii Explain this change in terms of quarks.

1   (a) K mesons were originally called 'strange' because they are produced in **one** type
         of interaction and they decay through a different type of interaction.
         (i)   In which type of interaction are they produced?
         (ii) Which type of interaction causes them to decay?
         (iii) In which type of interaction is strangeness always conserved?   *(3 marks)*
     (b) (i)   Describe the 3-quark model of hadrons.
         (ii) The 3-quark model originated from a theory that explained the properties
               of baryons and mesons. Show that the 3-quark model explains why there are
               just 4 charged mesons.   *(6 marks)*

2   From the following list of particles

         p $\bar{n}$ ν_e e^+ μ^- π^0

     identify all the examples of
     (i)   hadrons   (ii) leptons
     (iii) antiparticles   (iv) charged particles   *(4 marks)*
     AQA, 2006

3   (a) (i)   Write down the particles in the following list that may be affected by the weak interaction.
               positron   neutron   photon   neutrino   positive pion
         (ii) Write down the particles in the following list that may be affected by the
               electromagnetic force.
               electron   antineutrino   proton   neutral pion   negative muon   *(4 marks)*
     (b) A positive muon may decay in the following way:

               $\mu^+ \longrightarrow e^+ + \nu_e + \overline{\nu}_\mu$

         (i)   Exchange each particle for its corresponding antiparticle and complete the
               equation to show how a negative muon may decay.

               $\mu^- \longrightarrow$

         (ii) Give **one** difference and **one** similarity between a negative muon and an electron.   *(3 marks)*
     AQA, 2003

4   (a) State the quark substructure of a neutron.   *(2 marks)*
     (b) Which of the following terms can be used to describe a neutron?
         antiparticle   baryon   fundamental particle   hadron   lepton   meson   *(2 marks)*
     AQA, 2004

5   (a) A particle is made up from an up antiquark and a down quark.
         (i)   Name the classification of particles that has this type of structure.
         (ii) Find the charge on the particle.
         (iii) State the baryon number of the particle.   *(3 marks)*
     (b) A suggested decay for the positive muon (μ^+) is

               $\mu^+ \longrightarrow e^+ + \nu_e$

         Showing your reasoning clearly, deduce whether this decay satisfies the
         conservation rules that relate to baryon number, lepton number and charge. *(3 marks)*
     AQA, 2003

6   A sigma plus particle, Σ^+, is a baryon.
         (i)   How many quarks does the Σ^+ contain?
         (ii) If **one** of these quarks is an s quark, by what interaction will it decay?
         (iii) Which baryon will the Σ^+ eventually decay into?   *(3 marks)*
     AQA, 2005

7   Some subatomic particles are classified as *hadrons*.
    (a) What distinguishes a hadron from other subatomic particles?   *(1 mark)*
    (b) Hadrons fall into two subgroups.
        Name each subgroup and describe the general structure of each.   *(3 marks)*
    (c) The following equation represents an event in which a positive muon collides with a neutron to produce a proton and an antineutrino.
        $$n + \mu^+ \longrightarrow p + \bar{\nu}_\mu$$
        Show that this equation obeys the conservation laws of charge, lepton number and baryon number.   *(3 marks)*

        AQA, 2004

8   A negative pion (π^-) is a meson with a charge of –1e.
    State and explain the structure of the π^- in terms of the up and down quarks.   *(3 marks)*

        AQA, 2002

9   The following is an incomplete equation for the decay of a free neutron.
        $$^1_0n \longrightarrow {}^1_1p + {}^0_{-1}e + \ldots$$
    (a) Complete the equation by writing down the symbol for the missing particle.   *(2 marks)*
    (b) Use the principles of conservation of charge, baryon number and lepton number to demonstrate that decay is possible.   *(3 marks)*
    (c) The following reaction can take place when two protons meet head on, provided the two colliding protons have sufficient kinetic energy:
        $$p + p \longrightarrow p + p + \bar{p} + p$$
        If the two colliding protons each have the same amount of energy, calculate the minimum kinetic energy, in MeV, each must have for the reaction to proceed.   *(2 marks)*

        AQA, 2005

10 (a) (i) What class of particle is represented by the combination of three antiquarks, $\bar{q}\bar{q}\bar{q}$?
        (ii) Name a hadron that has an antiparticle identical to itself.   *(3 marks)*
    (b) The kaon K^+ has a strangeness of +1.
        (i)   Give its quark composition
        (ii) The K^+ may decay via the process
              $$K^+ \longrightarrow \pi^+ + \pi^0$$
              State the interaction responsible for this decay.
        (iii) The K^+ may also decay via the process
              $$K^+ \longrightarrow \mu^+ + \nu_\mu$$
              Change each particle of this equation to its corresponding antiparticle in order to complete an allowed decay process for the negative kaon K^-.
              $$K^- \longrightarrow$$
        (iv) Into what class of particle can both the μ^+ and the ν_μ be placed?
        (v)   State **one** difference between a positive muon and a positron, e^+.   *(6 marks)*

        AQA, 2002

11 The equation represents the collision of a neutral kaon with a proton, resulting in the production of a neutron and a positive pion.
        $$K^0 + p \longrightarrow n + \pi^+$$
    (a) Show that this collision obeys **three** conservation laws in addition to energy and momentum.   *(3 marks)*
    (b) The neutral kaon has a strangeness of +1.
        Write down the quark structure of the following particles.
        $$K^0 \qquad \pi^+ \qquad p$$ *(4 marks)*

        AQA, 2005

3 Quantum phenomena

3.1 Photoelectricity

Learning objectives:

■ What is photoelectricity?

■ What is a photon?

■ How was the photon model established?

Specification reference: 3.1.2

💡 How science works

Observing the photoelectric effect

ultraviolet radiation

zinc plate

gold leaf electroscope

Ultraviolet radiation from a UV lamp is directed at the surface of a zinc plate placed on the cap of a gold leaf electroscope, as shown above. This device is a very sensitive detector of charge. When it is charged, the thin gold leaf of the electroscope rises; it is repelled from the metal 'stem', because they both have the same type of charge.

■ If the electroscope is charged negatively, the leaf rises and stays in position. However, if ultraviolet light is directed at the zinc plate, the leaf gradually falls. The leaf falls because conduction electrons at the zinc surface leave the zinc surface when ultraviolet light is directed at it. The emitted electrons are referred to as **photoelectrons**.

■ If the electroscope is charged positively, the leaf rises and stays in position, regardless of whether or not ultraviolet light is directed at the zinc plate.

■ The discovery of photoelectricity

A metal contains conduction electrons, which move about freely inside the metal. These electrons collide with each other and with the positive ions of the metal. When Hertz discovered how to produce and detect radio waves, he found that the sparks produced in his spark gap detector when radio waves were being transmitted were stronger when ultraviolet radiation was directed at the spark gap. Further investigations on the effect of electromagnetic radiation on metals showed that electrons are emitted from the surface of a metal when electromagnetic radiation above a certain frequency was directed at the metal. This effect is known as the **photoelectric effect**.

Puzzling problems

The following observations were made about photoelectricity after Hertz's discovery. These observations were a major problem because they could not be explained using the wave theory of electromagnetic radiation.

1   Photoelectric emission of electrons from a metal surface does **not** take place if the frequency of the incident electromagnetic radiation is below a certain value known as the **threshold frequency**. This minimum frequency depends on the type of metal.

Note:

The **wavelength** of the incident light must be less than a **maximum** value equal to the speed of light divided by the threshold frequency.

2   The number of electrons emitted per second is proportional to the intensity of the incident radiation, provided the frequency is greater than the threshold frequency. If the frequency of the incident radiation is less than the threshold frequency, no photoelectric emission from that metal surface can take place, no matter how intense the incident radiation is.

3   Photoelectric emission occurs without delay as soon as the incident radiation is directed at the surface, provided the frequency of the radiation exceeds the threshold frequency. No matter how weak the intensity of the incident radiation is, electrons are emitted as soon as the source of radiation is switched on.

The wave theory of light cannot explain either the existence of a threshold frequency, or why photoelectric emission occurs without delay. According to wave theory, each conduction electron at the surface of a metal should gain some energy from the incoming waves, regardless of how many waves arrive each second. Wave theory incorrectly predicted that:

■ emission should take place with waves of any frequency,

■ emission would take longer using low intensity waves than using high intensity waves.

💡 Einstein's explanation of photoelectricity

The photon theory of light was put forward by Einstein in 1905 to explain photoelectricity. As explained in Topic 1.3, Einstein assumed that light is composed of wavepackets or **photons**, each of energy equal to hf, where f is the frequency of the light and h is the Planck constant. The accepted value for h is 6.63×10^{-34} J s.

$$\text{Energy of a photon} = hf$$

For electromagnetic waves of wavelength λ, the energy of each photon
$E = hf = \dfrac{hc}{\lambda}$ where c is the speed of the electromagnetic waves.

Remember, wavelength $\lambda = c/f$

To explain photoelectricity, Einstein said that:

■ When light is incident on a metal surface, an electron at the surface absorbs a **single** photon from the incident light and therefore gains energy equal to hf, where hf is the energy of a light photon.

■ An electron can leave the metal surface if the energy gained from a single photon exceeds the **work function**, ϕ, of the metal. This is the minimum energy needed by an electron to escape from the metal surface.

Hence the maximum kinetic energy of an emitted electron

$$E_{\text{Kmax}} = hf - \phi$$

Rearranging this equation gives

$$hf = E_{\text{Kmax}} + \phi$$

Emission can take place from a surface at zero potential, provided
$E_{\text{Kmax}} > 0$ or $hf > \phi$

Thus the threshold frequency of the metal,

$$f_{\text{min}} = \frac{\phi}{h}$$

photons

free electrons in the metal

photoelectron

metal

Figure 1 *Explaining photoelectricity*

Examiner's tip

Don't forget one electron absorbs one photon!

Summary questions

$h = 6.63 \times 10^{-34}$ J s, $c = 3.00 \times 10^8$ m s⁻¹

1 a What is meant by photoelectric emission from a metal surface?

b Explain why photoelectric emission from a metal surface only takes place if the frequency of the incident radiation is greater than a certain value.

2 a Calculate the frequency and energy of a photon of wavelength i 450 nm, ii 1500 nm.

b A metal surface at zero potential emits electrons from its surface if light of wavelength 450 nm is directed at it but not if light of wavelength 650 nm is used. Explain why photoelectric emission happens with light of wavelength 450 nm but not with light of wavelength 650 nm.

3 The work function of a certain metal plate is 1.1 $\times 10^{-19}$ J. Calculate a the threshold frequency of incident radiation, b the maximum kinetic energy of photoelectrons emitted from this plate when light of wavelength 520 nm is directed at the metal surface.

4 Light of wavelength 635 nm is directed at a metal plate at zero potential. Electrons are emitted from the plate with a maximum kinetic energy of 1.5 $\times$ 10⁻¹⁹ J. Calculate a the energy of a photon of this wavelength, b the work function of the metal, c the threshold frequency of electromagnetic radiation incident on this metal.

3.2 More about photoelectricity

Learning objectives:

- Why was Einstein's photon model revolutionary?
- What is a quantum?
- Why can't an electron absorb several photons to escape from a metal?

Specification reference: 3.1.2

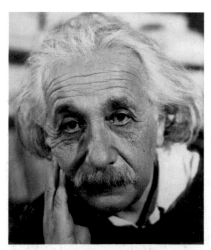

Figure 1 *The radiation curve for a hot object*

Figure 2 *Albert Einstein 1879–1955*

AQA Examiner's tip

Remember that the work function is characteristic of the metal and the threshold frequency relates the work function to the incident radiation.

How science works

Into the quantum world

Who was Planck? He made his name as a physicist at the end of the 19th century by solving a problem known as the **ultraviolet catastrophe**. Measurements on the spectrum of radiation from a hot object at a constant temperature showed that the intensity of the radiation varied with wavelength, as shown by Figure 1. But the theory of electromagnetic waves predicted infinite intensity at ultraviolet wavelengths.

Planck solved the problem by putting forward the idea that the energy of each vibrating atom is **quantised** – only certain levels of energy are allowed. He said the energy could only be in multiples of a basic amount or 'quantum', hf, where f is the frequency of vibration of the atom and h is a constant, which became known as the Planck constant. He imagined the energy levels to be like the rungs of a ladder with each atom absorbing or emitting radiation when it moved up or down a level. He used his ideas to produce a mathematical formula for the shape of the curves. But he never quite accepted the idea that energy is 'lumpy' (i.e. quantised).

There was one other problem that the physicists of the time couldn't solve – the photoelectric effect. They couldn't fully explain it using the wave theory of radiation. Einstein did so by 'inventing' a new theory of radiation – the photon model. His key idea was that electromagnetic radiation consists of photons or 'wavepackets' of energy hf, where f is the frequency of the radiation and h is the Planck constant. Einstein's photon model and Planck's theory of vibrating atoms showed that energy is quantised which means it is in 'lumps' that can't spread out evenly – a completely new way of thinking about energy. Welcome to the quantum world!

More about conduction electrons

The conduction electrons in a metal move about at random, like the molecules of a gas. The average kinetic energy of a conduction electron depends on the temperature of the metal. At $300\,\text{K}$, this is about $6 \times 10^{-21}\,\text{J}$ which is far too small for an electron to escape from the metal.

The work function of a metal is the **minimum** energy needed by a conduction electron to escape from the metal surface when the metal is at zero potential. The work function of a metal is of the order of $10^{-19}\,\text{J}$, which is about 20 times greater than the average kinetic energy of a conduction electron in a metal at $300\,\text{K}$. In other words, a conduction electron in a metal at about 20°C does not have sufficient kinetic energy to leave the metal.

When a conduction electron absorbs a photon, its kinetic energy increases by an amount equal to the energy of the photon. If the energy of the photon exceeds the work function of the metal, the conduction electron can leave the metal. If the electron does not leave the metal, it collides repeatedly with other electrons and positive ions and it quickly loses its extra kinetic energy.

▮ The vacuum photocell

A vacuum photocell is a glass tube that contains a metal plate, referred to as the photocathode, and a smaller metal electrode referred to as the anode. Figure 3 shows a vacuum photocell in a circuit. When light of a frequency greater than the threshold frequency for the metal is directed at the photocathode, electrons are emitted from the cathode to the anode. The microammeter in the circuit can be used to measure the photoelectric current. This is proportional to the number of electrons per second that transfer from the cathode to the anode.

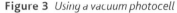

Figure 3 *Using a vacuum photocell*

▮ For a photoelectric current I, the number of photoelectrons per second that transfer from the cathode to the anode = I/e, where e is the charge of the electron.

▮ The photoelectric current is proportional to the intensity of the light incident on the cathode. The light intensity is a measure of the energy per second carried by the incident light, which is proportional to the number of photons per second incident on the cathode. Because each photoelectron must have absorbed one photon to escape from the metal surface, the number of photoelectrons emitted per second (i.e. the photoelectric current) is therefore proportional to the intensity of the incident light.

▮ The intensity of the incident light does *not* affect the maximum kinetic energy of a photoelectron. No matter how intense the incident light is, the energy gained by a photoelectron is due to the absorption of one photon only. Therefore, the maximum kinetic energy of a photoelectron is still given by $E_{Kmax} = hf - \phi$

▮ The maximum kinetic energy of the photoelectrons emitted for a given frequency of light can be measured using a photocell.

The details of this experiment are not required for your AS exam.

▮ If the measurements for different frequencies are plotted as a graph of E_{Kmax} against f, a straight line of the form $y = mx + c$ is obtained. This is in accordance with the above equation as $y = E_K$ and $x = f$. Note that the gradient, m, of the line = h and the y-intercept, $c = -\phi$. The x-intercept is equal to the threshold frequency.

▮ **Figure 4** *A graph of E_{Kmax} against frequency*

▮ Summary questions

$h = 6.63 \times 10^{-34}\,J\,s$, $c = 3.00 \times 10^8\,m\,s^{-1}$, $e = 1.6 \times 10^{-19}\,C$

1 A vacuum photocell is connected to a microammeter. Explain the following observations.

  a When the cathode was illuminated with blue light of low intensity, the microammeter showed a non-zero reading.

  b When the cathode was illuminated with an intense red light, the microammeter reading was zero.

2 A vacuum photocell is connected to a microammeter. When light is directed at the photocell, the microammeter reads 0.25 µA.

  a Calculate the number of photoelectrons emitted per second by the photocathode of the photocell.

  b Explain why the microammeter reading is doubled if the intensity of the incident light is doubled.

3 A narrow beam of light of wavelength 590 nm and of power 0.5 mW is directed at the photocathode of a vacuum photocell, which is connected to a microammeter which reads 0.4 µA. Calculate:

  a the energy of a single light photon of this wavelength,

  b the number of photons per second incident on the photocathode,

  c the number of electrons emitted per second from the photocathode.

4 **a** Use Figure 4 to estimate **i** the threshold frequency, **ii** the work function of the metal.

  b A metal surface has a work function of $1.9 \times 10^{-19}\,J$. Light of wavelength 435 nm is directed at the metal surface. Calculate the maximum kinetic energy of the photoelectrons emitted from this metal surface.

3.3 Collisions of electrons with atoms

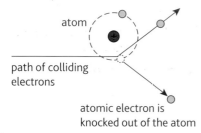

Learning objectives:

- What do we mean by ionisation of an atom?
- What do we mean by excitation of an atom?
- What happens inside an atom when it becomes excited?

Specification reference: 3.1.2

Figure 1 *Ionisation by collision*

atom

path of colliding electrons

atomic electron is knocked out of the atom

Ionisation

An ion is a charged atom. The number of electrons in an ion is not equal to the number of protons. An ion is formed from an uncharged atom by adding or removing electrons from the atom. Adding electrons makes the atom into a negative ion. Removing electrons makes the atom into a positive ion.

Any process of creating ions is called **ionisation**. For example:

- Alpha, beta and gamma radiation create ions when they pass through substances and collide with the atoms of the substance.
- Electrons passing through a fluorescent tube create ions when they collide with the atoms of the gas or vapour in the tube.

How science works

Measuring ionisation energy

We can measure the energy needed to ionise a gas atom by making electrons collide at increasing speed with the gas atoms in a sealed tube. The electrons are emitted from a heated filament in the tube and are attracted to a positive metal plate, the anode, at the other end of the tube. The gas needs to be at sufficiently low pressure otherwise there are too many atoms in the tube and the electrons cannot reach the anode.

The potential difference between the anode and the filament is increased so as to increase the speed of the electrons. The circuit is shown in Figure 2. The ammeter records a very small current due to electrons from the filament reaching the anode. No ionisation occurs until the electrons from the filament reach a certain speed. At this speed, each electron arrives near the anode with just enough kinetic energy to ionise a gas atom, by knocking an electron out of the atom. Ionisation near the anode causes a much greater current to pass through the ammeter.

By measuring the pd, V, between the filament and the anode, when the current starts to increase, we can calculate the ionisation energy of a gas atom, as this is equal to the work done W on each electron from the filament (and the work done is transformed to kinetic energy). The work done on each electron from the filament is given by its charge $e \times$ the tube potential difference V. Therefore, the **ionisation energy of a gas atom = eV**

Note:

You only need to know how ionisation occurs in a gas; the experimental details and the circuit are not required for your AS exam.

anode

gas at low pressure

electrons filament

Figure 2 *Measuring ionisation energy*

The electron volt

The **electron volt** is a unit of energy equal to the work done when an electron is moved through a pd of 1 volt. For a charge q moved through a pd V, the work done $= qV$. Therefore, the work done when an electron moves through a potential difference of 1 volt is equal to 1.6×10^{-19} J ($= 1.6 \times 10^{-19}$ C $\times$ 1 V). This amount of energy is defined as 1 electron volt (eV).

For example, the work done on:

■ an electron when it moves through a potential difference of 1000 V = 1000 eV

■ an ion of charge $+2e$ when it moves through a potential difference of 10 V = 20 eV

■ Excitation by collision

Using gas-filled tubes with a metal grid between the filament and the anode, we can show that gas atoms can absorb energy from colliding electrons without being ionised. This process, known as **excitation**, happens at certain energies, which are characteristic of the atoms of the gas. If a colliding electron loses all its kinetic energy when it causes excitation, the current due to the flow of electrons through the gas is reduced. If the colliding electron does not have enough kinetic energy to cause excitation, it is deflected by the atom, with no overall loss of kinetic energy.

The energy values at which an atom absorbs energy are known as its **excitation energies**. We can determine the excitation energies of the atoms in the gas-filled tube by increasing the potential difference between the filament and the anode and measuring the pd when the anode current falls. For example, two prominent excitation energies of a mercury atom are 4.9 eV and 5.7 eV.

When excitation occurs, the colliding electron makes an electron inside the atom move from an inner shell to an outer shell. Energy is needed for this process, because the atomic electron moves away from the nucleus of the atom. The excitation energy is always less than the ionisation energy of the atom, because the atomic electron is not removed completely from the atom when excitation occurs.

AQA Examiner's tip

Don't confuse atomic electrons with electrons that hit the atom.

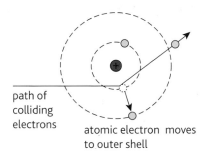

path of colliding electrons

atomic electron moves to outer shell

Figure 3 *Excitation by collision margin*

Summary questions

$e = 1.6 \times 10^{-19}$ C

1 State one difference and one similarity between ionisation and excitation.

2 a The mercury atom has an ionisation energy of 10.4 eV. Calculate this ionisation energy in joules.

   b An electron with 12.0 eV of kinetic energy collides with a mercury atom and ionises it. Calculate the kinetic energy, in eV, of the electron after the collision.

3 Complete the sentences below.

   a The ionisation energy of neon is much greater than that of sodium. Therefore, _____ energy is needed to remove an electron from a sodium atom than from a neon atom.

   b An electron that causes excitation of an atom by colliding with it has _____ kinetic energy before the collision than after the collision. The atom _____ the energy _____ by the electron.

4 a Describe what happens to a gas atom when an electron collides with it and causes it to absorb energy from the electron without being ionised.

   b Explain why a gas atom cannot absorb energy from a slow-moving electron that collides with it.

3.4 Energy levels in atoms

Learning objectives:

- What are energy levels?
- What happens when excited atoms 'de-excite'?
- How does a fluorescent tube work?

Specification reference: 3.1.2

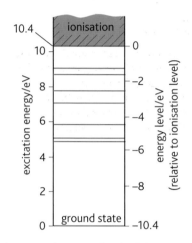

Figure 1 *The energy levels of the mercury atom*

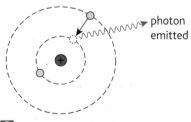

💡 **Figure 2** *De-excitation by photon emission*

Electrons in atoms

The electrons in an atom are trapped by the electrostatic force of attraction of the nucleus. They move about the nucleus in allowed orbits or 'shells' surrounding the nucleus. The energy of an electron in a shell is constant. An electron in a shell near the nucleus has less energy than an electron in a shell further away from the nucleus. Each shell can only hold a certain number of electrons. For example, the innermost shell (that is, the shell nearest to the nucleus) can only hold two electrons and the next nearest shell can only hold eight electrons.

Each type of atom has a certain number of electrons. For example, a helium atom has two electrons. Thus, in its lowest energy state, a helium atom has both electrons in the innermost shell.

The lowest energy state of an atom is called its **ground state**. When an atom in the ground state absorbs energy, one of its electrons moves to a shell at higher energy, so the atom is now in an **excited state**. We can use the excitation energy measurements to construct an energy level diagram for the atom, as shown in Figure 1. This shows the allowed energy values of the atom. Each allowed energy corresponds to a certain electron configuration in the atom. Note that the ionisation level may be considered as the 'zero' reference level for energy, instead of the ground state level.

De-excitation

Did you know that gases at low pressure emit light when they are made to conduct electricity? For example, a neon tube emits red-orange light when it conducts. The gas-filled tube used to measure excitation energies in Topic 3.3 emits light when excitation occurs. This happens because the atoms absorb energy as a result of excitation by collision but they do not retain the absorbed energy permanently.

The electron configuration in an excited atom is unstable because an electron that moves to an outer shell leaves a vacancy in the shell it moves from. Sooner or later, the vacancy is filled by an electron from an outer shell transferring to it. When this happens, the electron emits a photon. The atom therefore moves to a lower energy level.

The energy of the photon is equal to the energy lost by the electron and therefore by the atom. For example, when a mercury atom at an excitation energy level of 4.9 eV de-excites to the ground state, it emits a photon of energy 4.9 eV.

An atom in an excited state may de-excite to the ground state indirectly. For example, a mercury atom at an excitation energy of 5.7 eV may de-excite

- to the 4.9 eV level, emitting a 0.8 eV photon in the process; then
- to the ground state from the 4.9 eV level, emitting a 4.9 eV photon in this process.

In general, when an electron moves from energy level E_1 to a lower energy level E_2, **the energy of the emitted photon $hf = E_1 - E_2$**

Excitation using photons

An electron in an atom can absorb a photon and move to an outer shell where a vacancy exists – but only if the energy of the photon is exactly equal to the gain in the electron's energy (Figure 3). In other words, the photon energy must be exactly equal to the difference between the final and initial energy levels of the atom. If the photon's energy is smaller or larger than the difference between the two energy levels, it will not be absorbed by the electron.

Fluorescence

An atom in an excited state can de-excite directly or indirectly to the ground state, regardless of how the excitation took place. Therefore, an atom can absorb photons of certain energies and then emit photons of the same or lesser energies. For example, a mercury atom in the ground state could:

■ be excited to its 5.7 eV energy level by absorbing a photon of energy 5.7 eV; the mercury could then

■ de-excite to its 4.9 eV energy level by emitting a photon of energy 0.8 eV; then

■ de-excite to the ground state by emitting a photon of energy 4.9 eV.

Figure 4 represents these changes on an energy level diagram.

Figure 3 *Excitation by photon absorption*

■ **Hint**

A photon can be absorbed and cause ionisation if its energy is greater than or equal to the difference between the ionisation level and the ground state, although excitation requires photons of specific energies.

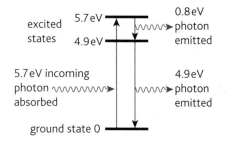

Figure 4 *Fluorescence*

This overall process explains why certain substances **fluoresce** or glow with visible light when they absorb ultraviolet radiation. Atoms in the substance absorb ultraviolet photons and become excited. When the atoms de-excite, they emit visible photons. When the source of ultraviolet radiation is removed, the substance stops glowing.

The **fluorescent tube** is a glass tube with a fluorescent coating on its inner surface. The tube contains mercury vapour at low pressure. When the tube is on, it emits visible light because:

■ ionisation and excitation of the mercury atoms occurs as they collide with each other and with electrons in the tube

■ the mercury atoms emit ultraviolet photons, as well as visible photons and photons of much less energy when they de-excite

■ the ultraviolet photons are absorbed by the atoms of the fluorescent coating, causing excitation of the atoms

■ the coating atoms de-excite and emit visible photons.

Figure 5 shows the circuit for a fluorescent tube. The tube is much more efficient than a filament lamp. A typical 100 W filament lamp releases about 10–15 W of light energy. The rest of the energy supplied to it is wasted as heat. In contrast, a fluorescent tube can produce the same light output with no more than a few watts of power wasted as heat.

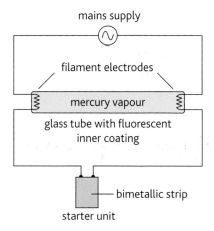

Figure 5 *The fluorescent tube*

Starting a fluorescent tube

The tube has a 'filament' electrode at each end. The starter unit is necessary because the mains voltage is too small to ionise the vapour in the tube when the electrodes are cold. When the tube is first switched on, the gas (argon) in the starter 'switch' unit conducts and heats the bimetallic strip, making it bend, so the switch closes. The current through the starter unit increases enough to heat the filament electrodes. When the bimetallic switch closes, the gas in the starter unit stops conducting, and so the bimetallic strip cools and the switch opens. The mains voltage now acts between the two electrodes, which are now hot enough for ionisation of the gas to occur.

Low energy light bulbs

Did you know that the UK government is stopping the sale of filament light bulbs? We will need to use low energy light bulbs instead. Such a light bulb uses much less power than a filament light bulb which has the same light output. This is because the light is produced by a folded-up fluorescent tube instead of a glowing filament so less energy is wasted as heat. A 100 W filament bulb emits about 15 W of light and wastes the rest. In contrast, a low energy light bulb with the same light output of 15 W wastes only about 5 W. Prove for yourself that the low energy light bulb is five times more efficient than the filament light bulb. Using them at home would cut your electricity bill considerably and help to cut carbon emissions.

Figure 6 *A filament light bulb and a low energy light bulb*

Summary questions

$e = 1.6 \times 10^{-19}$ C

1 Figure 1 shows some of the energy levels of the mercury atom.

  a Estimate the energy needed to excite the atom from the ground state to the highest excitation level shown in the diagram.

  b Mercury atoms in an excited state at 5.7 eV can de-excite directly or indirectly to the ground state. Show that the photons released could have six different energies.

2 a In terms of electrons, state two differences between excitation and de-excitation.

  b A certain type of atom has excitation energies of 1.8 eV and 4.6 eV.

  i Sketch an energy level diagram for the atom using these energy values.

  ii Calculate the possible photon energies from the atom when it de-excites from the 4.6 eV level, indicating on your diagram, by a downward arrow, the energy change responsible for each photon energy.

3 An atom absorbs a photon of energy 3.8 eV and subsequently emits photons of energy 0.6 eV and 3.2 eV.

  a Sketch an energy level diagram representing these changes.

  b In terms of electrons in the atom, describe how the above changes take place.

4 Explain why the gas atoms in a fluorescent tube stop emitting light when the electricity supply to it is switched off.

3.5 Energy levels and spectra

Learning objectives:

■ What is a line spectrum?

■ Why do atoms emit characteristic line spectra?

■ How do we calculate the wavelength of light for a given electron transition?

Specification reference: 3.1.2

Figure 1 *Observing a continuous spectrum*

Examiner's tip

Don't forget that lines in a spectrum are always due to energy levels.

💡 A colourful spectrum

A rainbow is a natural display of the colours of the spectrum of sunlight. Raindrops split sunlight into a continuous spectrum of colours. Figure 1 shows how we can use a prism to split a beam of white light from a filament lamp into a continuous spectrum. The wavelength of the light photons that produce the spectrum increases across the spectrum from deep violet at less than 400 nm to deep red at about 650 nm.

If we use a tube of glowing gas as the light source instead of a filament lamp, we see a spectrum of discrete lines of different colours, as shown in Figure 2, instead of a continuous spectrum.

Figure 2 *A line spectrum*

The wavelengths of the lines of a line spectrum of an element are characteristic of the atoms of that element. By measuring the wavelengths of a line spectrum, we can therefore identify the element that produced the light. No other element produces the same pattern of light wavelengths. This is because the energy levels of each type of atom are unique to that atom. So the photons emitted are characteristic of the atom.

■ Each line in a line spectrum is due to light of a certain colour and therefore a certain wavelength.

■ The photons that produce each line all have the same energy, which is different to the photons that produce any other line.

■ Each photon is emitted when an atom de-excites due to one of its electrons moving to an inner shell.

■ As explained in Topic 3.4, if the electron moves from energy level E_1 to a lower energy level E_2,

the energy of the emitted photon $hf = E_1 - E_2$

In Topic 13.7, we will see how to measure the wavelengths of the lines of a line spectrum. For each wavelength λ, we can calculate the energy of a photon of that wavelength as its frequency $f = c/\lambda$, where c is the speed of light. Given the energy level diagram for the atom, we can therefore identify on the diagram the transition that causes a photon of that wavelength to be emitted.

*Worked example:*_____

$c = 3.0 \times 10^8 \, \mathrm{m \, s^{-1}}$, $e = 1.6 \times 10^{-19} \, \mathrm{C}$, $h = 6.63 \times 10^{-34} \, \mathrm{J \, s}$

A mercury atom de-excites from its 4.9 eV energy level to the ground state. Calculate the wavelength of the photon released.

Solution

$$E_1 - E_2 = 4.9 - 0 = 4.9\,eV = 4.9 \times 1.6 \times 10^{-19}\,J = 7.84 \times 10^{-19}\,J$$

Therefore, $f = \dfrac{E_1 - E_2}{h} = \dfrac{7.84 \times 10^{-19}}{6.63 \times 10^{-34}} = 1.18 \times 10^{15}\,Hz$

$$\lambda = \frac{c}{f} = \frac{3.0 \times 10^8}{1.18 \times 10^{15}} = 2.54 \times 10^{-7}\,m$$

How science works

The Bohr atom

The hydrogen atom is the simplest type of atom – just one proton as its nucleus and one electron. The energy levels of the hydrogen atom, relative to the ionisation level, are given by the general formula:

$$E = -\frac{13.6\,eV}{n^2}$$

where $n = 1$ for the ground state, $n = 2$ for the next excited state, etc.

Therefore, when a hydrogen atom de-excites from energy level n_1 to a lower energy level n_2, the energy of the emitted photon is given by

$$E = \left| \frac{1}{n_2^2} - \frac{1}{n_1^2} \right| \times 13.6\,eV$$

Each energy level corresponds to the electron in a particular shell. Thus the above formula gives the energy of a photon released when an electron in the hydrogen atom moves from one shell to a shell at lower energy.

Figure 3 shows an example of a transition that can take place in an excited hydrogen atom. The energy level formula for hydrogen was first deduced from the measurements of the wavelengths of the lines. Later, the Danish physicist Niels Bohr applied the quantum theory to the motion of the electron in the hydrogen atom, and so produced the first theoretical explanation of the energy level formula for hydrogen.

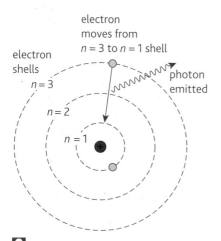

💡 **Figure 3** *An electron transition in the hydrogen atom*

Summary questions

$h = 6.63 \times 10^{-34}\,J\,s$,
$c = 3.00 \times 10^8\,m\,s^{-1}$,
$e = 1.6 \times 10^{-19}\,C$

1 State two differences between a continuous spectrum and a line spectrum

2 A mercury atom de-excites from 5.7 eV to 4.9 eV. For the photon emitted, calculate

a its energy in J,

b its wavelength.

3 A line spectrum has a line at a wavelength of 620 nm. Calculate

a the energy, in J, of a photon of this wavelength,

b the energy loss, in eV, of an atom that emits a photon of this wavelength.

4 Explain why the line spectrum of an element is unique to that element and can be used to identify it.

■ The discovery of helium

Measurements of the wavelength of light are important in branches of science such as astronomy and forensic science, as they enable us to identify the chemical elements in the light source. Helium was discovered from the spectrum of sunlight. A pattern of lines in the spectrum was observed at wavelengths that had never been observed from any known gas, and were therefore due to the presence of a previously unknown element in the Sun. Helium is produced as a result of the nuclear fusion of hydrogen nuclei in the Sun, and was given the name helium from *helios*, the Greek word for sun. Helium is also present in the Earth, produced as alpha particles from the radioactive decay of elements such as uranium. It can be collected at oil wells and stored for use in fusion reactors, helium-neon lasers and for very low temperature devices. In the liquid state, below a temperature of 2.17 K, it becomes a superfluid. This is a fluid with no resistance to flow, which escapes from an open container by creeping, as a thin film, up and over the sides of the container.

3.6 Wave particle duality

Learning objectives:

■ Why do we say photons have a dual nature?

■ How do we know that matter particles have a dual nature?

■ Why can we change the wavelength of a matter particle but not of a photon?

Specification reference: 3.1.2

The dual nature of light

Light is part of the electromagnetic spectrum of waves. The theory of electromagnetic waves predicted the existence of electromagnetic waves beyond the visible spectrum. The subsequent discovery of X-rays and radio waves confirmed these predictions and seemed to show that the nature of light had been settled. Many scientists in the late nineteenth century reckoned that all aspects of physics could be explained using Newton's laws of motion, and the theory of electromagnetic waves. They thought that the few minor problem areas, such as photoelectricity, would be explained sooner or later using Newton's laws of motion and Maxwell's theory of electromagnetic waves. However, as explained in Topic 3.1, photoelectricity was not explained until Einstein put forward the radical theory that light consists of photons, which are 'particle-like' packets of electromagnetic waves. Light has a dual nature, in that it can behave as a wave or as a particle, according to circumstances.

■ The **wave-like nature** is observed when **diffraction of light** takes place. This happens, for example, when light passes through a narrow slit. The light emerging from the slit spreads out in the same way as water waves spread out after passing through a gap. The narrower the gap or the longer the wavelength, the greater the amount of diffraction.

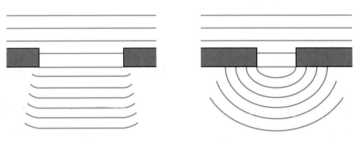

Figure 1 *Diffraction*

■ The **particle-like nature** is observed, for example, in the photoelectric effect. When light is directed at a metal surface and an electron at the surface absorbs a photon of frequency f, the kinetic energy of the electron is increased from a negligible value by hf. As described in Topic 3.1, the electron can escape if the energy it gains from a photon exceeds the work function of the metal.

💡 Matter waves

If light has a dual wave–particle nature, perhaps particles of matter also have a dual wave–particle nature. Electrons in a beam can be deflected by a magnetic field. This is evidence that electrons have a particle-like nature. The idea that matter particles also have a wave-like nature was first considered by de Broglie in 1923. By extending the ideas of duality from photons to matter particles, de Broglie put forward the hypothesis that:

■ matter particles have a dual wave–particle nature

■ the wave-like behaviour of a matter particle is characterised by a wavelength, its **de Broglie wavelength, λ,** which is related to the momentum, p, of the particle by means of the equation

$$\lambda = \frac{h}{p}$$

Since the momentum of a particle is defined as its mass × its velocity, according to de Broglie's hypothesis, a particle of mass m moving at velocity v has a de Broglie wavelength given by

$$\lambda = \frac{h}{mv}$$

Note:

The de Broglie wavelength of a particle can be altered by changing the velocity of the particle.

Examiner's tip

Don't mix up matter waves and electromagnetic waves and don't mix up their formulae!

Evidence for de Broglie's hypothesis

The wave-like nature of electrons was discovered when, 3 years after de Broglie put forward his hypothesis, it was demonstrated that a beam of electrons can be diffracted. Figure 2 shows in outline how this is done. After this discovery, further experimental evidence, using other types of particles, confirmed the correctness of de Broglie's theory.

pattern of rings seen on the screen

Figure 2 *Diffraction of electrons*

■ A narrow beam of electrons in a vacuum tube is directed at a thin metal foil. A metal is composed of many tiny crystalline regions. Each region or 'grain' consists of positive ions arranged in fixed positions in rows in a regular pattern. The rows of atoms cause the electrons in the beam to be diffracted, just as a beam of light is diffracted when it passes through a slit.

■ The electrons in the beam pass through the metal foil and are diffracted in certain directions only, as shown in Figure 2. They form a pattern of rings on a fluorescent screen at the end of the tube. Each ring is due to electrons diffracted by the same amount from grains of different orientations, at the same angle to the incident beam.

■ The beam of electrons is produced by attracting electrons from a heated filament wire to a positively charged metal plate, which has a small hole at its centre. Electrons that pass through the hole form the beam. The speed of these electrons can be increased by increasing the potential difference between the filament and the metal plate. This makes the diffraction rings smaller, because the increase of speed makes the de Broglie wavelength smaller. So less diffraction occurs and the rings become smaller.

How science works

Energy levels explained

An electron in an atom has a fixed amount of energy that depends on the shell it occupies. Its de Broglie wavelength has to fit the shape and size of the shell. This is why its energy depends on the shell it occupies.

For example, an electron in a spherical shell moves round the nucleus in a circular orbit. The circumference of its orbit must be equal to a whole number of de Broglie wavelengths (circumference $= n\lambda$, where $n = 1$ or 2 or 3, etc.). You don't need to know this for your AS level exam but this condition can be used to derive the energy level formula for the hydrogen atom – and it gives you a deeper insight into quantum physics.

Quantum technology

The PET scanner outlined on p10 is an example of quantum physics in use. Some further applications of quantum technology include

■ The STM (scanning tunneling microscope) is used to map atoms on solid surfaces (see Figure 1, Topic 1.1). The wave nature of electrons allows them to tunnel between the surface and a metal tip a few nanometres above the surface as the tip scans across the surface.

■ The TEM (transmission electron microscope) is used to obtain very detailed images of objects and surface features too small to see with optical microscopes. Electrons are accelerated in a TEM to high speed so their de Broglie wavelength is so small that they can give very detailed images.

■ The MR (magnetic resonance) body scanner used in hospitals. This detects radio waves emitted when hydrogen atoms in a patient in a strong magnetic field flip between energy levels.

■ SQUIDs (superconducting quantum interference devices) are used to detect very very weak magnetic fields, for example SQUIDs are used to detect magnetic fields produced by electrical activity in the brain.

Figure 3 *SQUIDS in use*

Summary questions

$h = 6.6 \times 10^{-34}$ J s,
the mass of an electron $= 9.1 \times 10^{-31}$ kg,
the mass of a proton $= 1.7 \times 10^{-27}$ kg

1 With the aid of an example in each case, explain what is meant by the dual wave–particle nature of
a light, b matter particles.

2 State whether each of the following experiments demonstrates the wave nature or the particle nature of matter or of light: a photoelectricity, b electron diffraction.

3 Calculate the de Broglie wavelength of
a an electron moving at a speed of 2.0×10^7 m s^{-1}
b a proton moving at the same speed.

4 Calculate the momentum and speed of
a an electron that has a de Broglie wavelength of 500 nm,
b a proton that has the same de Broglie wavelength.

1   When light at sufficiently high frequency, f, is incident on a metal surface, the maximum kinetic energy, E_{Kmax}, of a photoelectron is given by

$E_{Kmax} = hf - \phi$ where ϕ is the work function of the metal.

(a) State what is meant by the work function ϕ.   *(1 mark)*

(b) The following results were obtained in an experiment to measure E_{Kmax} for different frequencies, f.

f / 10^{14} Hz	5.6	6.2	6.8	7.3	8.3	8.9
E_{Kmax} / 10^{-19} J	0.8	1.2	1.7	2.1	2.9	3.4

   (i)   Use these results to plot a graph of E_{Kmax} against f.

   (ii) Explain why your graph confirms the equation above.

   (iii) Use your graph to determine the value of h and to calculate the work function of the metal.   *(13 marks)*

(c) Measurements like those above were first made to test the correctness of Einstein's explanation of photoelectricity. The equation above was a prediction by Einstein using the photon theory.
     Why is it important to test any new theory by testing its predictions experimentally?   *(2 marks)*

2   (a) One quantity in the photoelectric equation is a characteristic property of the metal that emits photoelectrons. Name and define this quantity.   *(2 marks)*

(b) A metal is illuminated with monochromatic light. Explain why the kinetic energy of the photoelectrons emitted has a range of values up to a certain maximum.   *(3 marks)*

(c) A gold surface is illuminated with monochromatic ultraviolet light of frequency 1.8×10^{15} Hz. The maximum kinetic energy of the emitted photoelectrons is 4.2×10^{-19} J. Calculate, for gold:

   (i)   the work function, in J,

   (ii) the threshold frequency.   *(5 marks)*

   AQA, 2006

3   **Figure 1** shows how the maximum kinetic energy of electrons emitted from the cathode of a photoelectric cell varies with the frequency of the incident radiation.

Figure 1

(a) Calculate the maximum wavelength of electromagnetic radiation that can release photoelectrons from the cathode surface.

speed of electromagnetic radiation in a vacuum $= 3.0 \times 10^8 \, \text{m s}^{-1}$ *(3 marks)*

(b) Another photoelectric cell uses a different metal for the photocathode. This metal requires twice the minimum energy for electron release compared to the metal in the first cell.

   (i) If drawn on the same axes, how would the graph line obtained for this second cell compare with the one for the first cell?

   (ii) Explain your answer with reference to the Einstein photoelectric equation.   *(3 marks)*

AQA, 2003

4   A fluorescent light tube contains mercury vapour at low pressure. The tube is coated on the inside, and contains two electrodes.

(a) Explain why the mercury vapour is at a low pressure.   *(1 mark)*

(b) Explain the purpose of the coating on the inside of the tube.   *(3 marks)*

AQA, 2003

5   The lowest energy levels of a mercury atom are shown below. The diagram is **not** to scale.

energy/$J \times 10^{-18}$

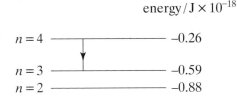

$n = 4$ ————————— −0.26

$n = 3$ ————————— −0.59

$n = 2$ ————————— −0.88

ground state $n = 1$ ————————— −2.18

(a) Calculate the frequency of an emitted photon due to a transition, shown by an arrow, from level $n = 4$ to level $n = 3$.   *(2 marks)*

(b) Which transition would cause the emission of a photon of a longer wavelength than that emitted in the transition from level $n = 4$ to level $n = 3$?   *(1 mark)*

AQA, 2002

6   (a) State what is meant by the duality of electrons. Give **one** example of each type of behaviour.   *(3 marks)*

(b) (i) Calculate the speed of an electron which has a de Broglie wavelength of $1.3 \times 10^{-10} \, \text{m}$.

   (ii) A particle when travelling at the speed calculated in (b)(i) has a de Broglie wavelength of $8.6 \times 10^{-14} \, \text{m}$.

    Calculate the mass of the particle.   *(4 marks)*

AQA, 2007

7   Electrons travelling at a speed of $5.00 \times 10^5 \, \text{m s}^{-1}$ exhibit wave properties.

(a) What phenomenon can be used to demonstrate the wave properties of electrons? Details of any apparatus used are not required.   *(1 mark)*

(b) Calculate the wavelength of these electrons.   *(2 marks)*

(c) Calculate the speed of muons with the same wavelength as these electrons.

Mass of muon $= 207 \times$ mass of electron   *(3 marks)*

(d) Both electrons and muons were accelerated from rest by the same potential difference. Explain why they have different wavelengths.   *(2 marks)*

AQA, 2003

4 Electric current

4.1 Current and charge

Learning objectives:

- What is an electric current?

- How can we calculate the charge flow in a circuit?

- What are charge carriers?

Specification reference: 3.1.3

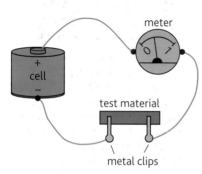

Figure 1 *Testing for conduction*

Figure 2 *Convention for current*

Electrical conduction

To make an electric current pass round a circuit, the circuit must be complete and there must be a source of potential difference, such as a battery, in the circuit. The electric current is the rate of flow of charge in the wire or component. The current is due to the passage of charged particles. These charged particles are referred to as **charge carriers**.

- In metals, the charge carriers are conduction electrons. They move about inside the metal, repeatedly colliding with each other and the fixed positive ions in the metal.

- In comparison, when an electric current is passed through a salt solution, the charge is carried by ions, which are charged atoms or molecules.

A simple test for conduction of electricity is shown in Figure 1. The meter shows a non-zero reading whenever any conducting material is connected into the circuit. The battery forces the charge carriers through the conducting material and causes electrons to pass through the battery and the meter. If the test material is a metal, electrons leave the battery at its negative terminal, pass through the conducting material then re-enter the battery at its positive terminal.

The convention for the direction of current in a circuit is from positive (+) to negative (−), as shown in Figure 2. The convention was agreed long before the discovery of electrons. When it was set up, it was known that an electric current is a flow of charge one way round a circuit. However, it was not known whether the current was due to positive charge flowing round the circuit from + to −, or if it was due to negative charge flowing from − to +.

The unit of current is the **ampere** (**A**), which is defined in terms of the magnetic force between two parallel wires when they carry the same current. The symbol for current is I.

The unit of charge is the **coulomb** (**C**), equal to the charge flow in one second when the current is one ampere. The symbol for charge is Q.

For a current I, the charge flow ΔQ in time Δt is given by

$$\Delta Q = I \Delta t$$

For example, the charge flow for a current of:

- 1 A in 10 s is 10 C

- 3 A in 10 s is 30 C

- 5 A in 200 s is 1000 C.

For charge flow ΔQ in a time interval Δt, the current I is given by

$$I = \frac{\Delta Q}{\Delta t}$$

The equation shows that a current of 1 A is due to a flow of charge of 1 coulomb per second. As the magnitude of the charge of the electron is

1.6×10^{-19} C, a current of 1 A along a wire must be due to 6.25×10^{18} electrons passing along the wire each second.

More about charge carriers

Materials can be classified in electrical terms as conductors, insulators or semiconductors.

- In an insulator, each electron is attached to an atom and cannot move away from the atom. When a voltage is applied across an insulator, no current passes through the insulator, because no electrons can move through the insulator.
- In a metallic conductor, most electrons are attached to atoms but some are not, and these are the charge carriers in the metal. When a voltage is applied across the metal, these conduction electrons are attracted towards the positive terminal of the metal.
- In a semiconductor, the number of charge carriers increases with an increase of temperature. The resistance of a semiconductor therefore decreases as its temperature is raised. A pure semiconducting material is referred to as an intrinsic semiconductor because conduction is due to electrons that break free from the atoms of the semiconductor.

How science works

Rechargeable batteries

A car battery is a 12 V rechargeable battery designed to supply a very large current to start the engine. The battery is recharged when the car engine is running. Smaller rechargeable batteries are used in portable electronic equipment, for example, in cameras and iPods. Such a battery supplies a much smaller current than a car battery. Disposable batteries can't be recharged. Once a disposable battery has 'run down', it is no longer of any use – not as environmentally friendly as a rechargeable battery!

Summary questions

$e = 1.6 \times 10^{-19}$ C

1. a The current in a certain wire is 0.35 A. Calculate the charge passing a point in the wire i in 10 s, ii in 10 min.
   b Calculate the average current in a wire through which a charge of 15 C passes in i 5 s, ii 100 s.

2. Calculate the number of electrons passing a point in the wire in 10 min when the current is:
   a 1.0 μA, b 5.0 A.

3. In an electron beam experiment, the beam current is 1.2 mA. Calculate
   a the charge flowing along the beam each minute
   b the number of electrons that pass along the beam each minute.

4. A certain type of rechargeable battery is capable of delivering a current of 0.2 A for 4000 s before its voltage drops and it needs to be recharged. Calculate:
   a the total charge the battery can deliver before it needs to be recharged,
   b the maximum time it could be used for without being recharged if the current through it was
   i 0.5 A, ii 0.1 A.

How science works

Physics and the human genome project

To map the human genome, fragments of DNA are tagged with amino acid bases. Each tagged fragment carries a negative charge. A voltage is applied across a strip of gel with a spot of liquid on it containing tagged fragments. The fragments are attracted to the positive electrode. The smaller the fragment, the faster it moves, so the fragments separate out according to size as they move to the positive electrode. The fragments pass through a spot of laser light, which causes a dye attached to each tag to fluoresce as it passes through the laser spot. Light sensors linked to a computer detect the glow from each tag. The computer is programmed to work out and display the sequence of bases in the DNA fragments.

4.2 Potential difference and power

Learning objectives:

- What do we mean by potential difference?

- How can we calculate electrical power?

- How do energy transfers take place in electrical devices?

Specification reference: 3.1.3

i Energy and potential difference

When a torch bulb is connected to a battery, electrons deliver energy from the battery to the torch bulb. Each electron takes a fixed amount of energy from the battery as it passes through it. The electrons then deliver energy to the bulb as they pass through it. After delivering energy to the bulb, each electron re-enters the battery via the positive terminal to be resupplied with more energy to deliver to the bulb.

Figure 1 *Energy transfer by electrons*

Each electron in the battery has the potential to deliver energy even if the battery is not part of a complete circuit. In other words, the battery supplies each electron with electrical potential energy. When the battery is in a circuit, each electron passing through a circuit component does work to pass through the component and therefore uses some or all of its electrical potential energy. The work done by an electron is equal to its loss of potential energy. The work done per unit charge is defined as the **potential difference** (abbreviated as pd) or **voltage** across the component.

Potential difference is defined as the work done (or energy transfer) per unit charge. The unit of pd is the volt which is equal to 1 joule per coulomb.

If work W is done when charge Q flows through the component, the pd across the component V is given by

$$V = \frac{W}{Q}$$

Rearranging this equation gives $W = QV$ for the work done or energy transfer when charge Q passes through a component which has a pd V across its terminals.

For example:

- If 30 J of work is done when 5 C of charge passes through a component, the pd across the component must be 6 V (= 30 J/5 C).

- If the pd across a component in a circuit is 12 V, then 3 C of charge passing through the component would transfer 36 J of energy from the battery to the component.

The emf of a source of electricity is defined as the electrical energy produced per unit charge passing through the source. The unit of emf is the volt, the same as the unit of pd.

For a source of emf ε in a circuit, the electrical energy produced when charge Q passes through the source $= Q\varepsilon$. This energy is transferred to other parts

Figure 2 *Power supplies*

of the circuit and some may be dissipated in the source itself due to the source's internal resistance. (See Topic 5.3 Emf and internal resistance.)

Energy transfer in different devices

Figure 3 *Electrical devices*

An electric current has a heating effect when it passes through a component with resistance. It also has a magnetic effect, which is made use of in electric motors and loudspeakers.

1 In a device that has resistance, such as an electrical heater, the work done on the device is transferred as thermal energy. This happens because the charge carriers repeatedly collide with atoms in the device and transfer energy to them, so the atoms vibrate more and the resistor becomes hotter.

2 In an electric motor, the work done on the motor is transferred as kinetic energy of the motor. The charge carriers are electrons that need to be forced through the wires of the spinning motor coil against the opposing force on the electrons due to the motor's magnetic field.

3 For a loudspeaker, the work done on the loudspeaker is transferred as sound energy. Electrons need to be forced through the wires of the vibrating loudspeaker coil against the force on them due to the loudspeaker magnet.

■ Electrical power and current

Consider a component or device that has a potential difference V across its terminals and a current I passing through it. In time Δt:

- the charge flow through it, $Q = I\Delta t$
- the work done by the charge carriers, $W = QV = (I\Delta t)V = IV\Delta t$

$$\text{Work done } W = IV\Delta t$$

The energy transfer ΔE in the component or device is equal to the work done W.

Because power $= \dfrac{\text{energy}}{\text{time}}$, the electrical power P supplied to the device is

$$\frac{IV\Delta t}{\Delta t} = IV$$

$$\text{Electrical power } P = IV$$

Notes

1 This equation can be rearranged to give $I = \dfrac{P}{V}$ or $V = \dfrac{P}{I}$

2 The unit of power is the watt (W). Therefore one volt is equal to one watt per ampere. For example, if the pd across a component is 4 V, then the power delivered to the component is 4 W per ampere of current.

4.3 Resistance

Learning objectives:

- What causes electrical resistance?
- When can we use Ohm's law?
- What is a superconductor?

Specification reference: 3.1.3

Definitions and laws

The resistance of a component in a circuit is a measure of the difficulty of making current pass through the component. Resistance is caused by the repeated collisions between the charge carriers in the material with each other and with the fixed positive ions of the material.

The resistance of any component is defined as

$$\frac{\text{the pd across the component}}{\text{the current through it}}$$

For a component which passes current I when the pd across it is V, its resistance R is given by the equation

$$R = \frac{V}{I}$$

The unit of resistance is the ohm (Ω), which is equal to 1 volt per ampere.

Rearranging the above equation gives $V = IR$ or $I = \frac{V}{R}$

Reminder about prefixes

Table 1 *Prefixes*

prefix	nano	micro	milli	kilo	mega	giga
symbol	n	μ	m	k	M	G
value	10^{-9}	10^{-6}	10^{-3}	10^{3}	10^{6}	10^{9}

Worked example:

The current through a component is 2.0 mA when the pd across it is 12 V. Calculate:

a its resistance at this current,

b the pd across the component when the current is 50 μA, assuming its resistance is unchanged.

Solution

a $R = \frac{V}{I} = \frac{12}{2.0 \times 10^{-3}} = 6000\,\Omega$

b $V = IR = 50 \times 10^{-6} \times 6000 = 0.30\,V$

Measurement of resistance

A resistor is a component designed to have a certain resistance, which is the same regardless of the current through it. The resistance of a resistor can be measured using the circuit shown in Figure 1.

- The ammeter is used to measure the current through the resistor. The ammeter must be in series with the resistor, so the same current passes through both the resistor and the ammeter.

- The voltmeter is used to measure the pd across the resistor. The voltmeter must be in parallel with the resistor so that they have the same pd. Also, no current should pass through the voltmeter, otherwise the ammeter will not record the exact current through the resistor. In theory, the voltmeter should have infinite resistance. In practice, a voltmeter with a sufficiently high resistance would be satisfactory.

- The variable resistor is used to adjust the current and pd as necessary. To investigate the variation of current with pd, the variable resistor is adjusted in steps. At each step, the current and pd are recorded from the ammeter and voltmeter respectively. The measurements can then be plotted on a graph of pd against current, as shown in Figure 2 (or current against pd – see Topic 4.4).

Figure 1 *Measuring resistance*

The graph for a resistor is a straight line through the origin. The resistance is the same, regardless of the current. The resistance is equal to the gradient of the graph because the gradient is constant and at any point is equal to the pd divided by the current. In other words, the pd across the resistor is proportional to the current. The discovery that the pd across a metal wire is proportional to the current through it was made by Georg Ohm in 1826, and is known as Ohm's law.

Ohm's law states that the pd across a metallic conductor is proportional to the current through it, provided the physical conditions do not change.

Notes:

1 Ohm's law is equivalent to the statement that the resistance of a metallic conductor under constant physical conditions (e.g. temperature) is constant.

2 For an ohmic conductor, $V = IR$ where R is constant. A resistor is a component designed to have a certain resistance.

3 If the current and pd measurements for an ohmic conductor are plotted with current on the y-axis and pd on the x-axis, the gradient of this graph gives $1/R$.

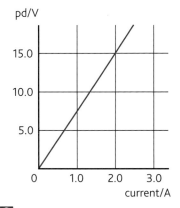

Figure 2 *Graph of pd v current for a resistor*

💡 ⚠ Resistivity

For a conductor of length L and uniform cross-sectional area A, as shown in Figure 3, its resistance R is

- proportional to L
- inversely proportional to A

Hence $R = \dfrac{\rho L}{A}$, where ρ is a constant for that material, known as its resistivity.

Figure 3 *Resistivity*

Rearranging this equation gives the following equation which can be used to calculate the resistivity of a sample of material of length L and uniform cross-sectional area A:

$$\text{resistivity, } \rho = \frac{RA}{L}$$

Notes:

1 The unit of resistivity is the ohm metre ($\Omega\,\text{m}$).

2 For a conductor with a circular cross-section of diameter d, $A = \dfrac{\pi d^2}{4}$ ($= \pi r^2$ where radius $r = d/2$)

Table 2 *Resistivity values of different materials at room temperature*

material	resistivity / $\Omega\,m$
copper	1.7×10^{-8}
constantan	5.0×10^{-7}
carbon	3×10^{-5}
silicon	2300
PVC	about 10^{14}

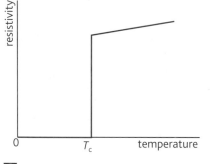

Figure 4 *Resistivity of a superconductor v temperature near the critical temperature*

Superconductivity

A superconductor is a wire or a device made of material that has zero resistivity at and below a **critical temperature** that depends on the material. This property of the material is called **superconductivity**. The wire or device has zero resistance below the critical temperature of the material. When a current passes through it, there is no pd across it because its resistance is zero. So the current has no heating effect.

A superconductor material loses its superconductivity if its temperature is raised above its critical temperature. The highest critical temperature currently claimed and awaiting verification is $150\,K$ $(-123\,°C)$ for a compound containing mercury, barium, calcium, copper and oxygen. Any material with a critical temperature above $77\,K$ $(-196\,°C)$, the boiling point of liquid nitrogen, is referred to as a high-temperature superconductor.

Superconductors are used to make high-power electromagnets that generate very strong magnetic fields and power cables that transfer electrical energy without wasting energy.

Summary questions

1 **a** Complete the table below by calculating the missing value for each resistor.

	1	2	3	4	5
current	2.0 A	0.45 A		5.0 mA	
pd	12.0 V		5.0 V	0.80 V	50 kV
resistance		22 Ω	40 kΩ		20 MΩ

b Use Figure 2 to find the resistance of the resistor that gave the results shown.

2 Calculate the resistance of a uniform wire of diameter 0.32 mm and length 5.0 m. The resistivity of the material = $5.0 \times 10^{-7}\,\Omega\,m$.

3 Calculate the resistance of a rectangular strip of copper of length 0.08 m, thickness 15 mm and width 0.80 mm. The resistivity of copper = $1.7 \times 10^{-8}\,\Omega\,m$.

4 A wire of uniform diameter 0.28 mm and length 1.50 m has a resistance of 45 Ω. Calculate:

a its resistivity,

b the length of this wire that has a resistance of 1.0 Ω.

4.4 Components and their characteristics

Specification reference: 3.1.3

Learning objectives:

- How does the current through a filament lamp vary with pd?

- What are the characteristics of a diode?

- What can we use a thermistor for?

—(A)—	ammeter
—(V)—	voltmeter
—⊣⊢—	cell
—⊗—	indicator or light source
—▷⊢—	diode
light-emitting diode	
resistor	
variable resistor	
thermistor	
light-dependent resistor	
heater	
—(M)—	electric motor

Figure 1 Circuit components

Circuit diagrams

Each type of component has its own symbol, which is used to represent the component in a circuit diagram. You need to recognise the symbols for different types of components to make progress – just like a motorist needs to know what different road signs mean. Note that on a circuit diagram, the direction of the current is always shown from + to – round the circuit.

You should be able to recognise the component symbols shown in Figure 1. Here are some notes about some of the components.

- A cell is a source of electrical energy. Note that a battery is a combination of cells.

- The symbol for an indicator or any light source (including a filament lamp, but not a light emitting diode) is the same.

- A diode allows current in one direction only. A light-emitting diode (or LED) emits light when it conducts. The direction in which the diode conducts is referred to as its 'forward' direction. The opposite direction is referred to as its 'reverse' direction. Examples of the use of diodes include the protection of dc circuits (in case the voltage supply is connected the wrong way round) and rectification (changing ac to dc).

- A resistor is a component designed to have a certain resistance.

- The resistance of a thermistor decreases with increasing temperature, if the thermistor is an intrinsic semiconductor such as silicon.

- The resistance of a light-dependent resistor (LDR) decreases with increasing light intensity.

Investigating the characteristics of different components

To measure the variation of current with pd for a component, use either

- a potential divider to vary the pd from zero, or
- a variable resistor to vary the current to a minimum.

Figure 2 Investigating component characteristics (a) using a potential divider (b) using a variable resistor

The advantage of using a potential divider is that the current through the component and the pd across it can be reduced to zero. This is not possible with a variable resistor circuit.

The measurements for each type of component are usually plotted as a graph of current (on the y-axis) against pd (on the x-axis). Typical graphs for a wire, a filament lamp, and a thermistor are shown in Figure 3. Note that the measurements are the same, regardless of which way the current passes through each of these components.

In both circuits, an ammeter sensor and a voltmeter sensor connected to a data logger could be used to capture data (i.e. to measure and record the readings) which could then be displayed directly on an oscilloscope or a computer.

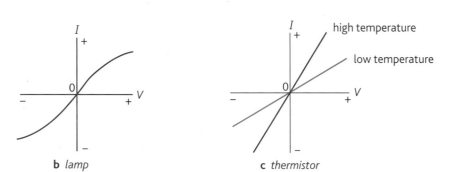

■ **Figure 3** *Current v pd for different components*

- A wire gives a straight line with a constant gradient equal to $1/$resistance R of the wire. Any resistor at constant temperature would give a straight line.
- A filament bulb gives a curve with a decreasing gradient because its resistance increases as it becomes hotter.
- ⚠ A thermistor at constant temperature gives a straight line. The higher the temperature, the greater the gradient of the line, as the resistance falls with increase of temperature. The same result is obtained for a light-dependent resistor in respect of light intensity.

⚠ The diode

To investigate the characteristics of the diode, one set of measurements is made with the diode in its 'forward direction' (i.e. forward biased) and another set with it in its 'reverse direction' (i.e. reverse biased). The current is very small when the diode is reverse biased and can only be measured using a milliammeter.

■ **Figure 4** *Current v pd for a diode*

Typical results for a silicon diode are shown in Figure 4. A silicon diode conducts easily in its 'forward' direction above a pd of about 0.6 V and hardly at all below 0.6 V or in the opposite direction.

Resistance and temperature

The resistance of a metal increases with increase of temperature. This is because the positive ions in the conductor vibrate more when its temperature is increased. The charge carriers (conduction electrons) therefore cannot pass through the metal as easily when a pd is applied across the conductor. A metal is said to have a **positive temperature coefficient** because its resistance increases with increase of temperature.

The resistance of an intrinsic semiconductor decreases with increase of temperature. This is because the number of charge carriers (conduction electrons) increases when the temperature is increased. A thermistor made from an intrinsic semiconductor therefore has a **negative temperature coefficient**. Its % change of resistance per kelvin change of temperature is much greater than for a metal. For this reason, thermistors are often used as the temperature-sensitive component in a temperature sensor.

Hint

Remember, a diode needs a certain pd to conduct.

Summary questions

1 A filament bulb is labelled '3.0V, 0.75W'.
   a Calculate its current and its resistance at 3.0V.
   b State and explain what would happen to the filament bulb if the current was increased from the value in **a**.

2 A certain thermistor has a resistance of 50 000 Ω at 20 °C and a resistance of 4000 Ω at 60 °C.

   It is connected in series with an ammeter and a 1.5 V cell. Calculate the ammeter reading when the thermistor is:
   a at 20 °C,
   b at 60 °C.

3 A silicon diode is connected in series with a cell and a torch bulb.
   a Sketch the circuit diagram showing the diode in its 'forward' direction.
   b Explain why the torch bulb would not light if the polarity of the cell were reversed in the circuit.

4 The resistance of a certain metal wire increased from 25.3 Ω at 0 °C to 35.5 Ω at 100 °C. Assuming the resistance over this range varies linearly with temperature, calculate:
   a the resistance at 50 °C,
   b the temperature when the resistance is 30.0 Ω.

1   The following measurements were made in an investigation to measure the resistivity of the material of a certain wire.

pd across the wire / V	0.0	2.0	4.0	6.0	8.0	10.0
current through the wire / A	0.00	0.15	0.31	0.44	0.62	0.74

Length of wire = 1.60 m

Diameter of wire = 0.28 mm

(a) Plot a graph of the pd against the current. *(4 marks)*

(b) Show that the pd, V, across the wire varies with the current I according to the equation

$$V = \frac{\rho L I}{A}$$

where ρ is the resistivity of the wire, L is its length and A is its area of cross-section. *(2 marks)*

(c) Use the graph to calculate the resistivity of the material of the wire. *(6 marks)*

2   A battery is connected across a uniform conductor. The current in the conductor is 40 mA.

(i)   Calculate the total charge that flows past a point in the conductor in 3 minutes.

(ii) Using data from the Data Booklet calculate the number of electron charge carriers passing the same point in the conductor in this time.

(iii) If 8.6 J of energy are transferred to the conductor in this time, calculate the potential difference across the conductor.

(iv) Calculate the resistance of the conductor. *(6 marks)*

AQA, 2004

3   (a) **Figure 1** shows a graph of V against I for a filament lamp. Calculate the maximum resistance of the lamp over the range shown by the graph. *(3 marks)*

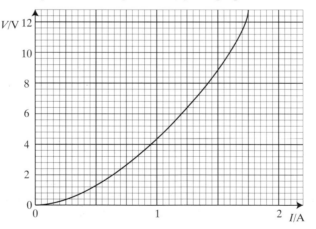

Figure 1

(b) Sketch on a copy of the axes below, a graph of current against potential difference for a diode. *(2 marks)*

AQA, 2002

4   **Figure 2** shows the general shape of the current–time graph during the 2 seconds after a 12 V filament lamp is switched on.

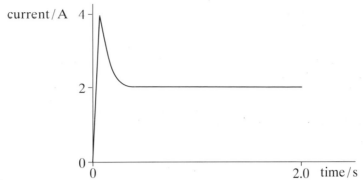

Figure 2

(a) A student wishes to perform an experiment to obtain this graph.

   (i)   Explain why sampling data using a sensor and a computer is a sensible option.

   (ii) Suggest a suitable sampling rate for such an experiment, giving a reason for your answer. *(3 marks)*

(b) Explain why the current rises to a high value before falling to a steady value and why a filament is more likely to fail when being switched on than at other times. *(6 marks)*

AQA, 2005

5   (a) A metal wire of length 1.4 m has a uniform cross-sectional area = $7.8 \times 10^{-7}\,m^2$. Calculate the resistance, R, of the wire.

   resistivity of the metal = $1.7 \times 10^{-8}\,\Omega\,m$ *(2 marks)*

(b) The wire is now stretched to twice its original length by a process that keeps its volume constant.

   If the resistivity of the metal of the wire remains constant, show that the resistance increases to $4R$. *(2 marks)*

AQA, 2003

6   (a) The resistivity of a material in the form of a uniform resistance wire is to be measured. The area of cross-section of the wire is known.

   The apparatus available includes a battery, a switch, a variable resistor, an ammeter and a voltmeter.

   (i)   Draw a circuit diagram using some or all of this apparatus, which would enable you to determine the resistivity of the material.

   (ii) Describe how you would make the necessary measurements, ensuring that you have a range of values.

   (iii) Show how a value of the resistivity is determined from your measurements. *(9 marks)*

(b) A sheet of carbon-reinforced plastic measuring 80 mm × 80 mm × 1.5 mm has its two large surfaces coated with highly conducting metal film. When a potential difference of 240 V is applied between the metal films, there is a current of 2.0 mA in the plastic. Calculate the resistivity of the plastic. *(3 marks)*

AQA, 2002

7   (a) (i)   What is a *superconductor*?

   (ii) With the aid of a sketch graph, explain the term *transition temperature*. *(3 marks)*

(b) Explain why superconductors are very useful for applicatons which require very large electric currents and name **two** such applicatons. *(3 marks)*

AQA, 2006

Direct current circuits

5.1 Circuit rules

Current rules

1 **At any junction in a circuit, the total current leaving the junction is equal to the total current entering the junction.**

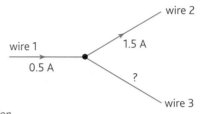

Figure 1 *At a junction*

For example, Figure 1 shows a junction of three wires where the current in two of the wires (wire 1 and wire 2) is given. The current in wire 3 must be 1.0 A into the junction, because the total current into the junction (= 1.0 A along wire 3 + 0.5 A along wire 1) is the same as the total current out of the junction (= 1.5 A along wire 2).

The junction rule holds because the rates of charge flowing into and out of a junction are always equal. The current along a wire is the charge flow per second. In Figure 1, the charge *entering* the junction each second is 0.5 C along wire 1 and 1.0 C along wire 3. The charge *leaving* the junction each second must therefore be 1.5 C as the junction does not retain charge.

2 **Components in series**

■ **The current entering a component is the same as the current leaving the component**. In other words, components do not use up current. The charge per second entering a component is equal to the charge per second leaving it. In Figure 2, ammeters A_1 and A_2 show the same reading because they are measuring the same current.

■ **The current passing through two or more components in series is the same through each component**. This is because the rate of flow of charge through each component is the same at any instant. The same amount of charge passing through any one component each second passes through every other component each second. In Figure 2, the ammeters read the same because the same amount of charge each second passes through each component.

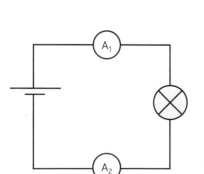

Figure 2 *Components in series*

Potential difference rules

The potential difference (abbreviated as pd), or voltage, between any two points in a circuit is defined as the energy transfer per coulomb of charge that flows from one point to the other.

- If the charge carriers lose energy, the potential difference is a potential drop.
- If the charge carriers gain energy, which happens when they pass through a battery or cell, the potential difference is a potential rise equal to the pd across the battery or cell's terminals.

Examiner's tip

Learn the basic rules.

The rules for potential differences are listed below with an explanation of each rule in energy terms.

1 **For two or more components in series, the total pd across all the components is equal to the sum of the potential differences across each component.**

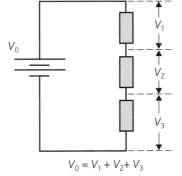

$$V_0 = V_1 + V_2 + V_3$$

■ **Figure 3** *Adding potential differences*

In Figure 3, the pd across the battery terminals is equal to the sum of the potential differences across the three resistors. This is because the pd across each resistor is the energy delivered per coulomb of charge to that resistor. So the sum of potential differences across the three resistors is the total energy delivered to the resistors per coulomb of charge passing through them, which is the pd across the battery terminals.

2 **The pd across components in parallel is the same.**

$$V_0 = V_1 + V_2$$

■ **Figure 4** *Components in parallel*

In Figure 4, charge carriers can pass through either of the two resistors in parallel. The same amount of energy is delivered by a charge carrier regardless of which of the two resistors it passes through.

Suppose the variable resistor is adjusted so the pd across it is 4 V. If the battery pd is 12 V, the pd across the two resistors in parallel is 8 V (= 12 V − 4 V). This is because each coulomb of charge leaves the battery with 12 J of electrical energy and uses 4 J on passing through the variable resistor. Therefore, each coulomb of charge has 8 J of electrical energy to deliver to either of the two parallel resistors.

3 For any complete loop of a circuit, the sum of the emfs round the loop is equal to the sum of the potential drops round the loop. This follows from the fact that the total emf in a loop is the total electrical energy per coulomb produced in the loop and the sum of the potential drops is the electrical energy per coulomb delivered round the loop. The above statement follows therefore from the conservation of energy.

Figure 5 *The loop rule*

For example, in Figure 5, the battery has an emf of 9 V. If the variable resistor is adjusted so that the pd across the light bulb is 6 V, the pd across the variable resistor is 3 V (= 9 V – 6 V). The total emf in the circuit is 9 V due to the battery. This is equal to the sum of the potential differences round the circuit (= 3 V across the variable resistor + 6 V across the light bulb). In other words, every coulomb of charge leaves the battery with 9 J of electrical energy and supplies 3 J to the variable resistor and 6 J to the light bulb.

Summary questions

1 A battery, which has an emf of 6 V and negligible internal resistance, is connected to a 6 V 6 W light bulb in parallel with a 6 V 24 W light bulb, as shown in Figure 6.

Figure 6

Calculate **a** the current through each light bulb, **b** the current from the battery, **c** the power supplied by the battery.

2 A 4.5 V battery of negligible internal resistance is connected in series with a variable resistor and a 2.5 V 0.5 W torch bulb.

a Sketch the circuit diagram for this circuit.

b The variable resistor is adjusted so that the pd across the torch bulb is 2.5 V. Calculate **i** the pd across the variable resistor, **ii** the current through the torch bulb.

3 A 6.0 V battery of negligible internal resistance is connected in series with an ammeter, a 20 Ω resistor and an unknown resistor *R*.

a Sketch the circuit diagram.

b The ammeter reads 0.20 A. Calculate **i** the pd across the 20 Ω resistor, **ii** the pd across *R*, **iii** the resistance of *R*.

4 In Question 3, when the unknown resistor is replaced with a torch bulb, the ammeter reads 0.12 A. Calculate **a** the pd across the torch bulb, **b** the resistance of the torch bulb.

5.2 More about resistance

Learning objectives:

- How can we calculate resistances in series or in parallel?

- What is resistance heating?

- How can we calculate the current and pds for each component in a circuit?

Specification reference: 3.1.3

Resistors in series

Figure 1 *Resistors in series*

Resistors in series pass the same current. The total pd is equal to the sum of the individual pds.

- For two resistors R_1 and R_2 in series, as in Figure 1, when current I passes through the resistors,

    the pd across R_1, $V_1 = IR_1$, and

    the pd across R_2, $V_2 = IR_2$

The total pd across two resistors, $V = V_1 + V_2 = IR_1 + IR_2$

Therefore, the total resistance $\quad R = \dfrac{V}{I} = \dfrac{IR_1 + IR_2}{I} = R_1 + R_2$

- For two or more resistors R_1, R_2, R_3, etc. in series, the theory can easily be extended to show that the **total resistance is equal to the sum of the individual resistances**.

$$R = R_1 + R_2 + R_3 + \ldots$$

Resistors in parallel

Figure 2 *Resistors in parallel*

Resistors in parallel have the same pd. The current through a parallel combination of resistors is equal to the sum of the individual currents.

- For two resistors R_1 and R_2 in parallel, as in Figure 2, when the pd across the combination is V,

    the current through resistor R_1, $I_1 = \dfrac{V}{R_1}$

    the current through resistor R_2, $I_2 = \dfrac{V}{R_2}$

The total current through the combination, $I = I_1 + I_2 = \dfrac{V}{R_1} + \dfrac{V}{R_2}$

Since the total resistance $R = \dfrac{V}{I}$, then the total current $I = \dfrac{V}{R}$

Therefore $\dfrac{V}{R} = \dfrac{V}{R_1} + \dfrac{V}{R_2}$

Cancelling V from each term gives the following equation, which is used to calculate the total resistance R:

$$\frac{1}{R} = \frac{1}{R_1} + \frac{1}{R_2}$$

- For two or more resistors R_1, R_2, R_3, etc. in parallel, the theory can easily be extended to show that the total resistance R is given by

$$\frac{1}{R} = \frac{1}{R_1} + \frac{1}{R_2} + \frac{1}{R_3} + \dots$$

Resistance heating

The heating effect of an electric current in any component is due to the resistance of the component. As explained in Topic 4.2, the charge carriers repeatedly collide with the positive ions of the conducting material. There is a net transfer of energy from the charge carriers to the positive ions as a result of these collisions. After a charge carrier loses kinetic energy in such a collision, the force due to the pd across the material accelerates it until it collides with another positive ion.

Figure 3 *Heating elements*

For a component of resistance R, when current I passes through it, the pd across the component, $V = IR$

Therefore the power supplied to the component, $P = IV = I^2R \left(= \dfrac{V^2}{R}\right)$

Hence the energy per second transferred to the component as thermal energy $= I^2R$

If the component is at constant temperature, heat transfer to the surroundings takes place at the same rate. Therefore,

$$\text{the rate of heat transfer } = I^2R$$

- If the component heats up, its temperature rise depends on the power supplied to it (I^2R) and the rate of heat transfer to the surroundings.
- The energy transferred to the object by the electric current in time $t =$ power $\times$ time $= I^2Rt$

The energy transfer per second to the component (that is, the power supplied to it) does not depend on the direction of the current. For example, the heating effect of an alternating current at a given instant depends only on the magnitude of the current, not on the direction of the current.

Summary questions

1 Calculate the total resistance of each of the resistor combinations in Figure 4.

Figure 4

2 A 3 Ω resistor and a 6 Ω resistor are connected in parallel with each other. The parallel combination is connected in series with a 6.0 V battery and a 4 Ω resistor, as shown in Figure 5. Assume the battery itself has negligible internal resistance.

Figure 5

Calculate:

a the combined resistance of the 3 Ω resistor and a 6 Ω resistor in parallel,

b the total resistance of the circuit,

c the battery current,

d the power supplied to the 4 Ω resistor.

3 A 2 Ω resistor and a 4 Ω resistor are connected in series with each other. The series combination is connected in parallel with a 9 Ω resistor and a 3 V battery of negligible internal resistance, as shown in Figure 6.

Figure 6

Calculate:

a the total resistance of the circuit,

b the battery current,

c the power supplied to each resistor,

d the power supplied by the battery.

4 Calculate:

a the power supplied to a 10 Ω resistor when the pd across it is 12 V,

b the resistance of a heating element designed to operate at 60 W and 12 V.

5.3 Emf and internal resistance

Emf, ε

internal resistance, r

Figure 1 *Internal resistance*

Figure 2 *Emf and internal resistance*

■ Internal resistance

The **internal resistance** of a source of electricity is due to opposition to the flow of charge through the source. This causes electrical energy produced by the source to be dissipated inside the source when charge flows through it.

- The **electromotive force** (emf, symbol ε) of the source is the electrical energy per unit charge produced by the source. If electrical energy E is given to a charge Q in the source,

$$\varepsilon = \frac{E}{Q}$$

- The **pd across the terminals** of the source is the electrical energy per unit charge delivered by the source when it is in a circuit. The terminal pd is less than the emf whenever current passes through the source. The difference is due to the internal resistance of the source.

The internal resistance of a source is the loss of potential difference per unit current in the source when current passes through the source.

In circuit diagrams, the internal resistance of a source may be shown as a resistor (labelled 'internal resistance') in series with the usual symbol for a cell or battery, as in Figure 1.

When a cell of emf ε and internal resistance r is connected to an external resistor of resistance R, as shown in Figure 2, all the current through the cell passes through its internal resistance and the external resistor. So the two resistors are in series, which means that the total resistance of the circuit is $r + R$. Therefore, the current through the cell, $I = \frac{\varepsilon}{R + r}$

In other words, the cell emf $\varepsilon = I(R + r) = IR + Ir =$ the terminal pd + the 'lost' pd

$$\varepsilon = IR + Ir$$

The 'lost' pd inside the cell (i.e. the pd across the internal resistance of the cell) is equal to the difference between the cell emf and the pd across its terminals. In energy terms, the 'lost' pd is the energy per coulomb dissipated or wasted inside the cell due to its internal resistance.

■ Power

Multiplying each term of the above equation by the cell current I gives

Power supplied by the cell, $I\varepsilon = I^2R + I^2r$

In other words, the power supplied by the cell = the power delivered to R + the power wasted in the cell due to its internal resistance.

The power delivered to $R = I^2R = \frac{\varepsilon^2}{(R + r)^2}R.$ since $I = \frac{\varepsilon}{R + r}$

Figure 3 shows how the power delivered to R varies with the value of R.

It can be shown that the peak of this power curve is at $R = r$. In other words, when a source delivers power to a 'load', **maximum power is delivered to the load when the load resistance is equal to the internal resistance of the source.** The load is then said to be 'matched ' to the source. (Although this particular point is not in this AS specification, you might find it useful if you ever need to replace an amplifier or a speaker.)

Figure 3 *Power delivered to a load v load resistance*

⚠ 💡 Measurement of internal resistance

The pd across the terminals of a cell, when the cell is in a circuit, can be measured by connecting a high-resistance voltmeter directly across the terminals of the cell. Figure 4 shows how the terminal pd can be measured for different values of current. The current is changed by adjusting the variable resistor. The lamp (or a fixed resistor) limits the maximum current that can pass through the cell. The ammeter is used to measure the cell current. The measurements of terminal pd and current for a given cell may be plotted on a graph, as shown in Figure 5.

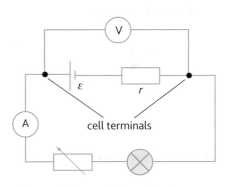

Figure 4 *Measuring internal resistance*

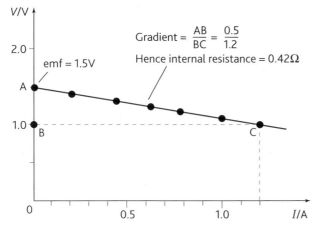

Gradient = $\dfrac{AB}{BC} = \dfrac{0.5}{1.2}$

Hence internal resistance = 0.42 Ω

emf = 1.5V

Figure 5 *A graph of terminal pd v current*

The terminal pd decreases as the current increases. This is because the 'lost' pd increases as the current increases.

■ The terminal pd is equal to the cell emf at zero current. This is because the 'lost' pd is zero at zero current.

■ The graph is a straight line with a negative gradient. This can be seen by rearranging the equation $\varepsilon = IR + Ir$ to become $IR = \varepsilon - Ir$. Because IR represents the terminal pd V, then

$$V = \varepsilon - Ir$$

By comparison with the standard equation for a straight line, $y = mx + c$, a graph of V on the y-axis against I on the x-axis gives a straight line with a gradient $-r$ and a y-intercept ε.

Examiner's tip

Ensure you can relate $V = \varepsilon - Ir$ to $y = mx + c$

Figure 5 shows the gradient triangle ABC in which AB represents the lost pd and BC represents the current. So the gradient AB/BC = lost voltage / current = internal resistance r.

Note: the internal resistance and the emf of a cell can be calculated if the terminal pd is known for two different values of current.

■ For current I_1, the terminal pd $V_1 = \varepsilon - I_1 r$
■ For current I_2, the terminal pd $V_2 = \varepsilon - I_2 r$

Subtracting the first equation from the second gives:

$$V_1 - V_2 = (\varepsilon - I_1 r) - (\varepsilon - I_2 r) = I_2 r - I_1 r = (I_2 - I_1)r$$

Therefore, $r = \dfrac{V_1 - V_2}{I_2 - I_1}$

So r can be calculated from the above equation and then substituted into either equation for the cell pd to enable ε to be calculated.

Summary questions

1 A battery of emf 12 V and internal resistance 1.5 Ω was connected to a 4.5 Ω resistor. Calculate:

a the total resistance of the circuit,

b the current through the battery,

c the lost pd,

d the pd across the cell terminals.

2 A cell of emf 1.5 V and internal resistance 0.5 Ω is connected to a 2.5 Ω resistor. Calculate:

a the current,

b the terminal pd,

c the power delivered to the 2.5 Ω resistor,

d the power wasted in the cell.

3 The pd across the terminals of a cell was 1.1 V when the current from the cell was 0.20 A, and 1.3 V when the current was 0.10 A. Calculate:

a the internal resistance of the cell,

b the cell's emf.

4 A battery of unknown emf ε and internal resistance r is connected in series with an ammeter and a resistance box R. The current was 2.0 A when $R = 4.0$ Ω and 1.5 A when $R = 6.0$ Ω. Calculate ε and r.

5.4 More circuit calculations

Specification reference: 3.1.3

Learning objectives:

- How do we calculate currents in circuits with:
  - resistors in series and parallel?
  - more than one cell?
  - diodes in the circuit?

Circuits with a single cell and one or more resistors

Here are some rules:

1   Sketch the **circuit diagram** if it is not drawn.

2   To calculate the **current** passing through the cell, calculate the total circuit resistance using the resistor combination rules. Don't forget to add on the internal resistance of the cell if that is not negligible.

$$\text{cell current} = \frac{\text{cell emf}}{\text{total circuit resistance}}$$

3   To work out the current and pd for each resistor, start with the **resistors in series with the cell** which therefore pass the same current as the cell current.

Pd across each resistor in series with the cell
= current × the resistance of each resistor.

4   To work out the current through **parallel resistors**, work out the combined resistance and multiply by the cell current to give the pd across each resistor.

$$\text{current through each resistor} = \frac{\text{pd across the parallel combination}}{\text{resistor's resistance}}$$

Circuits with cells in series

The same rules as above apply except the current through the cells is calculated by dividing the overall (net) emf by the total resistance.

- If the cells are connected in the same direction in the circuit, as in Figure 1a), the net emf is the sum of the individual emfs. For example, in Figure 1a), the net emf is 3.5 V.

- If the cells are connected in opposite directions to each other in the circuit, as in Figure 1b), the net emf is the difference between the emfs in each direction. For example, in Figure 1b), the net emf is 0.5 V in the direction of the 2.0 V cell.

- The total internal resistance is the sum of the individual internal resistances. This is because the cells, and therefore the internal resistances, are in series.

AQA Examiner's tip

Check the pds round a circuit add up to the battery pd.

a

b

Figure 1 *Cells in series*

Worked example:

A cell of emf 3.0 V and internal resistance 2.0 Ω and a cell of emf 2.0 V and internal resistance 1.0 Ω are connected in series with each other and with a 7.0 Ω resistor, as in Figure 2. Calculate the pd across the 7.0 Ω resistor.

Solution

The net emf of the two batteries = 3.0 + 2.0 = 5.0 V in the direction of the 3.0 V cell.

The total circuit resistance = 1.0 Ω + 2.0 Ω + 7.0 Ω = 10.0 Ω

Figure 2

Therefore the cell current $= \dfrac{\text{net emf}}{\text{total circuit resistance}} = \dfrac{5.0\,V}{10.0\,\Omega} = 0.50\,A$

The pd across the $7.0\,\Omega$ resistor = current × resistance = $0.50\,A \times 7.0\,\Omega = 3.5\,V$

🔬 Circuits with identical cells in parallel

For a circuit with n identical cells in parallel, the current through each cell $= I/n$, where I is the total current supplied by the cells.

Therefore, the 'lost' pd in each cell $= \dfrac{I}{n}r = \dfrac{Ir}{n}$, where r is the internal resistance of each cell.

Hence the terminal pd across the cells, $V = \varepsilon - \dfrac{Ir}{n}$

Therefore, the cells act as a source of emf ε and internal resistance r/n.

Solar panels

A solar panel consists of many parallel rows of identical solar cells in series. For example, using single solar cells with a maximum emf of $0.45\,V$ and an internal resistance of $1.0\,\Omega$, a row of 20 cells in series would have a maximum emf of $9.0\,V$ and an internal resistance of $20\,\Omega$. Forty such rows in parallel would still give a maximum emf of $9.0\,V$ but would have an internal resistance of $0.5\,\Omega$ $(= 20\,\Omega/40)$.

Figure 3 *Cells in parallel*

Figure 4 *Solar cell panel*

◼ Diodes in circuits

Assume that a silicon diode has:

- ◼ a 'forward' pd of $0.6\,V$ whenever a current passes through it,
- ◼ infinite resistance in the reverse direction or at pds less than $0.6\,V$ in the forward direction.

Therefore, in a circuit with one or more diodes:

- ◼ a pd of $0.6\,V$ exists across a diode that is forward-biased and passing a current,
- ◼ a diode that is reverse-biased has infinite resistance.

For example, suppose a diode is connected in its forward direction in series with a 1.5 V cell of negligible internal resistance and a 1.5 kΩ resistor, as in Figure 5.

The pd across the diode is 0.6 V because it is forward-biased. Therefore, the pd across the resistor is 0.9 V (= 1.5 V – 0.6 V). The current through the resistor is therefore 6.0×10^{-4} A (= 0.9 V/1500 Ω).

Figure 5 *Using a diode*

Summary questions

1 A cell of emf 3.0 V and negligible internal resistance is connected to a 4.0 Ω resistor in series with a parallel combination of a 24.0 Ω resistor and a 12.0 Ω resistor, as shown in Figure 6. Calculate:

a the total resistance of the circuit,

b the cell current,

c the current and pd for each resistor.

Figure 6

2 A 15.0 Ω resistor, a battery of emf 12.0 V with an internal resistance of 3.0 Ω and a battery of emf 9.0 V with an internal resistance of 2.0 Ω are connected in series. The batteries act in the same direction in the circuit. Sketch the circuit diagram and calculate:

a the total resistance of the circuit,

b the cell current,

c the current and pd across the 15 Ω resistor.

3 a Two 8 Ω resistors and a battery of emf 12.0 V and internal resistance 8 Ω are connected in series with each other. Sketch the circuit diagram and calculate i the power delivered to each external resistor, ii the power wasted due to internal resistance.

b The two 8 Ω resistors in a are reconnected in parallel with each other then connected to the same battery. Sketch the circuit diagram and calculate i the power delivered to each external resistor, ii the power wasted due to internal resistance.

4 a For the circuit shown in Figure 7, calculate the pd and current for each resistor and diode.

b In Figure 7, both diodes are reversed. Sketch the new circuit and calculate the pd and current for each resistor and diode for this new arrangement.

Figure 7

5.5 The potential divider

Learning objectives:

- What is a potential divider?
- How can we supply a variable pd from a battery?
- How can we design sensor circuits?

Specification reference: 3.1.3

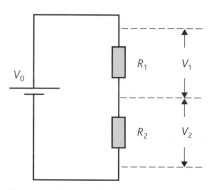

Figure 1 *A potential divider*

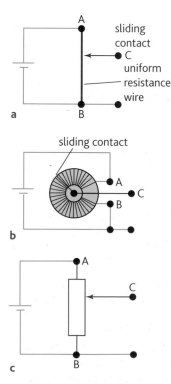

Figure 2 *Potential dividers used to supply a variable pd*
(a) a linear track using resistance wire
(b) a circular track (c) circuit symbol

💡 The theory of the potential divider

A potential divider consists of two or more resistors in series with each other and with a source of fixed potential difference. The potential difference of the source is divided between the components in the circuit, as they are in series with each other. By making a suitable choice of components, a potential divider can be used:

- to supply a pd which is fixed at any value between zero and the source pd
- to supply a variable pd
- to supply a pd that varies with a physical condition such as temperature or pressure.

To supply a fixed pd

Consider two resistors $R_1 + R_2$ in series connected to a source of fixed pd V_0, as shown in Figure 1.

The total resistance of the combination $= R_1 + R_2$

Therefore, the current I through the resistors is given by:

$$I = \frac{\text{pd across the resistors}}{\text{total resistance}} = \frac{V_0}{R_1 + R_2}$$

So the pd V_1 across resistor R_1 is given by:

$$V_1 = IR_1 = \frac{V_0 R_1}{R_1 + R_2}$$

and the pd V_2 across resistor R_2 is given by:

$$V_2 = IR_2 = \frac{V_0 R_2}{R_1 + R_2}$$

These two equations show that the pd across each resistor as a proportion of the source pd is the same as the resistance of the resistor in proportion to the total resistance. In other words, if the resistances are $5\,k\Omega$ and $10\,k\Omega$, respectively:

- the pd across the $5\,k\Omega$ resistor is $\frac{1}{3}$ ($= \frac{5}{15}$) of the source pd, and
- the pd across the $10\,k\Omega$ resistor is $\frac{2}{3}$ ($= \frac{10}{15}$) of the source pd.

Also, dividing the equation for V_1 by the equation for V_2 gives

$$\frac{V_1}{V_2} = \frac{R_1}{R_2}$$

This equation shows that

> **the ratio of the pds across each resistor is equal to the resistance ratio of the two resistors.**

To supply a variable pd

The source pd is connected to a fixed length of uniform resistance wire. A sliding contact on the wire can then be moved along the wire, as illustrated in Figure 2, giving a variable pd between the contact and one end of the wire. A uniform track of a suitable material may be used instead of resistance wire. The track may be linear or circular, as in Figure 2. The circuit symbol for a variable potential divider is also shown in Figure 2.

A variable potential divider can be used:

- as a simple audio 'volume control' to change the loudness of the sound from a loudspeaker. The audio signal pd is supplied to the potential divider in place of a cell or battery. The variable output pd from the potential divider is supplied to the loudspeaker.

- to vary the brightness of a light bulb between zero and normal brightness. In contrast with using a variable resistor in series with the light bulb and the source pd, the use of a potential divider enables the current through the light bulb to be reduced to zero. If a variable resistor in series with the light bulb had been used, there would be a current through the light bulb when the variable resistor is at maximum resistance.

⁊ Sensor circuits

A **sensor circuit** produces an output pd which changes as a result of a change of a physical variable such as temperature or light intensity.

1 A **temperature sensor** consists of a potential divider made using a thermistor and a variable resistor, as in Figure 4.

   With the temperature of the thermistor constant, the source pd is divided between the thermistor and the variable resistor. By adjusting the variable resistor, the pd across the thermistor can then be set at any desired value. When the temperature of the thermistor changes, its resistance changes so the pd across it changes. For example, suppose the variable resistor is adjusted so that the pd across the thermistor at 20 °C is exactly half the source pd. If the temperature of the thermistor is then raised, its resistance falls, so the pd across it falls.

2 A **light sensor** uses a light-dependent resistor (LDR) and a variable resistor, as in Figure 5. The pd across the LDR changes when the incident light intensity on the LDR changes. If the light intensity increases, the resistance of the LDR falls and the pd across the LDR falls.

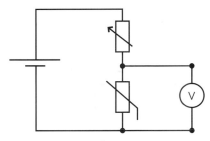

Figure 3 *Brightness control using a variable potential divider*

Figure 4 *A temperature sensor*

Figure 5 *A light sensor*

Summary questions

1 A potential divider consists of a 1.0 kΩ resistor in series with a 5.0 kΩ resistor and a battery of emf 4.5 V and negligible internal resistance.

   a Sketch the circuit and calculate the pd across each resistor.

   b A second 5.0 kΩ resistor is connected in the above circuit in parallel with the first 5.0 kΩ resistor. Calculate the pd across each resistor in this new circuit.

2 A 12 V battery of negligible internal resistance is connected to the fixed terminals of a variable potential divider which has a maximum resistance of 50 Ω. A 12 V light bulb is connected between the sliding contact and the negative terminal of the potential divider. Sketch the circuit diagram and describe how the brightness of the light bulb changes when the sliding contact is moved from the negative to the positive terminal of the potential divider.

3 **a** A potential divider consists of an 8.0 Ω resistor in series with a 4.0 Ω resistor and a 6.0 V battery of negligible internal resistance. Calculate **i** the current, **ii** the pd across each resistor.

   b In the circuit in **a**, the 4 Ω resistor is replaced by a thermistor with a resistance of 8 Ω at 20 °C and a resistance of 4 Ω at 100 °C. Calculate the pd across the fixed resistor at **i** 20 °C, **ii** 100 °C.

4 A light sensor consists of a 5.0 V cell, an LDR and a 5.0 kΩ resistor in series with each other. A voltmeter is connected in parallel with the resistor. When the LDR is in darkness, the voltmeter reads 2.2 V.

   a Calculate **i** the pd across the LDR, **ii** the resistance of the LDR when the voltmeter reads 2.2 V.

   b Describe and explain how the voltmeter reading would change if the LDR were exposed to daylight with no adjustment made to the variable resistor.

AQA Examination-style questions

1 A student is given three resistors of resistance $3.0\,\Omega$, $4.0\,\Omega$ and $6.0\,\Omega$, respectively.
   - (i) Draw the arrangement, using all three resistors, which will give the largest resistance.
   - (ii) Calculate the resistance of the arrangement you have drawn.
   - (iii) Draw the arrangement, using all three resistors, which will give the smallest resistance.
   - (iv) Calculate the resistance of the arrangement you have drawn. *(5 marks)*

AQA, 2005

2 In the circuit shown in **Figure 1**, the battery has negligible internal resistance.

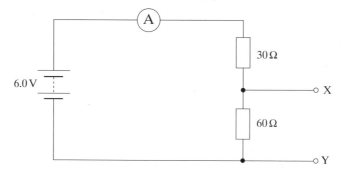

Figure 1

Calculate the current in the ammeter when
   - (a) the terminals X and Y are short-circuited i.e. connected together, *(2 marks)*
   - (b) the terminals X and Y are connected to a $30\,\Omega$ resistor. *(4 marks)*

AQA, 2002

3 (a) Define the electrical resistance of a component. *(2 marks)*
   (b) Calculate the total resistance of the arrangement of resistors in **Figure 2**. *(3 marks)*

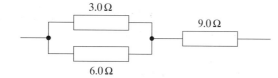

Figure 2

   (c) (i) Calculate the current in the $3.0\,\Omega$ resistor in **Figure 2** when the current in the $9.0\,\Omega$ resistor is $2.4\,A$.

   (ii) Calculate the total power dissipated by the arrangement of resistors in **Figure 2** when the current in the $9.0\,\Omega$ resistor is $2.4\,A$. *(4 marks)*

AQA, 2006

4 In the circuit shown in **Figure 3** the resistor network between the points P and Q is connected in series to a resistor R, an ammeter and a battery of negligible internal resistance.

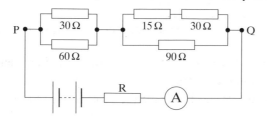

Figure 3

   (a) Determine the equivalent resistance of the network between the points P and Q. *(3 marks)*

(b) (i) If the current through the ammeter is 50 mA, calculate the total charge that flows through the resistor R in 4 minutes.

   (ii) If 18 J of energy are transferred to the resistor R in this time, calculate the potential difference across R.

   (iii) Calculate the resistance of R.

   (iv) Calculate the emf of the battery.

(6 marks)

AQA, 2007

5   In the circuit shown in **Figure 4**, the battery has an emf of 12 V and an internal resistance of 2.0 Ω. The resistors A and B each have resistance of 30 Ω.

Figure 4

Calculate:

(i) the total current in the circuit,

(ii) the voltage between the points P and Q,

(iii) the power dissipated in resistor A,

(iv) the energy dissipated by resistor A in 20 s.

(8 marks)

AQA, 2003

6   In the circuit shown in **Figure 5** cell X has an emf of 12 V and a negligible internal resistance. The resistances of R_A and R_B are 10 Ω and 15 Ω, respectively.

Figure 5

(a) Calculate the potential difference across R_B.   *(2 marks)*

(b) Cell **X** is replaced by cell **Y** that has an emf of 12 V and an internal resistance of 7.5 Ω. Calculate the terminal potential difference across cell **Y**.   *(3 marks)*

AQA, 2003

7   **Figure 6** shows an EHT supply of emf 5000 V and internal resistance 2 MΩ.

Figure 6

(a) A lead of negligible resistance is connected between the supply terminals producing a short circuit.

   (i) State the magnitude of the terminal potential difference between the supply terminals.

   (ii) Calculate the current in the circuit.

   (iii) Calculate the minimum power rating for the resistor used to provide the internal resistance.   *(4 marks)*

(b) Explain briefly why the supply is designed with such a high internal resistance.   *(1 mark)*

AQA, 2005

6.1 Alternating current and power

Learning objectives:

- What is an alternating current?

- What do we mean by the rms value of an alternating current?

- How can we calculate the power supplied by an alternating current?

Specification reference: 3.1.3

Alternating current measurements

An alternating current (ac) is a current that repeatedly reverses its direction. In one cycle of an alternating current, the charge carriers move one way in the circuit then reverse direction then re-reverse direction.

The **frequency** (*f*) of an alternating current is the number of cycles it passes through each second. The unit of frequency is the hertz (Hz), equal to 1 cycle per second. Mains electricity has a frequency of 50 Hz. In a mains circuit, each cycle therefore takes 0.020 s (= $^1/_{50}$ s). Note that the time for one full cycle, the time period *T*, is given by $T = 1/f$.

The **peak value** of an alternating current (or pd) is the maximum current (or pd) which is the same in either direction. The peak current in a circuit depends on the peak pd of the alternating current source and on the components in the circuit. For example, the peak pd in a mains circuit is 325 V. If this pd is applied to a 100 Ω heating element, the peak current through the heating element would be 3.25 A (= 325 V/100 Ω). Note that the peak-to-peak value is the difference between the peak value one way and the peak value in the opposite direction (i.e. twice the peak value).

Figure 1 shows how the mains pd varies with time. This type of variation is described as 'sinusoidal' because its shape is that of a sine wave. Using transformers, we can change the peak pd of an alternating current but not its frequency.

How science works

Inside a phone charger

A phone charger contains a step-down transformer that steps the mains pd down to a much lower pd (still alternating) then a diode circuit is used to convert the alternating pd to a direct pd.

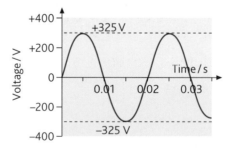

Figure 1 *The variation of mains pd with time*

Observing alternating current

1 Use an oscilloscope to display the waveform (i.e. variation with time) of the alternating pd from a signal generator.

- Increasing the output pd from the signal generator makes the oscilloscope trace taller. This shows that the peak value of the alternating pd has been made larger.

Figure 2 *Using an oscilloscope*

■ Increasing the frequency of the signal generator increases the number of cycles on the screen. This is because the number of cycles per second of the alternating pd has increased.

2 Connect the signal generator to a torch lamp and make the frequency low enough so you can see the brightness of the lamp vary.

■ At a very low frequency, you can see the lamp light up and then fade out repeatedly. The lamp is at its brightest each time the current is at its peak value. This happens twice each cycle corresponding to the current at its peak value in each direction.

■ If the frequency is raised gradually, the lamp flickers faster and faster until the variation of brightness is too fast to notice. The mains frequency is too high to cause flickering.

⚑ The heating effect of an alternating current

Imagine an electric heater supplied with alternating current at a very low frequency. The heater would heat up then cool down, then heat up, etc. The heater would repeatedly heat up then go cold.

As explained in Topic 5.2, the heating effect of an electric current varies according to the square of the current. This is because the electrical power P supplied to the heater for a current I is given by

$P = IV = I^2R$, where R is the resistance of the heater element.

Figure 3 shows how the power $(= I^2R)$ varies with time.

Figure 3 *Variation of power with time for an alternating current*

■ At peak current I_0, maximum power is supplied equal to $I_0^2 R$.

■ At zero current, zero power is supplied.

For a sinusoidal current, the **mean power** over a full cycle is half the peak power. This can be seen from the symmetrical shape of the power curve in Figure 4 about the mean power. The mean power is therefore $\frac{1}{2}I_0^2 R$.

The direct current that would give the same power as the mean power is called the **root mean square value** of the alternating current, I_{rms}.

The root mean square value of an alternating current is the value of direct current that would give the same heating effect as the alternating current in the same resistor.

Therefore,

$$I_{rms}^2 R = \tfrac{1}{2}I_0^2 R$$

Cancelling R from this equation gives:

$$I_{rms}^2 = \tfrac{1}{2}I_0^2$$

Therefore

$$I_{rms} = \frac{1}{\sqrt{2}}I_0$$

Also, the root mean square value of an alternating pd is given by:

$$V_{rms} = \frac{1}{\sqrt{2}}V_0$$

The root mean square value of an alternating current or pd

$$= \frac{1}{\sqrt{2}} \times \text{the peak value.}$$

Note that for any known value of resistance in an alternating circuit, if we know the rms pd or current for the resistor, we can calculate the mean power supplied to it using the rms value.

$$P = I_{rms}^2 R = V_{rms}^2/R = I_{rms}V_{rms}$$

For example, if an alternating current of rms value 4 A is passed through a 5 Ω resistor, the mean power supplied to the resistor $= 4^2 \times 5 = 80\,\text{W}$.

Summary questions

1 An alternating current has a frequency of 200 Hz and a peak value of 0.10 A. Calculate:

   a the time for 1 cycle,

   b the rms current.

2 An alternating current of peak value 3.0 A is passed through a 4.0 Ω resistor. Calculate:

   a i the rms current, ii the rms pd across the resistor,

   b i the peak power, ii the mean power supplied to the resistor.

3 A mains electric heater gives a mean output power of 1.0 kW when the rms pd across it is 230 V. Calculate:

   a i the rms current, ii the peak current, iii the peak power.

   b The heater plug is fitted with a 5 A fuse. Explain why the fuse does not blow even though the peak current through it is more than 5 A.

4 A 12 V, 48 W lamp lights at its normal brightness when it is connected to a source of alternating pd.

   a Calculate i the rms current through it, ii the peak current through it, iii the peak pd across it.

   b The cable connecting the lamp to the source has a resistance of 0.5 Ω.

   i   Show that the rms pd across the cable is 2.0 V when the lamp is on.

   ii Calculate the peak pd of the source when the lamp is on.

6.2 Using an oscilloscope

Learning objectives:

- How do we use an oscilloscope as a dc voltmeter?

- How do we use it as an ac voltmeter?

- How do we use an oscilloscope to measure frequency?

Specification reference: 3.1.3

How to use an oscilloscope

An oscilloscope consists of a specially made electron tube and associated control circuits. An electron gun at one end of the glass tube emits electrons in a beam towards a fluorescent screen at the other end of the tube, as shown in Figure 1. Light is emitted from the spot on the screen where the beam hits the screen.

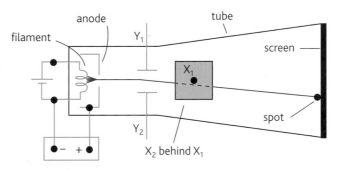

Figure 1 *An oscilloscope tube*

The position of the spot of light on the screen is affected by the pd across either pair of deflecting plates. With no pd across either set of deflecting plates, the spot on the screen stays in the same position. If a pd is applied across the X-plates, the spot deflects horizontally. A pd across the Y-plates makes it deflect vertically. In both cases, the displacement of the spot is proportional to the applied pd.

To display a waveform:

- the X-plates are connected to the oscilloscope's **time base circuit** which makes the spot move at constant speed left to right across the screen, then back again much faster. Because the spot moves at constant speed across the screen, the x scale can be calibrated, usually in milliseconds or microseconds per centimetre.

- the pd to be displayed is connected to the Y-plates via the Y-input so the spot moves up and down as it moves left to right across the screen. As it does so, it traces out the waveform on the screen. Because the vertical displacement of the spot is proportional to the pd applied to the Y-plates, the Y-input is calibrated in volts per centimetre (or per division if the grid on the oscilloscope screen is not a centimetre grid). The calibration value is usually referred to as the y-sensitivity or y-gain of the oscilloscope.

Figure 2 shows the trace produced when an alternating pd is applied to the Y-input. The screen is marked with a centimetre grid.

1   To measure the peak pd, observe that the waveform height from the bottom to the top of the wave is 5.0 cm. The amplitude (i.e. peak height) of the wave is therefore 2.5 cm. As the y-gain is set at $0.5\,\text{V cm}^{-1}$, the peak pd is therefore 1.25 V (= $0.5\,\text{V cm}^{-1} \times 2.5\,\text{cm}$).

2   To measure the frequency of the alternating pd, we need to measure the time period T (the time for 1 cycle) of the waveform. Then we can calculate the frequency f as $f = 1/T$.

Figure 2 *Using an oscilloscope*

3 We can see from the waveform that one full cycle corresponds to a distance of 3.8 cm across the screen horizontally. As the time base control is set at $2\,\text{ms}\,\text{cm}^{-1}$, the time period T is therefore 7.6 ms (= $2\,\text{ms}\,\text{cm}^{-1} \times$ 3.8 cm). Therefore, the frequency of the alternating pd is 132 Hz.

■ Using an oscilloscope as a dc voltmeter

a *Applied pd = 0*

Figure 3 *Measuring a constant pd*

b *Applied pd = +4 V*

c *Applied pd = −3 V*

An oscilloscope can be used to measure a constant pd as well as the peak value of an alternating pd. Applying a constant pd to the Y-input makes the spot move across the screen at a constant height. Its vertical displacement does not change for a constant pd. The spot therefore traces a horizontal line on the screen above or below the 'zero pd' line according to whether the applied pd is positive or negative. By measuring the vertical displacement of the line and using the y-gain, we can therefore calculate the direct pd.

Note that an oscilloscope has a very high input resistance so the current it draws from a circuit is negligible, as it should be for any voltmeter.

🔺 Measuring the speed of ultrasound

The time base circuit of an oscilloscope can be used to trigger an ultrasonic transmitter so it sends out a short pulse of ultrasonic waves. An ultrasonic receiver can be used to detect the transmitted pulse. If the receiver signal is applied to the Y-input of the oscilloscope, the waveform of the received pulse can be seen on the oscilloscope screen, as shown in Figure 4.

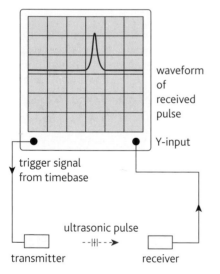

Figure 4 *Measuring the speed of ultrasound*

Because the pulse takes time to travel from the transmitter to the receiver, it is displayed on the screen at the point reached by the spot as it sweeps across from left to right. By measuring the horizontal distance on the screen from the leading edge of the pulse to the start of the spot's sweep, the travel time of the pulse from the transmitter to the receiver can be determined. For example, if the pulse is 3.5 cm from the start of the spot's sweep and the time base control is set at $0.2\,\text{ms}\,\text{cm}^{-1}$, the travel time of the pulse must be 0.7 ms (= $0.2\,\text{ms}\,\text{cm}^{-1} \times$ 3.5 cm). If the distance from the transmitter to receiver is known, the speed of ultrasound can be calculated (from distance / travel time).

Summary questions

1 The trace of an oscilloscope is displaced vertically by 0.9 cm when a pd of 4.5 V is applied to the Y-input.

a Calculate i the y-gain of the oscilloscope, ii the displacement of the spot when a pd of 12 V is applied to the Y-input.

b An alternating pd is applied to the Y-input instead. The height of the waveform from the bottom to the top is 6.5 cm when the y-gain is 0.5 V cm⁻¹. Calculate i the peak value of the alternating pd, ii the rms pd.

2 The time base control of an oscilloscope is set at 10 ms cm⁻¹ and an alternating pd is applied to the Y-input. The horizontal distance across two complete cycles is observed to be 4.4 cm. Calculate:

a the time period of the alternating pd,

b its frequency.

3 Figure 5 shows the waveform on an oscilloscope screen when an alternating pd was applied to the Y-plates.

a The y-gain of the oscilloscope is 5.0 V cm⁻¹. Calculate the peak value and the rms value of the alternating pd.

b The time base setting of the oscilloscope was 5 ms cm⁻¹. Calculate the time period and the frequency of the alternating pd.

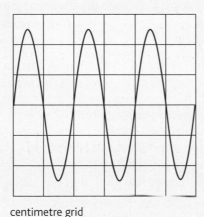

centimetre grid

Figure 5

4 Copy the grid of Figure 5 and sketch the trace you would observe if

a a constant pd of 10.0 V was applied to the Y-input,

b a 10.0 V rms alternating pd of frequency 50 Hz was applied to the Y-input.

1   The travel time of ultrasound pulses from a transmitter to a receiver via a reflector
    was measured using an oscilloscope. **Figure 1** shows the arrangement.

Figure 1

(a) For each pulse transmitted, the transmitted pulse and the received pulse were
     displayed on the oscilloscope screen, as shown in **Figure 1**. The screen is marked
     with a cm grid.

(i)   The time base of the oscilloscope was $2.0\,\mathrm{ms\,cm^{-1}}$. Calculate the time taken
      by each pulse to travel from the transmitter to the receiver.

(ii) The speed of the ultrasonic waves was $340\,\mathrm{m\,s^{-1}}$. Calculate the distance from
      the transmitter to the reflector.   (5 marks)

(b) Discuss the accuracy of this distance measurement.   (4 marks)

2   (a) (i)   What is meant by the *root mean square* (rms) value of an alternating current?
              Write down an expression that shows how the rms value is related to the peak
              value of the current.   (5 marks)

(ii) Explain why it is generally more useful to specify the magnitude of an ac
      quantity by giving its rms value rather than its peak value.   (4 marks)

(b) The standard mains electrical supply in the USA is specified as '110 V, 60 Hz'.

(i)   Calculate the maximum instantaneous voltage provided by this supply.

(ii) How does the frequency of the USA supply compare with that of the mains
      supply in Britain?

(iii) State **one** advantage and **one** disadvantage of supplying mains electricity at
      the lower voltage.   (4 marks)

3   An alternating current (ac) source is connected to a resistor to form a complete
    circuit. The trace obtained on an oscilloscope connected across the resistor is shown in **Figure 2**.

Figure 2

The oscilloscope settings are: Y sensitivity 4.0 V per division, time base 1.0 ms per division.

(i)   Determine the peak voltage of the ac source

(ii) Hence calculate the rms voltage

(iii) Determine the time period of the ac signal

(iv) Hence calculate the frequency of the ac signal   (4 marks)

AQA, 2001

4 (a) (i) Calculate the time period of an alternating current of frequency 50 Hz.

(ii) On a copy of the outline axes in **Figure 3**, draw one complete cycle of a sinusoidal alternating current of peak value 0.20 A and frequency 50 Hz.   *(3 marks)*

Figure 3

(b) An alternating current of peak value 0.20A passes through a resistor of resistance 47 Ω. Calculate

(i) the peak voltage across the resistor,

(ii) the rms voltage across the resistor,

(iii) the maximum rate of supply of electrical energy to the resistor.   *(3 marks)*

(c) An alternating voltage is applied to a resistor. Describe the effect this has on a conduction electron in the resistor.   *(3 marks)*

AQA, 2006

5 An oscilloscope is connected to a sinusoidal ac source as shown in **Figure 4**. The frequency and the voltage output of the ac source can be varied.

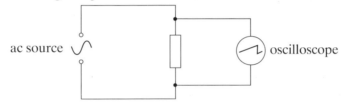

Figure 4

At a certain frequency the ac signal has an rms output of 7.1 V. **Figure 5** shows the trace obtained on the screen of the oscilloscope when one horizontal division corresponded to a time of 5.0 ms.

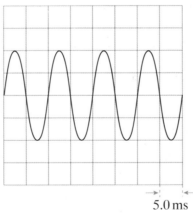

5.0 ms

Figure 5

(a) Calculate, for the signal shown in **Figure 5**:

(i) the peak voltage,

(ii) the frequency.   *(3 marks)*

(b) The voltage output and frequency of the signal are now changed so that the peak voltage is 80 V and the frequency is 200 Hz.

State which two controls on the oscilloscope have to be altered so that **four** full cycles again appear on the screen but the peak to peak distance occupies the **full** screen.

Determine the values at which these two controls have to be set.   *(5 marks)*

AQA, 2004

AQA Examination-style questions

Unit 1 questions: Particles, quantum phenomena and electricity

1 (a) An ion of plutonium $^{239}_{94}$Pu has an overall charge of $+1.6 \times 10^{-19}$ C. For this ion state the number of

   (i)   protons

   (ii) neutrons

   (iii) electrons   *(3 marks)*

   (b) Plutonium has several *isotopes*. Explain the meaning of the word isotopes.   *(2 marks)*

AQA, 2006

2 (a) (i)   State the quark composition of a π^+ meson.

   (ii) The equation below represents the production of a π^+ meson when two protons collide.

   $$p + p \longrightarrow p + \pi^+ + X$$

   Identify particle X and state its quark composition.   *(3 marks)*

   (b) π^+ mesons at rest decay into muons which are always emitted at a certain speed.

   The equation below represents the decay of a π^+ meson into a positive muon and another particle Y.

   $$\pi^+ \longrightarrow \mu^+ + Y$$

   Identify particle Y and state **one** of its properties.   *(4 marks)*

AQA, 2006

3 A physicist, who is attempting to analyse a nuclear event, suggests that a π^- particle and a proton collided and were annihilated with the creation of a neutron, a π^+ particle and a K^- particle.

   π and K particles are mesons. The baryon and lepton numbers of both these mesons are zero.

   (a) Write down the equation that represents this interaction.   *(1 mark)*

   (b) Show in terms of the conservation of charge, baryon number and lepton number, that this transformation is permitted.   *(4 marks)*

AQA, 2002

4 (i)   A negative muon, μ^- is 207 times more massive than an electron.

   Calculate the de Broglie wavelength of a negative muon travelling at 3.0×10^6 ms^{-1}.

   (ii) Using values from the data sheet (page 245) calculate the ratio $\dfrac{\text{rest mass of } \pi^0}{\text{rest mass of } \mu^-}$ where π^0 is a neutral pion.

   (iii) Calculate the speed necessary for a π^0 to have the same de Broglie wavelength as that of the μ^- in part (i).   *(6 marks)*

AQA, 2006

5 (a) State what is meant by the *photoelectric effect* and explain how **two** observations made in photoelectric experiments suggest that electromagnetic radiation behaves like a stream of particles rather than a wave.   *(7 marks)*

   (b) Photons with energy 1.1×10^{-18} J are incident on a metal surface. The maximum energy of electrons emitted from the surface is 4.8×10^{-19} J.

   (i)   Calculate the work function of the metal.

   (ii) Calculate the wavelength of the de Broglie wave associated with the emitted electrons of maximum energy.   *(4 marks)*

AQA, 2006

6 The quantum theory suggests that the electron in a hydrogen atom can only exist in certain well-defined energy states. Some of these are shown in **Figure 1**.

energy / 10^{-19} J

$n = \infty$ ———————— 0
$n = 4$ ———————— −1.4
$n = 3$ ———————— −2.4

$n = 2$ ———————— −5.4

$n = 1$ ———————— −21.8

Figure 1

An electron **E** of energy 2.5×10^{-18} J collides with a hydrogen atom that is in its ground state and excites the electron in the hydrogen atom to the $n = 3$ level.

Calculate

(i) the energy that is needed to excite an electron in the hydrogen atom from the ground state to the $n = 3$ level,

(ii) the kinetic energy of the incident electron **E** after the collision,

(iii) the wavelength of the lowest energy photon that could be emitted as the excited electron returns to the ground state. *(5 marks)*

AQA, 2006

7 (a) An electron is trapped in a solid between a group of atoms where the potential is +2.8 V. The de Broglie wavelength of this electron is 1.2 nm. Calculate

(i) its speed,

(ii) its kinetic energy,

(iii) the sum of its kinetic energy and its potential energy. *(5 marks)*

(b) (i) Calculate the energy of a photon of wavelength 650 nm.

(ii) State and explain whether or not the electron in part (a) can escape from this group of atoms as a result of absorbing this photon. *(3 marks)*

AQA, 2005

8 (a) (i) State what is meant by the *wave–particle duality* of electromagnetic radiation.

(ii) Which aspect of the dual nature of electromagnetic radiation is demonstrated by the photoelectric effect? *(2 marks)*

(b) A metal plate is illuminated with ultraviolet radiation of frequency 1.67×10^{15} Hz. The maximum kinetic energy of the liberated electrons is 3.0×10^{-19} J.

(i) Calculate the work function of the metal.

(ii) The radiation is maintained at the same frequency but the intensity is doubled. State what changes, if any, occur to the number of electrons released per second and to the maximum kinetic energy of these electrons.

(iii) The metal plate is replaced by another metal plate of different material. When illuminated by radiation of the same frequency no electrons are liberated.

Explain why this happens and what can be deduced about the work function of the new metal. *(7 marks)*

AQA, 2001

9   (a) A filament lamp labelled '12 V, 2.0 A' has a constant resistance of $2.0\,\Omega$ for electrical currents up to 0.50 A.

Sketch on graph paper the current–voltage graph for this lamp for positive voltages up to 12 V and currents up to 2.0 A. Show clearly any calculations you made in order to answer the question.   *(3 marks)*

(b) Sketch on a copy of the axes below the current–voltage characteristic for a semi-conductor diode.   *(3 marks)*

AQA, 2003

10   The filament of a 60 W, 230 V mains lamp is a coil of thin tungsten wire.

Figure 2

(a) When the lamp is new, the filament wire has a radius of $80\,\mu m$ and operates at a temperature of 2500 K.

   (i) Calculate the resistance of the filament at 2500 K.

   (ii) Show that the length of the wire in the filament is 0.25 m.

   resistivity of tungsten = $7.0 \times 10^{-5}\,\Omega\,m$ *(4 marks)*

(b) Near the end of its working life, the radius of the filament has decreased to $70\,\mu m$ and its working temperature is 2300 K. At this temperature, the resistivity of tungsten is $6.4 \times 10^{-5}\,\Omega\,m$. Discuss whether the lamp consumes electrical energy at a rate of 60 W near the end of its working life.   *(3 marks)*

AQA, 2006

11   **Figure 3** shows a circuit that is to be used as a sensor to monitor light intensity.

Figure 3

(a) State the full name of the component labelled **X**.   *(1 mark)*

(b) Calculate the output voltage when the resistance of **X** is 1.8 kΩ. *(2 marks)*

(c) (i) State and explain how the resistance of component **X** changes when the light intensity falls.

    (ii) State how the output voltage of the sensor will change when the light intensity falls. *(3 marks)*

AQA, 2007

12 **Figure 4** shows how the resistance R of three electrical components varies with temperature θ in °C.

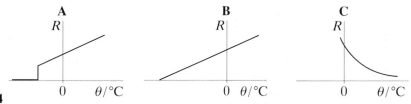

Figure 4

(a) Indicate below which one of **A**, **B** or **C** shows the correct graph for

a wire-wound resistor,

a thermistor,

a superconductor. *(2 marks)*

(b) The metal wire used to manufacture the wire-wound resistor has a resistance per metre of 26 Ω and a diameter of 0.23 mm. Calculate the resistivity of the material from which the wire is made. *(4 marks)*

AQA, 2007

13 The circuits in **Figure 5** and **Figure 6** both contain a 6.0 V supply of negligible internal resistance. Each circuit is designed to operate a 2.5 V, 0.25 A filament lamp **L**.

Figure 5   **Figure 6**

(a) Calculate the resistance of the filament lamp when working normally. *(2 marks)*

(b) Calculate the resistance of the resistor that should be used for **R** in **Figure 5**. *(2 marks)*

(c) Calculate the total resistance of the circuit in **Figure 6**. *(3 marks)*

(d) Explain which circuit dissipates the lower total power. *(3 marks)*

AQA, 2005

14 The heating circuit of a hairdryer is shown in **Figure 7**. It consists of two heating elements, R_1 and R_2, connected in parallel. Each element is controlled by its own switch.

Figure 7

The elements are made from the same resistance wire. This wire has a resistivity of $1.1 \times 10^{-6}\,\Omega\,m$ at its working temperature. The cross-sectional area of the wire is $1.7 \times 10^{-8}\,m^2$ and the length of the wire used to make R_1 is $3.0\,m$.

(a) Show that the resistance of R_1 is about $190\,\Omega$. *(3 marks)*

(b) Calculate the power output from the heating circuit with only R_1 switched on when it is connected to a 240 V supply. *(2 marks)*

(c) With both elements switched on, the total power output is three times that of R_1 on its own.
   (i) Calculate the length of wire used to make the coil R_2.
   (ii) Calculate the total current with both elements switched on. *(5 marks)*

AQA, 2004

15   **Figure 8** shows a power supply connected to a car battery in order to charge the battery. The terminals of the same polarity are connected together to achieve this.

Figure 8

(a) The power supply has an emf of 22V and internal resistance $0.75\,\Omega$. When charging begins, the car battery has an emf of 10 V and internal resistance of $0.15\,\Omega$. They are connected together via a variable resistor.
   (i) Calculate the total emf of the circuit when charging begins.
   (ii) The resistor R is adjusted to give an initial charging current of 0.25 A. Calculate the value of R. *(4 marks)*

(b) The car battery takes 8.0 hours to charge. Calculate the charge that flows through it in this time assuming that the current remains at 0.25 A. *(1 mark)*

AQA, 2003

16   A manufacturer asks you to design the heating element in a car rear-window demister. The design brief calls for an output of 48 W at a potential difference of 12 V. **Figure 9** shows where the eight elements will be on the car window before electrical connections are made to them.

Figure 9

(a) Calculate the current supplied by the power supply. *(1 mark)*

(b) One design possibility is for the eight elements to be connected in parallel.
   (i) Calculate the current in each element in this parallel arrangement.
   (ii) Calculate the resistance required for each element. *(3 marks)*

(c) Another design possibility is to have the eight elements connected in series.
   (i) Calculate the current in each element in this series arrangement.
   (ii) Calculate the resistance required for each element. *(4 marks)*

(d) State **one** disadvantage of the series design compared to the parallel arrangement. *(1 mark)*

(e) The series design is adopted. Each element is to have a rectangular cross-section of 0.12 mm by 3.0 mm. The length of each element is to be 0.75 m.

    (i) State the unit of resistivity.

    (ii) Calculate the resistivity of the material from which the element must be made.   *(3 marks)*

AQA, 2002

17   (a) The circuit in **Figure 10** may be used to determine the internal resistance, r, of a battery.

An oscilloscope is connected across the battery. **Figure 11** represents the screen of the oscilloscope.

Figure 10

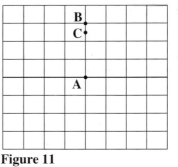

Figure 11

The vertical sensitivity of the oscilloscope is set at 2.0 V per division.

The time base of the oscilloscope is switched off throughout the experiment.

With both switches, S_1 and S_2, open, the spot on the oscillosocpe screen is at **A**.

    (i) Switch S_1 is closed with switch S_2 remaining open. The spot moves to **B**. State what the deflection **AB** represents and determine its value.

    (ii) With switch S_1 kept closed, switch S_2 is now also closed. The spot moves to **C**. Explain why the voltage represented by **AC** is less than the voltage measured by the oscilloscope in part (i).

    (iii) Calculate the current through the 15 Ω resistor with both switches closed.

    (iv) Calculate the internal resistance, r, of the battery.   *(8 marks)*

(b) The oscilloscope is now connected to an alternating voltage source of rms value 5.3 V, as shown in **Figure 12**.

Figure 12

    (i) Calculate the peak value of the alternating voltage.

    (ii) Draw on a copy of the grid below what you would expect to see on the oscilloscope screen, if the time base remains switched off and the voltage sensitivity is changed to 5.0 V per division.   *(3 marks)*

AQA, 2007

UNIT 2

Mechanics, materials and waves

Chapters in this unit

■ Introduction

This unit builds on your GCSE studies of motion, force, energy and waves. You will learn about the principles and applications of mechanics, materials and waves including optics. All these topic areas underpin many work-related areas including communications, engineering, transport and technology. Many new technologies and devices have developed from the topic areas in this unit, including vehicle safety features and nanotechnology. Nanotechnology is the discipline that develops devices too small to see without a powerful microscope.

Mechanics

In the study of mechanics, we will analyse the forces that maintain objects at rest or in uniform motion. We will be describing and calculating the effect of the forces acting on an object when it is not in **equilibrium**. We also consider **work** in terms of the **energy** transfer when a force moves its point of application, and we look at **power** in terms of rate of energy transfer. Applications, such as **terminal velocity**, **drag forces**, road and vehicle safety features, and the **efficiency** of machines are studied in detail.

Materials

In considering materials, we look at the important properties of materials, such as **density**, strength, **elasticity**, and the limits that determine the reliable and safe use of materials.

Waves

The study of waves in this unit encompasses wave measurements, the nature of **longitudinal waves** and **transverse waves**, and why polarisation is a property of transverse waves but not of longitudinal waves. We also consider in detail general wave properties, including **refraction**, **diffraction** and **interference**. In addition, we will find out how to create **stationary waves**. We will study some of the widespread applications of wave properties, including satellite TV dishes and the sounds created by musical strings when they vibrate.

In the optics chapter, we look at refraction of light in detail, including **total internal reflection** and the endoscope. We will study the experiments that demonstrate the wave nature of light and enable us to measure the wavelengths of different colours of light accurately.

Physicists discovered that the distant galaxies are all moving away from each other, concluding the universe is expanding. How they did this by measuring the wavelength of light from stars and galaxies is described. Therefore, the study of waves and optics in this unit takes us into direct and useful applications and also into fundamental discoveries about our place in the universe.

What you already know:

From your GCSE studies on force and energy, you should know that:

- Speed is distance travelled per unit time and velocity is speed in a given direction.

- The acceleration of an object is its rate of change of velocity.

- An object acted on by two equal and opposite forces is at rest or it moves at constant velocity.

- When an object accelerates or decelerates:
  - the greater the resultant force acting on the object, the greater its acceleration is,
  - the greater the mass of the object, the less its acceleration is.

- The gravitational field strength g at any point is the force per unit mass on a small object due to the earth's gravitational attraction on the object.

- The weight of an object in newtons = its mass in kilograms × g.

- Work is done by a force when the force moves its point of application in the direction of the force.

- Energy is transferred by a force when it does work.

- Energy cannot be created or destroyed. It can only be transformed from one form into other forms.

- Energy exists in different forms and can be changed from any form into other forms.

- Power is the rate of transfer of energy.

From your GCSE studies on waves, you should know that:

- Sound is a longitudinal waveform and all electromagnetic waves are transverse waveforms.

- A complete wave is from one peak to the next peak.

- Wavelength is the distance between adjacent wave peaks.

- Frequency is the number of complete waves passing a point per second.

- The speed of a wave = wavelength × frequency.

- All waves undergo reflection and refraction.

- The spectrum of electromagnetic waves in order of increasing frequency is radio waves, microwaves, infrared radiation, visible light, ultraviolet radiation, X-rays and gamma (γ) radiation.

Forces in equilibrium

7.1 Vectors and scalars

Learning objectives:

- What is a vector quantity?
- How do we represent vectors?
- How do we add and resolve vectors?

Specification reference: 3.2.1

Figure 1 *Map of locality*

a A force of 40 N due East
(Scale: 1 cm ≡ 10 N)

b A velocity of 10 m s⁻¹ at
45° West of due North
(Scale: 1 cm ≡ 4 m s⁻¹)

Figure 2 *Representing vectors
(a) a force of 40 N due east, (b) a velocity
of 10 m s⁻¹ at 45° west of north*

Representing a vector

Imagine you are planning to cycle to a friend's home several kilometres away from your home. The **distance** you travel depends on your route. However, the direct distance from your home to your friend's home is the same, whichever route you choose. Distance in a given direction, or **displacement**, is an example of a **vector** quantity because it has magnitude and direction. In Figure 1, suppose your home is at point O on the map and your friend's home is at A. The road distance you would cycle from O to A is greater than the direct distance or displacement from O to A. This is represented by the arrow from O to A.

> A vector is any physical quantity that
> has a direction as well as a magnitude.

Further examples of vectors include velocity, acceleration and force.

> A scalar is any physical quantity that is not directional.

For example, distance is a scalar because it takes no account of direction. Further examples of scalars include mass, density, volume and energy.

Any vector can be represented as an arrow. The length of the arrow represents the magnitude of the vector quantity. The direction of the arrow gives the direction of the vector.

- **Displacement** is distance in a given direction. As shown in Figure 1, the displacement from one point to another can be represented on a map or a scale diagram as an arrow from the first point to the second point. The length of the arrow must be in proportion to the least distance between the two points.

- **Velocity** is speed in a given direction. The velocity of an object can be represented by an arrow of length in proportion to the speed pointing in the direction of motion of the object.

- **Force and acceleration** are both vector quantities and therefore can each be represented by an arrow in the appropriate direction and of length in proportion to the magnitude of the quantity.

Addition of vectors using a scale diagram

Let's go back to the cycle journey in Figure 1. Suppose when you reach your friend's home at A you then go on to another friend's home at B. Your journey is now a two-stage journey.

Stage 1 from O to A is represented by the displacement vector **OA**.

Stage 2 from A to B is represented by the displacement vector **AB**.

Figure 3 shows how the overall displacement from O to B, represented by vector OB, is the result of adding vector AB to vector OA. The resultant is the third side of a triangle where OA and AB are the other two sides.

$$OB = OA + AB$$

Use Figure 1 to show that the resultant displacement **OB** is 5.1 km in a direction 11° north of due east.

Any two vectors of the same type together can be added together using a scale diagram. For example, Figure 4a) shows a ship pulled via cables by two tugboats. The two 'pull' forces F_1 and F_2 acting on the ship are at 40° to each other. Suppose the forces are both 8.0 kN. Figure 4b) shows how we can find the resultant (combined effect) of the two forces using a scale diagram.

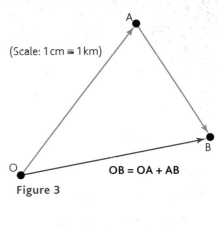

(Scale: 1 cm ≡ 1 km)

$OB = OA + AB$

Figure 3

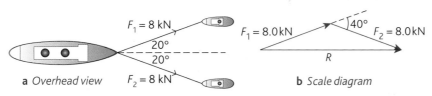

a *Overhead view*

b *Scale diagram*

Figure 4 *Adding two forces using a scale diagram*

Addition of two perpendicular vectors using a calculator

1 Adding two displacement vectors that are at right angles to each other:

Suppose you walk 10.0 m forward then turn through exactly 90° and walk 7.0 m. At the end, how far will you be from your starting point? The vector diagram to add the two displacements is shown in Figure 5, drawn to a scale of 1 cm to 2.0 m. The two displacements form the two shorter sides of a right-angled triangle with the overall displacement, the **resultant**, as the hypotenuse. Using a ruler and a protractor, the resultant displacement can be shown to be a distance of 12.2 m at an angle of 35° to the initial direction. You can check this using

- ■ Pythagoras' theorem for the distance $(= (10.0^2 + 7.0^2)^{1/2})$
- ■ the trigonometry equation, $\tan \theta = 7.0/10.0$ for the angle θ between the resultant and the initial direction.

2 Two forces acting at right angles to each other:

Figure 6 shows an object O acted on by two forces F_1 and F_2 at right angles to each other. The vector diagram for this situation is also shown. The two forces in the vector diagram form two of the sides of a right-angled triangle in which the resultant force is represented by the hypotenuse.

Figure 5 *Adding two displacements at right angles to each other*

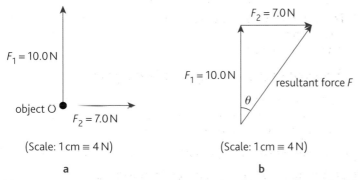

a

b

Figure 6 *(a) An object acted on by two perpendicular forces, (b) Vector diagram for (a)*

a *Forces acting*

b *Vector diagram*

Figure 7 *Two forces acting in the same direction*

a *Forces acting*

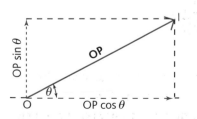

b *Vector diagram*

Figure 8 *Two forces acting in opposite directions*

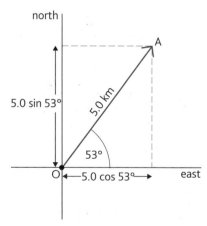

Figure 9 *Resolving a vector*

The vector diagram drawn to scale can therefore be used to find the resultant if the magnitudes of F_1 and F_2 are given. For example, the resultant of a force of 10.0 N acting at right angles to a force of 7.0 N has a magnitude of 12.2 N in a direction of 35° to the direction of the force of 10.0 N. You could check this using Pythagoras' theorem and the appropriate trigonometry equation. You might, however, recognise that you have already done this! See addition of displacement vectors on page 91.

In general, if the two perpendicular forces are F_1 and F_2, then

■ **the magnitude of the resultant $F = (F_1^2 + F_2^2)^{1/2}$, and**

■ **the angle θ between the resultant and F_1 is given by $\tan \theta = \dfrac{F_2}{F_1}$**

Note:

The resultant of two vectors that act **along the same line** has a magnitude that is

■ the sum, if the two vectors are in the same direction. For example, if an object is acted on by a force of 6.0 N and a force of 4.0 N both acting in the same direction, the resultant force is 10.0 N (Figure 7).

■ the difference, if the two vectors are in opposite directions. For example, if an object is acted on by a 6.0 N force and a 4.0 N force in opposite directions, the resultant force is 2.0 N in the direction of the 6.0 N force (Figure 8).

■ Resolving a vector into two perpendicular components

This is the process of working out the components of a vector in two perpendicular directions from the magnitude and direction of the vector. Figure 9 shows the displacement vector OA represented on a scale diagram that also shows lines due north and due east. The components of this vector along these two lines are $5.0 \cos 53°$ km (= 3.0 km) along the line due east and $5.0 \sin 53°$ km (= 4.0 km) along the line due north.

In general, to resolve any vector into two perpendicular components, draw a diagram showing the two perpendicular directions and an arrow to represent the vector. Figure 10 shows this diagram for a vector OP. The components are represented by the projection of the vector onto each line. If the angle θ between the vector OP and one of the lines is known,

■ the component along that line = $OP \cos \theta$, and

■ the component perpendicular to that line (i.e. along the other line) = $OP \sin \theta$

Thus a force F can be resolved into two perpendicular components:

■ **$F \cos \theta$ parallel to a line at angle θ to the line of action of the force, and**

■ **$F \sin \theta$ perpendicular to the line.**

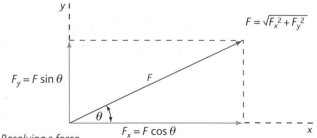

Figure 10 *The general rule for resolving a vector*

Figure 11 *Resolving a force*

Worked example:

A paraglider is pulled along at constant height at steady speed by a cable attached to a speedboat as shown in Figure 12. The cable pulls on the paraglider with a force of 500 N at an angle of 35° to the horizontal. Calculate the horizontal and vertical components of this force.

Solution

Because the force on the paraglider is at an angle of 35° below the horizontal, the horizontal and vertical components of this force are, in N,

- 500 cos 35° horizontally

- 500 sin 35° vertically downwards.

Figure 12

Summary questions

1 Figure 13 shows three situations a–c where two or more known forces act on an object. For each situation, calculate the magnitude and direction of the resultant force.

Figure 13

2 Calculate the magnitude and direction of the resultant force on an object which is acted on by a force of 4.0 N and a force of 10 N that are i in the same direction, ii in opposite directions, iii at right angles to each other.

3 A crane is used to raise one end of a steel girder off the ground, as shown in Figure 14. When the cable attached to the end of the girder is at 20° to the vertical, the force of the cable on the girder is 6.5 kN. Calculate the horizontal and vertical components of this force.

Figure 14

4 A yacht is moving due north as a result of a force, due to the wind, of 350 N in a horizontal direction of 40° east of due north, as shown in Figure 15.

Figure 15

Calculate the component of the force of the wind:

a in the direction the yacht is moving,

b perpendicular to the direction in which the yacht is moving.

7.2 Balanced forces

Specification reference: 3.2.1

Learning objectives:

- Why do we have to consider the direction in which a force acts?

- When do two (or more) forces have no overall effect on a point object?

- What is the parallelogram of forces?

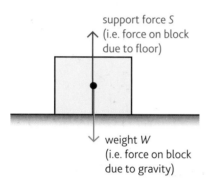

Figure 1 *Balanced forces*

support force S
(i.e. force on block due to floor)

weight W
(i.e. force on block due to gravity)

■ Equilibrium of a point object

When two forces act on a point object, the object is in equilibrium (at rest or moving at constant velocity) only if the two forces are equal and opposite to each other. The resultant of the two forces is therefore zero. The two forces are said to be **balanced**.

For example, an object resting on a horizontal surface is acted on by its weight W (i.e. the force of gravity on it) acting downwards, and a support force S from the surface, acting upwards. Hence S is equal and opposite to W, provided the object is at rest (or moving at constant velocity).

$$S = W$$

When three forces act on a point object, their combined effect (the resultant) is zero only if the resultant of any two of the forces is equal and opposite to the third force. To check the combined effect of the three forces is zero:

- resolve each force along the same parallel and perpendicular lines
- balance the components along each line.

Worked example 1: _____

A child of weight W on a swing is at rest due to the swing seat being pulled to the side by a horizontal force F_1. The rope supporting the seat is then at an angle θ to the vertical, as shown in Figure 2.

Assuming the swing seat is of negligible weight, the swing seat is acted on by three forces, which are: the weight of the child, the horizontal force F_1 and the tension T in the rope. Resolving the tension T vertically and horizontally gives $T\cos\theta$ for the vertical component of T (which is upwards) and $T\sin\theta$ for the horizontal component of T. Therefore, the balance of forces:

1) horizontally: $F_1 = T\sin\theta$

2) vertically: $W = T\cos\theta$

Because $\sin^2\theta + \cos^2\theta = 1$ (see 16.2), then $F_1^2 + W^2 = T^2\sin^2\theta + T^2\cos^2\theta = T^2$

$$\therefore T^2 = F_1^2 + W^2$$

Also, because $\tan\theta = \dfrac{\sin\theta}{\cos\theta}$, then $\dfrac{F_1}{W} = \dfrac{T\sin\theta}{T\cos\theta} = \tan\theta$

$$\therefore \tan\theta = \frac{F_1}{W}$$

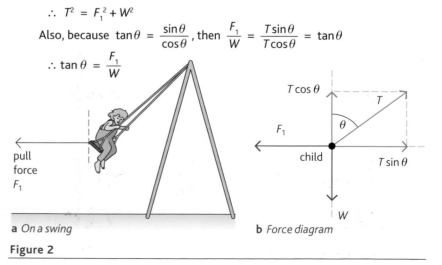

pull force F_1

a *On a swing*

$T\cos\theta$

F_1

θ

T

child

$T\sin\theta$

W

b *Force diagram*

Figure 2

Worked example 2 :

An object of weight W is at rest on a rough slope (i.e. a slope with a roughened surface). The object is acted on by a frictional force F, which prevents it sliding down the slope, and a support force S from the slope, perpendicular to the slope.

Resolving the three forces parallel and perpendicular to the slope gives:

1) horizontally: $F = W\sin\theta$

2) vertically: $S = W\cos\theta$

Because $\sin^2\theta + \cos^2\theta = 1$ (see Topic 16.2 if necessary), then $F^2 + S^2 = W^2\sin^2\theta + W^2\cos^2\theta = W^2$

$\therefore W^2 = F^2 + S^2$

Also, because $\tan\theta = \dfrac{\sin\theta}{\cos\theta}$, then $\dfrac{F}{S} = \dfrac{W\sin\theta}{W\cos\theta} = \tan\theta$

$\therefore \tan\theta = \dfrac{F}{S}$

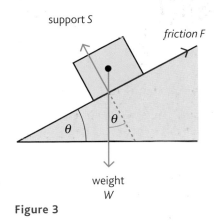

Figure 3

Worked example 3:

An object of weight W is supported by a vertical string, which is supported by two strings at different angles θ_1 and θ_2 to the vertical, as shown in Figure 4. Suppose the tension in the string at angle θ_1 to the vertical is T_1 and the tension in the other string is T_2.

At the point P where the strings meet, the forces T_1, T_2 and W are in equilibrium.

Resolving T_1 and T_2 vertically and horizontally gives:

1) horizontally: $T_1\sin\theta_1 = T_2\sin\theta_2$

2) vertically: $T_1\cos\theta_1 + T_2\cos\theta_2 = W$

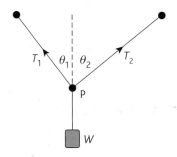

Figure 4 *A suspended weight*

⚠ Testing three forces in equilibrium

Figure 5 shows a practical arrangement to test three forces acting on a point object P. The tension in each string pulls on P and is due to the weight it supports, either directly or indirectly over a pulley. Provided the pulleys are frictionless, each tension force acting on P is equal to the weight supported by its string.

a *Using pulleys*

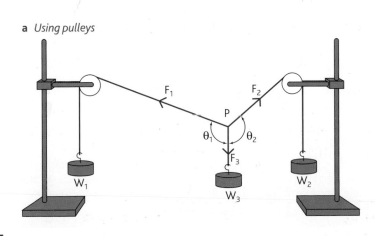

b *Using the parallelogram rule*

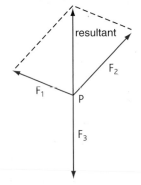

💡 **Figure 5** *Testing three forces*

The three forces F_1, F_2 and F_3 acting on P are in equilibrium, so any two should give a resultant equal and opposite to the third force. For example, the resultant of F_1 and, F_2 is equal and opposite to F_3. You can test this by measuring the angle between each of the upper strings and the lower string which is vertical. A scale diagram can then be constructed using the fact that the magnitudes of F_1, F_2 and F_3 are equal to W_1, W_2 and W_3 respectively. Your diagram should show that the resultant of F_1 and, F_2 is equal and opposite to F_3.

Note:

Greater accuracy can be obtained by drawing a parallelogram, using the two force vectors F_1 and, F_2 as adjacent sides. The resultant is the diagonal of the parallelogram **between** the two force vectors. This should be equal and opposite to F_3.

Summary questions

1 A point object of weight 6.2 N is acted on by a horizontal force of 3.8 N.

  a Calculate the resultant of these two forces.

  b Determine the magnitude and direction of a third force acting on the object for it to be in equilibrium.

2 A small object of weight 5.4 N is at rest on a rough slope, which is at an angle of 30° to the horizontal.

  a Sketch a diagram and show the three forces acting on the object.

  b Calculate i the frictional force on the object, ii the support force from the slope on the object.

3 An archer pulled a bowstring back until the two halves of the string are at 140° to each other (Figure 6). The force needed to hold the string in this position was 95 N.

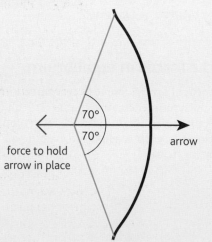

Figure 6

Calculate:

  a the tension in each part of the bowstring in this position,

  b the resultant force on an arrow at the instant the bowstring is released from this position.

4 An elastic string is stretched horizontally between two fixed points 0.80 m apart. An object of weight 4.0 N is suspended from the midpoint of the string, causing the midpoint to drop a distance of 0.12 m. Calculate:

  a the angle of each part of the string to the vertical,

  b the tension in each part of the string.

7.3 The principle of moments

Learning objectives:

- Under what conditions does a force produce a turning effect?

- How can the turning effect of a given force be increased?

- What is required to balance a force that produces a turning effect?

- Why is the centre of mass an important idea?

Specification reference: 3.2.1

Figure 1 *A turning force*

■ Turning effects

Whenever you use a lever or a spanner, you are using a force to turn an object about a pivot. For example, if you use a spanner to loosen a wheel nut on a bicycle, you need to apply a force to the spanner to make it turn about the wheel axle. The effect of the force depends on how far it is applied from the wheel axle. The longer the spanner, the less force needed to loosen the nut. However, if the spanner is too long and the nut is too tight, the spanner could snap if too much force is applied to it.

The moment of a force about any point is defined as the force × the perpendicular distance from the line of action of the force to the point.

The unit of the moment of a force is the newton metre (Nm).

For a force F acting along a line of action at perpendicular distance d from a certain point,

$$\text{the moment of the force} = F \times d$$

Notes:

1 The greater the distance d, the greater the moment.
2 The distance d is the **perpendicular** distance from the line of action of the force to the point.

▲ ⚲ The principle of moments

An object that is not a point object is referred to as a body. Any such object turns if a force is applied to it anywhere other than through its centre of gravity. If a body is acted on by more than one force and it is in equilibrium, the turning effects of the forces must balance out. In more formal terms, considering the **moments** of the forces about any point, for equilibrium

$$\text{the sum of the clockwise moments} = \text{the sum of the anticlockwise moments}$$

This statement is known as **the principle of moments**.

For example, consider a uniform metre rule balanced on a pivot at its centre, supporting weights W_1 and W_2 suspended from the rule on either side of the pivot.

- Weight W_1 provides an anticlockwise moment about the pivot = $W_1 d_1$, where d_1 is the distance from the line of action of the weight to the pivot.
- Weight W_2 provides a clockwise moment about the pivot = $W_2 d_2$, where d_2 is the distance from the line of action of the weight to the pivot.

For equilibrium, applying the principle of moments:

$$W_1 d_1 = W_2 d_2$$

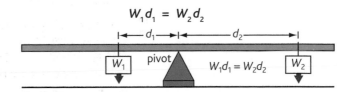

⚲ **Figure 2** *The principle of moments*

Figure 3 *A centre of mass test*

Summary questions

1 A child of weight 200 N sits on a seesaw at a distance of 1.2 m from the pivot at the centre. The seesaw is balanced by a second child sitting on it at a distance of 0.8 m from the centre. Calculate the weight of the second child.

2 A metre rule, pivoted at its centre of mass, supports a 3.0 N weight at its 5.0 cm mark, a 2.0 N weight at its 25 cm mark and a weight W at its 80 cm mark.

   a Sketch a diagram to represent this situation.

   b Calculate the weight W.

3 In Q2, the 3.0 N weight and the 2.0 N weight are swapped with each other. Sketch the new arrangement and work out the new distance of weight W from the pivot.

4 A uniform metre rule supports a 4.5 N weight at its 100 mm mark. The rule is balanced horizontally on a horizontal knife-edge at its 340 mm mark. Sketch the arrangement and calculate the weight of the rule.

Note:

If a third weight W_3 is suspended from the rule on the same side of the pivot as W_2 at distance d_3 from the pivot, then the rule can be rebalanced by increasing distance d_1.

At this new distance d_1' for W_1,

$$W_1 d_1' = W_2 d_2 + W_3 d_3$$

■ Centre of mass

A tightrope walker knows just how important the centre of mass of an object can be. One slight off-balance movement can be catastrophic. The tightrope walker uses a horizontal pole to ensure his or her overall centre of mass is always directly above the rope. The support force from the rope then acts upwards through the centre of mass of the walker.

The centre of mass of a body is the point through which a single force on the body has no turning effect. In effect, it is the point where we consider the weight of the body to act when studying the effect of forces on the body.

Centre of mass tests

1 Support a ruler at its centre on the end of your finger. The centre of mass of the ruler is directly above the point of support. Tip the ruler too much and it falls off because the centre of mass is no longer above the point of support.

2 Find the centre of mass of a triangular card. Figure 3 shows how to do this. It should be possible to balance the card at its centre of mass on the end of a pencil.

■ Calculating the weight of a metre rule

1 Locate the centre of mass of a metre rule by balancing it horizontally on a horizontal knife-edge. Note the position of the centre of mass. The rule is **uniform** if its centre of mass is exactly at the middle of the rule.

2 Balance the metre rule off-centre on a knife-edge, using a known weight W_1 as shown in Figure 4. The position of the known weight needs to be adjusted gradually until the rule is exactly horizontal.

At this position

■ the known weight W_1 provides an anticlockwise moment about the pivot $= W_1 d_1$, where d_1 is the perpendicular distance from the line of action of W_1 to the pivot

■ the weight of the rule W_0 provides a clockwise moment $= W_0 d_0$, where d_0 is the distance from the centre of mass of the rule to the pivot.

Applying the principle of moments,

$$W_0 d_0 = W_1 d_1$$

By measuring distance d_0 and d_1, the weight W_0 of the rule can therefore be calculated.

Figure 4 *Finding the weight of a beam*

7.4 More on moments

Learning objectives:

- What can we say about the support force on a pivoted body?

- When a body in equilibrium is supported at two places, how much force is exerted on each support?

- What is meant by a couple?

Specification reference: 3.2.1

Figure 1 *Support forces*

Figure 2 *A two-support problem*

AQA Examiner's tip

In calculations, you can always eliminate the turning effect of a force by taking moments about a point through which it acts.

▲ *i* Support forces

Single support problems

When an object in equilibrium is supported at one point only, the support force on the object is equal and opposite to the total downward force acting on the object. For example, in Figure 1, a uniform rule is balanced on a knife-edge at its centre of mass, with two additional weights W_1 and W_2 attached to the rule. The support force S on the rule from the knife-edge must be equal to the total downward weight. Therefore

$$S = W_1 + W_2 + W_0, \text{ where } W_0 \text{ is the weight of the rule.}$$

As explained in Topic 7.3, taking moments about the knife-edge gives

$$W_1 d_1 = W_2 d_2$$

Note:

What difference is made by taking moments about a different point? Consider moments about the point where W_1 is attached to the rule.

The sum of the clockwise moments $= W_0 d_1 + W_2 (d_1 + d_2)$

The sum of the anticlockwise moments $= S d_1 = (W_1 + W_2 + W_0) d_1$

$$\therefore (W_1 + W_2 + W_0) d_1 = W_0 d_1 + W_2 (d_1 + d_2)$$

Multiplying out the brackets gives:

$$W_1 d_1 + W_2 d_1 + W_0 d_1 = W_0 d_1 + W_2 d_1 + W_2 d_2$$

which simplifies to become $W_1 d_1 = W_2 d_2$

This is the same as the equation obtained by taking moments about S. So moments can be taken about any point. It makes sense therefore to choose a point through which one or more unknown forces act, as such forces have zero moment about this point.

Two support problems

Consider a uniform beam supported on two pillars X and Y, which are at distance D apart. The weight of the beam is 'shared' between the two pillars according to how far the beam's centre of mass is from each pillar. For example:

- If the centre of mass of the beam is midway between the pillars, the weight of the beam is 'shared' equally between the two pillars. In other words, the support force on the beam from each pillar is equal to half the weight of the beam.

- If the centre of mass of the beam is at distance d_x from pillar X and distance d_y from pillar Y, as shown in Figure 2, then taking moments about

  1 where X is in contact with the beam,
  $$S_y D = W d_x, \text{ where } S_y \text{ is the support force from pillar}$$
  $$\text{gives } S_y = \frac{W d_x}{D}$$

2 where Y is in contact with the beam,

$S_x D = W d_y$, where S_y is the support force from pillar

gives $S_x = \dfrac{W d_y}{D}$

Therefore, if the centre of mass is closer to X than to Y, $d_x < d_y$ so $S_y < S_x$.

■ Couples

A **couple** is a pair of equal and opposite forces acting on a body, but not along the same line. Figure 3 shows a couple acting on a beam. The couple turns or tries to turn the beam.

The moment of a couple is sometimes referred to as a **torque**.

The moment, or torque, of a couple = force × perpendicular distance between the lines of action of the forces.

To prove this, consider the couple in Figure 3. Taking moments about an arbitrary point P between the ends at distance x along the beam from one end,

1 the moment due to the force F at that end = Fx clockwise

2 the moment due to the force F at the other end = $F(d - x)$, where d is the perpendicular distance between the lines of action of the forces.

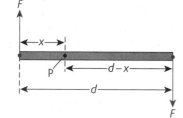

Figure 3 *A couple*

Therefore the total moment = $Fx + F(d - x) = Fx + Fd - Fx = Fd$.

The total moment is the same, regardless of the point about which moments are taken.

Summary questions

1 A uniform metre rule of weight 1.2 N rests horizontally on two knife-edges at the 100 mm mark and the 800 mm mark. Sketch the arrangement and calculate the support force on the rule due to each knife-edge.

2 A uniform beam of weight 230 N and of length 10 m rests horizontally on the tops of two brick walls, 8.5 m apart, such that a length of 1.0 m projects beyond one wall and 0.5 m projects beyond the other wall. Figure 4 shows the arrangement.

Figure 4

Calculate:

a the support force of each wall on the beam,

b the force of the beam on each wall.

3 A uniform bridge span of weight 1200 kN and of length 17.0 m rests on a support of width 1.0 m at either end. A stationary lorry of weight 60 kN is the only object on the bridge. Its centre of mass is 3.0 m from the centre of the bridge.

Figure 5

Calculate the support force on the bridge at each end.

4 A uniform plank of weight 150 N and of length 4.0 m rests horizontally on two bricks. One of the bricks is at the end of the plank. The other brick is 1.0 m from the other end of the plank.

a Sketch the arrangement and calculate the support force on the plank from each brick.

b A child stands on the free end of the plank and just causes the other end to lift off its support.

Sketch this arrangement and calculate the weight of the child.

7.5 Stability

Learning objectives:

■ What is the difference between stable and unstable equilibrium?

■ When is a tilted object going to topple over?

■ Why is a vehicle more stable, the lower its centre of mass?

Specification reference: 3.2.1

■ Stable and unstable equilibrium

If a body in **stable equilibrium** is displaced then released, it returns to its equilibrium position. For example, if an object such as a coat hanger hanging from a support is displaced slightly, it swings back to its equilibrium position.

Why does an object in stable equilibrium return to equilibrium when it is displaced and then released? The reason is that the centre of mass of the object is directly below the point of support when the object is at rest. The weight of the object is considered to act at its centre of mass. Thus the support force and the weight are directly equal and opposite to each other when the object is in equilibrium. However, when it is displaced, at the instant of release, the line of action of the weight no longer passes through the point of support, so the weight returns the object to equilibrium.

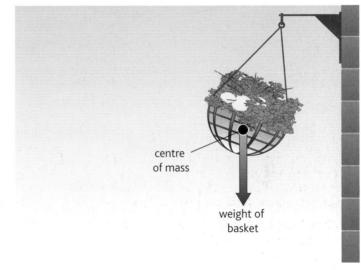

centre of mass

weight of basket

Figure 1 *Returning to equilbrium*

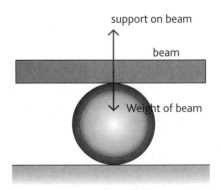

support on beam

beam

Weight of beam

Figure 2 *Unstable equilbrium*

A plank balanced on a drum is in **unstable equilibrium** (Figure 2). If it is displaced slightly from equilibrium then released, the plank will roll off the drum. The reason is that the centre of mass of the plank is directly above the point of support when it is in equilibrium. The support force is exactly equal and opposite to the weight. If the plank is displaced slightly, the centre of mass is no longer above the point of support. The weight therefore acts to turn the plank further from the equilibrium position.

■ Tilting and toppling

Skittles at a bowling alley are easy to knock over because they are tall, so their centre of gravity is too high and the base is too narrow. A slight nudge from a ball causes a skittle to tilt then tip over.

Tilting

This is where an object at rest on a surface is acted on by a force that raises it up on one side. For example, if a horizontal force F is applied to the top of a tall free-standing bookcase, the force can make the bookcase tilt about its base along one edge.

In Figure 3, to make the bookcase tilt, the force must turn it clockwise about point P. The entire support from the floor acts at point P. The weight of the bookcase provides an anticlockwise moment about P.

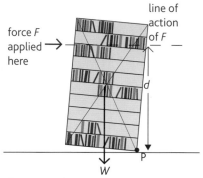

1 The clockwise moment of F about P $= Fd$, where d is the perpendicular distance from the line of action of F to the pivot.

2 The anticlockwise moment of W about P $= Wb/2$ where b is the width of the base.

Therefore, for tilting to occur $Fd > Wb/2$

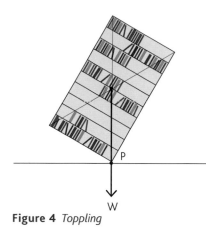

Figure 3 *Tilting*

Toppling

A tilted object will topple over if it is tilted too far. If an object on a flat surface is tilted more and more, the line of action of its weight (which is through its centre of mass) passes closer and closer to the pivot. If the object is tilted so much that the line of action of its weight passes beyond the pivot, the object will topple over if allowed to. The position where the line of action of the weight passes through the pivot is the furthest it can be tilted without toppling. Beyond this position, it topples over if it is released.

■ On a slope

A tall object on a slope will topple over if the slope is too great. For example, a high-sided vehicle on a road with a sideways slope will topple over if the slope is too great. This will happen if the line of action of the weight (passing through the centre of mass of the object) lies outside the wheelbase of the vehicle. In Figure 5, the vehicle will not topple over because the line of action of the weight lies within the wheelbase.

Figure 4 *Toppling*

> ### ■ Hint
> The lower the centre of mass of an object, the more stable it is.

Figure 5 *Unstable equilbrium*

Consider the forces acting on the vehicle on a sideways slope when it is at rest. The sideways friction F, the support forces S_x and S_y and the force of gravity on the vehicle (i.e. its weight) act as shown in Figure 5. For equilibrium, resolving the forces parallel and perpendicular to the slope gives:

1 parallel to the slope:

$F = W \sin\theta$

2 perpendicular to the slope:

$S_x + S_y = W \cos\theta$

Note that S_x is greater than S_y because X is lower than Y.

Summary questions

1 Explain why a bookcase with books on its top shelf only is less stable than if the books were on the bottom shelf.

2 An empty wardrobe of weight 400 N has a square base 0.8 m × 0.8 m and a height of 1.8 m. A horizontal force is applied to the top edge of the wardrobe to make it tilt. Calculate the force needed to lift the wardrobe base off the floor along one side.

force applied here

1.8 m

0.8 m

Figure 6

3 A vehicle has a wheelbase of 1.8 m and a centre of mass, when unloaded, which is 0.8 m from the ground.

0.8 m

1.8 m

Figure 7

   a The vehicle is tested for stability on an adjustable slope. Calculate the maximum angle of the slope to the horizontal if the vehicle is not to topple over.

   b If the vehicle carries a full load of people, will it be more or less likely to topple over on a slope? Explain your answer.

4 Discuss whether or not a high-sided heavy goods lorry is more or less likely to be affected by strong side winds when it is fully loaded, compared to when it is empty.

7.6 Equilibrium rules

Learning objectives:

- What condition must apply to the forces on an object in equilibrium?

- What condition must apply to the turning effects of the forces?

- How can we apply these conditions to predict the forces acting on a body in equilibrium?

Specification reference: 3.2.1

Free body force diagrams

When two objects interact, they always exert equal and opposite forces on one another. A diagram showing the forces acting on an object can become very complicated, if it also shows the forces the object exerts on other objects as well. A free body force diagram shows only the forces acting on the object.

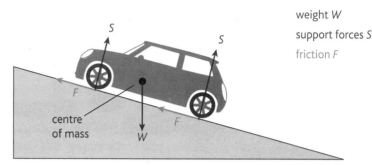

weight W

support forces S

friction F

Figure 1 *A free body diagram of a parked car on a slope*

The triangle of forces

For a point object acted on by three forces to be in equilibrium, the three forces must give an overall resultant of zero. The three forces as vectors should form a triangle. In other words, for three forces F_1, F_2 and F_3 to give zero resultant,

$$\text{their vector sum } F_1 + F_2 + F_3 = 0$$

As explained in Topic 7.1, any two of the forces gives a resultant that is equal and opposite to the third force. For example, the resultant of $F_1 + F_2$ is equal and opposite to F_3 ($F_1 + F_2 = -F_3$).

The same rule applies to a body in equilibrium acted on by three forces. In addition, their lines of action must intersect at the same point, otherwise the body cannot be in equilibrium, as the forces will have a net turning effect. Consider the example of a rectangular block on a rough slope, as shown in Figure 3.

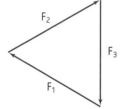

Figure 2 *The triangle of forces for a point object*

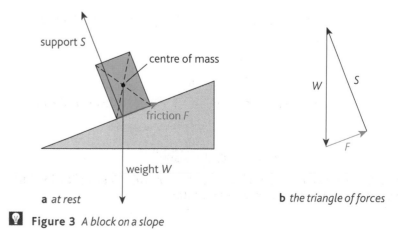

a *at rest*

b *the triangle of forces*

Figure 3 *A block on a slope*

■ The weight W of the block acts vertically down through the centre of mass of the block.

■ The frictional force F on the block due to the slope prevents the block from sliding down the slope, so it acts up the slope.

■ The support force S on the block due to the slope acts normal to the slope through the point where the lines of action of W and F act. Figure 3 also shows the triangle of forces for the three forces W, F, and S acting on the block.

We can draw a scale diagram of the triangle of forces to find an unknown force or angle, given the other forces and angles in the triangle. For example, to find the unknown force, F_3, in the triangle of forces in Figure 4:

1 Draw one of the known force vectors, F_1, to scale, as one side of the force triangle.

2 Use a protractor and ruler to draw the other known force (e.g. F_2) at the correct angle to F_1 as the second side of the triangle. The third side of the triangle can then be drawn in to give the unknown force (F_3).

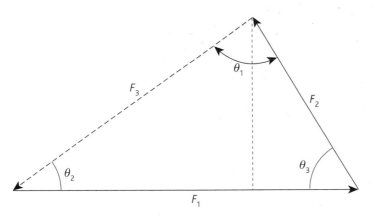

Figure 4 *Constructing a scale diagram*

You could calculate the unknown force by resolving it and F_2 parallel and perpendicular to the 'base' force F_1. Labelling θ_2 as the angle opposite F_2 and θ_3 as the angle opposite F_3, the perpendicular components of the resolved forces, $F_2\sin\theta_3$ and $F_3\sin\theta_2$, correspond to the height of the triangle and are equal and opposite to each other:

$$F_2\sin\theta_3 = F_3\sin\theta_2$$

Thus the unknown force can be calculated if F_2, θ_2 and θ_3 are known.

Rearranging this equation gives

$$\frac{F_2}{\sin\theta_2} = \frac{F_3}{\sin\theta_3}$$

By applying the same theory to F_1 and either F_2 or F_3, it can be shown that

$$\frac{F_1}{\sin\theta_1} = \frac{F_2}{\sin\theta_2} = \frac{F_3}{\sin\theta_3}$$

This rule, known as the sine rule, is not part of this AS specification but you might meet it if you study A level Maths.

■ The conditions for equilibrium of a body

An object in equilibrium is either at rest or moving with a constant velocity. The forces acting on it must give zero resultant and their turning effects must balance out as well.

Therefore, for a body in equilibrium:

1 The resultant force must be zero. If there are only three forces, they must form a closed triangle.

2 The principle of moments must apply (i.e. the moments of the forces about the same point must balance out).

See Topics 7.3 and 7.4 again if necessary.

Worked example:

A uniform shelf of width 0.6 m and of weight 12 N is attached to a wall by hinges and is supported horizontally by two parallel cords attached at two corners of the shelf, as shown in Figure 5. The other end of each cord is fixed to the wall 0.4 m above the hinge. Calculate:

a the angle between each cord and the shelf,

b the tension in each cord.

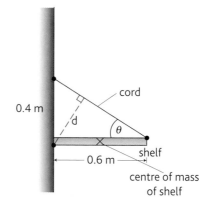

Figure 5

Solution

a Let the angle between each cord and the shelf = θ

From Figure 5, $\tan\theta = \dfrac{0.4}{0.6}$, so $\theta = 34°$.

b Taking moments about the hinge gives:

1 The sum of the clockwise moments = weight of shelf × distance from hinge to the centre of mass of the shelf = 12 × 0.3 = 3.6 N m.

2 The sum of the anticlockwise moments = $2Td$, where T is the tension in each cord and d is the perpendicular distance from the hinge to either cord.

From the diagram above, it can be seen that $d = 0.6\sin\theta = 0.6\sin 34 = 0.34\,\text{m}$

Applying the principle of moments gives:

2 × 0.34 × T = 3.6

$T = 5.3\,\text{N}$

Summary questions

1 A uniform plank of length 5.0 m rests horizontally on two bricks that are 0.5 m from either end. A child of weight 200 N stands on one end of the plank and causes the other end to lift, so it is no longer supported at that end. Calculate:

a the weight of the plank,

b the support force acting on the plank from the supporting brick.

Figure 6

2 A security camera is supported by a frame that is fixed to a wall and ceiling as shown in Figure 7. The support structure must be strong enough to withstand the effect of a downward force of 1500 N acting on the camera (in case the camera is gripped by someone below it). Calculate

a the moment of a force of 1500 N on the camera about the point where the support structure is attached to the wall,

b the extra force on the vertical strut supporting the frame, when the camera is pulled with a downward force of 1500 N.

Figure 7

3 A crane is used to raise one end of a 15 kN girder of length 10.0 m off the ground. When the end of the girder is at rest 6.0 m off the ground, the crane cable is perpendicular to the girder, as shown in Figure 8.

Figure 8

a Calculate the tension in the cable.

b Show that the support force on the girder from the ground has a horizontal component of 3.6 N and a vertical component of 10.2 kN. Hence calculate the magnitude of the support force.

4 A small toy of weight 2.8 N is suspended from a horizontal beam by means of two cords that are attached to the same point on the toy (Figure 9). One cord makes an angle of 60° to the beam and the other makes an angle of 40° to the vertical. Calculate the tension in each cord.

Figure 9

7.7 Statics calculations

■ What are the important principles that always apply to a body in equilibrium?

Specification reference: 3.2.1

AQA Examiner's tip

Get as far as you can using force diagrams, resolving and common sense.

7.5 N

Figure 1

Figure 3

1 Calculate the magnitude of the resultant of a 6.0 N force and a 9.0 N force acting on a point object when the two forces act:

 a in the same direction,

 b in opposite directions,

 c at 90° to each other.

2 A point object in equilbrium is acted on by a 3 N force, a 6 N force and a 7 N force. What is the resultant force on the object if the 7 N force is removed?

3 A point object of weight 5.4 N in equilibrium is acted on by a horizontal force of 4.2 N and a second force F.

 a Draw a free body force diagram for the object and determine the magnitude of F.

 b Calculate the angle between the direction of F and the horizontal.

4 An object of weight 7.5 N hangs on the end of a cord, which is attached to the midpoint of a wire stretched between two points on the same horizontal level, as shown in Figure 1. Each half of the wire is at 12° to the horizontal. Calculate the tension in each half of the wire.

5 A ship is towed at constant speed by two tugboats, each pulling the ship with a force of 9.0 kN. The angle between the tugboat cables is 40°, as shown in Figure 2.

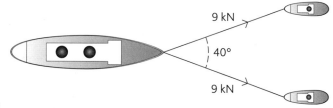

9 kN

40°

9 kN

Figure 2

 a Calculate the resultant force on the ship due to the two cables.

 b Calculate the drag force on the ship.

6 A metre rule of weight 1.0 N is pivoted on a knife-edge at its centre of mass, supporting a weight of 5.0 N and an unknown weight W as shown in Figure 3. To balance the rule horizontally with the unknown weight on the 250 mm mark of the rule, the position of the 5.0 N weight needs to be at the 810 mm mark.

 a Calculate the unknown weight.

 b Calculate the support force on the rule from the knife-edge.

7 In Figure 3, a 2.5 N weight is also suspended from the rule at its 400 mm mark. What adjustment needs to be made to the position of the 5.0 N weight to rebalance the rule?

8 A uniform metre rule is balanced horizontally on a knife-edge at its 350 mm mark, by placing a 3.0 N weight on the rule at its 10 mm mark.

   a Sketch the arrangement and calculate the weight of the rule.

   b Calculate the support force on the rule from the knife-edge.

9 A uniform diving board has a length 4.0 m and a weight of 250 N, as shown in Figure 4. It is bolted to the ground at one end and projects by a length of 3.0 m beyond the edge of the swimming pool. A person of weight 650 N stands on the free end of the diving board. Calculate:

   a the force on the bolts,

   b the force on the edge of the swimming pool.

Figure 4

10 A uniform beam XY of weight 1200 N and of length 5.0 m is supported horizontally on a concrete pillar at each end. A person of weight 500 N sits on the beam at a distance of 1.5 m from end X.

   a Sketch a free body force diagram of the beam.

   b Calculate the support force on the beam from each pillar.

11 A bridge crane used at a freight depot consists of a horizontal span of length 12 m fixed at each end to a vertical pillar, as shown in Figure 5.

   a When the bridge crane supports a load of 380 kN at its centre, a force of 1600 kN is exerted on each pillar. Calculate the weight of the horizontal span.

   b The same load is moved across a distance of 2.0 m by the bridge crane. Sketch a free body force diagram of the horizontal span and calculate the force exerted on each pillar.

Figure 5

12 A uniform curtain pole of weight 24 N and of length 3.2 m is supported horizontally by two wall-mounted supports X and Y, which are 0.8 m and 1.2 m from each end, respectively.

   a Sketch the free body force diagram for this arrangement and calculate the force on each support when there are no curtains on the pole.

   b When the pole supports a pair of curtains of total weight 90 N drawn along the full length of the pole, what will be the force on each support?

13 A uniform steel girder of weight 22 kN and of length 14 m is lifted off the ground at one end by means of a crane. When the raised end is 2.0 m above the ground, the cable is vertical.

   a Sketch a free body force diagram of the girder in this position.

   b Calculate the tension in the cable at this position and the force of the girder on the ground.

14 A rectangular picture 0.80 m deep and 1.0 m wide, of weight 24 N, hangs on a wall, supported by a cord attached to the frame at each of the top corners, as shown in Figure 6. Each section of the cord makes an angle of 25° with the picture, which is horizontal along its width.

   a Copy the diagram and mark the forces acting on the picture on your diagram.

   b Calculate the tension in each section of the cord.

You will find the answers to these questions at the back of the book.

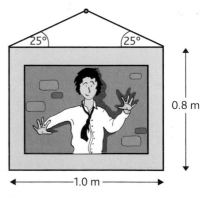

Figure 6

1　A student set up a model bridge crane to find out how the support forces change with the position of a load of weight W on the horizontal beam of the crane. With the load at different measured distances d from the fixed support at X, she used a newtonmeter to measure the support force S at Y near the other end, when the beam was horizontal. She repeated the measurements and also measured the distance D from X to Y.

newtonmeter used to measure support force S

Figure 1

The measurements she obtained are in the table below.

Distance XY = 480 mm

distance d / mm		40	120	200	280	360	440
support force S / N	1st set	1.4	2.6	4.4	5.6	7.3	8.6
	2nd set	1.2	2.9	4.3	5.9	7.0	8.8
	mean						

(a) (i) Complete the table.

(ii) Plot a graph of S on the y-axis against d on the x-axis. *(5 marks)*

(b) (i) By taking moments about X, show that $S = \dfrac{Wd}{D} + 0.5\, W_0$, where W_0 is the weight of the beam.

(ii) Use your graph to determine the weight of the load, W. *(6 marks)*

(c) The distances were measured to an accuracy of ± 1 mm and the newtonmeter readings to an accuracy of ± 0.1 N.

(i) Show that the percentage uncertainty in S is significantly greater than the percentage uncertainty in d.

(ii) Without using additional apparatus, discuss what further measurements you could make to improve the accuracy of your measurements. *(3 marks)*

2　(a) An object is acted upon by forces of 9.6 N and 4.8 N, with an angle of 40° between them. Draw a vector diagram of these forces, using a scale of 1 cm representing 1 N. Complete the vector diagram to determine the magnitude of the resultant force acting on the object. Measure the angle between the resultant force and the 9.6 N force. *(3 marks)*

(b) **Calculate** the magnitude of the resultant force when the same two forces act at right angles to each other.

You must not use a scale diagram for this part. *(2 marks)*

AQA, 2007

3　**Figure 2** shows a uniform steel girder being held horizontally by a crane. Two cables are attached to the ends of the girder and the tension in each of these cables is T.

(a) If the tension, T, in each cable is 850 N, calculate:

(i) the horizontal component of the tension in each cable,

(ii) the vertical component of the tension in each cable,

(iii) the weight of the girder. *(4 marks)*

(b) Describe the line of action of the weight of the girder. *(1 mark)*

Figure 2

AQA, 2005

4 (a) Define the moment of a force. *(2 marks)*

(b) **Figure 3** shows the force, *F*, acting on bicycle pedal.

Figure 3

(i) The moment of the force about O is 46 N m in the position shown. Calculate the value of the force, *F*.

(ii) Force, *F*, is constant in magnitude and direction while the pedal is moving downwards. State and explain how the moment of *F* changes as the pedal moves through 80°, from the position shown. *(4 marks)*

AQA, 2007

5 **Figure 4** shows a student standing on a plank that pivots on a log. The student intends to cross the stream.

Figure 4

(a) The plank has a mass of 25 kg and is 3.0 m long with a uniform cross-section. The log pivot is 0.50 m from the end of the plank. The student has a mass of 65 kg and stands at the end of the plank. A load is placed on the far end in order to balance the plank horizontally.

Draw on a copy of **Figure 4** the forces that act on the plank. *(3 marks)*

(b) By taking moments about the log pivot, calculate the load, in N, needed on the right-hand end of the plank in order to balance the plank horizontally. *(3 marks)*

(c) Explain why the load will eventually touch the ground as the student walks toward the log. *(2 marks)*

AQA, 2003

8 On the move

8.1 Speed and velocity

Learning objectives:

- How does displacement differ from distance?

- What is the difference between instantaneous speed and average speed?

- When is it necessary to consider velocity rather than speed?

Specification reference: 3.2.1

Hint

1 km = 1000 m; 1 hour = 3600 s;
108 km h^{-1} = 30 m s^{-1}

Speed

Displacement is distance in a given direction.

Speed is defined as change of distance per unit time.

Velocity is defined as change of displacement per unit time. In other words, velocity is speed in a given direction.

Speed and distance are scalar quantities. Velocity and displacement are vector quantities.

The unit of speed and of velocity is the metre per second (m s^{-1}).

Motion at constant speed

An object moving at a constant speed travels equal distances in equal times. For example, a car travelling at a speed of 30 m s^{-1} on a motorway travels a distance of 30 m every second or 1800 m every minute. In 1 hour, the car would therefore travel a distance of 108 000 m or 108 km. So 30 m s^{-1} = 108 km h^{-1}.

For an object which travels distance s in time t at constant speed,

$$\text{speed } v = \frac{s}{t}$$

$$\text{distance travelled } s = vt$$

For an object moving at constant speed on a circle of radius r, its speed

$$v = \frac{2\pi r}{T}$$

where T is the time to move round once and $2\pi r$ is the circumference of the circle.

Motion at changing speed

There are two types of speed cameras. One type measures the speed of a vehicle as it passes the camera. The other type is linked to a second speed camera and a computer, which works out the average speed of the vehicle between the two cameras. This will catch drivers who slow down for a speed camera then speed up again!

For an object moving at changing speed that travels a distance s in time t,

$$\text{average speed } = \frac{s}{t}$$

In a short time interval Δt, the distance Δs it travels is given by $\Delta s = v \Delta t$, where v is the speed at that time (i.e. its instantaneous speed). Rearranging this equation gives:

$$v = \frac{\Delta s}{\Delta t}$$

Figure 1

Distance–time graphs

For an object moving at **constant speed**, its graph of distance against time is a straight line with a constant gradient.

$$\text{The speed of the object} = \frac{\text{distance travelled}}{\text{time taken}} = \text{gradient of the line}$$

For an object moving at **changing speed**, the gradient of the line changes. The gradient of the line at any point can be found by drawing a tangent to the line at that point and then measuring the gradient of the tangent. This is shown in Figure 3 where PR is the tangent at point Y on the line. Show for yourself that the speed at point X on the line is $2.5\,\text{m s}^{-1}$.

Figure 2 *Constant speed*

Speed at Y $= \dfrac{PQ}{QR} = \dfrac{192-52}{20}$

$= 7\,\text{m s}^{-1}$

Figure 3 *Changing speed*

Velocity

An object moving at **constant velocity** moves at the same speed without changing its direction of motion.

If an object changes its direction of motion or its speed or both, its velocity changes. For example, the velocity of an object moving on a circular path at constant speed changes continuously because its direction of motion changes continuously.

Displacement–time graphs

An object travelling along a straight line has two possible directions of motion. To distinguish between the two directions, we need a direction code where positive values are in one direction and negative values in the opposite direction.

For example, consider an object thrown vertically into the air. The direction code is + for upwards and – for downwards. Figure 4 shows how its displacement changes with time. The object has an initial positive velocity and a negative return velocity. The displacement and velocity are both positive when the object is ascending. However, when it is descending, its velocity is negative and its displacement is positive until it returns to its initial position. We will consider displacement–time graphs in more detail in Topic 8.5.

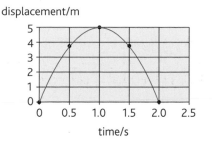

Figure 4 *A displacement–time graph*

8.2 Acceleration

Learning objectives:

■ When do moving objects accelerate and decelerate?

■ Why is uniform acceleration a special case?

■ Why is acceleration considered to be a vector?

Specification reference: 3.2.1

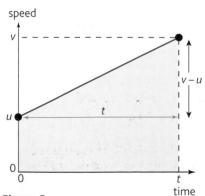

Figure 1 *A sports car on a test track*

Performance tests

A car maker wants to compare the performance of a new model with the original model. To do this, the velocity of each car is measured on a test track. Each vehicle accelerates as fast as possible to top velocity from a standstill. The results are listed in the table below.

Table 1

time from a standing start / s	0	2	4	6	8	10
velocity of old model / m s⁻¹	0	8	16	24	32	32
velocity of new model / m s⁻¹	0	10	20	30	30	30

Which car accelerates fastest?

The old model took 8 s to reach its top velocity of $32\,\text{m s}^{-1}$. Its velocity must have increased by $4.0\,\text{m s}^{-1}$ every second when it was accelerating.

The new model took 6 s to reach its top velocity of $30\,\text{m s}^{-1}$. Its velocity must have increased by $5.0\,\text{m s}^{-1}$ every second when it was accelerating.

Clearly, the velocity of the new model increases at a faster rate than the old model. In other words, its acceleration is greater.

Acceleration is defined as change of velocity per unit time.

■ The unit of **acceleration** is the metre per second per second (m s^{-2}).
■ Acceleration is a vector quantity.
■ Deceleration values are negative and signify that the velocity decreases with respect to time.

For a moving object that does not change direction, its acceleration at any point can be worked out from its rate of change of speed, because there is no change of direction. For example:

The acceleration of the old model above is $4.0\,\text{m s}^{-2}$ because its velocity increased by $4.0\,\text{m s}^{-1}$ every second.

The acceleration of the new model above is $5.0\,\text{m s}^{-2}$ because its velocity increased by $5.0\,\text{m s}^{-1}$ every second.

Uniform acceleration

Uniform acceleration is where the velocity of an object moving along a straight line changes at a constant rate. In other words, the acceleration is constant. Consider an object that accelerates uniformly from velocity u to velocity v in time t along a straight line. Figure 2 shows how its velocity changes with time.

The acceleration, a, of the object $= \dfrac{\text{change of velocity}}{\text{time taken}} = \dfrac{v - u}{t}$

$$a = \frac{v - u}{t}$$

Figure 2

To calculate the velocity v at time t, rearranging this equation gives

$$at = v - u$$

$$v = u + at$$

Worked example:

The driver of a vehicle travelling at $8\,m\,s^{-1}$ applies the brakes for 30 s and reduces the velocity of the vehicle to $2\,m\,s^{-1}$. Calculate the deceleration of the vehicle during this time.

Solution

$u = 8\,m\,s^{-1}, v = 2\,m\,s^{-1}, t = 30\,s$

$a = \dfrac{v - u}{t} = \dfrac{2 - 8}{30} = \dfrac{-6}{30} = -0.2\,m\,s^{-2}$

AQA Examiner's tip

Compare the appearance of uniform acceleration and uniform velocity on velocity–time graphs and on displacement–time graphs.

Non-uniform acceleration

Non-uniform acceleration is where the direction of motion of an object changes, or its speed changes, at a varying rate. Figure 3 shows how the speed of an object increases for an object moving along a straight line with an increasing acceleration. This can be seen directly from the graph because the gradient increases with time (the graph becomes steeper and steeper) and the gradient represents the acceleration.

The acceleration at any point is the gradient of the tangent to the curve at that point. In Figure 3,

the gradient of the tangent at point P $= \dfrac{\text{height of gradient triangle}}{\text{base of gradient triangle}}$

$= \dfrac{4.0\,m\,s^{-1} - 1.0\,m\,s^{-1}}{2.0\,s} = 1.5\,m\,s^{-2}$

Therefore the acceleration at P is $1.5\,m\,s^{-2}$.

Acceleration = gradient of the line on the velocity–time graph.

Figure 3

Summary questions

1 **a** An aeroplane taking off accelerates uniformly on a runway from a velocity of $4\,m\,s^{-1}$ to a velocity of $64\,m\,s^{-1}$ in 40 s. Calculate its acceleration.

b A car travelling at a velocity of $20\,m\,s^{-1}$ brakes sharply to a standstill in 8.0 s. Calculate its deceleration, assuming its velocity decreases uniformly.

2 A cyclist accelerates uniformly from a velocity of $2.5\,m\,s^{-1}$ to a velocity of $7.0\,m\,s^{-1}$ in a time of 10 s. Calculate **a** Its acceleration, **b** its velocity 2.0 s later if it continued to accelerate at the same rate.

3 A train on a straight journey between two stations accelerates uniformly from rest for 20 s to a velocity of $12\,m\,s^{-1}$. It then travelled at constant velocity for a further 40 s before decelerating uniformly to rest in 30 s.

a Sketch a velocity–time graph to represent its journey,

b Calculate its acceleration in each part of the journey.

4 The velocity of an object released in water increased as shown in Figure 4.

Figure 4

Describe how **a** the velocity of the object changed with time, **b** the acceleration of the object changed with time.

8.3 Motion along a straight line at constant acceleration

Learning objectives:

- What is the difference between u and v?

- How can we calculate the displacement of an object moving with uniform acceleration?

- What else do we need to know to calculate the acceleration of an object if we know its displacement in a given time?

Specification reference: 3.2.1

The dynamics equations for constant acceleration

Consider an object that accelerates uniformly from initial speed u to final speed v in time t without change of direction. Figure 2 in 8.2 shows how its speed changes with time.

1 The acceleration $a = \dfrac{(v - u)}{t}$, as explained in 8.2

Rearranging this equation gives

$$v = u + at \qquad \text{(equation 1)}$$

2 The distance moved, s = average speed × time taken

Because the acceleration is uniform, the average speed $= \dfrac{(u + v)}{2}$

Therefore $$s = \dfrac{(u + v)t}{2} \qquad \text{(equation 2)}$$

3 By combining the two equations above to eliminate v, a further useful equation is produced.

To do this, substitute $u + at$ in place of v in equation 2. This gives

$$s = \frac{(u + (u + at))}{2}t = \frac{(u + u + at)\,t}{2} = \frac{(2ut + at^2)}{2}$$

Therefore $$s = ut + \tfrac{1}{2}at^2 \qquad \text{(equation 3)}$$

4 A fourth useful equation is obtained by combining (1) and (2) to eliminate t. This can be done by multiplying

$a = \dfrac{(v - u)}{t}$ and $s = \dfrac{(u + v)t}{2}$ together to give

$$as = \frac{(v - u)}{t} \times \frac{(u + v)t}{2}$$

This simplifies to become

$$as = \frac{(v - u)(v + u)}{2} = \frac{(v^2 - uv + uv - u^2)}{2} = \frac{(v^2 - u^2)}{2}$$

Therefore $2as = v^2 - u^2$

Rearranging this equation gives

$$v^2 = u^2 + 2as \qquad \text{(equation 4)}$$

The four equations, sometimes referred to as the 'suvat' equations, are invaluable in any situation where the acceleration is constant.

Note:

If $a = 0$ (i.e. constant velocity), the equations all reduce to $s = vt$.

Worked example:

A driver of a vehicle travelling at a speed of $30\,\mathrm{m\,s^{-1}}$ on a motorway brakes sharply to a standstill in a distance of $100\,\mathrm{m}$. Calculate the deceleration of the vehicle.

Solution

$u = 30\,\mathrm{m\,s^{-1}}, v = 0, s = 100\,\mathrm{m}, a = ?$

To find a, use $v^2 = u^2 + 2as$

Therefore $0 = u^2 + 2as$ because $v = 0$

Rearranging this equation gives

$2as = -u^2$

$a = -\dfrac{u^2}{2s} = -\dfrac{30^2}{2 \times 100} = -4.5\,\mathrm{m\,s^{-2}}$

Note:

The acceleration is negative which means it is a deceleration as it is in the opposite direction to the velocity.

Using a speed–time graph to find the distance moved

1 **Consider an object moving at constant speed, v,** as shown in Figure 1.

   The distance moved in time t, $s = $ speed $\times$ time taken $= vt$.
   This distance is represented on the graph by the area under the line between the start and time t. This is a rectangle of height corresponding to speed v and of base corresponding to the time t.

Figure 1

2 **Consider an object moving at constant acceleration, a,** from initial speed u to speed v at time t, as shown in Figure 2. From equation 2 above, the distance s moved in this time is given by

   $$s = \frac{(u + v)t}{2}$$

   This distance is represented on the graph by the area under the line between the start and time t. This is a trapezium which has a base corresponding to time t and an average height corresponding to the average speed $\frac{1}{2}(u + v)$.

   Therefore the area of the trapezium (= average height $\times$ base) corresponds to $\frac{1}{2}(u + v)t$

   This is the distance moved.

Figure 2

3 **Consider an object moving with a changing acceleration,** as shown in Figure 3. Let v represent the speed at time t and $v + \delta v$ represent the speed a short time later at $t + \delta t$. (δ is pronounced 'delta'.)

   Because the speed change δv is small compared with the speed v, the distance travelled δs in the short time interval δt is given by $\delta s = v\,\delta t$.

   This is represented on the graph by the area of the shaded strip under the line, which has a base corresponding to δt and a height corresponding to v. In other words, $\delta s = v\,\delta t$ is represented by the area of this strip.

   By considering the whole area under the line in strips of similar width, the total distance travelled from the start to time t is therefore represented by the sum of the area of every strip, which is therefore the total area under the line.

Figure 3

Examiner's tip

Always begin a 'suvat' calculation by identifying which three variables are known. Remember the acceleration must be constant for these equations to apply.

Whatever the shape of the line of a speed–time graph,

distance travelled = area under the line of a speed–time graph.

The equations for constant acceleration are:

$$v = u + at$$

$$s = \tfrac{1}{2}(u + v)t$$

$$s = ut + \tfrac{1}{2}at^2$$

$$v^2 = u^2 + 2as$$

Summary questions

1 A vehicle accelerates uniformly along a straight road, increasing its speed from $4.0\,\mathrm{m\,s^{-1}}$ to $30.0\,\mathrm{m\,s^{-1}}$ in 13 s. Calculate:

  a its acceleration,

  b the distance it moves in this time.

2 An aircraft lands on a runway at a speed of $40\,\mathrm{m\,s^{-1}}$ and brakes to a halt in a distance of 860 m. Calculate:

  a the braking time,

  b the deceleration of the aircraft.

3 A cyclist accelerates uniformly from rest to a speed of $6.0\,\mathrm{m\,s^{-1}}$ in 30 s then brakes at uniform deceleration to a halt in a distance of 24 m.

  a For the first part of the journey, calculate **i** the acceleration, **ii** the distance travelled.

  b For the second part of the journey, calculate **i** the deceleration, **ii** the time taken.

  c Sketch a speed–time graph for this journey.

  d Use the graph to determine the average speed for the journey.

4 The speed of an athlete for the first 5 s of a sprint race is shown in Figure 4. Use the graph to determine:

  a the initial acceleration of the athlete,

  b the distance moved in the first 2 s,

  c the distance moved in the next 2 s,

  d the average speed over the first 4 s.

Figure 4

8.4 Free fall

Learning objectives:

■ What does 'free fall' mean?

■ How does the velocity of a freely falling object change as it falls?

■ Do objects of different masses or sizes all fall with the same acceleration?

Specification reference: 3.2.1

Figure 1 *Galileo Galilei 1564-1642*

■ Experimental tests

Does a heavy object fall faster than a lighter object?

Release a stone and a small coin at the same time. Which one hits the ground first? The answer to this question was first discovered by Galileo about four centuries ago. He reasoned that because any number of identical objects must fall at the same rate, then any one such object must fall at the same rate as the rest put together. So he concluded that any two objects must fall at the same rate, regardless of their relative weights. He was reported to have demonstrated the correctness of his theory by releasing two different weights from the top of the Leaning Tower of Pisa.

■ How science works

The inclined plane test

Galileo wanted to know if a falling object speeds up as it falls, but clocks and stopwatches were devices of the future. The simplest test he could think of was to time a ball as it rolled down a plank. He devised a 'dripping water' clock, counting the volume of the drips as a measure of time. He measured how long the ball took to travel equal distances down the slope from rest. His measurements showed that the ball gained speed as it travelled down the slope. In other words, he showed that the ball accelerated as it rolled down the slope. He reasoned that the acceleration would be greater the steeper the slope. So he concluded that an object falling vertically accelerates.

⠿ Acceleration due to gravity

One way to investigate the free fall of a ball is to make a multiflash photo or video clip of the ball's flight as it falls after being released from rest. A vertical metre rule can be used to provide a scale. To obtain a multiflash photo, an ordinary camera with a slow speed shutter may be used to record the ball's descent in a dark room illuminated by a stroboscope (a flashing light). The flashing light needs to flash at a known constant rate of about 20 flashes per second. Figure 2 on the next page shows a possible arrangement using a steel ball and a multiflash photo taken with this arrangement. If you make a video clip, you need to be able to rerun the clip at slow speed with the time displayed.

For each image of the ball on the photograph, the time of descent of the ball and the distance fallen by the ball from rest can be measured directly. The photograph shows that the ball speeds up as it falls, because it travels further between successive images. Measurements from this photograph are given in the table on the next page.

Figure 2 *Investigating free fall*

Table 1 *Free fall measurements*

number of flashes after start	0	2	3	4	5	6	7	8	9
time of descent t / s	0	0.06	0.10	0.13	0.16	0.19	0.23	0.26	0.29
distance fallen s / m	0	0.02	0.04	0.07	0.12	0.17	0.24	0.33	0.42

How can we tell if the acceleration is constant from these results? One way is to consider how the distance fallen, s, would vary with time, t, for constant acceleration. From Topic 8.3, we know that

$s = ut + \frac{1}{2}at^2$, where u = the initial speed and a = acceleration.

In this experiment, $u = 0$

Therefore $s = \frac{1}{2}at^2$ for constant acceleration, a.

Compare this equation with the general equation for a straight line graph, $y = mx + c$, where m is the gradient and c is the y-intercept. If we let y represent s and let x represent t^2, then $m = \frac{1}{2}a$ and $c = 0$. See Topic 16.5 if necessary.

So a graph of s against t^2 should therefore give a straight line through the origin. In addition, the gradient of the line $(= \frac{1}{2}a)$ can be measured, enabling the acceleration $(= 2 \times \text{gradient})$ to be calculated.

Figure 3 shows this graph. As you can see, it is a straight line through the origin. We can therefore conclude that the equation $s = \frac{1}{2}at^2$ applies here so the acceleration of a falling object is constant. Show for yourself that the gradient of the line is $5.0\,\text{m s}^{-2}$ ($\pm 0.2\,\text{m s}^{-2}$), giving an acceleration of $10\,\text{m s}^{-2}$.

Because there are no external forces acting on the object apart from the force of gravity, this value of acceleration is known as the **acceleration of free fall** and is represented by the symbol, g. Accurate measurements give a value of $9.8\,\text{m s}^{-2}$ near the Earth's surface.

The 'suvat' equations from Topic 8.3 may be applied to any free fall situation where air resistance is negligible.

The equations can also be applied to situations where objects are thrown vertically upwards. As a general rule, apply the direction code + for *upwards* and – for *downwards* when values are inserted into the suvat equations.

Figure 3 *A graph of s against t²*

How science works

⚠ *Practical*

Use an electronic timer or motion sensor to make your own measurements of *s* and *t*. Repeat your measurements to obtain an average timing for each measured distance and plot a suitable graph to find *g*.

Worked example:

$g = 9.8\,\text{m}\,\text{s}^{-2}$

A coin was released at rest at the top of a well. It took 1.6 s to hit the bottom of the well. Calculate **a** the distance fallen by the coin, **b** its speed just before impact.

Solution

$u = 0$, $t = 1.6\,\text{s}$, $a = -9.8\,\text{m}\,\text{s}^{-2}$ (− as *g* acts downwards)

a To find *s*, use $s = \frac{1}{2}at^2$ as $u = 0$

Therefore $s = \frac{1}{2} \times -9.8 \times 1.6^2$

$= -12.5\,\text{m}$ (− indicates 12.5 m downwards)

b To find *v*, use $v = u + at$

$= 0 + (-9.8 \times 1.6) = -15.7\,\text{m}\,\text{s}^{-1}$ (− indicates downward velocity)

Summary questions

$g = 9.8\,\text{m}\,\text{s}^{-2}$

1 A pebble, released at rest from a canal bridge, took 0.9 s to hit the water. Calculate:

  a the distance it fell before hitting the water,

  b its speed just before hitting the water.

2 A spanner was dropped from a hot air balloon when the balloon was at rest 50 m above the ground. Calculate:

  a the time taken for the spanner to hit the ground,

  b the speed of impact of the spanner on hitting the ground.

3 A bungee jumper jumped off a platform 75 m above a lake, releasing a small object at the instant she jumped off the platform.

  a Calculate **i** the time taken by the object to fall to the lake, **ii** the speed of impact of the object on hitting the water, assuming air resistance is negligible.

  b Explain why the bungee jumper would take longer to descend than the time taken in **a**.

4 An astronaut on the Moon threw an object 4.0 m vertically upwards and caught it again 4.5 s later. Calculate:

  a the acceleration due to gravity on the Moon,

  b the speed of projection of the object,

  c how high the object would have risen on the Earth, for the same speed of projection.

8.5 Motion graphs

Learning objectives:

■ What is the difference between a distance–time graph and a displacement–time graph?

■ What does the gradient of a velocity–time graph represent?

■ What does the area under a velocity–time graph represent?

Specification reference: 3.2.1

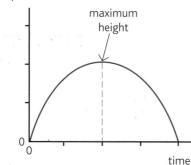

Figure 1 *Displacement–time for an object projected upwards*

Figure 2 *Distance–time for an object projected upwards*

■ The difference between a distance–time graph and a displacement–time graph

Displacement is distance in a given direction from a certain point. Consider a ball thrown directly upwards and caught when it returns. If the ball rises to a maximum height of 2.0 m, on returning to the thrower, its displacement from its initial position is zero. However, the distance it has travelled is 4.0 m.

The displacement of the ball changes with time as shown by Figure 1. The line in this graph fits the equation $s = ut - \frac{1}{2}gt^2$, where s is the displacement, t is the time taken and u is the initial velocity of the object.

The gradient of the line in Figure 1 represents the velocity of the object.

■ Immediately after leaving the thrower's hand, the velocity is positive and large so the gradient is positive and large.

■ As the ball rises, its velocity decreases so the gradient decreases.

■ At maximum height, its velocity is zero so the gradient is zero.

■ As the ball descends, its velocity becomes increasingly negative, corresponding to increasing speed in a downward direction. So the gradient becomes increasingly negative.

The distance travelled by the object changes with time as shown by Figure 2. The gradient of this line represents the speed. From projection to maximum height, the shape is exactly the same as in Figure 1. After maximum height, the distance continues to increase so the line curves up, not down like Figure 1.

■ The difference between a speed–time graph and a velocity–time graph

Velocity is speed in a given direction. Consider how the velocity of an object thrown into the air changes with time. The object's velocity decreases from its initial positive (upwards) value to zero at maximum height then increases in the negative (downwards) direction as it falls.

Figure 3 shows how the velocity of the object changes with time.

1 **The gradient of the line represents the object's acceleration.** This is constant and negative, equal to the acceleration of free fall, g. The acceleration of the object is the same when it descends as when it ascends so the gradient of the line is always equal to $-9.8\,\mathrm{m\,s^{-2}}$.

2 **The area under the line represents the displacement of the object from its starting position.**

■ The area between the positive section of the line and the time axis represents the displacement during the ascent.

■ The area under the negative section of the line and the time axis represents the displacement during the descent.

Taking the area for a) as positive and the area for b) as negative, the total area is therefore zero. This corresponds to zero for the total displacement.

Worked example:

$g = 9.8\,m\,s^{-2}$

A ball released from a height of 1.20 m above a concrete floor rebounds to a height of 0.82 m.

a Calculate **i** its time of descent, **ii** the speed of the ball immediately before it hits the floor.

b Calculate **i** the speed of the ball immediately after it leaves the floor, **ii** its time of ascent.

c Sketch a velocity–time graph for the ball. Assume the contact time is negligible compared with the time of descent or ascent.

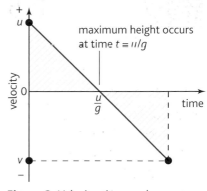

Figure 3 *Velocity–time graph*

Solution

a $u = 0$, $a = -9.8\,m\,s^{-2}$, $s = -1.2\,m$

i To find t, use $s = ut + \frac{1}{2}at^2$

$-1.2 = 0 + 0.5 \times -9.8 \times t^2$ so $-1.2 = -4.9\,t^2$

$t^2 = \dfrac{-1.2}{-4.9} = 0.245$ so $t = 0.49\,s$

ii To find v, use $v = u + at$

$v = 0 + -9.8 \times 0.49 = -4.8\,m\,s^{-1}$ (− for downwards)

b $v = 0$, $a = -9.8\,m\,s^{-2}$, $s = +0.82\,m$

i To find u, use $v^2 = u^2 + 2as$

$0 = u^2 + 2 \times -9.8 \times 0.82$

$u^2 = 16.1\,m^2\,s^{-2}$ so $u = +4.0\,m\,s^{-1}$ (+ for upwards)

ii To find t, use $v = u + at$

$0 = 4.0 + -9.8 \times t$

$9.8\,t = 4.0$ so $t = 0.41\,s$

c See Figure 4. Note that the line has a constant gradient equal to the acceleration due to gravity, $-9.8\,m\,s^{-2}$.

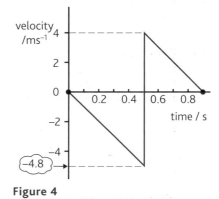

Figure 4

Summary questions

$g = 9.8\,m\,s^{-2}$

1 A swimmer swims 100 m from one end of a swimming pool to the other end at a constant speed of 1.2 m s⁻¹, then swims back at constant speed, returning to the starting point 210 s after starting.

   a Calculate how long the swimmer takes to swim from **i** the starting end to the other end, **ii** back to the start from the other end.

   b For the swim from start to finish, sketch **i** a displacement–time graph, **ii** a distance–time graph, **iii** a velocity–time graph.

2 A motorcyclist travelling along a straight road at a constant speed of 8.8 m s⁻¹ passes a cyclist travelling in the same direction at a speed of 2.2 m s⁻¹. After 200 s, the motorcyclist stops.

   a Calculate how long the motorcyclist has to wait before the cyclist catches up.

   b On the same axes, sketch a velocity–time graph for **i** the motorcyclist, **ii** the cyclist.

3 A hot air balloon is ascending vertically at a constant velocity of 3.5 m s⁻¹ when a small metal object falls from its base and hits the ground 3.0 s later.

   a Sketch a graph to show how the velocity of the object changed with time during its descent.

   b Show that the balloon base was 33.6 m above the ground when the object fell off the base.

4 A ball is released from a height of 1.8 m above a level surface and rebounds to a height of 0.90 m.

   a Given $g = 9.8\,m\,s^{-2}$, calculate **i** the duration of its descent, **ii** its velocity just before impact, **iii** the duration of its ascent, **iv** its velocity just after impact.

   b Sketch a graph to show how its velocity changes with time from release to rebound at maximum height.

   c Sketch a further graph to show how the displacement of the object changes with time.

8.6 More calculations on motion along a straight line

Learning objectives:

- How do we calculate the motion of an object with constant acceleration if its velocity reverses?

- Should the overall motion be broken down into stages?

- How do we use signs to work out if an object is moving forwards or backwards?

Specification reference: 3.2.1

Figure 1 *A space vehicle docking*

Motion along a straight line at constant acceleration

The equations for motion at constant acceleration, a, are

$$v = u + at \qquad \text{(equation 1)}$$

$$s = \tfrac{1}{2}(u + v)t \qquad \text{(equation 2)}$$

$$s = ut + \tfrac{1}{2}at^2 \qquad \text{(equation 3)}$$

$$v^2 = u^2 + 2as \qquad \text{(equation 4)}$$

where s is the displacement in time t, u is the initial velocity and v is the final velocity.

For motion along a straight line at constant acceleration, one direction along the line is positive and the opposite direction is negative.

Worked example:

A space vehicle moving towards a docking station at a velocity of $2.5 \, \text{m s}^{-1}$ is $26 \, \text{m}$ from the docking station when its reverse thrust motors are switched on to slow it down and stop it when it reaches the station. The vehicle decelerates uniformly until it comes to rest at the docking station when its motors are switched off.

Calculate **a** its deceleration, **b** how long it takes to stop, **c** its velocity if its motors remained on for $5.0 \, \text{s}$ longer than necessary.

Solution

Let the + direction represent motion towards the docking station and − represent motion away from the station.

Initial velocity, $u = +2.5 \, \text{m s}^{-1}$, final velocity, $v = 0$, displacement, $s = +26 \, \text{m}$

a To find its deceleration, a, use $v^2 = u^2 + 2as$

$$0 = 2.5^2 + 2a \times 26$$

$$-52a = 2.5^2$$

$$a = \frac{2.5^2}{52} = -0.12 \, \text{m s}^{-2}$$

b To find the time taken, use $v = u + at$

$$0 = 2.5 - 0.12t$$

$$0.12t = 2.5$$

$$t = \frac{2.5}{0.12} = 21 \, \text{s}$$

c Initial velocity, $u = 2.5 \, \text{m s}^{-1}$, acceleration, $a = -0.12 \, \text{m s}^{-2}$, time taken $t = 26 \, \text{s}$

To calculate its velocity v after $26 \, \text{s}$, use $v = u + at$

$$= 2.5 - 0.12 \times 26 = -0.62 \, \text{m s}^{-1}$$

The velocity of the space vehicle would be $0.62 \, \text{m s}^{-1}$ away from the docking station after $26 \, \text{s}$.

Two-stage problems

Consider an object released from rest, falling then hitting a bed of sand.

The motion is in two stages:

1 Falling motion due to gravity: acceleration = g (downwards)

2 Deceleration in the sand: initial velocity = velocity of object just before impact.

The acceleration in each stage is **not** the same. The link between the two stages is that the velocity at the end of the first stage is the same as the velocity at the start of the second stage.

For example, a ball is released from a height of 0.85 m above a bed of sand, and creates an impression in the sand of depth 0.025 m. For directions, let + represent upwards and – represent downwards.

Stage 1: $u = 0$, $s = -0.85$ m, $a = -9.8$ m s^{-2}.

To calculate the speed of impact v, use $v^2 = u^2 + 2as$

$$v^2 = 0^2 + 2 \times -9.8 \times -0.85 = 16.7 \text{ m}^2\text{s}^{-2} \qquad v = -4.1 \text{ m s}^{-1}$$

Note:
$v^2 = 16.7 \text{ m}^2\text{s}^{-2}$ so $v = -4.1$ or $+ 4.1$ m s^{-1}. The negative answer is chosen as the ball is moving downwards.

Stage 2: $u = -4.1$ m s^{-1}, $v = 0$ (as the ball comes to rest in the sand), $s = -0.025$ m

To calculate the deceleration, a, use $v^2 = u^2 + 2as$

$$0^2 = (-4.1)^2 + 2a \times -0.025$$

$$2a \times 0.025 = 16.7$$

$$a = \frac{16.7}{2 \times 0.025} = 334 \text{ m s}^{-2}$$

Note:
$a > 0$ and therefore in the opposite direction to the direction of motion, which is downwards. Thus the ball slows down in the sand with a deceleration of 334 m s^{-2}.

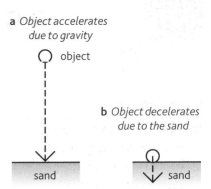

a *Object accelerates due to gravity*

b *Object decelerates due to the sand*

Figure 2 *A two-stage problem*

Examiner's tip

Applying the sign convention ' + for forwards (or up), – for backwards (or down)', for an object

- moving forwards and accelerating, $v > 0$ and $a > 0$
- moving forwards and decelerating, $v > 0$ and $a < 0$
- moving backwards and accelerating, $v < 0$ and $a < 0$
- moving backwards and decelerating, $v < 0$ and $a > 0$

Summary questions

$g = 9.8$ m s^{-2}

1 A vehicle on a straight downhill road accelerated uniformly from a speed of 4.0 m s^{-1} to a speed of 29 m s^{-1} over a distance of 850 m. The driver then braked and stopped the vehicle in 28 s.

   a Calculate **i** the time taken to reach 29 m s^{-1} from 4 m s^{-1}, **ii** its acceleration during this time.

   b Calculate **i** the distance it travelled during deceleration, **ii** its deceleration for the last 28 s.

2 A rail wagon moving at a speed of 2.0 m s^{-1} on a level track reached a steady incline which slowed it down to rest in 15.0 s and caused it to reverse. Calculate:

   a the distance it moved up the incline,

   b its acceleration on the incline,

   c its velocity and position on the incline after 20.0 s.

3 A cyclist accelerated from rest at a constant acceleration of 0.4 m s^{-2} for 20 s, then stopped pedalling and slowed to a standstill at constant deceleration over a distance of 260 m.

   a Calculate **i** the distance travelled by the cyclist in the first 20 s, **ii** the speed of the cyclist at the end of this time.

   b Calculate **i** the time taken to cover the distance of 260 m after she stopped pedalling,

   ii her deceleration during this time.

4 A rocket was launched directly upwards from rest. Its motors operated for 30 s after it left the launch pad, providing it with a constant vertical acceleration of 6.0 m s^{-2} during this time. Its motors then switched off.

   a Calculate **i** its velocity, **ii** its height above the launch pad when its motors switched off.

   b Calculate the maximum height reached after its motors switched off.

   c Calculate the velocity with which it would hit the ground if it fell from maximum height without the support of a parachute.

8.7 Projectile motion 1

Learning objectives:

- Why is the acceleration of a projectile always vertically downwards?

- What is the horizontal component of a vertical vector?

- What is the effect of gravity on horizontal speed?

Specification reference: 3.2.1

Figure 1 *Upward projection*

Figure 2 *Testing horizontal projection*

Figure 3 *Multiflash photo of two falling balls*

A **projectile** is any object acted upon only by the force of gravity. Three key principles apply to all projectiles:

1 The acceleration of the object is always equal to *g* and is always downwards because the force of gravity acts downwards. The acceleration therefore only affects the vertical motion of the object.

2 The horizontal velocity of the object is constant because the acceleration of the object does not have a horizontal component.

3 The motions in the horizontal and vertical directions are independent of each other.

Vertical projection

Such an object moves vertically as it has no horizontal motion. Its acceleration is $9.8\,\mathrm{m\,s^{-2}}$ downwards. Using the direction code ' + is upwards, – is downwards', its displacement, *y*, and velocity, *v*, after time *t* are given by

$$v = u - gt$$

$$y = ut - \tfrac{1}{2}gt^2$$

where *u* is its initial velocity.

See Topic 8.4 for more about vertical projection.

Horizontal projection

A stone thrown from a cliff top follows a curved path downwards before it hits the water. If its initial projection is horizontal:

- its path through the air becomes steeper and steeper as it drops,

- the faster it is projected, the further away it will fall into the sea,

- the time taken for it to fall into the sea does not depend on how fast it is projected.

Suppose two balls are released at the same time above a level floor such that one ball drops vertically and the other is projected horizontally. Which one hits the floor first? In fact, they both hit the floor simultaneously. Try it!

Why should the two balls in Figure 2 hit the ground at the same time? They are both pulled to the ground by the force of gravity, which gives each ball a downward acceleration *g*. The ball that is projected horizontally experiences the same downward acceleration as the other ball. This downward acceleration does not affect the horizontal motion of the ball projected horizontally; only the vertical motion is affected.

Investigating horizontal projection

A stroboscope and a camera with a slow shutter (or a video camera) may be used to record the motion of a projectile as outlined in Topic 8.4. Figure 3 shows a multiflash photograph of two balls A and B released at the same time. A was released from rest and dropped vertically. B was given an initial horizontal projection so it followed a curved path. The stroboscope flashed at a constant rate so images of both balls were recorded at the same time.

- **The horizontal position** of B changes by equal distances between successive flashes. This shows that the horizontal component of B's velocity is constant.
- **The vertical position** of A and B changes at the same rate. At any instant, A is at the same level as B. This shows that A and B have the same vertical component of velocity at any instant.

The projectile path of a ball projected horizontally

An object projected horizontally falls in an arc towards the ground. If its initial velocity is U, then at time t after projection:

- The horizontal component of its displacement,

$$x = Ut$$

(because it moves horizontally at a constant speed).

- The vertical component of its displacement,

$$y = \tfrac{1}{2}gt^2$$

(because it has no vertical component of its initial velocity).

- Its velocity has
  a horizontal component $v_x = U$, and
  a vertical component $v_y = -gt$

Note that, at time t, the speed $= (v_x^2 + v_y^2)^{1/2}$

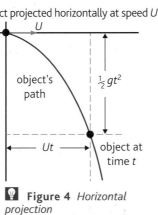

object projected horizontally at speed U

object's path

$\tfrac{1}{2}gt^2$

Ut — object at time t

Figure 4 *Horizontal projection*

Worked example:

$g = 9.8\,\mathrm{m\,s^{-2}}$

An object is projected horizontally at a speed of $15\,\mathrm{m\,s^{-1}}$ from the top of a tall tower of height $35.0\,\mathrm{m}$. Calculate:

a how long it takes to fall to the ground,

b how far it travels horizontally,

c its speed just before it hits the ground.

Solution

a $y = -35\,\mathrm{m}$, $a = -9.8\,\mathrm{m\,s^{-2}}$ (– for downwards)

$y = \tfrac{1}{2}gt^2$

$t^2 = \dfrac{2y}{a} = 2 \times \dfrac{-35}{-9.8} = 7.14\,\mathrm{s^2}$

$t = 2.67\,\mathrm{s}$

b $U = 15\,\mathrm{m\,s^{-1}}$, $t = 2.67\,\mathrm{s}$

$x = Ut = 15 \times 2.67 = 40\,\mathrm{m}$

c Just before impact, $v_x = U = 15\,\mathrm{m\,s^{-1}}$ and $v_y = -gt = -9.8 \times 2.67 = 26.2\,\mathrm{m\,s^{-1}}$

Therefore speed just before impact $v = (v_x^2 + v_y^2)^{1/2} = (15^2 + 26.2^2)^{1/2} = 30.2\,\mathrm{m\,s^{-1}}$

AQA Examiner's tip

The horizontal and vertical motions of a projectile take the same time.

Summary questions

$g = 9.8\,\mathrm{m\,s^{-2}}$

1 An object is released, 50 m above the ground, from a hot air balloon, which is descending vertically at a speed of $4.0\,\mathrm{m\,s^{-1}}$. Calculate:

a the velocity of the object at the ground,

b the duration of descent of the object,

c the height of the balloon above the ground when the object hits the ground.

2 An object is projected horizontally at a speed of $16\,\mathrm{m\,s^{-1}}$ into the sea from a cliff top of height $45.0\,\mathrm{m}$. Calculate:

a how long it takes to reach the sea,

b how far it travels horizontally,

c its impact velocity.

3 A dart is thrown horizontally along a line passing through the centre of a dartboard, 2.3 m away from the point at which the dart was released. The dart hits the dartboard at a point 0.19 m below the centre. Calculate:

a the time of flight of the dart,

b its horizontal speed of projection.

4 A parcel is released from an aircraft travelling horizontally at a speed of $120\,\mathrm{m\,s^{-1}}$ above level ground. The parcel hits the ground 8.5 s later. Calculate:

a the height of the aircraft above the ground,

b the horizontal distance travelled in this time by i the parcel, ii the aircraft,

c the speed of impact of the parcel at the ground.

8.8 Projectile motion 2

Learning objectives:

- Where else do we meet projectile motion?

- What would happen if we could switch gravity off?

Specification reference: 3.2.1

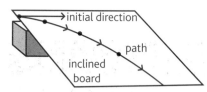

Figure 1 *Using an inclined board*

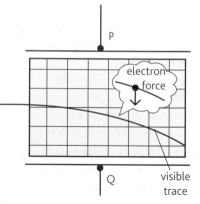

Figure 2 *An electron beam on a parabolic path*

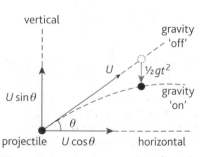

Figure 3 *Imagination at work*

💡 Projectile-like motion

Any form of motion where an object experiences a constant acceleration in a different direction to its velocity will be like projectile motion. For example:

- The path of a ball rolling across an inclined board will be a projectile path. Figure 1 shows the idea. The object is projected across the top of the board from the side. Its path curves down the board and is **parabolic**. This is because the object is subjected to constant acceleration acting down the board, and its initial velocity is across the board. The same equations as for projectile motion apply with the motion down the board replacing the vertical motion.

- The path of a beam of electrons directed between two oppositely charged parallel plates is also parabolic, as shown in Figure 2. Each electron in the beam is acted on by a constant force towards the positive plate, because the charge of an electron is negative. Therefore, each electron experiences a constant acceleration towards the positive plate. Its path is parabolic because its motion parallel to the plates is at **zero** acceleration whereas its motion perpendicular to the plates is at constant (non-zero) acceleration.

Imagination at work

Imagine if gravity could be switched off. An object projected into the air would follow a straight line with no change in its velocity. Suppose it had been launched at speed U in a direction at angle θ above the horizontal. Its initial velocity would therefore have a horizontal component $U\cos\theta$ and a vertical component $U\sin\theta$.

Without gravity, its velocity would be unchanged, so its displacement at time t after projection would have

- a horizontal component $x = Ut\cos\theta$, and
- a vertical component $y = Ut\sin\theta$

Let's now consider the difference made to its displacement and velocity if we 'bring back' gravity. At time t after its launch,

- its vertical position with gravity 'on' would be $\frac{1}{2}gt^2$ lower than if gravity had been 'off'

- its vertical component of velocity would be changed by $-gt$ from its initial value $U\sin\theta$

Note:

- We can extend the analysis to cover projection at angle θ below the horizontal by assigning a positive value of θ for projection at angle θ *above* the horizontal, and a negative value of θ for projection at angle θ *below* the horizontal.

- Its speed v at time t is given by $v = (v_x^2 + v_y^2)^{1/2}$

- **Only horizontal projection and vertical projection are required in your specification.** The general method above gives the correct results for horizontal projection of an object if we make the angle of projection $\theta = 0$. As $\sin\theta = 0$ for $\theta = 0°$, we get $\frac{1}{2}gt^2$ for the object's vertical drop at time t projecting it horizontally and $-gt$ (– for downwards) for its vertical component of velocity. Prove for yourself that we get the equations for vertical projection in Topic 8.7 if we make the angle of projection $\theta = 90°$.

Worked example:

g = 9.8 m s⁻²

An arrow is fired horizontally at a speed of 48 m s⁻¹ from a height of 1.50 m above a level field. The arrow hits the target at a point 1.20 m above the ground. Calculate:

a how long it takes the arrow to hit the target,

b the horizontal distance travelled by the arrow.

Solution

$U = 48\,\text{m s}^{-1}, \theta = 0$

a The arrow would have travelled horizontally in the absence of gravity. Its vertical drop due to gravity is therefore 0.30 m (= 1.50 – 1.20 m).

Therefore, its time of flight t is given by $\frac{1}{2}gt^2 = 0.30\,\text{m}$

Rearranging this equation gives $t^2 = \dfrac{2 \times 0.30}{9.8} = 6.1 \times 10^{-2}\,s^2$

Therefore $t = 0.247\,s$

b The arrow's horizontal motion is unaffected by gravity. Hence, the horizontal distance travelled by the arrow = $Ut = 48 \times 0.247 = 11.9\,\text{m}$

AQA Examiner's tip

A question like Q4b) below won't be on your exam paper but it is here to help you develop your grasp of projectile motion.

Summary questions

g = 9.8 m s⁻²

1 A ball was projected horizontally at a speed of 0.52 m s⁻¹ across the top of an inclined board of width 600 mm and length 1200 mm. It reached the bottom of the board 0.9 s later (Figure 4). Calculate:

a the distance travelled by the ball across the board,

b its acceleration on the board,

c its speed at the bottom of the board.

initial velocity = 0.52 m s⁻¹

1200 mm
600 mm

Figure 4

2 An arrow hits the ground after being fired horizontally at a speed of 25 m s⁻¹ from the top of a tower 20 m above the ground. Calculate:

a how long the arrow takes to fall to the ground,

b the distance travelled horizontally by the arrow.

3 A cannonball fired horizontally from a seaside tower hit the sea 2.7 s later at a distance of 58 m away from the foot of the tower. Calculate:

a the horizontal component of velocity of the cannon ball at the instant it was fired,

b the height of the tower above the sea,

c the speed of impact of the cannonball at the sea.

4 A cable car was travelling at a speed of 4.6 m s⁻¹ in a direction 40° above the horizontal, when an object was released from the cable car (Figure 5).

cable
4.6 m s⁻¹
40°
object released

Figure 5

a Calculate the horizontal and vertical components of velocity of the object at the instant it was released.

b The object took 5.8 s to fall to the ground below. Calculate **i** the distance fallen by the object from the point of release, **ii** the horizontal distance travelled by the object from the point of release to where it hit the ground.

1 A car accelerates uniformly from rest to a speed of $100\,\text{km}\,\text{h}^{-1}$ in $5.8\,\text{s}$.
    (a) Calculate the magnitude of the acceleration of the car in $\text{m}\,\text{s}^{-2}$.   *(3 marks)*
    (b) Calculate the distance travelled by the car while accelerating.   *(2 marks)*

                                      AQA, 2005

2 **Figure 1** shows how the velocity of a toy train moving in a straight line varies over a period of time.

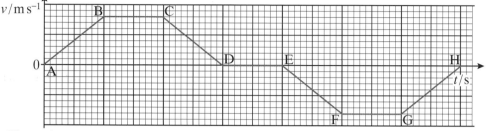

Figure 1

    (a) Describe the motion of the train in the following regions of the graph.
        AB   BC   CD   DE   EF   *(5 marks)*
    (b) What feature of the graph represents the displacement of the train?   *(1 mark)*
    (c) Explain, with reference to the graph, why the distance travelled by the train is different from its displacement.   *(2 marks)*

                                        AQA, 2002

3 A vehicle accelerates uniformly from a speed of $4.0\,\text{m}\,\text{s}^{-1}$ to a speed of $12\,\text{m}\,\text{s}^{-1}$ in $6.0\,\text{s}$
    (a) Calculate the vehicle's acceleration.   *(2 marks)*
    (b) Sketch a graph of speed against time for the vehicle covering the $6.0\,\text{s}$ period in which it accelerates.   *(2 marks)*
    (c) Calculate the distance travelled by the vehicle during its $6.0\,\text{s}$ period of acceleration.   *(2 marks)*

                                        AQA, 2002

4 A supertanker, cruising at an initial speed of $4.5\,\text{m}\,\text{s}^{-1}$, takes one hour to come to rest.
    (a) Assuming that the force slowing the tanker down is constant, calculate
        (i) the deceleration of the tanker,
        (ii) the distance travelled by the tanker while slowing to a stop.   *(4 marks)*
    (b) Sketch a distance–time graph representing the motion of the tanker until it stops.   *(2 marks)*
    (c) Explain the shape of the graph you have sketched in part (b).   *(2 marks)*

                                        AQA, 2006

5 (a) A cheetah accelerating uniformly from rest reaches a speed of $29\,\text{m}\,\text{s}^{-1}$ in $2.0\,\text{s}$ and then maintains this speed for $15\,\text{s}$. Calculate:
        (i) its acceleration,
        (ii) the distance it travels while accelerating,
        (iii) the distance it travels while it is moving at constant speed.   *(4 marks)*
    (b) The cheetah and an antelope are both at rest and $100\,\text{m}$ apart. The cheetah starts to chase the antelope. The antelope takes $0.50\,\text{s}$ to react. It then accelerates uniformly for $2.0\,\text{s}$ to a speed of $25\,\text{m}\,\text{s}^{-1}$ and then maintains this speed. **Figure 2** shows the speed–time graph for the cheetah.

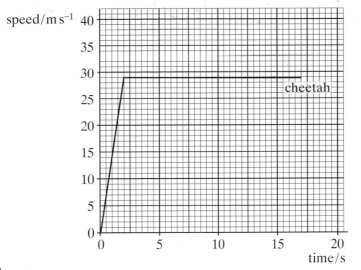

Figure 2

(i) Using the same axes plot the speed–time graph for the antelope during the chase.

(ii) Calculate the distance covered by the antelope in the 17 s after the cheetah started to run.

(iii) How far apart are the cheetah and the antelope after 17 s? *(6 marks)*

AQA, 2007

6   The following data were obtained when two students performed an experiment to determine the acceleration of free fall. One student released a lump of lead the size of a tennis ball from a window in a tall building and the other measured the time for it to reach the ground.

    distance fallen by lump of lead = 35 m

    time to reach the ground = 2.7 s

(a) Calculate a value for the acceleration of free fall, *g*, from these observations. *(2 marks)*

(b) State and explain the effect on the value of *g* obtained by the students if a tennis ball were used instead of the lump of lead. *(3 marks)*

(c) The graph in **Figure 3** shows how the velocity changes with time for the lump of lead from the time of release until it hits the ground. Sketch on the same axes a graph to show how the velcity would change with time if a tennis ball were used by the students instead of a lump of lead.

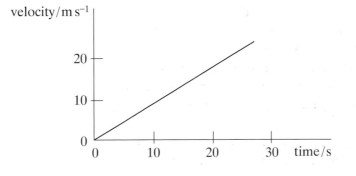

Figure 3 *(2 marks)*

AQA, 2004

7   (a) A man jumps from a plane that is travelling horizontally at a speed of 70 m s⁻¹. If air resistance can be ignored, and before he opens his parachute, determine

(i) his horizontal velocity 2.0 s after jumping,

(ii) his vertical velocity 2.0 s after jumping,

(iii) the magnitude and direction of his resultant velocity 2.0 s after jumping. *(5 marks)*

AQA, 2003

9.1 Force and acceleration

Learning objectives:

- What does a resultant force always produce?
- What would happen to a body that was already in motion if there was no resultant force acting on it?
- How is weight different from mass?

Specification reference: 3.2.1

Figure 1 *Overcoming friction*

◼ Motion without force

Motorists on icy roads in winter need to be very careful, because the tyres of a car have little or no grip on the ice. Moving from a standstill on ice is very difficult. Stopping on ice is almost impossible, as a car moving on ice will slide when the brakes are applied. **Friction** is a hidden force that we don't usually think about until it is absent!

If you have ever pushed a heavy crate across a rough concrete floor, you will know all about friction. The push force is opposed by friction and as soon as you stop pushing, friction stops the crate moving. If the crate had been pushed onto a patch of ice, it would have moved across the ice without any further push needed.

Figure 2 shows an air track which allows motion to be observed in the absence of friction. The glider on the air track floats on a cushion of air. Provided the track is level, the glider moves at constant velocity along the track because friction is absent.

Figure 2 *The linear air track*

Newton's first law of motion

Objects either stay at rest or remain in uniform motion unless acted on by a force.

Sir Isaac Newton was the first person to realise that a moving object stays moving at constant velocity unless acted on by a force. He recognised that when an object is acted on by a resultant force, the result is to change the object's velocity. In other words, an object moving at constant velocity is either

- acted on by no forces, or
- the forces acting on it are balanced (the resultant force is zero).

◼ Investigating force and motion

How does the velocity of an object change if it is acted on by a constant force? Figure 3 shows how this can be investigated, using a dynamics trolley and a motion sensor connected to a computer. The computer is used to process a signal from the motion sensor and to display a graph showing how the velocity of the trolley changes with time.

The trolley is pulled along a sloping runway using one or more elastic bands stretched to the same length. The runway is sloped just enough to compensate for friction. To test for the correct slope, the trolley should move down the runway at constant speed after being given a brief push.

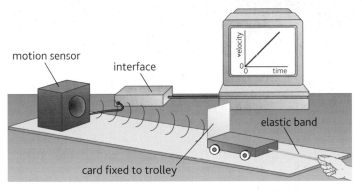

motion sensor
interface
velocity
0
0 time
elastic band
card fixed to trolley

Figure 3 *Investigating force and motion*

As a result of pulling the trolley with a constant force, the velocity–time graph should show that the velocity increases at a constant rate. The acceleration of the trolley is therefore constant and can be measured from the velocity–time graph. Table 1 below shows typical measurements using different amounts of force (one, two or three elastic bands in parallel stretched to the same length each time) and different amounts of mass (i.e. a single, double or triple trolley).

Table 1

force (no of elastic bands)	1	2	3	1	2	3
mass (no. of trolleys)	1	1	1	2	2	2
acceleration (in m s⁻²)	12	24	36	6	12	18
mass × acceleration	12	24	36	12	24	36

The results in the table show that the force is proportional to the mass × the acceleration. In other words, if a resultant force F acts on an object of mass m, the object undergoes acceleration a such that

$$F \text{ is proportional to } ma$$

By defining the unit of force, the **newton**, as the amount of force that will give an object of mass 1 kg an acceleration of $1\,\mathrm{m\,s^{-2}}$, the above proportionality statement can be expressed as an equation

$$F = ma$$

where F = resultant force (in N), m = mass (in kg), a = acceleration (in $\mathrm{m\,s^{-2}}$).

This equation is known as **Newton's second law** for constant mass.

Worked example:

A vehicle of mass 600 kg accelerates uniformly from rest to a velocity of $8.0\,\mathrm{m\,s^{-1}}$ in 20 s. Calculate the force needed to produce this acceleration.

Solution

Acceleration $a = \dfrac{v - u}{t} = \dfrac{8.0 - 0}{20} = 0.4\,\mathrm{m\,s^{-2}}$

Force $F = ma = 600 \times 0.4 = 240\,\mathrm{N}$

Hint

The acceleration is always in the same direction as the resultant force. For example, a freely moving projectile in motion experiences a force vertically downwards due to gravity. Its acceleration is therefore vertically downwards, no matter what its direction of motion is.

AQA Examiner's tip

The mass m must be in kg and a in $\mathrm{m\,s^{-2}}$ when calculating a force in N.

spring

weight of parcel
= 5.3 N

this part is the cylinder
inside the balance tube
that slides out when
weight is added

parcel

Figure 4 *Using a newtonmeter to weigh an object*

coin on postcard

postcard

flick
card
here

tumbler

Figure 5 *An 'inertia trick'*

How science works

Why does a heavy object fall at the same rate as a lighter object?

As outlined on p119, Galileo used his imagination to prove that objects fall at the same rate, regardless of their weight. He also reasoned that if two objects joined by a string were released and they initially fell at different rates, the faster one would be slowed down by the slower one, which would be speeded up by the faster one until they fell at the same rate. Many years later, Newton explained their identical falling motion because, for an object of mass m in free fall,

$$\text{acceleration} = \frac{\text{force of gravity } mg}{\text{mass } m}$$

$$= g \text{ which is independent of } m$$

■ Weight

■ The acceleration of a falling object acted on by gravity only is g. Because the force of gravity on the object is the only force acting on it, its **weight** (in newtons), $W = mg$, where m = the mass of the object (in kg).

■ When an object is in equilibrium, the support force on it is equal and opposite to its weight. Therefore, an object placed on a weighing balance (e.g. a newtonmeter or a top pan balance) exerts a force on the balance equal to the weight of the object. Thus the balance measures the weight of the object. See Figure 4.

■ g is also referred to as the **gravitational field strength** at a given position, as it is the force of gravity per unit mass on a small object at that position. So the gravitational field strength at the Earth's surface is $9.81\,\text{N}\,\text{kg}^{-1}$. Note that the weight of a fixed mass depends on its location. For example, the weight of a 1 kg object is 9.81 N on the Earth's surface and 1.62 N on the Moon's surface.

■ The mass of an object is a measure of its **inertia**, which is its resistance to change of motion. More force is needed to give an object a certain acceleration than to give an object with less mass the same acceleration. Figure 5 shows an entertaining demonstration of inertia. When the card is flicked, the coin drops into the glass because the force of friction on it due to the moving card is too small to shift it sideways.

■ The scale of a top pan balance is usually calibrated for convenience in grams or kilograms.

Summary questions

$g = 9.81\,\text{N}\,\text{kg}^{-1}$

1 A car of mass 800 kg accelerates uniformly along a straight line from rest to a speed of 12 m s⁻¹ in 50 s. Calculate:

  a the acceleration of the car,

  b the force on the car that produced this acceleration,

  c the ratio of the accelerating force to the weight of the car.

2 An aeroplane of mass 5000 kg lands on a runway at a speed of 60 m s⁻¹ and stops 25 s later.

  Calculate:

  a the deceleration of the aeroplane,

  b the braking force on the aircraft.

3 **a** A vehicle of mass 1200 kg on a level road accelerates from rest to a speed of 6.0 m s⁻¹ in 20 s, without change of direction. Calculate the force that accelerated the car.

  b The vehicle in **a** is fitted with a trailer of mass 200 kg. Calculate the time taken to reach a speed of 6.0 m s⁻¹ from rest for the same force as in **a**.

4 A bullet of mass 0.002 kg travelling at a speed of 120 m s⁻¹ hit a tree and penetrated a distance of 55 mm into the tree. Calculate:

  a the deceleration of the bullet,

  b the impact force of the bullet on the tree.

9.2 Using $F = ma$

Learning objectives:

- How do we apply $F = ma$ when the forces on an object are in opposite directions?

- Why do you experience less support as an ascending lift stops?

- Are there any situations in which $F = ma$ cannot be applied?

Specification reference: 3.2.1

⚠ Two forces in opposite directions

When an object is acted on by two unequal forces acting in opposite directions, the object accelerates in the direction of the larger force. If the forces are F_1 and F_2 where $F_1 > F_2$

$$\text{Resultant force, } F_1 - F_2 = ma,$$

where m is the mass of the object and a is its acceleration which is in the same direction as F_1.

If the object is on a horizontal surface and F_1 and F_2 are horizontal and in opposite directions, the above equation still applies. The support force on the object is equal and opposite to its weight.

Figure 1 *Unbalanced forces*

Some examples are given below where two forces act in different directions on an object.

Towing a trailer

Consider the example of a car of mass M fitted with a trailer of mass m on a level road. When the car and the trailer accelerate, the car pulls the trailer forward and the trailer holds the car back. Assume friction and air resistance are negligible.

Figure 2 *Car and trailer*

- The car is subjected to a driving force F pushing it forwards (from its engine thrust) and the tension T in the tow bar holding it back.

  Therefore the resultant force on the car $= F - T = Ma$

- The force on the trailer is due to the tension T in the tow bar pulling it forwards.

  Therefore $T = ma$

Combining the two equations gives $F = Ma + ma = (M + m)a$

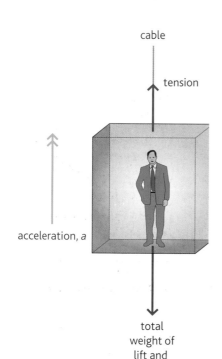

Figure 3 *Rocket launch*

Figure 4 *In a lift*

Rocket problems

If T is the thrust of the rocket engine when its mass is m and the rocket is moving upwards, its acceleration a is given by $T - mg = ma$

Rocket thrust $T = mg + ma$.

The rocket thrust must therefore overcome the weight of the rocket for the rocket to take off (Figure 3).

Lift problems

Using 'upwards is positive' gives the resultant force on the lift as $T - mg$, where T is the tension in the lift cable and m is the total mass of the lift and occupants (Figure 4).

$T - mg = ma$, where a = acceleration.

a If the lift is moving at constant velocity, then $a = 0$
so $T = mg$ (tension = weight).

b If the lift is moving up and accelerating, then $a > 0$
so $T = mg + ma > mg$

c If the lift is moving up and decelerating, then $a < 0$
so $T = mg + ma < mg$

d If the lift is moving down and accelerating, then $a < 0$ (velocity and acceleration are both downwards, therefore negative)
so $T = mg + ma < mg$.

e If the lift is moving down and decelerating, then $a > 0$ (velocity downwards and acceleration upwards, therefore positive)
so $T = mg + ma > mg$

The tension in the cable is less than the weight if

- the lift is moving up and decelerating (velocity > 0 and acceleration < 0)
- the lift is moving down and accelerating (velocity < 0 and acceleration < 0)

The tension in the cable is greater than the weight if

- the lift is moving up and accelerating (velocity > 0 and acceleration > 0)
- the lift is moving down and decelerating (velocity < 0 and acceleration > 0)

Worked example:

$g = 9.8\,\text{m s}^{-2}$

A lift of total mass 650 kg moving downwards decelerates at $1.5\,\text{m s}^{-2}$ and stops. Calculate the tension in the lift cable during the deceleration.

Figure 5

Solution

The lift is moving down so its velocity $v < 0$. Since it decelerates, its acceleration a is in the opposite direction to its velocity, so $a > 0$.

Therefore, inserting $a = +1.5\,\text{m s}^{-2}$ in the equation $T - mg = ma$ gives

$T = mg + ma = (650 \times 9.8) + (650 \times 1.5) = 7300\,\text{N}$

AQA **Examiner's tip**

Identify the separate forces acting, then work out the resultant force; show these steps by clear working (usually starting in algebra, such as $T - mg = ma$).

Further F = ma problems

Pulley problems

Consider two masses M and m (where $M > m$) attached to a thread hung over a frictionless pulley, as in Figure 6. When released, mass M accelerates downwards and mass m accelerates upwards. If a is the acceleration and T is the tension in the thread, then

▪ the resultant force on mass M, $Mg - T = Ma$

▪ the resultant force on mass m, $T - mg = ma$

Therefore, adding the two equations gives

$$Mg - mg = (M + m)a$$

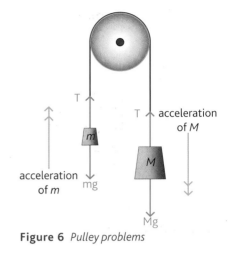

Figure 6 *Pulley problems*

Sliding down a slope

Consider a block of mass m sliding down a slope, as in Figure 7.

The component of the block's weight down the slope $= mg\sin\theta$

If the force of friction on the block $= F_0$, then the resultant force on the block $= mg\sin\theta - F_0$

Therefore **$mg\sin\theta - F_0 = ma$**, where a is the acceleration of the block.

Note:

With the addition of an engine force F_E, the above equation can be applied to a vehicle on a downhill slope of constant gradient. Thus the acceleration is given by $F_E + mg\sin\theta - F_0 = ma$, where F_0 is the combined sum of the force of friction and the braking force.

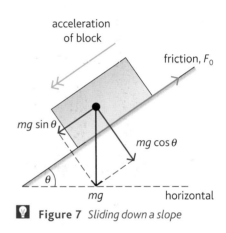

Figure 7 *Sliding down a slope*

Summary questions

$g = 9.8\,\mathrm{m\,s^{-2}}$.

1 A rocket of mass 550 kg blasts vertically from the launch pad at an acceleration of $4.2\,\mathrm{m\,s^{-2}}$. Calculate:

  a the weight of the rocket,

  b the thrust of the rocket engines.

2 A car of mass 1400 kg, pulling a trailer of mass 400 kg, accelerates from rest to a speed of $9.0\,\mathrm{m\,s^{-1}}$ in a time of 60 s on a level road. Assuming air resistance is negligible, calculate:

  a the tension in the tow bar,

  b the engine force.

3 A lift and its occupants have a total mass of 1200 kg. Calculate the tension in the lift cable when the lift is:

  a stationary,

  b ascending at constant speed,

  c ascending at a constant acceleration of $0.4\,\mathrm{m\,s^{-2}}$,

  d descending at a constant deceleration of $0.4\,\mathrm{m\,s^{-2}}$.

4 A brick of mass 3.2 kg on a sloping flat roof, at 30° to the horizontal, slides at constant acceleration $2.0\,\mathrm{m}$ down the roof in 2.0 s from rest. Calculate:

  a the acceleration of the brick,

  b the frictional force on the brick due to the roof.

9.3 Terminal speed

Learning objectives:

■ Why does the speed reach a maximum when a driving force is still acting?

■ What do we mean by a drag force?

■ What determines the terminal speed of a falling object or a vehicle?

Specification reference: 3.2.1

a *Falling in a fluid*

b *Skydiving*

Figure 1 *At terminal speed*

AQA Examiner's tip

The magnitude of the acceleration at any instant is the gradient of the speed–time curve.

Any object moving through a fluid experiences a force that drags on it due to the fluid. The **drag force** depends on

■ the shape of the object

■ its speed

■ the viscosity of the fluid which is a measure of how easily the fluid flows past a surface.

The faster an object travels in a fluid, the greater the drag force on it.

⚠ Motion of an object falling in a fluid

The speed of an object released from rest in a fluid increases as it falls, so the drag force on it due to the fluid increases. The resultant force on the object is the difference between the force of gravity on it (its weight) and the drag force. As the drag force increases, the resultant force decreases, so the acceleration becomes less as it falls. If it continues falling, it attains **terminal speed**, when the drag force on it is equal and opposite to its weight. Its acceleration is then zero and its speed remains constant as it falls (Figure 1).

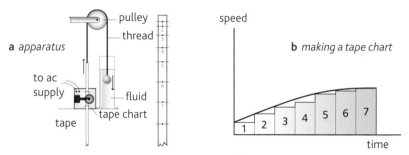

a *apparatus*   **b** *making a tape chart*

Figure 2 *Investigating the motion of an object falling in a fluid*

Figure 2 shows how to investigate the motion of an object falling in a fluid. When the object is released, the thread attached to the object pulls a tape through a tickertimer, which prints dots on the tape. The spacing between successive dots is a measure of the speed of the object as the dots are printed on the tape at a constant rate. A tape chart can be made from the tape to show how the speed changes with time. This is done by cutting the tape at each dot and pasting successive lengths side by side on graph paper, as shown in Figure 2b. The results show that:

■ the speed increases and reaches a constant value, which is the terminal speed,

■ the acceleration at any instant is the gradient of the speed-time curve.

At any instant, the resultant force $F = mg - D$, where m is the mass of the object and D is the drag force.

Therefore, the acceleration of the object $= \dfrac{mg - D}{m} = g - \dfrac{D}{m}$

■ The initial acceleration $= g$ because the speed is zero, and therefore the drag force is zero, at the instant the object is released.

■ At the terminal speed, the potential energy lost by the object is converted, as it falls, to internal energy of the fluid by the drag force.

Motion of a powered vehicle

The top speed of a road vehicle or an aircraft depends on its engine power, also referred to as its motive power, and its shape. A vehicle with a streamlined shape can reach a higher top speed than a vehicle with the same motive power that is not streamlined.

For a powered vehicle of mass m moving on a level surface, if F_E represents the engine force driving the vehicle (sometimes called the motive force), the resultant force on it $= F_E - F_R$, where F_R is the **resistive force** opposing the motion of the vehicle. (F_R = the sum of the drag force and friction forces acting on the vehicle.)

Therefore its acceleration $a = \dfrac{F_E - F_R}{m}$

Because the drag force increases with speed, the maximum speed (the terminal speed) of the vehicle v_{max} is reached when the resistive force becomes equal and opposite to the engine force.

Figure 3 *Vehicle power*

Worked example:

A car of mass 1200 kg has an engine which provides an engine force of 600 N. Calculate:

a its initial acceleration,

b its acceleration when the resistive force is 400 N.

Solution

a Maximum acceleration is when the resistive force is zero (i.e. when the car starts). The resultant force on the car is therefore 600 N at the start.

Therefore, its initial acceleration $= \dfrac{\text{force}}{\text{mass}} = \dfrac{600}{1200} = 0.5\,\text{m s}^{-2}$

b When the resistive force = 400 N, the resultant force = weight − drag force = 600 − 400 = 200 N

Acceleration $= \dfrac{\text{force}}{\text{mass}} = \dfrac{200}{1200} = 0.16\,\text{m s}^{-2}$

How science works

Hydrofoil physics

A hydrofoil boat travels much faster than an ordinary boat because it has a powerful jet engine that enables it to 'ski' on its hydrofoils when the jet engine is switched on.

- When the jet engine is switched on and takes over from the less powerful propeller engine, the boat speeds up and the hydrofoils are extended. The boat rides on the hydrofoils, so the drag force is reduced, as its hull is no longer in the water. At top speed, the motive force of the jet engine is equal to the drag force on the hydrofoils.

- When the jet engine is switched off, the drag force on the hydrofoils reduces the speed of the boat and the hydrofoils are retracted. The speed drops further until the drag force is equal to the motive force of the propeller engine. The boat then moves at a constant speed, which is much less than its top speed with the jet engine on.

Summary questions

$g = 9.8\,\text{m s}^{-2}$

1 a A steel ball of mass 0.15 kg, released from rest in a liquid, falls a distance of 0.20 m in 5.0 s. Assuming the ball reaches terminal speed within a fraction of a second, calculate **i** its terminal speed, **ii** the drag force on it when it falls at terminal speed.

b State and explain whether or not a smaller steel ball would fall at the same rate in the same liquid.

2 Explain why a cyclist can reach a higher top speed by crouching over the handlebars instead of sitting upright while pedalling.

3 A vehicle of mass 32 000 kg has an engine which has a maximum engine force of 4.4 kN and a top speed of 36 m s⁻¹ on a level road.

Calculate **a** its maximum acceleration from rest, **b** the distance it would travel at maximum acceleration to reach a speed of 12 m s⁻¹ from rest.

4 Explain why a vehicle has a higher top speed on a downhill stretch of road than on a level road.

9.4 On the road

Learning objectives:

- What is happening to a vehicle's speed whilst a driver is reacting to a hazard ahead?

- What is the difference between braking distance and stopping distance?

- How do road conditions affect these distances?

Specification reference: 3.2.1

Stopping distances

Traffic accidents often happen because vehicles are being driven too fast and too close. A driver needs to maintain a safe distance between his or her own vehicle and the vehicle in front. If a vehicle suddenly brakes, the driver of the following vehicle needs to brake as well to avoid a crash.

Thinking distance is the distance travelled by a vehicle in the time it takes the driver to react. For a vehicle moving at constant speed v, the thinking distance s_1 = speed × reaction time = vt_0, where t_0 is the reaction time of the driver. The reaction time of a driver is affected by distractions, drugs and alcohol, which is why drivers in the UK are banned from using mobile phones while driving and breathalyser tests are carried out on drivers.

Braking distance is the distance travelled by a car in the time it takes to stop safely, from when the brakes are first applied. Assuming constant deceleration, a, to zero speed from speed v,

the braking distance $s_2 = v^2/2a$ since $v^2 = 2as_2$.

Stopping distance = thinking distance + braking distance = $vt_0 + \dfrac{v^2}{2a}$ where v is the speed before the brakes were applied.

Figure 1 shows how thinking distance, braking distance and stopping distance vary with speed for a reaction time of 0.67 s and a deceleration of 6.75 m s^{-2}. Using these values for reaction time and deceleration in the above equations, Figure 1 gives the shortest stopping distances on a dry road as recommended in the Highway Code.

Figure 1 *Stopping distances*

How science works

Skidding

On a front-wheel drive vehicle, the engine turns the front wheels via the transmission system. Friction between the tyres and the road prevent 'wheel spin' (slipping) so the driving wheels therefore 'roll' along the road. If the driver tries to accelerate too fast, the wheels skid. This is because there is an upper limit to the amount of friction between the tyres and the road (Figure 2).

When the brakes are applied, the wheels are slowed down by the brakes. The vehicle therefore slows down, provided the wheels do not skid. If the braking force is increased, the friction force between

Examiner's tip

A car can only move forwards by pushing backwards on the road. The same applies when you take a forward step.

the tyres and the road increases. However, if the upper limit of friction (usually referred to as 'limiting frictional force') between the tyres and the road is reached, the wheels skid. When this happens, the brakes lock and the vehicle slides uncontrollably forward. Most vehicles are now fitted with an anti-lock brake system (ABS), which consists of a speed sensor on each wheel linked to a central electronic control unit that controls hydraulic valves in the brake system. When the brakes are applied, if a wheel starts to lock, the control unit senses that the wheel is rotating much more slowly than the other wheels; as a result, the valves are activated, so the brake pressure on the wheel is reduced to stop it locking.

friction due to braking

friction caused by motive force

Figure 2 *Stopping and starting*

Testing friction

Measure the limiting friction between the underside of a block and the surface it is on. Pull the block with an increasing force until it slides. The limiting frictional force on the block is equal to the pull force on the block just before sliding occurs. Find out how this force depends on the weight of the block.

Figure 3 *Testing friction*

How science works

More about braking distance

The braking distance for a vehicle depends on the speed of the vehicle at the instant the brakes are applied, on the road conditions and on the condition of the vehicle tyres.

- On a greasy or icy road, skidding is more likely because the limiting frictional force is reduced from its 'dry' value. To stop a vehicle safely on a greasy or icy road, the brakes must be applied with less force than on a dry road otherwise skidding will occur. Therefore the braking distance (the distance to stop safely) is longer than on a dry road. In fast-moving traffic, a driver must ensure there is a bigger gap to the car in front so as to be able to slow down safely if the vehicle in front slows down.

- The condition of the tyres of a vehicle also affects braking distance. The tread of a tyre must not be less than a certain depth, otherwise any grease, oil or water on the road reduces friction very considerably. In the United Kingdom, the absolute minimum legal requirement is that every tyre of a vehicle must have a tread depth of at least 1.6 mm across three-quarters of the width of the tyre all the way round. If the pressure on a tyre is too small or too great, or the wheel is 'unbalanced', then the tyre will wear unevenly and will quickly become unsafe. Clearly, a driver must check the condition of the tyres regularly. If you are a driver or hope to become one, remember that the vehicle tyres are the only contacts between the vehicle and the road and must therefore be looked after.

Figure 4 *Tyre treads*

*Worked example:*_____

$g = 9.8\,\mathrm{m\,s^{-2}}$

A vehicle of mass 900 kg, travelling on a level road at a speed of $15\,\mathrm{m\,s^{-1}}$, can be brought to a standstill without skidding by a braking force equal to $0.5 \times$ its weight. Calculate **a** the deceleration of the vehicle, **b** the braking distance.

Solution

a Weight $= 900 \times 9.8 = 8800\,\mathrm{N}$

Braking force $= 0.5 \times 8800 = 4400\,\mathrm{N}$

$$\text{Deceleration} = \frac{\text{braking force}}{\text{mass}} = \frac{4400}{900} = 4.9\,\mathrm{m\,s^{-2}}$$

b $u = 15\,\mathrm{m\,s^{-1}},\ v = 0,\ a = -4.9\,\mathrm{m\,s^{-2}}$

To calculate s, use $v^2 = u^2 + 2as$

$$s = \frac{-u^2}{2a} = \frac{-15^2}{2 \times -4.9} = 23\,\mathrm{m}$$

Summary questions

$g = 9.8\,\mathrm{m\,s^{-2}}$

1 A vehicle is travelling at a speed of $18\,\mathrm{m\,s^{-1}}$ on a level road, when the driver sees a pedestrian stepping off the pavement into the road 45 m ahead. The driver reacts within 0.4 s and applies the brakes, causing the car to decelerate at $4.8\,\mathrm{m\,s^{-2}}$.

  a Calculate **i** the thinking distance, **ii** the braking distance.

  b How far does the driver stop from where the pedestrian stepped into the road?

2 The braking distance of a vehicle for a speed of $18\,\mathrm{m\,s^{-1}}$ on a dry level road is 24 m. Calculate:

  a the deceleration of the vehicle from this speed to a standstill over this distance,

  b the frictional force on a vehicle of mass 1000 kg on this road when it stops.

3 **a** What is meant by the braking distance of a vehicle?

  b Explain in terms of the forces acting on the wheels of a car, why a vehicle slows down when the brakes are applied.

4 The frictional force on a vehicle travelling on a certain type of level road surface is $0.6 \times$ the vehicle's weight. For a vehicle of mass 1200 kg,

  a show that the maximum deceleration on this road is $5.9\,\mathrm{m\,s^{-2}}$,

  b calculate the braking distance on this road for a speed of $30\,\mathrm{m\,s^{-1}}$.

9.5 Vehicle safety

- In a road accident, what can we say about the force on a moving body if it is suddenly stopped?

- What should be increased to give a smaller deceleration from a given speed?

- Which design features attempt to achieve this in a modern vehicle?

Specification reference: 3.2.1

Impact forces

Figure 1 *Head on collision*

Measuring impacts

The effect of a collision on a vehicle can be measured in terms of the acceleration or deceleration of the vehicle. By expressing an acceleration or deceleration in terms of g, the acceleration due to gravity, the force of the impact can then easily be related to the weight of the vehicle. For example, suppose a vehicle hits a wall and its acceleration is $-30\,\text{m s}^{-2}$. In terms of g, the acceleration $= -3g$. So the **impact force** of the wall on the vehicle must have been 3 times its weight ($= 3mg$, where m is the mass of the vehicle). Such an impact is sometimes described as being 'equal to $3g$'. This statement, although technically wrong because the acceleration not the impact force is equal to $3g$, is a convenient way of expressing the effect of an impact on a vehicle or a person.

How science works

How much acceleration or deceleration can a person withstand?

The duration of the impact as well as the magnitude of the acceleration affects the person. A person who is sitting or upright can survive a deceleration of $20g$ for a time of a few milliseconds, although not without severe injury. A deceleration of over $5g$ lasting for a few seconds can cause injuries. Car designers carry out tests using dummies in remote-control vehicles to measure the change of motion of different parts of a vehicle or a dummy. Sensors linked to data recorders and computers are used, as well as video cameras that record the motion to allow video clips to be analysed.

Figure 2 *A video clip of a side-on impact*

⤤ ⚠ Contact time and impact time

When objects collide and bounce off each other, they are in contact with each other for a certain time, which is the same for both objects. The shorter the contact time, the greater the impact force for the same initial velocities of the two objects. When two vehicles collide, they may or may not separate from each other after the collision. If they remain tangled together, they exert forces on each other until they are moving at the same velocity. The duration of the impact force is not the same as the contact time in this situation.

The impact time, t, (the duration of the impact force) can be worked out by applying the equation $s = \frac{1}{2}(u + v)t$ to one of the vehicles, where s is the distance moved by that vehicle during the impact, u is its initial velocity and v is its final velocity. If the vehicle mass is known, the impact force can also be calculated.

For a vehicle of mass m in time t,

$$\text{the impact time } t = \frac{2s}{u + v}$$

$$\text{the acceleration } a = \frac{v - u}{t}$$

$$\text{the impact force } F = ma$$

For example, suppose a 1000 kg vehicle moving at 20 m s⁻¹ slows down in a distance of 4.0 m to a velocity of 12 m s⁻¹, as a result of hitting a stationary vehicle. Rearranging the above equation gives

$$t = \frac{2s}{(u + v)} = \frac{2 \times 4.0}{(20 + 12)} = 0.25\,\text{s}$$

The acceleration, $a = \frac{(v - u)}{t} = \frac{12 - 20}{0.25} = -32\,\text{m s}^{-2} = -3.3g$ (where $g = 9.8\,\text{m s}^{-2}$)

The impact force $F = ma = 1000 \times -32 = -32\,000\,\text{N}$.

Note:

The work done by the impact force F over an impact distance s ($= Fs$) is equal to the change of kinetic energy of the vehicle. The impact force can also be worked out using the equation

$$F = \frac{\text{change of kinetic energy}}{\text{impact distance}}$$

You will learn in Topic 10.2 that the kinetic energy of a vehicle of mass m moving at speed v can be calculated using the formula $\frac{1}{2}mv^2$. Prove for yourself that the vehicle in the example above has 200 kJ of kinetic energy at 20 ms⁻¹ and 72 kJ at 12 ms⁻¹. You can then show the change of kinetic energy ÷ impact distance gives −32000 N for the impact force.

How science works

Car safety features

Figure 3 *Vehicle safety features*

In the example on page 144, the vehicle's deceleration and hence the impact force would be lessened if the impact time was greater. So design features that would increase the impact time reduce the impact force. With a reduced impact force, the vehicle occupants are less affected. The following vehicle safety features are designed to increase the impact time and so reduce the impact force.

■ **Vehicle bumpers** give way a little in a low-speed impact and so increase the impact time. The impact force is therefore reduced as a result. If the initial speed of impact is too high, the bumper and/or the vehicle chassis are likely to be damaged.

■ **Crumple zones** The engine compartment of a car is designed to give way in a front-end impact. If the engine compartment were rigid, the impact time would be very short, so the impact force would be very large. By designing the engine compartment so it crumples in a front-end impact, the impact time is increased and the impact force is therefore reduced.

■ **Seat belts** In a front-end impact, a correctly-fitted seat belt restrains the wearer from crashing into the vehicle frame after the vehicle suddenly stops. The restraining force on the wearer is therefore much less than the impact force would be if the wearer hit the vehicle frame. With the seat belt on, the wearer is stopped more gradually than without it.

■ **Collapsible steering wheel** In a front-end impact, the seat belt restrains the driver without holding the driver rigidly. If the driver makes contact with the steering wheel, the impact force is lessened as a result of the steering wheel collapsing in the impact.

■ **Airbags** An airbag reduces the force on a person, because the airbag acts as a cushion and increases the impact time on the person. More significantly, the force of the impact is spread over the contact area, which is greater than the contact area with a seat belt. So the pressure on the body is less.

Summary questions

$g = 9.8 \, \text{m s}^{-2}$

1 A car of mass 1200 kg travelling at a speed of 15 m s⁻¹ is struck from behind by another vehicle, causing its speed to increase to 19 m s⁻¹ in a time of 0.20 s. Calculate:

  a the acceleration of the car, in terms of g,

  b the impact force on the car.

2 The front end of a certain type of car of mass 1500 kg travelling at a speed of 20 m s⁻¹ is designed to crumple in a distance of 0.8 m, if the car hits a wall. Calculate:

  a the impact time if it hits a wall at 20 m s⁻¹,

  b the impact force.

3 The front bumper of a car of mass 900 kg is capable of withstanding an impact with a stationary object, provided the car is not moving faster than 3.0 m s⁻¹, when the impact occurs. The impact time at this speed is 0.40 s. Calculate:

  a the deceleration of the car from 3.0 m s⁻¹ to rest in 0.40 s,

  b the impact force on the car.

4 In a crash, a vehicle travelling at a speed of 25 m s⁻¹ is stopped in a distance of 4.5 m. A passenger of mass 68 kg is wearing a seat belt, which restrains her forward movement relative to the car to a distance of 0.5 m.

  a Show that the deceleration of the passenger is 62.5 m s⁻²,

  b Calculate i the deceleration of the passenger in terms of g, ii the resultant force on the passenger.

1   A car moving at a velocity of $20\,\text{m s}^{-1}$ brakes to a standstill in a distance of $40\,\text{m}$. A child of mass $15\,\text{kg}$ is sitting in a forward-facing child car seat fitted to the back seat of the car.

   (a) Calculate (i) the deceleration of the car, (ii) the force on the child.   *(3 marks)*

   (b) In 2006, the UK government passed a law requiring that children in cars must travel in child car seats. If the child had not been in the child car seat, explain why the force on her would have been much greater than the value calculated in (a) (ii).   *(2 marks)*

   (c) Road accidents involving children could be reduced by reducing the speed limit outside a school to $20\,\text{mph}$ ($9\,\text{m s}^{-1}$). Discuss the effect this would have on road safety near a school where the speed limit is currently $30\,\text{mph}$.   *(3 marks)*

2   A packing case is being lifted vertically at a constant speed by a cable attached to a crane.

   (a) With reference to one of Newton's laws of motion, explain why the tension, T, in the cable must be equal to the weight of the packing case.   *(3 marks)*

   (b) A $12.0\,\text{N}$ force and a $8.0\,\text{N}$ force act on a body of mass $6.5\,\text{kg}$ at the same time. For this body, calculate

   (i)   the maximum resultant acceleration that it could experience,

   (ii) the minimum resultant acceleration that it could experience.   *(4 marks)*

   AQA, 2005

3   **Figure 1** shows how the velocity of a motor car increases with time as it accelerates from rest along a straight horizontal road.

Figure 1

   (a) The acceleration is approximately constant for the first five seconds of the motion. Show that, over the first five seconds of the motion, the acceleration is approximately $2.7\,\text{m s}^{-2}$.   *(3 marks)*

   (b) Throughout the motion shown in **Figure 1** there is a constant driving force of $2.0\,\text{kN}$ acting on the car.

   (i)   Calculate the mass of the car and its contents.

   (ii) What is the magnitude of the resistive force acting on the car after $40\,\text{s}$?   *(3 marks)*

   (c) Find the distance travelled by the car during the first $40\,\text{s}$ of the motion.   *(3 marks)*

   AQA, 2006

4   A constant resultant horizontal force of $1.8 \times 10^3\,\text{N}$ acts on a car of mass $900\,\text{kg}$, initially at rest on a level road.

   (a) Calculate:

   (i)   the acceleration of the car,

     (ii) the speed of the car after 8.0 s,

     (iii) the distance travelled by the car in the first 8.0 s of its motion.   *(5 marks)*

  (b) In practice the resultant force on the car changes with time. Air resistance is one factor that affects the resultant force acting on the vehicle.

     (i)   Suggest, with a reason, how the resultant force on the car changes as its speed increases.

     (ii) Explain, using Newton's laws of motion, why the vehicle has a maximum speed.   *(5 marks)*

                                                   AQA, 2004

5   A passenger aircraft has a mass of 3.2×10^5 kg when fully laden. It is powered by four jet engines each producing a maximum thrust of 270 kN.

  (a) (i)   Calculate the total force of the engines acting on the aircraft.

     (ii) Show that the initial acceleration of the aircraft with the engines set to full thrust is about 3.4 m s^{-2}. Ignore any frictional forces.   *(3 marks)*

  (b) The aircraft starts from rest at the beginning of its take-off and has a take-off speed of 90 m s^{-1}.

     (i)   Calculate the time taken for the aircraft to reach its take-off speed if frictional forces are ignored.

     (ii) Frictional forces reduce the actual acceleration of the aircraft to 2.0 m s^{-2}. Calculate the mean total frictional force acting against the aircraft during the time taken to reach its take off speed.   *(4 marks)*

  (c) Calculate the minimum runway length required by this aircraft for take-off when the acceleration is 2.0 m s^{-2}.   *(2 marks)*

  (d) The cruising speed of the aircraft in level flight with the engines at maximum thrust is a constant 260 m s^{-1}. The pilot adjusts the thrust so that the **horizontal** acceleration is always 2.0 m s^{-2}.

     Calculate the time taken from take-off to reach its cruising speed.   *(2 marks)*

  (e) When it is at cruising speed, the aircraft travels at a constant velocity and at a constant height. Explain in terms of the horizontal and vertical forces acting on the aircraft, how this is achieved.   *(2 marks)*

                                                   AQA, 2002

6   A fairground ride ends with the car moving up a ramp at a slope of 30° to the horizontal as shown in **Figure 2.**

Figure 2

  (a) The car and its passengers have a total weight of 7.2×10^3 N. Show that the component of the weight parallel to the ramp is 3.6×10^3 N.   *(1 mark)*

  (b) Calculate the deceleration of the car assuming the only force causing the car to decelerate is that calculated in part (a).   *(2 marks)*

  (c) The car enters at the bottom of the ramp at 18 m s^{-1}. Calculate the minimum length of the ramp for the car to stop before it reaches the end. The length of the car should be neglected.   *(2 marks)*

  (d) Explain why the stopping distance is, in practice, shorter than the value calculated in part (c).   *(2 marks)*

                                                   AQA, 2005

7   A ball bearing is released into a tall cylinder of clear oil. The ball bearing initially accelerates but soon reaches terminal velocity.

  (a) By considering the forces acting on the ball bearing, explain its motion.   *(3 marks)*

  (b) How would you demonstrate that the ball bearing had reached terminal velocity?   *(2 marks)*

                                                   AQA, 2002

10 Work, energy and power

10.1 Work and energy

Learning objectives:

■ What is energy and how do we measure it?

■ Does energy ever disappear?

■ What is meant by work (in the scientific sense)?

Specification reference: 3.2.1

Energy rules

Energy is needed to make stationary objects move, to change their shape or to warm them up. When you lift an object, you transfer energy from your muscles to the object.

Objects can possess energy in different forms, including:

■ potential energy – energy due to position

■ kinetic energy – energy due to motion

■ thermal energy – energy due to the temperature of an object

■ chemical or nuclear energy – energy associated with chemical or nuclear reactions

■ electrical energy – energy of electrically charged objects

■ elastic energy – energy stored in an object when it is stretched or compressed.

Energy is measured in **joules (J)**. One joule is equal to the energy needed to raise a 1 N weight through a vertical height of 1 m.

Energy can be changed from one form into other forms. In any change, the total amount of energy after the change is always equal to the total amount of energy before the change. The total amount of energy is unchanged.

Energy cannot be created or destroyed.

This statement is known as the **principle of conservation of energy.**

Forces at work

Work is done on an object when a force acting on it makes it move. As a result, energy is transferred to the object. The amount of work done depends on the force and the distance the object moved. The greater the force or the further the distance, the greater the work done.

Work done = force × distance moved in the direction of the force.

The unit of work is the joule (J), equal to the work done when a force of 1 N moves its point of application by a distance of 1 m in the direction of the force. For example, a force of 2 N needs to be applied to an object of weight 2 N to raise the object steadily. If the object is raised by 1.5 m, the work done by the force is 3 J (= 2 N × 1.5 m). Therefore, the gain of potential energy of the object is 3 J.

💡 **Figure 1** *Using joules*

Force and displacement

Imagine a yacht acted on by a wind force F at an angle θ to the direction in which the yacht moves. The wind force has a component $F\cos\theta$ in the direction of motion of the yacht and a component $F\sin\theta$ at right angles to the direction of motion. If the yacht is moved a distance s by the wind, the work done on it, W, is equal to the component of force in the direction of motion × the distance moved.

$$W = Fs\cos\theta$$

Figure 2 *Force and displacement*

Note that if $\theta = 90°$ (which means that the force is perpendicular to the direction of motion) then, because $\cos 90° = 0$, the work done is zero.

Force–distance graphs

- If a constant force F acts on an object and makes it move a distance s in the direction of the force, the work done on the object $W = Fs$. Figure 3 shows a graph of force against distance in this situation. The area under the line is a rectangle of height representing the force and of base length representing the distance moved. **Therefore the area under the line represents the work done.**

- If a variable force F acts on an object and causes it to move in the direction of the force, the work done for a small amount of distance Δs, $\Delta W = F\Delta s$. This is represented on a graph of the force F against distance s by the area of a strip under the line of width Δs and height F (Figure 4). The total work done is therefore the sum of the areas of all the strips (i.e. the total area under the line).

The area under the line of a force–distance graph represents the total work done.

Hint

No work is done when F and s are at right angles to each other.

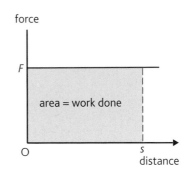

Figure 3 *Force–distance graph for a constant force*

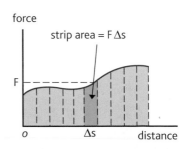

Figure 4 *Force–distance graph for a variable force*

Figure 5 *Force against extension for a spring*

For example, consider the force needed to stretch a spring. The greater the force, the more the spring is extended from its unstretched length. Figure 5 shows how the force needed to stretch a spring changes with the extension of the spring. The graph is a straight line through the origin. Therefore, the force needed is proportional to the extension of the spring. This is known as **Hooke's law**. See Topic 11.2 for more about springs.

Figure 5 is a graph of force against distance, in this case the distance the spring is extended. Therefore, the area under the line represents the work done to stretch the spring. If F is the force needed to extend the spring to extension ΔL, the area under the line from the origin to extension ΔL represents the work done to stretch the spring to extension ΔL. As this area is a triangle, the work done $= \frac{1}{2} \times$ height $\times$ base $= \frac{1}{2} F \Delta L$

The work done to stretch the spring to extension ΔL = $\frac{1}{2} F \Delta L$

Summary questions

$g = 9.8\,\mathrm{m\,s^{-2}}$

1 Calculate the work done when:

a a weight of 40 N is raised by a height of 5.0 m,

b a spring is stretched to an extension of 0.45 m by a force of 20 N.

2 Calculate the energy transferred by a force of 12 N when it moves an object by a distance of 4.0 m:

a in the direction of the force,

b in a direction at 60° to the direction of the force,

c in a direction at right angles to the direction of the force.

3 A luggage trolley of total weight 400 N is pushed at steady speed 20 m up a slope, by a force of 50 N acting in the same direction as the object moves in. At the end of this distance, the trolley is 1.5 m higher than at the start. Calculate:

a the work done pushing the trolley up the slope,

b the gain of potential energy of the trolley,

c the energy wasted due to friction.

4 A spring that obeys Hooke's law requires a force of 1.2 N to extend it to an extension of 50 mm. Calculate:

a the force needed to extend it to an extension of 100 mm,

b the work done when the spring is stretched to an extension of 100 mm from zero extension.

10.2 Kinetic energy and potential energy

Learning objectives:

■ When an object is lifted, what happens to the work done on it?

■ If it is then allowed to fall, what energy change takes place?

■ What is the effect on the kinetic energy of a car if its speed is doubled?

Specification reference: 3.2.1

■ Kinetic energy

Kinetic energy is the energy of an object due to its motion. The faster an object moves, the more kinetic energy it has. To see the exact link between kinetic energy and speed, consider an object of mass m, initially at rest, acted on by a constant force F for a time t.

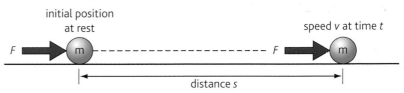

Figure 1 *Gaining kinetic energy*

Let the speed of the object at time t be v.

Therefore, distance travelled, $\quad s = \frac{1}{2}(u + v)t = \frac{1}{2}vt \qquad$ because $u = 0$

$\qquad$ acceleration $\qquad a = \dfrac{(v - u)}{t} = \dfrac{v}{t}$

Using Newton's second law, $\quad F = ma = \dfrac{mv}{t}$

Therefore, the work done W by force F to move the object through distance s,

$$W = Fs = \frac{mv}{t} \times \frac{vt}{2} = \frac{1}{2}mv^2$$

Because the gain of kinetic energy is due to the work done, then

$$\text{kinetic energy, } E_K = \tfrac{1}{2}mv^2$$

■ Hint

The formula does not hold at speeds approaching the speed of light. Einstein's theory of special relativity tells us that the mass of an object increases with speed and that the energy of an object can be worked out from the equation $E = mc^2$, where c is the speed of light in free space and m is the mass of the object.

⚗ Potential energy

Potential energy is the energy of an object due to its position.

If an object of mass m is raised through a vertical height Δh at steady speed, the force needed to raise it is equal and opposite to its weight mg. Therefore,

$$\text{the work done to raise the object } = \text{ force} \times \text{distance moved } = mg\,\Delta h$$

The work done on the object increases its gravitational potential energy.

$$\text{Change of gravitational potential energy } \Delta E_P = mg\,\Delta h$$

At the Earth's surface, $g = 9.8\,\text{m s}^{-2}$

■ Energy changes involving kinetic and potential energy

Consider an object of mass m released above the ground. If air resistance is negligible, the object gains speed as it falls. Its potential energy therefore decreases and its kinetic energy increases.

After falling through a vertical height Δh, its kinetic energy is equal to its loss of potential energy.

$$\tfrac{1}{2}mv^2 = mg\,\Delta h$$

■ Hint

The formula only holds if the change of height h is much smaller than the Earth's radius. If height h is not insignificant compared with the Earth's radius, the value of g is not the same over height h. The force of gravity on an object decreases with increased distance from the Earth.

Summary questions

$g = 9.8\,\mathrm{m\,s^{-2}}$

1 A ball of mass 0.50 kg was thrown directly up at a speed of 6.0 m s⁻¹. Calculate:

  a its kinetic energy at 6 m s⁻¹,

  b its maximum gain of potential energy,

  c its maximum height gain.

2 A ball of mass 0.20 kg at a height of 1.5 m above a table is released from rest and it rebounds to a height of 1.2 m above the table. Calculate:

  a the loss of potential energy on descent,

  b the gain of potential energy at maximum rebound height,

  c the loss of energy due to the impact.

3 A cyclist of mass 80 kg (including the bicycle) freewheels from rest 500 m down a hill. The foot of the hill is 20 m lower than the cyclist's starting point and the cyclist reaches a speed of 12 m s⁻¹ at the foot of the hill. Calculate:

  a the loss of potential energy,

  b the gain of kinetic energy of the cyclist and cycle,

  c the work done against friction and air resistance during the descent,

  d the average resistive force during the descent.

4 A fairground vehicle of total mass 1200 kg moving at a speed of 2 m s⁻¹ descends through a height of 50 m to reach a speed of 28 m s⁻¹ after travelling a distance of 75 m along the track. Calculate:

  a its loss of potential energy,

  b its initial kinetic energy,

  c its kinetic energy after the descent,

  d the work done against friction,

  e the average frictional force on it during the descent.

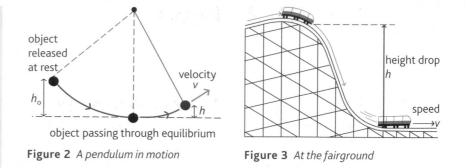

Figure 2 *A pendulum in motion*

Figure 3 *At the fairground*

A pendulum bob

A pendulum bob is displaced from its equilibrium position and then released with the thread taut. The bob passes through the equilibrium position at maximum speed then slows down to reach maximum height on the other side of the equilibrium position. If its initial height above equilibrium position = h_0, then whenever its height above the equilibrium position = h, its speed v at this height is such that

kinetic energy = loss of potential energy from maximum height

$$\tfrac{1}{2}mv^2 = mg(h_0 - h)$$

A fairground vehicle of mass *m* on a downward track

If a fairground vehicle was initially at rest at the top of the track and its speed is v at the bottom of the track, then at the bottom of the track

■ its kinetic energy = $\tfrac{1}{2}mv^2$

■ its loss of potential energy = mgh, where h is the vertical distance between the top and the bottom of the track

■ the work done to overcome friction and air resistance = $mgh - \tfrac{1}{2}mv^2$

Worked example: _____

$g = 9.8\,\mathrm{m\,s^{-2}}$

On a fairground ride, the track descends by a vertical drop of 55 m over a distance of 120 m along the track. A train of mass 2500 kg on the track reaches a speed of 30 m s⁻¹ at the bottom of the descent after being at rest at the top. Calculate (a) the loss of potential energy of the train, (b) its gain of kinetic energy, (c) the average frictional force on the train during the descent.

Solution

a Loss of potential energy = $mg\,\Delta h = 2500 \times 9.8 \times 55 = 1.35 \times 10^6\,\mathrm{J}$

b Its gain of kinetic energy = $\tfrac{1}{2}mv^2 = 0.5 \times 2500 \times 30^2 = 1.13 \times 10^6\,\mathrm{J}$

c Work done to overcome friction = $mg\,\Delta h - \tfrac{1}{2}mv^2 = 1.35 \times 10^6 - 1.13 \times 10^6$

$$= 2.2 \times 10^5\,\mathrm{J}$$

Because the work done to overcome friction = frictional force × distance moved along track,

the frictional force = $\dfrac{\text{work done to overcome friction}}{\text{distance moved}}$

$$= \frac{2.2 \times 10^5}{120} = 1830\,\mathrm{N}$$

10.3 Power

Learning objectives:

■ Which physical quantities are involved in power?

■ How could you develop more power as you go up a flight of stairs?

■ Why is a 100 W light bulb more powerful than a 40 W light bulb when each works at the same mains voltage?

Specification reference: 3.2.1

Power and energy

Energy can be transferred from one object to another by means of

■ **work done** by a force due to one object making the other object move

■ **heat transfer** from a hot object to a cold object. Heat transfer can be due to conduction or convection or radiation.

In addition, electricity, sound waves and **electromagnetic radiation** such as light or radio waves transfer energy.

In any energy transfer process, the more energy transferred per second, the greater the power of the transfer process. For example, in a tall building where there are two elevators of the same total weight, the more powerful elevator is the one that can reach the top floor fastest. In other words, its motor transfers energy from electricity at a faster rate than the motor of the other elevator. The energy transferred per second is the **power** of the motor.

Power is defined as the rate of transfer of energy.

The unit of power is the watt (W), equal to an energy transfer rate of 1 joule per second. Note that 1 kilowatt (kW) = 1000 W, and 1 megawatt (MW) = 10^6 W.

If energy ΔE is transferred steadily in time Δt,

$$\text{power } P = \frac{\Delta E}{\Delta t}$$

Where energy is transferred by a force doing work, the energy transferred is equal to the work done by the force. Therefore, the rate of transfer of energy is equal to the work done per second. In other words, if the force does work ΔW in time Δt,

$$\text{power } P = \frac{\Delta W}{\Delta t}$$

200 N

1 m in 2 s

Figure 1 *A 100 watt worker*

Power measurements

Muscle power

Test your own muscle power by timing how long it takes you to walk up a flight of steps. To calculate your muscle power, you will need to know your weight and the total height gain of the flight of steps.

■ Your gain of potential energy = your weight × total height gain

■ Your muscle power = $\dfrac{\text{energy transferred}}{\text{time taken}} = \dfrac{\text{weight} \times \text{height gain}}{\text{time taken}}$

For example, a person of weight 480 N who climbs a flight of stairs of height 10 m in 12 s has leg muscles of power 400 W (= 480 N × 10 m/12 s). Each leg would therefore have muscles of power 200 W.

Electrical power

The power of a 12 V light bulb can be measured using a joulemeter, as shown in Figure 2. The joulemeter is read before and after the light bulb is switched on. The difference between the readings is the energy supplied to the light bulb. If the light bulb is switched on for a measured time, the power of the light bulb can be calculated from the energy supplied to it / the time taken.

battery

joulemeter

torch bulb

02602 J
ON
OFF

switch

Figure 2 *Using a joulemeter*

constant velocity

total resistive forces

total engine force

💡 **Figure 3** *Engine power*

💡 Engine power

Vehicle engines, marine engines and aircraft engines are all designed to make objects move. The output power of an engine is sometimes called its **motive power**.

When a powered object moves at constant velocity at constant height, the resistive forces (e.g. friction, air resistance, drag) are equal and opposite to the motive force.

The work done by the engine is converted to internal energy of the surroundings by the resistive forces.

For a powered vehicle driven by a constant force F moving at speed v,

the work done per second = force × distance moved per second

Therefore, the output power of the engine $P = Fv$

Worked example:

> An aircraft powered by engines that exert a force of 40 kN is in level flight at a constant velocity of 80 m s⁻¹. Calculate the output power of the engine at this speed.
>
> *Solution*
>
> $F = 40\,kN = 40\,000\,N$
>
> Power = force × velocity = $40\,000 \times 80 = 3.2 \times 10^6\,W$

When a powered object gains speed, the output force exceeds the resistive forces on it.

Consider a vehicle that speeds up on a level road. The output power of its engine is the work done by the engine per second. The work done by the engine increases the kinetic energy of the vehicle and enables the vehicle to overcome the resistive forces acting on it. Because the resistive forces increase the internal energy of the surroundings,

the motive power = energy per second wasted due to the resistive force + the gain of kinetic energy per second

How science works

Juggernaut physics

The maximum weight of a truck with six or more axles on UK roads must not exceed 44 tonnes, which corresponds to a total mass of 44 000 kg. This limit is set so as to prevent damage to roads and bridges. European Union regulations limit the output power of a large truck to a maximum of 6 kW per tonne. Therefore, the maximum output power of a 44 tonne truck is 264 kW. Prove for yourself that a truck with an output power of 264 kW moving at a constant speed of 31 m s⁻¹ (= 70 miles per hour) along a level road experiences a drag force of 8.5 kN.

Summary questions

$g = 9.8\,m\,s^{-2}$

1. A student of weight 450 N climbed 2.5 m up a rope in 18 s. Calculate:

   a the gain of potential energy of the student,

   b the energy transferred per second.

2. Calculate the power of the engines of an aircraft at a speed of 250 m s⁻¹ if the total engine thrust to maintain this speed is 2.0 MN.

3. A rocket of mass 5800 kg accelerates vertically from rest to a speed of 220 m s⁻¹ in 25 s. Calculate:

   a its gain of potential energy,

   b its gain of kinetic energy,

   c the power output of its engine, assuming no energy is wasted due to air resistance.

4. Calculate the height through which a 5 kg mass would need to drop to lose the same energy as a 100 W light bulb would radiate in 1 min.

10.4 Energy and efficiency

Learning objectives:

- What force is mainly responsible for energy 'loss' when mechanical energy is converted from one form to another?

- Into what form of energy is wasted energy almost always converted?

- Can any device ever achieve 100% efficiency?

Specification reference: 3.2.1

Machines at work

A machine that lifts or moves an object applies a force to the object to move it. If the machine exerts a force F on an object to make it move through a distance s in the direction of the force, the work done W on the object by the machine can be calculated using the equation

$$\text{Work done, } W = Fs$$

If the object moves at a constant velocity v due to this force being opposed by an equal and opposite force caused by friction, the object moves a distance $s = vt$ in time t.

Therefore, the output power of the machine

$$P_{OUT} = \frac{\text{work done by the machine}}{\text{time taken}} = \frac{Fvt}{t} = Fv$$

$$\text{Output power, } P_{OUT} = Fv$$

where F = output force of the machine, and v = speed of the object

Examples

1 An electric motor operating a sliding door exerts a force of $125\,\text{N}$ on the door, causing it to open at a constant speed of $0.40\,\text{m s}^{-1}$. The output power of the motor is $125\,\text{N} \times 0.40\,\text{m s}^{-1} = 50\,\text{W}$. The motor must therefore transfer $50\,\text{J}$ every second to the sliding door while the door is being opened.

   Friction in the motor bearings and also electrical resistance of the motor wires means that some of the electrical energy supplied to the motor is wasted. For example, if the motor is supplied with electrical energy at a rate of $150\,\text{J s}^{-1}$ and it transfers $50\,\text{J s}^{-1}$ to the door, the difference of $100\,\text{J s}^{-1}$ is wasted as a result of friction and electrical resistance in the motor.

2 A pulley system is used to raise a load of $80\,\text{N}$ at a speed of $0.15\,\text{m s}^{-1}$ by means of a constant 'effort' of $30\,\text{N}$ applied to the system. Figure 1 shows the arrangement. Note that for every metre the load rises, the effort needs to act over a distance of 3 metres because the load is supported by three sections of rope. The effort must therefore act at a speed of $0.45\,\text{m s}^{-1}$ ($= 3 \times 0.15\,\text{m s}^{-1}$).

   - The work done on the load each second = load × distance raised per second $= 80\,\text{N} \times 0.15\,\text{m s}^{-1} = 12\,\text{J s}^{-1}$

   - The work done by the effort each second = effort × distance moved by the effort each second
     $= 30\,\text{N} \times 0.45\,\text{m s}^{-1} = 13.5\,\text{J s}^{-1}$

The difference of $1.5\,\text{W}$ is the energy wasted each second in the pulley system. This is due to friction in the bearings and also because energy must be supplied to raise the lower pulley.

Figure 1 Using pulleys

Figure 2 *Efficiency*

Summary questions

1 In a test of muscle efficiency, an athlete on an exercise bicycle pedals against a brake force of 30 N at a speed of 15 m s⁻¹.

a Calculate the useful energy supplied per second by the athlete's muscles.

b If the efficiency of the muscles is 25%, calculate the energy per second supplied to the athlete's muscles.

2 A 60 W electric motor raises a weight of 20 N through a height of 2.5 m in 8.0 s. Calculate:

a the electrical energy supplied to the motor,

b the useful energy transferred by the motor,

c the efficiency of the motor.

3 A power station has an overall efficiency of 35% and it produces 200 MW of electrical power. The fuel used in the power station releases 80 MJ per kilogram of fuel burned. Calculate:

a the energy per second supplied by the fuel,

b the mass of fuel burned per day.

4 A vehicle engine has a power output of 6.2 kW and uses fuel which releases 45 MJ per kilogram when burned. At a speed of 30 m s⁻¹ on a level road, the fuel usage of the vehicle is 18 km per kilogram. Calculate:

a the time taken by the vehicle to travel 18 km at 30 m s⁻¹,

b the useful energy supplied by the engine in this time,

c the overall efficiency of the engine.

⚡ Efficiency measures

Useful energy is energy transferred for a purpose. In any machine where friction is present, some of the energy transferred by the machine is wasted. In other words, not all the energy supplied to the machine is transferred for the intended purpose. For example, suppose a 500 W electric winch raises a weight of 150 N by 6.0 m in 10 s.

■ The electrical energy supplied to the winch
= 500 W × 10 s = 5000 J

■ The useful energy transferred by the machine
= potential energy gain of the load = 150 N × 6 m = 900 J

Therefore, in this example, 4100 J of energy is wasted.

$$\text{The efficiency of a machine} = \frac{\text{useful energy transferred by the machine}}{\text{energy supplied to the machine}}$$

$$= \frac{\text{work done by the machine}}{\text{energy supplied to the machine}}$$

Notes:

■ **Efficiency** can be expressed as $\dfrac{\text{the output power of a machine}}{\text{the input power to the machine}}$

■ **Percentage efficiency** = efficiency × 100 %. In the above example, the efficiency of the machine is therefore 0.18 or 18%.

How science works

Improving efficiency

In any process or device where energy is transferred for a purpose, the efficiency of the transfer process or the device is the fraction of the energy supplied that is used for the intended purpose. The rest of the energy supplied is wasted, usually as heat and/or sound. The devices we use could be made more efficient. For example:

■ A filament light bulb that is 12% efficient emits 12 J of energy as light for every 100 J of energy supplied to it by electricity. It therefore wastes 88 J of energy per second as heat.

■ A fluorescent lamp with the same light output that is 80% efficient wastes just 3 J per second as heat. It gives the same light output for only 15 J of electrical energy supplied each second.

Is it possible to stop energy being wasted as heat? If the petrol engine of a car were insulated to stop heat loss, the engine would overheat. Less energy is wasted in an electric motor because it doesn't burn fuel so an electric car would be more efficient than a petrol car. However, the power stations where our electricity is generated are typically less than 40% efficient. This is partly because we need to burn fuel to produce the steam or hot gases used to drive turbines, which turn the electricity generators. If the turbines were not kept cool, they would stop working because the pressure inside would build up and prevent the steam or hot gas from entering. Stopping the heat transfer to the cooling system would stop the generators working.

10.5 Renewable energy

Learning objectives:

- How much power can we generate from different renewable energy resources?

- Could we meet all our energy needs from renewable energy resources?

- Can we meet our demand for energy and cut carbon emissions at the same time?

Specification reference: 3.2.1

Figure 1 *A wind farm*

Renewable energy sources will contribute increasingly to the world's energy supplies in the future. Most of the energy we use at present is obtained from fossil fuels. But scientists think that the use of fossil fuels is causing increased global warming, due to the increasing amount of carbon dioxide in the atmosphere. Increased global warming could have disastrous consequences (e.g. rising sea levels, changing weather patterns, etc.). To cut carbon emissions, many countries are now planning to build new nuclear power stations and to develop more renewable energy resources. The UK's demand for power is about 500 000 MW. Our nuclear power stations currently provide about a quarter of our electricity, which is about 7% of our total energy supply. In terms of physics, let's consider how much energy could be supplied from typical renewable energy resources.

Wind power

A wind turbine is an electricity generator on a tall tower, driven by large blades pushed round by the force of the wind. A typical modern wind turbine on a suitable site can generate about 2 MW of electrical power. Let's consider how this estimate is obtained.

- The kinetic energy of a mass m of wind moving at speed $v = \frac{1}{2}mv^2$

- Therefore, the kinetic energy per unit volume of air from the wind at speed $v = \frac{1}{2}\rho v^2$, where ρ is the density (i.e. mass per unit volume) of air.

- Suppose the blades of a wind turbine sweep out an area A when they rotate. For wind at speed v, a cylinder of air of area A and length v passes every second through the area swept out by the blades. So the volume of air passing per second $= vA$

Therefore, the kinetic energy per second of the wind passing through a wind turbine $= \frac{1}{2}\rho v^2 vA = \frac{1}{2}\rho v^3 A$

For a wind turbine with blades of length 20 m, $A = \pi(20)^2 = 1300\,\text{m}^2$

The density of air, $\rho = 1.2\,\text{kg m}^{-3}$

The power of the wind at $v = 15\,\text{m s}^{-1}$

$$= \frac{1}{2} \times 1.2 \times 15^3 \times 1300$$

$$= 2.6 \times 10^6\,\text{W} = 2.6\,\text{MW}$$

The calculation shows that the maximum power output of a large wind turbine at a windy site could not be more than about 2 MW. To generate the same power as a 5000 MW power station, about 2500 wind turbines would need to be constructed and connected to the electricity network. Britain has many coastal sites where wind turbines could be located. Thousands of wind turbines would be needed to make a significant contribution to UK energy needs.

Water power

Hydroelectricity and tidal power stations both make use of the potential energy released by water when it runs to a lower level.

■ A tidal power station covering an area of 100 km² could trap a depth of 6 m of sea water twice per day. This would mean releasing a volume of 6×10^8 m² of sea water over a few hours. The mass of such a volume is about 6×10^{11} kg and if its centre of mass drops through an average height of about 1 m, the potential energy released would be about 6×10^{12} J. Prove for yourself this would give an energy transfer rate of more than 250 MW if released over about 6 hours. Several tidal power stations would make a significant contribution to UK energy needs.

Figure 2 *A tidal power station*

■ A hydroelectric power station releases less water per second than a tidal power station but the water drops through a much greater height. However, even a large height drop of 500 m with rainfall over an area of 1000 km² at a depth of about 10 mm per day would transfer no more than about 500 MW. Lots of hydroelectric power stations would be needed to make a big contribution to UK energy needs.

Solar power

A solar panel of area 1 m² in space would absorb solar energy at a rate of about 1400 J s⁻¹ if it absorbed all the incident solar energy. At the Earth's surface, the incident energy would be less, because some would be absorbed in the atmosphere. In addition, some of the Sun's energy would be reflected by the panel itself.

■ A solar heating panel can heat water running though it to 70°C on a hot sunny day. In Britain in summer, a typical solar heating panel can absorb up to 500 J s⁻¹ of solar energy.

■ A solar cell panel produces electricity directly. A potential difference is produced across each solar cell when light is incident on the cell. A large array of solar cells and plenty of sunshine is necessary to produce useful amounts of power.

To make a significant contribution to UK energy needs, millions of homes and buildings would need to be fitted with solar panels.

Figure 3 *(a) A solar heating panel, (b) A solar cell panel*

Renewable energy overview

The UK demand for electricity uses about 30% of our total energy supply. If nuclear energy continues to meet a quarter of this electricity demand, could renewable energy meet the rest of the demand – approximately 100 000 MW!

10 million buildings each with a 0.5 kW solar panel could produce 5000 MW.

100 off-shore wind farms, each producing 100 MW, could produce 10 000 MW.

100 tidal and hydroelectric power stations could produce 25 000 MW.

Other renewable resources such as ground source heat (geothermal power) could contribute in some areas. But the simplified analysis above fails to take account of the unreliable nature of renewables. Supply and demand could be smoothed out by using renewable energy to pump water into upland reservoirs ('pumped storage'). Hundreds more reservoirs would be needed for this purpose.

Better insulation in homes and buildings and more efficient machines would help to reduce demand and so help to cut carbon emissions. Carbon capture of carbon emissions from fossil-fuel power stations could cut overall carbon emissions significantly. Road transport would need to switch from fossil fuels if overall carbon emissions are to be cut even more and the UK is to avoid overdependence on imported fuel. Biofuels for transport could contribute and more electricity would be needed if more people use electric vehicles.

Summary questions

1 A solar cell panel of area 1 m² can produce 200 W of electrical power on a sunny day. Calculate the area of panels that would be needed to produce 2000 MW of electrical power.

2 The maximum power that can be obtained from a wind turbine is proportional to the cube of the wind speed. When the wind speed is 10 m s⁻¹, the power output of a certain wind turbine is 1.2 MW. Calculate the power output of this wind turbine when the wind speed is 15 m s⁻¹.

3 A hydroelectric power station produces electrical power at an overall efficiency of 25%. The power station is driven by water that has descended from an upland reservoir 650 m above the power station.

Calculate the volume of water passing through the power station per second when it produces 200 MW of electrical power.

The density of water = 1000 kg m⁻³

4 At a tidal power station, water is trapped over an area of 200 km² when the tide is 3.0 m above the power station turbines. The trapped water is released gradually over a period of 6 hours. Calculate:

a the mass of trapped water,

b the average loss of potential energy per second of this trapped water when it is released over a period of 6 hours.

The density of sea water = 1050 kg m⁻³

1   (a)   An electric car is fitted with a battery, which is used to drive an electric motor that drives the car. The battery has a maximum power output of 12 kW, which gives a maximum driving force of 600 N.

         Calculate (i) the top speed of the car, (ii) the car's maximum range, if the battery lasts for 90 minutes at maximum power output without being recharged.   *(4 marks)*

    (b)   A hybrid vehicle has a battery-driven electric motor and a petrol engine, which takes over from the electric motor when the vehicle has reached a certain speed. Above this speed, the petrol engine also recharges the battery. The vehicle has an overall fuel efficiency of 18 km per litre, compared with 10 km per litre for an equivalent petrol-only car, which has a carbon emission of 180 grams per km. Discuss the benefits of the use of such hybrid cars instead of petrol-only cars, in terms of carbon emissions, given the average annual distance travelled by a driver in the UK is about 20 000 km. The average annual carbon emission per UK household, including driving, is about 10 000 kg.   *(5 marks)*

2   **Figure 1** shows apparatus that can be used to investigate energy changes.

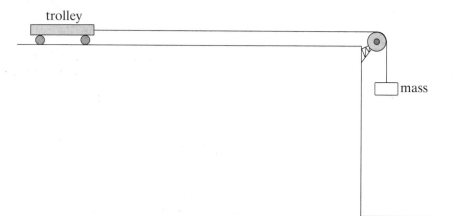

    Figure 1

The trolley and the mass are joined by an inextensible string. In an experiment to investigate energy changes, the trolley is initially held at rest, and is then released so that the mass falls vertically to the ground.

    (a)   (i)   State the energy changes of the falling mass.

         (ii)   Describe the energy changes that take place in this system.   *(4 marks)*

    (b)   State what measurements would need to be made to investigate the conservation of energy.   *(2 marks)*

    (c)   Describe how the measurements in part (b) would be used to investigate the conservation of energy.   *(4 marks)*

                                                     AQA, 2006

3   A small hydroelectric power station uses water which falls through a height of 4.8 m

    (a)   Calculate the change in potential energy of a 1.0 kg mass of water falling through a vertical height of 4.8 m.   *(2 marks)*

    (b)   Calculate the maximum power available from the water passing through this power station when water flows through it at a rate of 6.7×10^7 kg per hour.   *(3 marks)*

    (c)   State **two** factors that affect the usefulness of hydroelectric power stations for electricity production.   *(2 marks)*

                                                     AQA, 2002

4 **Figure 2** represents the motion of a car of mass 1.4×10^3 kg, travelling in a straight line.

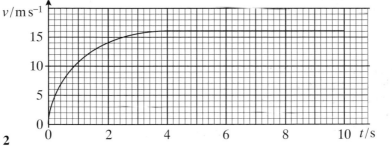

Figure 2

(a) Describe, without calculation, how the *resultant* force acting on the car varies over this 10 second interval. *(2 marks)*

(b) Calculate the maximum kinetic energy of the car. *(2 marks)*

(c) At some time later, when the car is travelling at a steady speed of $30 \, \text{m s}^{-1}$, the useful power developed by the engine is 20 kW. Calculate the driving force required to maintain this speed. *(2 marks)*

AQA, 2002

5 A skydiver of mass 70 kg, jumps from a stationary balloon and reaches a speed of $45 \, \text{m s}^{-1}$ after falling a distance of 150 m.

(a) Calculate the skydiver's:
  (i) loss of gravitational potential energy,
  (ii) gain in kinetic energy. *(4 marks)*

(b) The difference between the loss of gravitational potential energy and the gain in kinetic energy is equal to the work done against air resistance. Use this fact to calculate:
  (i) the work done against air resistance,
  (ii) the average force due to air resistance acting on the skydiver. *(3 marks)*

AQA, 2004

6 **Figure 3** shows a car traveling at constant velocity along a horizontal road.

Figure 3

(a) The car has an effective power output of 18 kW and is travelling at a constant velocity of $10 \, \text{m s}^{-1}$. Show that the total resistive force acting is 1800 N. *(1 mark)*

(b) The total resistive force consists of two components. One of these is a constant frictional force of 250 N and the other is the force of air resistance, which is proportional to the square of the car's speed. Calculate:
  (i) the force of air resistance when the car is travelling at $10 \, \text{m s}^{-1}$,
  (ii) the force of air resistance when the car is travelling at $20 \, \text{m s}^{-1}$,
  (iii) the effective output power of the car required to maintain a constant speed of $20 \, \text{m s}^{-1}$ on a horizontal road. *(4 marks)*

AQA, 2001

7 (a) A ball bearing is released when near the top of a tall cylinder containing oil. Discuss the energy changes which take place when the ball bearing (i) accelerates from rest, (ii) travels at constant velocity. *(6 marks)*

(b) A pump-operated hydraulic jack is used to raise a large object of mass 470 kg. The jack is used by pushing down on the handle of a lever connected to the pump. During each stroke, a force of 50 N is applied downward on the handle which is moved through a distance of 0.42 m. 52 strokes of the handle are needed to raise the object through a vertical height of 0.58 m. Calculate the efficiency of this process. *(5 marks)*

11 Materials

11.1 Density

Learning objectives:

- How do we define density?
- What is the unit of density?
- How do we measure the density of an object?

Specification reference: 3.2.2

How science works

More about units

mass: 1 kg = 1000 grams

length: 1 m = 100 cm

                  = 1000 mm

volume: $1 m^3 = 10^6 cm^3$

density: $1000 kg m^{-3} = \dfrac{10^6 g}{10^6 cm^3}$

                  $= 1 g cm^{-3}$

AQA Examiner's tip

Unit errors are commonplace in density calculations. Avoid such errors by writing the unit and the numerical value of each quantity in your working.

Table 1 *Density*

substance	density / kg m^{-3}
air	1.2
aluminium	2700
copper	8900
gold	19300
hydrogen	0.083
iron	7900
lead	11300
oxygen	1.3
silver	10500
water	1000

Density and its measurement

Lead is much more dense than aluminium. Sea water is more dense than tap water. To find how much more dense one substance is compared with another, we need to measure the mass of equal volumes of the two substances. The substance with the greater mass in the same volume is more dense. For example, a lead sphere of volume $1 cm^3$ has a mass of 11.3 g whereas an aluminium sphere of the same volume has a mass of 2.7 g.

The density of a substance is defined as its mass per unit volume.

For a certain amount of a substance of mass m and volume V, its density ρ (pronounced 'rho'), may be calculated using the equation

$$\text{density } \rho = \frac{m}{V}$$

The unit of density is the kilogram per cubic metre (kg m^{-3}).

Rearranging the above equation gives $m = \rho V$ or $V = \dfrac{m}{\rho}$

Table 1 shows the density of some common substances in kg m^{-3}. You can see that gases are much less dense than solids or liquids. This is because the average separation between the molecules in a gas is much greater than in a liquid or solid.

Worked example:

Using the data above, calculate:

a the mass, in kilograms, of a piece of aluminium of volume $3.6 \times 10^{-5} m^3$,

b the volume, in m^3, of a mass of 0.50 kg of iron.

Solution

a $\rho = 2700$ kg m^{-3}; mass $m = \rho V = 2700$ kg m$^{-3} \times 3.6 \times 10^{-5} m^3 = 9.7 \times 10^{-2}$ kg

b $\rho = 7900$ kg m^{-3}; volume $= \dfrac{m}{\rho} = \dfrac{0.50 \text{ kg}}{7900 \text{ kg m}^{-3}} = 6.3 \times 10^{-5} m^3$

Density measurements

An unknown substance can often be identified if its density is measured and compared with the density of known substances. The following procedures could be used to measure the density of a substance.

1 A regular solid

- Measure its mass using a top pan balance.
- Measure its dimensions using vernier callipers or a micrometer and calculate its volume using the appropriate formula (e.g. for a sphere of radius r, volume $= \frac{4}{3}\pi r^3$; see Figure 1 for other volume formulae). Calculate the density from mass/volume.

2 A liquid

■ Measure the mass of an empty measuring cylinder. Pour some of the liquid into the measuring cylinder and measure the volume of the liquid directly. Use as much liquid as possible to reduce the percentage error in your measurement.

■ Measure the mass of the cylinder and liquid to enable the mass of the liquid to be calculated. Calculate the density from mass/volume.

3 An irregular solid

■ Measure the mass of the object.

■ Immerse the object on a thread in liquid in a measuring cylinder, observe the increase in the liquid level, this is the volume of the object.

■ Calculate the density of the object from its mass/volume.

Density of alloys

An alloy is a solid mixture of two or more metals. For example, brass is an alloy of copper and zinc that has good resistance to corrosion and wear.

For an alloy, of volume V, that consists of two metals A and B,

■ if the volume of metal A $= V_A$, the mass of metal A $= \rho_A V_A$, where ρ_A is the density of metal A,

■ if the volume of metal B $= V_B$, the mass of metal B $= \rho_B V_B$, where ρ_B is the density of metal B.

Therefore, the mass of the alloy, $m = \rho_A V_A + \rho_B V_B$

Hence the density of the alloy $\rho = \dfrac{m}{V} = \dfrac{\rho_A V_A + \rho_B V_B}{V} = \dfrac{\rho_A V_A}{V} + \dfrac{\rho_B V_B}{V}$

Worked example:

A brass object consists of $3.3 \times 10^{-5}\,m^3$ of copper and $1.7 \times 10^{-5}\,m^3$ of zinc. Calculate the mass and the density of this object. The density of copper $= 8900\,kg\,m^{-3}$. The density of zinc $= 7100\,kg\,m^{-3}$.

Solution

Mass of copper   = density of copper × volume of copper

               = $8900 \times 3.3 \times 10^{-5}\,m^3 = 0.294\,kg$

Mass of zinc   = density of zinc × volume of zinc

               = $7100 \times 1.7 \times 10^{-5}\,m^3 = 0.121\,kg$

Total mass, $m = 0.294 + 0.121 = 0.415\,kg$

Total volume, $V = 5.0 \times 10^{-5}\,m^3$

Density of alloy $\rho = \dfrac{m}{V} = \dfrac{0.415\,kg}{5.0 \times 10^{-5}\,m^3} = 8300\,kg\,m^{-3}$

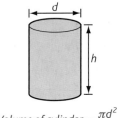

a *Volume of cuboid* $= a \times b \times c$

b *Volume of cylinder* $= \dfrac{\pi d^2}{4} \times h$

Figure 1 *Volume formulae*

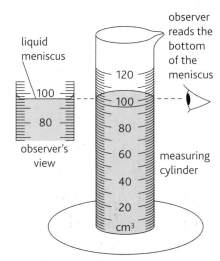

Figure 2 *Using a measuring cylinder*

AQA Examiner's tip

Make sure that you are familiar with the formulae for volumes of spheres and cylinders.

Summary questions

1 A rectangular brick of dimensions $5.0\,cm \times 8.0\,cm \times 20.0\,cm$ has a mass of $2.5\,kg$. Calculate **a** its volume, **b** its density.

2 An empty paint tin of diameter $0.150\,m$ and of height $0.120\,m$ has a mass of $0.22\,kg$. It is filled with paint to within $7\,mm$ of the top. Its total mass is then $6.50\,kg$. Calculate **a** the mass, **b** the volume, **c** the density of the paint in the tin.

3 A solid steel cylinder has a diameter of $12\,mm$ and a length of $85\,mm$. Calculate **a** its volume in m^3, **b** its mass in kg. The density of steel $= 7800\,kg\,m^{-3}$.

4 An alloy tube of volume $1.8 \times 10^{-4}\,m^3$ consists of 60% aluminium and 40% magnesium by volume. Calculate **a** the mass of **i** aluminium, **ii** magnesium in the tube, **b** the density of the alloy. The density of aluminium $= 2700\,kg\,m^{-3}$. The density of magnesium $= 1700\,kg\,m^{-3}$.

11.2 Springs

Learning objectives:

- Is there any limit to the linear graph of force against extension for a spring?

- What is the meaning of spring constant, and in what unit is it measured?

- If the extension of a spring is doubled, how much more energy does it store?

Specification reference: 3.2.2

🔆 **Figure 1** *Testing the extension of a spring*

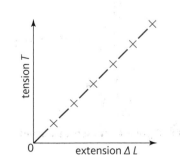

Figure 2 *Hooke's law*

⚠ Hooke's law

A stretched spring exerts a pull on the object holding each end of the spring. This pull, referred to as the **tension** in the spring, is equal and opposite to the force needed to stretch the spring. The more a spring is stretched, the greater the tension in it. Figure 1 shows a stretched spring supporting a weight at rest. This arrangement may be used to investigate how the tension in a spring depends on its extension from its unstretched length. The measurements may be plotted on a graph of tension against extension, as shown in Figure 2. The graph shows that the force needed to stretch a spring is proportional to the extension of the spring. This is known as **Hooke's law**, after its discoverer, Robert Hooke, a seventeenth century scientist.

Hooke's law states that the force needed to stretch a spring is directly proportional to the extension of the spring from its natural length.

Hooke's law may be written as

$$\text{Force } F = k\Delta L$$

where k is the spring constant (sometimes referred to as the stiffness constant) and ΔL is the extension from its natural length L.

- The greater the value of k, the stiffer the spring is. The unit of k is N m^{-1}.

- The graph of F against ΔL is a straight line of gradient k through the origin.

- If a spring is stretched beyond its **elastic limit**, it does not regain its initial length when the force applied to it is removed.

- AS/A level maths students may meet Hooke's law in the form $F = \lambda \Delta L/L$, where L is the unstretched length of the spring and λ $(= kL)$ is the spring modulus. Note that λ is not in the specification for AS/A level physics.

Worked example: _____

A vertical steel spring fixed at its upper end has an unstretched length of 300 mm. Its length is increased to 385 mm when a 5.0 N weight attached to the lower end is at rest. Calculate:

a the spring constant,

b the length of the spring when it supports an 8.0 N weight at rest.

Solution

a Use $F = k\Delta L$ with $F = 5.0$ N and $\Delta L = 385 - 300$ mm = 85 mm = 0.085 m.

Therefore $k = \dfrac{F}{\Delta L} = \dfrac{5.0\,\text{N}}{0.085\,\text{m}} = 59\,\text{N m}^{-1}$.

b Use $F = k\Delta L$ with $F = 8.0$ N and $k = 59\,\text{N m}^{-1}$ to calculate ΔL.

$$\Delta L = \frac{F}{k} = \frac{8.0\,\text{N}}{59\,\text{N m}^{-1}} = 0.136\,\text{m}$$

Therefore the length of the spring $= 0.300\,\text{m} + 0.136\,\text{m} = 0.436\,\text{m}$

Spring combinations

Springs in parallel

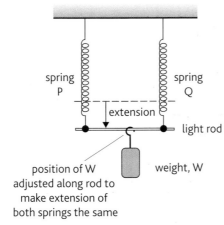

Figure 3 *Two springs in parallel*

Figure 3 shows a weight W supported by means of two springs P and Q in parallel with each other. The extension, ΔL, of each spring is the same. Therefore

- the force needed to stretch P, $F_P = k_P \Delta L$
- the force needed to stretch Q, $F_Q = k_Q \Delta L$

where k_P and k_Q are the spring constants of P and Q, respectively.

Since the weight W is supported by both springs, $W = F_P + F_Q = k_P \Delta L + k_Q \Delta L = k \Delta L$

where the effective spring constant, $k = k_P + k_Q$

Springs in series

Figure 4 shows a weight W supported by means of two springs joined end-on in 'series' with each other. The tension in each spring is the same and is equal to the weight W.

Therefore

- the extension of spring P, $\Delta L_P = \dfrac{W}{k_P}$

- the extension of spring Q, $\Delta L_Q = \dfrac{W}{k_Q}$

where k_P and k_Q are the spring constants of P and Q, respectively.

Therefore the total extension, $\Delta L = \Delta L_P + \Delta L_Q = \dfrac{W}{k_P} + \dfrac{W}{k_Q} = \dfrac{W}{k}$

where k, the effective spring constant, is given by the equation

$$\frac{1}{k} = \frac{1}{k_P} + \frac{1}{k_Q}$$

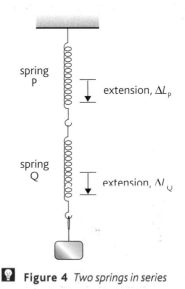

Figure 4 *Two springs in series*

■ The energy stored in a stretched spring

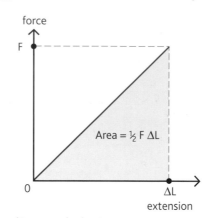

Figure 4 *Energy stored in a stretched spring*

Elastic potential energy is stored in a stretched spring. If the spring is suddenly released, the elastic energy stored in it is suddenly converted to kinetic energy of the spring. As explained in 10.1, the work done to stretch a spring by extension ΔL from its unstretched length $= \frac{1}{2} F \Delta L$, where F is the force needed to stretch the spring to extension ΔL. The work done on the spring is stored as elastic potential energy. Therefore, the elastic potential energy E_p in the spring $= \frac{1}{2} F \Delta L$. Also, since $F = k \Delta L$ where k is the spring constant, then $E_p = \frac{1}{2} k \Delta L^2$.

Elastic potential energy stored in a stretched spring, $E_p = \frac{1}{2} F \Delta L = \frac{1}{2} k \Delta L^2$

■ Summary questions

$g = 9.8 \, \text{m s}^{-2}$

1 A steel spring has a spring constant of $25 \, \text{N m}^{-1}$. Calculate:

　a the extension of the spring when the tension in it is equal to 10 N,

　b the tension in the spring when it is extended by 0.50 m from its unstretched length.

2 Two identical steel springs of length 250 mm are suspended vertically side-by-side from a fixed point. A 40 N weight is attached to the ends of the two springs. The length of each spring is then 350 mm. Calculate:

　a the tension in each spring,

　b the extension of each spring,

　c the spring constant of each spring.

3 Repeat 2a and b for the two springs in 'series' and vertical.

4 An object of mass 0.150 kg is attached to the lower end of a vertical spring of unstretched length 300 mm, which is fixed at its upper end. With the object at rest, the length of the spring becomes 420 mm as a result. Calculate:

　a the spring constant,

　b the energy stored in the spring,

　c the weight that needs to be added to extend the spring to 600 mm.

11.3 Deformation of solids

Learning objectives:

- How is stress related to force, and strain to extension?

- What is meant by tensile?

- Why do we bother with stress and strain, when force and extension are more easily measured?

Specification reference: 3.2.2

extension / mm

Figure 1 *Typical curves*

Force and solid materials

Look around at different materials and think about the effect of force on each material. To stretch or twist or compress the material, a pair of forces is needed. For example, stretching a rubber band requires the rubber band to be pulled by a force at either end. Some materials, such as rubber, bend or stretch easily. The **elasticity** of a solid material is its ability to regain its shape after it has been deformed or distorted, and the forces that deformed it have been released. Deformation that stretches an object is **tensile**, whereas deformation that compresses an object is **compressive**.

The arrangement shown in Topic 11.2 Figure 1 shows how to test different materials to see how easily they stretch. In each case, the material is held at its upper end and loaded by hanging weights at its lower end. A set square or pointer attached to the bottom of the weights may be used to measure the extension of the material, as the weight of the load is increased in steps then decreased to zero. The extension of the strip of material at each step is its increase of length from its unloaded length. The tension in the material is equal to the weight. The measurements may be plotted as a tension–extension graph, as shown in Figure 1.

- A steel spring gives a straight line, in accordance with Hooke's law (see Topic 11.2).

- A rubber band at first extends easily when it is stretched. However, it becomes fully stretched and very difficult to stretch further when it has been lengthened considerably.

- A polythene strip 'gives' and stretches easily after its initial stiffness is overcome. However, after 'giving' easily, it extends little and becomes difficult to stretch.

Stress and strain

The extension of a wire under tension may be measured using Searle's apparatus, as shown in Figure 2 on the next page (or similar apparatus with a vernier scale). A micrometer attached to the control wire is adjusted so the spirit level between the control and test wire is horizontal. When the test wire is loaded, it extends slightly, causing the spirit level to drop on one side. The micrometer is then readjusted to make the spirit level horizontal again. The change of the micrometer reading is therefore equal to the extension. The extension may be measured for different values of tension by increasing the test weight in steps.

For a wire of length L and area of cross-section A under tension,

- the **tensile stress** in the wire, $\sigma = T/A$, where T is the tension. The unit of stress is the **pascal** (Pa) equal to $1\,\mathrm{N\,m^{-2}}$.

- the **tensile strain** in the wire, $\varepsilon = \Delta L / L$, where ΔL is the extension (increase in length) of the wire. Strain is a ratio and therefore has no unit.

■ **Hint**

Some materials can be strong and brittle, whilst others can be plastic and tough. Toughness is a measure of the energy needed to break a material.

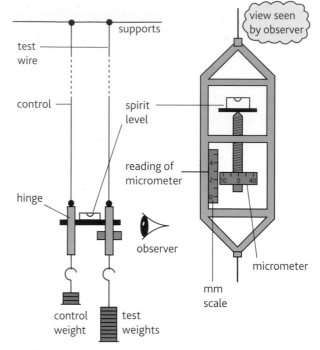

Figure 2 *Searle's apparatus*

AQA **Examiner's tip**

Don't forget the italicised words in the definitions below:

Stress is tension per unit *cross-sectional area*

Strain is extension per *unit length*

Figure 3 shows how the stress in a wire varies with strain. Note the stress is on the *y*-axis and the strain on the *x*-axis.

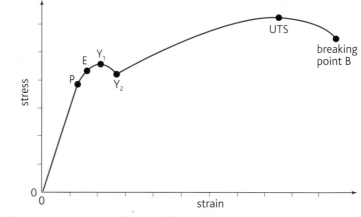

💡 **Figure 3** *Stress v strain for a metal wire*

■ From 0 to the **limit of proportionality** P, the stress is proportional to the strain.

The value of stress/strain is a constant, known as the **Young modulus** of the material.

$$\text{Young modulus } E = \frac{\text{stress}, \sigma}{\text{strain}, \varepsilon} = \frac{T}{A} \div \frac{\Delta L}{L} = \frac{TL}{A\,\Delta L}$$

Note that, for a wire of uniform diameter, *d*, the area of cross-section

$$A = \frac{\pi d^2}{4}$$

■ Beyond P, the line curves and continues beyond the **elastic limit** E to the **yield point** Y_1 which is where the wire weakens temporarily. The **elastic limit** is the point beyond which the wire is permanently stretched and suffers **plastic deformation**.

Beyond Y_2, a small increase in the stress causes a large increase in strain as the material of the wire undergoes plastic flow. Beyond maximum stress, the **ultimate tensile stress** (UTS), the wire loses its strength, extends and becomes narrower at its weakest point. Increase of stress occurs due to the reduced area of cross-section at this point until the wire breaks at point B. The ultimate tensile stress is sometimes called the **breaking stress**.

Worked example:

A crane fitted with a steel cable of uniform diameter 2.3 mm and length 28 m is used to lift an iron girder of weight 3200 N off the ground. Calculate the extension of the cable when it supports the girder at rest.

The Young modulus for steel = 2.1×10^{11} Pa

Solution

Tension $T = 3200$ N, $L = 28$ m

Area of cross-section of wire = $\dfrac{\pi (2.3 \times 10^{-3})^2}{4} = 4.15 \times 10^{-6}$ m²

To find the extension, rearranging the Young modulus equation $E = \dfrac{TL}{A\,\Delta L}$ gives:

$$\Delta L = \frac{TL}{AE} = \frac{3200 \times 28}{4.15 \times 10^{-6} \times 2.1 \times 10^{11}} = 0.103 \text{ m}$$

Stress–strain curves for different materials

The **stiffness** of different materials can be compared using the **gradient** of the stress–strain line which is equal to the Young modulus of the material. Thus steel is stiffer than copper.

The **strength** of a material is its ultimate tensile stress (UTS) which is its maximum stress. Steel is stronger than copper because its maximum stress is greater.

A **brittle** material snaps without any noticeable yield. For example, glass breaks without any 'give'.

A **ductile** material can be drawn into a wire. Copper is more ductile than steel.

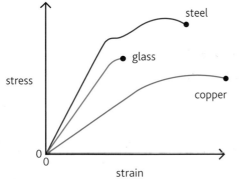

Figure 4 *Stress–strain curves*

Summary questions

1. Calculate the stress in a wire of diameter 0.25 mm when the tension in the wire is 50 N.

2. A metal wire of diameter 0.23 mm and of unstretched length 1.405 m was suspended vertically from a fixed point. When a 40 N weight was suspended from the lower end of the wire, the wire stretched by an extension of 10.5 mm. Calculate the Young modulus of the wire material.

3. A vertical steel wire of length 2.5 m and diameter 0.35 mm supports a weight of 90 N. Calculate:

   a the stress in the wire,

   b the extension of the wire.
   The Young modulus of steel = 2.1×10^{11} Pa.

4. Compare the stress–strain curves in Figure 5. Use the curves to decide:

   a which material is i stiffest, ii strongest?

   b which material is i brittle, ii ductile?

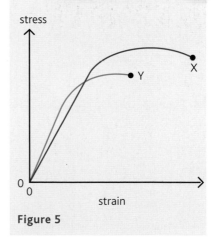

Figure 5

11.4 More about stress and strain

Learning objectives:

Learning objectives:

- If a metal wire is stretched to a point below its elastic limit and then unloaded, does it return to its original length?

- What happens when a metal wire is stretched beyond its elastic limit and then unloaded?

- How does the deformation of other materials such as rubber and polythene compare with a metal wire?

Specification reference: 3.2.2

Loading and unloading of different materials

How does the strength of a material change as a result of being stretched? The arrangement shown in Topic 11.2 Figure 2 may be used to investigate this question. The tension in a strip of material is increased by increasing the weight it supports in steps. At each step, the extension of the material is measured. Typical results for different materials are shown in Figure 1. For each material, the loading curve and the subsequent unloading curve are shown.

- For a metal wire, its unloading curve and the loading curve are the same straight line. Provided its elastic limit is not exceeded, the wire, when unloaded, returns to the same length as it had before it was loaded. If the wire is stretched beyond its elastic limit, the unloading line is parallel to the loading line. In this case, when it is completely unstretched, the wire is slightly longer so it has a **permanent extension**.

- For a rubber band, the change of length during unloading for a given change in tension is greater than during loading. The rubber band returns to the same unstretched length, but the unloading curve is below the loading curve, except at zero extension and maximum extension. The rubber band remains elastic as it regains its initial length, but it has a **low limit of proportionality**.

a *Metal wire*

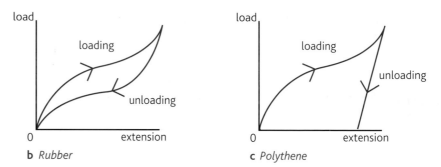

b *Rubber* **c** *Polythene*

Figure 1 *Loading and unloading curves*

- For a polythene strip, the extension during unloading is also greater than during loading. However, the strip does not return to the same initial length when it is completely unloaded. The polythene strip has a low limit of proportionality and suffers **plastic deformation**.

How science works

Cross-links

Polythene is a polymer, which means each molecule is a long chain of atoms. Before being stretched, the molecules are tangled together. Weak bonds or 'cross-links' form between the molecules. When under tension, polythene easily stretches as the weak crosslinks break. New weak cross-links form in the stretched state and when the tension is removed, the polythene strip remains stretched.

Strain energy

As explained in Topic 11.2, the area under the line of a force–extension graph is equal to the work done to stretch the wire. The work done to deform an object is referred to as **strain energy**. Consider the energy changes for each of the three materials above when each material is loaded then unloaded.

1 Metal wire (or spring)

Provided the limit of proportionality is not exceeded, to stretch a wire to an extension ΔL, the work done $= \frac{1}{2}T\Delta L$, where T is the tension in the wire at this extension. Because the elastic limit is not reached, the work done is stored as elastic energy in the wire. Therefore,

the elastic energy stored in a stretched wire $= \frac{1}{2}T\Delta L$

Because the graph of tension against extension is the same for unloading as for loading, all the energy stored in the wire can be recovered when the wire is unloaded.

Worked example:

A steel wire of uniform diameter 0.35 mm and of length 810 mm is stretched to an extension of 2.5 mm. Calculate (a) the tension in the wire, (b) the elastic energy stored in the wire.

The Young modulus for steel = 2.1×10^{11} Pa

Solution

a Extension, $\Delta L = 2.5$ mm $= 2.5 \times 10^{-3}$ m

Area of cross-section of wire $= \dfrac{\pi (0.35 \times 10^{-3})^2}{4} = 9.6 \times 10^{-8}$ m^2

To find the tension, rearranging the Young modulus equation

$E = \dfrac{TL}{A\,\Delta L}$ gives

$T = \dfrac{EA\,\Delta L}{L} = \dfrac{2.1 \times 10^{11} \times 9.6 \times 10^{-8} \times 2.5 \times 10^{-3}}{0.810} = 62$ N

b Elastic energy stored in the wire $= \frac{1}{2}T\Delta L = 0.5 \times 62 \times 2.5 \times 10^{-3} = 7.8 \times 10^{-2}$ J

2 Rubber band

The work done to stretch the rubber band is represented in Figure 1 by the area under the loading curve. The work done by the rubber band, when it is unloaded, is represented by the area under the unloading curve. The area between the loading curve and the unloading curve therefore represents the difference between energy stored in the rubber band when it is stretched, and useful energy recovered from it when it is unstretched. The difference occurs because some of the energy stored in the rubber band becomes internal energy of the molecules when the rubber band unstretches. Figure 2 shows how the area between the loading and unloading curves can be used to determine the internal energy retained, when the rubber band is stretched then released.

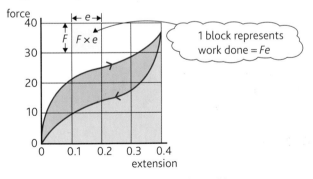

Figure 2 *Energy changes when loading and unloading rubber*

3 Polythene

As it does not regain its initial length, the area between the loading and unloading curve represents work done to deform the material permanently, as well as internal energy retained by the polythene when it unstretches.

Rubber is also a polymer but its molecules are curled up and tangled together when it is in an unstretched state. When placed under tension, its molecules are straightened out. When the tension is removed, its molecules curl up again and it regains its initial length.

How science works

Check your tyre pressure

When a car is in motion, the parts of the tyres that make contact with the road are deformed. They then regain shape as they lose contact with the road. This repeated deformation causes the tyre to become warm. The greater the amount of deformation, the more energy is wasted, so the fuel consumption of the vehicle is greater. Under-inflated tyres therefore waste fuel. Over-inflated tyres are unsafe as they have less contact with the road so the brakes are less effective. See Topic 9.5.

Summary questions

The Young modulus for
steel = 2.1×10^{11} Pa
copper = 1.3×10^{11} Pa

1 A vertical steel cable of diameter 24 mm and of length 18 m supports a weight of 1500 N attached to its lower end. Calculate **a** the tensile stress in the cable, **b** the extension of the cable, **c** the elastic energy stored in the cable, assuming its elastic limit has not been reached.

2 A vertical steel wire of diameter 0.28 mm and of length 2.0 m is fixed at its upper end, and has a weight of 15 N suspended from its lower end. Calculate **a** the extension of the wire, **b** the elastic energy stored in the wire.

3 A steel bar of length 40 mm and cross-sectional area 4.5 $\times 10^{-4}$ m^2 is placed in a vice and compressed by 0.20 mm when the vice is tightened. Calculate **a** the compressive force exerted on the bar, **b** the work done to compress it.

4 Figure 2 shows a force against extension curve for rubber band. Use the graph to determine **a** the work done to stretch the rubber band to an extension of 0.40 m, **b** the internal energy retained by the rubber band when it unstretches.

1   (a) Define the *density* of a material.   *(1 mark)*

     (b) Brass, an alloy of copper and zinc, consists of 70% **by volume** of copper and 30%
          by volume of zinc.

          density of copper = $8.9 \times 10^3\,\mathrm{kg\,m^{-3}}$
          density of zinc = $7.1 \times 10^3\,\mathrm{kg\,m^{-3}}$

          (i)   Determine the mass of copper and the mass of zinc required to make a rod
                of brass of volume $0.80 \times 10^{-3}\,\mathrm{m^3}$.

          (ii) Calculate the density of brass.   *(5 marks)*

                                                                                                 AQA, 2004

2   **Figure 1** shows a lorry of mass $1.2 \times 10^3\,\mathrm{kg}$ parked on a platform used to weigh
     vehicles. The lorry compresses the spring that supports the platform by 0.030 m.

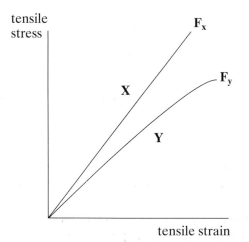

     Figure 1

     Calculate the energy stored in the spring.   *(3 marks)*

                                                                                                 AQA, 2002

3   (a) **Figure 2** shows the variation of tensile stress with tensile strain for two wires
          X and **Y**, having the same dimensions, but made of different materials. The
          materials fracture at the points $\mathbf{F_X}$ and $\mathbf{F_Y}$ respectively.

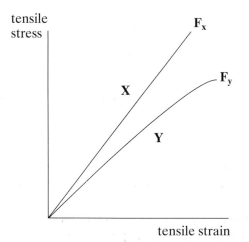

     Figure 2

     State, with a reason for each, which material, **X** or **Y**,

     (i)   obeys Hooke's law up to the point of fracture,

     (ii) is the weaker material,

     (iii) is ductile,

     (iv) has the greater elastic strain energy for a given tensile stress.   *(8 marks)*

(b) An elastic cord of unstretched length 160 mm has a cross-sectional area of 0.64 mm². The cord is stretched to a length of 190 mm. Assume that Hooke's law is obeyed for this range and that the cross-sectional area remains constant.

the Young modulus for the material of the cord = 2.0×10^7 Pa

   (i) Calculate the tension in the cord at this extension.

  (ii) Calculate the energy stored in the cord at this extension.

(5 marks)

AQA, 2003

4 A material in the form of a wire, 3.0 m long and cross-sectional area = 2.8×10^{-7} m² is suspended from a support so that it hangs vertically. Different masses may be suspended from its lower end. The table shows the extension of the wire when it is subjected to an increasing load and then a decreasing load.

load / N	0	24	52	70	82	88	94	101	71	50	16	0
extension / mm	0	2.2	4.6	6.4	7.4	8.2	9.6	13.0	10.2	8.0	4.8	3.2

(a) Plot a graph of load (on the *y* axis) against extension (on the *x* axis) both for increasing and decreasing loads.

(4 marks)

(b) Explain what the shape of the graph tells us about the behaviour of the material in the wire.

(4 marks)

(c) Using the graph, determine a value of the Young modulus for the material of the wire.

(3 marks)

AQA, 2003

5 **Figure 3** shows two wires, one made of steel and the other of brass, firmly clamped together at their ends. The wires have the same unstretched length and the same cross-sectional area. One of the clamped ends is fixed to a horizontal support and a mass M is suspended from the other end, so that the wires hang vertically.

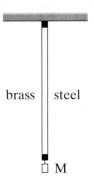

brass steel

M

Figure 3

   (i) Since the wires are clamped together the extension of each wire will be the same. If E_S is the Young modulus for steel and E_B the Young modulus for brass, show that

$$\frac{E_S}{E_B} = \frac{F_S}{F_B}$$

where F_S and F_B are the respective forces in the steel and brass wire.

  (ii) The mass M produces a total force of 15 N. Show that the magnitude of the force $F_S = 10$ N.

the Young modulus for steel = 2.0×10^{11} Pa

the Young modulus for brass = 1.0×10^{11} Pa

(iii) The cross-sectional area of each wire is 1.4×10^{-6} m² and the unstretched length is 1.5 m. Determine the extension produced in either wire.

(6 marks)

AQA, 2005

12.1 Waves and vibrations

Learning objectives:

■ What are the differences between transverse and longitudinal waves?

■ What is a plane-polarised wave?

■ What physical test can distinguish transverse waves from longitudinal waves?

Specification reference: 3.2.3

signal
generator

loudspeaker

vibrations
of air

sound
waves

Figure 1 *Creating sound waves in air*

Types of waves

Waves that pass through a substance are vibrations that pass through the substance. For example, sound waves in air are created by making a surface vibrate so it sends compression waves through the surrounding air. Sound waves, seismic waves and waves on strings are examples of waves that pass through a substance. These types of waves are often referred to as **mechanical waves**. When waves progress through a substance, the particles of the substance vibrate in a certain way which makes nearby particles vibrate in the same way, and so on.

Electromagnetic waves are vibrating electric and magnetic fields that progress through space without the need for a substance. The vibrating electric field generates a vibrating magnetic field, which generates a vibrating electric field further away, and so on. Electromagnetic waves include radio waves, microwaves, infrared radiation, light, ultraviolet radiation, X-rays and gamma radiation. The full spectrum of electromagnetic waves is listed in Topic 1.3.

Longitudinal and transverse waves

Longitudinal waves are waves in which the direction of vibration of the particles is **parallel** to (along) the direction in which the wave travels. Sound waves, primary seismic waves and compression waves on a 'slinky' are all longitudinal waves. Figure 2 shows how to send longitudinal waves along a slinky. When one end of the slinky is moved to and fro repeatedly, each 'forward' movement causes a compression wave to pass along the slinky as the coils push into each other. Each 'reverse' movement causes the coils to move apart so a 'rarefaction' (expansion) wave passes along the slinky.

direction of travel

hand moved backwards and forwards
along the line of the slinky

compression   compression

Figure 2 *Longitudinal waves on a slinky*

Transverse waves are waves in which the direction of vibration is **perpendicular** to the direction in which the wave travels. Electromagnetic waves, secondary seismic waves and waves on a string or a wire are all transverse waves.

Figure 3 shows transverse waves travelling along a rope. When one end of the rope is moved from side to side repeatedly, these sideways movements travel along the rope, as each unaffected part of the rope is pulled sideways when the part next to it moves sideways.

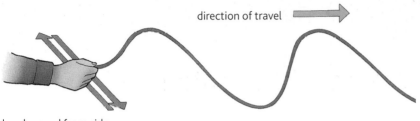

direction of travel

hand moved from side
to side repeatedly

Figure 3 *Making rope waves*

Polarisation

Transverse waves are **plane-polarised** if the vibrations stay in one plane only. If the vibrations change from one plane to another, the waves are **unpolarised**. Longitudinal waves cannot be polarised.

Figure 3 shows unpolarised waves being created on a rope. When they pass through a slit in a board, as in Figure 4, they become polarised because only the vibrations parallel to the slit pass through it.

Light from a filament lamp or a candle is unpolarised. If unpolarised light is passed through a polaroid filter, the transmitted light is polarised as the filter only allows through light which vibrates in a certain direction, according to the alignment of its molecules.

If unpolarised light is passed through two polaroid filters, the transmitted light intensity changes if one polaroid is turned relative to the other one. The filters are said to be 'crossed' when the transmitted intensity is a minimum. At this position, the polarised light from the first filter cannot pass through the second filter, as the alignment of molecules in the second filter is at 90° to the alignment in the first filter. This is like passing rope waves through two 'letter boxes' at right angles to each other, as shown in Figure 4.

Light is part of the spectrum of electromagnetic waves. The plane of polarisation of an electromagnetic wave is defined as the plane in which the electric field oscillates.

Polaroid sunglasses reduce the glare of light reflected by water or glass. Such light is partly polarised when it reflects and so its intensity is reduced using polaroid sunglasses.

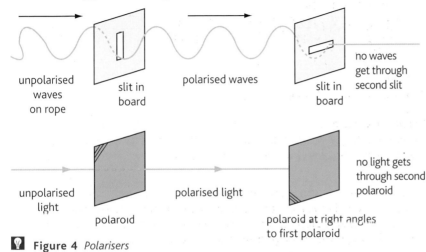

unpolarised
waves
on rope

slit in
board

polarised waves

slit in
board

no waves
get through
second slit

unpolarised
light

polaroid

polarised light

polaroid at right angles
to first polaroid

no light gets
through second
polaroid

Figure 4 *Polarisers*

How science works

Good reception

Radio waves from a transmitter are polarised. The aerial of a radio receiver needs to be aligned in the same plane as the radio waves to obtain the best reception.

Summary questions

1 Classify the following types of waves as either longitudinal or transverse:

radio waves

microwaves

sound waves

secondary seismic waves

2 Sketch a snapshot of a longitudinal waves travelling on a slinky coil, indicating the direction in which the waves are travelling and areas of high density (compression) and low density (rarefaction).

3 Sketch a snapshot of a transverse wave travelling along a rope, indicating the direction in which the waves are travelling and the direction of motion of the particles at the peaks and troughs.

4 a What is meant by a polarised wave?

b A light source is observed through two pieces of polaroid which are initially aligned parallel to each other. Describe and explain what you would expect to observe when one of the polaroids is rotated through 360°.

12.2 Measuring waves

Figure 1 *Measuring electrical waves*

When we make an intercontinental phone call, sound waves are converted to electrical waves. These waves are carried by electromagnetic waves from ground transmitters to satellites in space and back to ground receivers, where they are converted back to electrical waves then back to sound waves. The electronic circuits ensure that these sound waves are very similar to the original sound waves. The engineers who design and maintain communications systems need to measure the different types of waves at different stages, to make sure the waves are not distorted.

■ Key terms

The following terms, some of which are illustrated in Figure 2, are used to describe waves.

- The **displacement** of a vibrating particle is its distance and direction from its equilibrium position.

- The **amplitude** of a wave is the maximum displacement of a vibrating particle. For a transverse wave, this is the height of a wave crest or the depth of a wave trough from the middle.

- The **wavelength** of a wave is the least distance between two adjacent vibrating particles with the same displacement and velocity at the same time (e.g. distance between adjacent crests).

- **One complete cycle of a wave** is from maximum displacement to the next maximum displacement (e.g. from one wave peak to the next).

- The **period** of a wave is the time for one complete wave to pass a fixed point.

- The **frequency** of a wave is the number of cycles of vibration of a particle per second, or the number of complete waves passing a point per second. The unit of frequency is the hertz (Hz).

For waves of frequency f, the period of the wave $= \dfrac{1}{f}$

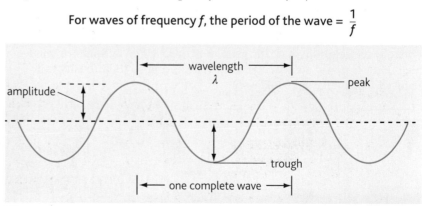

Figure 2 *Parts of a wave*

⚠ Wave speed

The higher the frequency of a wave, the shorter its wavelength. For example, if waves are sent along a rope, the higher the frequency at which they are produced, the closer together the wave peaks are. The same effect can be seen in a ripple tank when straight waves are produced at a constant frequency. If the frequency is raised to a higher value, the waves are closer together.

Figure 3 represents the crests of straight waves in a ripple tank travelling at constant speed.

- Each wave crest travels a distance equal to one wavelength (λ) in the time for one cycle.
- The time taken for one cycle = $1/f$, where f is the frequency of the waves.

Therefore, the speed of the waves, $c = \dfrac{\text{distance travelled in one cycle}}{\text{time taken for one cycle}}$

$$= \frac{\lambda}{1/f} = f\lambda$$

For waves of frequency f and wavelength λ

$$\text{wave speed } c = f\lambda$$

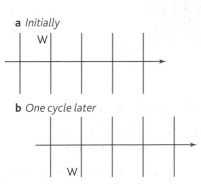

a *Initially*

b *One cycle later*

Figure 3 *Wave speed*

Note:

The symbol c is used as a general symbol for the speed of waves. In the data booklet, c refers to the speed of electromagnetic waves in free space.

Phase difference

The **phase difference** between two vibrating particles is the fraction of a cycle between the vibrations of the two particles, measured either in degrees or radians, where 1 cycle = 360° = 2π radians. For two points at distance d apart along a wave of wavelength λ

$$\text{the phase difference in radians} = \frac{2\pi d}{\lambda}$$

Figure 4 shows three successive snapshots of the particles of a transverse wave progressing from left to right across the diagram. Particles O, P, Q, R and S are spaced approximately $\frac{1}{4}$ of a wavelength apart. Table 1 shows the phase difference between O and each of the other particles.

Table 1 *Phase differences*

	P	Q	R	S
distance from O in terms of wavelength, λ	¼λ	½λ	¾λ	λ
phase difference relative to O / radians	½π	π	$\frac{3}{2}\pi$	2π

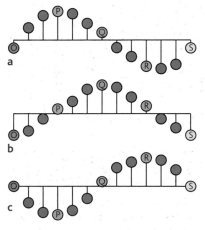

a
b
c

Figure 4 *Progressive waves*

Summary questions

1 Sound waves in air travel at a speed of 340 m s^{-1} at 20 °C. Calculate the wavelength of sound waves in air which have a frequency of a 3400 Hz, b 18 000 Hz.

2 Electromagnetic waves in air travel at a speed of 3.0 × 10^8 m s^{-1}. Calculate the frequency of light waves of wavelength of a 0.030 m, b 600 nm

3 Figure 5 shows a waveform on an oscilloscope screen when the y-sensitivity of the oscilloscope was 0.50 V cm^{-1} and the time base was set at 0.5 ms cm^{-1}. Determine the amplitude and the frequency of this waveform.

4 For the waves in Figure 4,
   a determine i the amplitude and the wavelength, ii the phase difference between P and R, iii the phase difference between P and S,

b what would be the displacement and direction of motion of Q three-quarters of a cycle after the last snapshot?

Figure 5

12.3 Wave properties 1

Learning objectives:

■ What causes waves to refract when they pass across a boundary?

■ In which direction do light waves bend when they travel out of glass and into air?

■ What do we mean by diffraction?

Specification reference: 3.2.3

Wave properties such as reflection, refraction and diffraction occur with many different types of waves. A **ripple tank** may be used to study these wave properties. The tank is a shallow transparent tray of water with sloping sides. The slopes prevent waves reflecting off the sides of tank. If they did reflect, it would be difficult to see the waves.

■ The waves observed in a ripple tank are referred to as **wavefronts**, which are lines of constant phase (e.g. crests).

■ The direction in which a wave travels is at right angles to the wavefront.

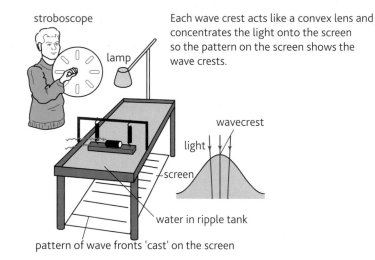

stroboscope

lamp

Each wave crest acts like a convex lens and concentrates the light onto the screen so the pattern on the screen shows the wave crests.

wavecrest

light

screen

water in ripple tank

pattern of wave fronts 'cast' on the screen

Figure 1 *The ripple tank*

Figure 2 *Reflection of plane waves*

Figure 3 *Refraction*

Reflection

Straight waves directed at a certain angle to a hard flat surface (the 'reflector') reflect off at the same angle, as shown in Figure 2. The angle between the reflected wavefront and the surface is the same as the angle between the incident wavefront and the surface. Therefore the direction of the reflected wave is at the same angle to the reflector as the direction of the incident wave. This effect is observed when a light ray is directed at a plane mirror. The angle between the incident ray and the mirror is equal to the angle between the reflected ray and the mirror.

Refraction

When waves pass across a boundary at which the wave speed changes, the wavelength also changes. If the wave fronts are at a non-zero angle to the boundary, they change direction as well as changing speed. This effect is known as **refraction**. We will consider refraction and reflection of light in more detail in Topics 13.1 and 13.2.

Figure 3 shows the refraction of water waves in a ripple tank when they pass across a boundary from deep to shallow water at a non-zero angle to the boundary. Because they move more slowly in the shallow water, the wavelength is smaller in the shallow water and therefore they change direction.

The direction of the refracted waves is closer to the normal, the line perpendicular to the boundary, than the direction of the incident waves.

Refraction of light is observed when a light ray is directed into a glass block non-normally. The light ray changes direction when it crosses the glass boundary. This happens because light waves travel more slowly in glass than in air.

Diffraction

Diffraction occurs when waves spread out after passing through a gap or round an obstacle. The effect can be seen in a ripple tank when straight waves are directed at a gap, as shown in Figure 4.

- The narrower the gap, the more the waves spread out.
- The longer the wavelength, the more the waves spread out.

To explain why the waves are diffracted on passing through the gap, consider each point on a wavefront as a secondary emitter of 'wavelets'. The wavelets from the points along a wavefront travel only in the direction in which the wave is travelling, not in the reverse direction, and they combine to form a new wavefront spreading beyond the gap. We will consider diffraction of light in more detail in Topic 13.6.

Figure 4 *The effect of the gap width*

Dish design

Satellite TV dishes in Europe need to point south, because the satellites orbit the Earth directly above the equator. The bigger the dish, the stronger the signal it can receive, because more radio waves are reflected by the dish onto the aerial. But a bigger dish reflects the radio waves to a smaller focus, because it diffracts the waves less. The dish therefore needs to be aligned more carefully than a smaller dish, otherwise it will not focus the radio waves onto the aerial.

Figure 5 *A satellite TV dish*

Summary questions

1 Copy and complete the diagram in Figure 6 by showing the wavefront after it has reflected from the straight reflector. Also, show the direction of the reflected wavefront.

reflector

30°

Figure 6

2 A circular wave spreads out from a point P on a water surface, which is 0.50 m from a flat reflecting wall. The wave travels at a speed of 0.20 m s⁻¹. Sketch the arrangement and show the position of the wavefront **a** 2.5 s, **b** 4.0 s after the wavefront was produced at P.

3 Copy and complete the diagram in Figure 7 by showing the wavefronts after they passed across the boundary and have been refracted. Also, show the direction of the refracted waves.

boundary

Figure 7

4 Water waves are diffracted on passing through a gap. How is the amount of diffraction changed as a result of:

a widening the gap without changing the wavelength?

b increasing the wavelength of the water waves without changing the gap width?

c increasing the wavelength of the water waves and reducing the gap width?

d widening the gap and increasing the wavelength of the waves?

12.4 Wave properties 2

Learning objectives:

- What features of two waves must combine in order to produce reinforcement?

- What is the phase difference between two waves if they produce maximum cancellation?

- Why is total cancellation rarely achieved in practice?

Specification reference: 3.2.3

Reinforcement

Cancellation

Figure 1 *Superposition*

AQA Examiner's tip

Be careful when using the term 'minimum'. When two troughs meet at the same point, they superpose to produce maximum negative displacement, not 'a minimum'.

Figure 2 *Making stationary waves*

The principle of superposition

When waves meet, they pass through each other. At the point where they meet, they combine for an instant before they move apart. This combining effect is known as **superposition**. Imagine a boat hit by two wave crests at the same time from different directions. Anyone on the boat would know it had been hit by a 'supercrest', the combined effect of two wave crests.

The principle of superposition states that when two waves meet, the total displacement at a point is equal to the sum of the individual displacements at that point.

- Where a crest meets a crest, a **supercrest** is created; the two waves reinforce each other.

- Where a trough meets a trough, a **supertrough** is created; the two waves reinforce each other.

- Where a crest meets a trough, the resultant displacement is **zero**; the two waves cancel each other out.

Further examples of superposition

1 Stationary waves on a rope

Stationary waves are formed on a rope if two people send waves continuously along a rope from either end, as shown in Figure 2. The two sets of waves are referred to as **progressive waves** to distinguish them from stationary waves. They combine at fixed points along the rope to form points of no displacement or **nodes** along the rope. At each node, the two sets of waves are always 180° out of phase, so they cancel each other out. Stationary waves are described in more detail in Topics 12.5 and 12.6.

2 Water waves in a ripple tank

A vibrating dipper on a water surface sends out circular waves. Figure 3 shows a snapshot of two sets of circular waves produced in this way in a ripple tank. The waves pass through each other continuously.

- Points of cancellation are created where a crest from one dipper meets a trough from the other dipper. These points of cancellation are seen as gaps in the wavefronts.

- Points of reinforcement are created where a crest from one dipper meets a crest from the other dipper, or where a trough from one dipper meets a trough from the other dipper.

As the waves are continuously passing through each other at constant frequency and at a constant phase difference, cancellation and reinforcement occurs at fixed positions. This effect is known as **interference**. **Coherent** sources of waves produce an interference pattern where they overlap, because they vibrate at the same frequency with a constant phase difference. If the phase difference changed at random, the points of cancellation and reinforcement would move about at random, and no interference pattern would be seen. Interference of light is described in more detail in Topic 13.4.

Tests using microwaves

A microwave transmitter and receiver can be used to demonstrate reflection, refraction, diffraction, interference and polarisation of microwaves. The transmitter produces microwaves of wavelength 3.0 cm. The receiver can be connected to a suitable meter, which gives a measure of the intensity of the microwaves at the receiver.

1 Place the receiver in the path of the microwave beam from the transmitter. Move the receiver gradually away from the transmitter and note that the receiver signal decreases with distance from the transmitter. This shows that the microwaves become weaker as they travel away from the transmitter.

2 Place a metal plate between the transmitter and the receiver to show that microwaves cannot pass through metal.

3 Use two metal plates to make a narrow slit and show that the receiver detects microwaves that have been diffracted as they pass through the slit. Show that if the slit is made wider, less diffraction occurs.

4 Use a narrow metal plate with the two plates from step 3 above to make a pair of slits as in Figure 4. Direct the transmitter at the slits and use the receiver to find points of cancellation and reinforcement, where the microwaves from the two slits overlap.

Figure 3 *Interference of water waves*

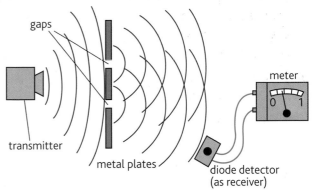

Figure 4 *Interference of microwaves*

Summary questions

1 Figure 5 shows two wave pulses on a rope travelling towards each other. Sketch a snapshot of the rope

Figure 5

a when the two waves are passing through each other,

b when the two waves have passed through each other.

2 How would you expect the interference pattern in Figure 3 to change if

a the two dippers are moved further apart?

b the frequency of the waves produced by the dippers is reduced?

3 Microwaves from a transmitter are directed at a narrow slit between two metal plates. A receiver is placed in the path of the diffracted microwaves, as shown in Figure 6.

How would you expect the receiver signal to change if a the receiver is moved directly away from the slit? b the slit is then made narrower?

4 Microwaves from a transmitter are directed at two parallel slits in a metal plate. A receiver is placed on the other side of the metal plate on a line AB parallel to the plate. When the receiver is moved a short distance towards B, the receiver signal decreases then increases again.

a Explain why the signal decreased when it was moved towards B along the line AB.

b Explain why the signal increased as it moved towards B.

Figure 6

12.5 Stationary and progressive waves

Learning objectives:

- What is the necessary condition for the formation of a stationary wave?

- Is a stationary wave formed by superposition?

- Why are nodes formed in fixed positions?

Specification reference: 3.2.3

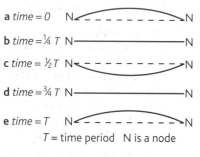

Figure 1 *Vibrations of a guitar string*

a *time = 0*   N ⌒ ⌒ ⌒ ⌒ N

b *time = ¼ T* N ――――― N

c *time = ½ T* N ⌣ ⌣ ⌣ ⌣ N

d *time = ¾ T* N ――――― N

e *time = T*   N ⌒ ⌒ ⌒ ⌒ N

   T = time period   N is a node

Figure 2 *Fundamental vibrations*

N   N   N Initially

N   N   N ¼ cycle later

N   N ½ cycle later

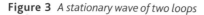

(N = node)

Figure 3 *A stationary wave of two loops*

Formation of stationary waves

When a guitar string is plucked, the sound produced depends on the way in which the string vibrates. If the string is plucked gently at its centre, a stationary wave of constant frequency is set up on the string. The sound produced therefore has a constant frequency. If the guitar string is plucked harshly, the string vibrates in a more complicated way and the note produced contains other frequencies, as well as the frequency produced when it is plucked gently.

As explained in Topic 12.4, a stationary wave is formed when two progressive waves pass through each other. This can be achieved on a string in tension by fixing both ends and making the middle part vibrate, so progressive waves travel towards each end, reflect at the ends and then pass through each other.

The simplest stationary wave pattern on a string is shown in Figure 2. This is the **fundamental mode of vibration** of the string. It consists of a single loop that has a **node** (a point of no displacement) at either end. The string vibrates with maximum amplitude midway between the nodes. This position is referred to as an **antinode**. In effect, the string vibrates from side-to-side repeatedly. For this pattern to occur, the distance between the nodes at either end (i.e. the length of the string) must be equal to one half-wavelength of the waves on the string.

$$\text{Distance between adjacent nodes} = \tfrac{1}{2}\lambda$$

If the frequency of the waves sent along the rope from either end is raised steadily, the pattern in Figure 2 disappears and a new pattern is observed with two equal loops along the rope. This pattern, shown in Figure 3, has a node at the centre as well as at either end. It is formed when the frequency is twice as high as in Figure 2, corresponding to half the previous wavelength. Because the distance from one node to the next is equal to half a wavelength, the length of the rope is therefore equal to one full wavelength.

Stationary waves that vibrate freely do not transfer energy. The amplitude of vibration is zero at the nodes so there is no energy at the nodes. The amplitude of vibration is a maximum at the antinodes, so there is maximum energy at the antinodes. Because the nodes and antinodes are at fixed positions, no energy is transferred in a freely-vibrating stationary wave pattern.

Explanation of stationary waves

Consider a snapshot of two progressive waves passing through each other.

- When they are in phase, they reinforce each other to produce a large wave as shown in Figure 4a).

- A quarter of a cycle later, the two waves have each moved one-quarter of a wavelength in opposite directions. As shown in Figure 4b), they are now in antiphase so they cancel each other.

- After a further quarter cycle, the two waves are back in phase. The resultant is again a large wave as in a) except reversed.

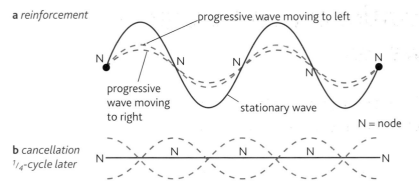

a *reinforcement*

progressive wave moving to left

progressive wave moving to right

stationary wave

N = node

b *cancellation*
¹/₄-*cycle later*

Figure 4 *Explaining stationary waves*

The points where there is no displacement (i.e. the nodes) are fixed in position throughout. Between these points, the stationary wave oscillates between the nodes. In general, in any stationary wave pattern:

1. **The amplitude** of a vibrating particle in a stationary wave pattern varies with position from zero at a node to maximum amplitude at an antinode.

2. **The phase difference** between two vibrating particles is
   - zero if the two particles are between adjacent nodes or separated by an even number of nodes
   - $180°$ (= π radians) if the two particles are separated by an odd number of nodes.

	stationary waves	progressive waves
frequency	All particles except at the nodes vibrate at the same frequency.	All particles vibrate at the same frequency.
amplitude	The amplitude varies from zero at the nodes to a maximum at the antinodes.	The amplitude is the same for all particles.
phase difference between two particles	Equal to $m\pi$, where m is the number of nodes between the two particles.	Equal to $2\pi d/\lambda$ where d = distance apart and λ is the wavelength.

🔅 ⚠ More examples of stationary waves

1 Sound in a pipe

Sound resonates at certain frequencies in an air-filled tube or pipe. In a pipe closed at one end, these resonant frequencies occur when there is an antinode at the open end and a node at the other end.

2 Using microwaves

Microwaves from a transmitter are directed normally at a metal plate, which reflects the microwaves back towards the transmitter. When a detector is moved along the line between the transmitter and the metal plate, the detector signal is found to be zero at equally spaced positions along the line. The reflected waves and the waves from the transmitter form a stationary wave pattern. The positions where no signal is detected are where nodes occur. They are spaced at intervals of half-a-wavelength.

transmitter

λ

detector

metal plate

Figure 5 *Using microwaves*

Summary questions

1

  a Sketch the stationary wave pattern seen on a rope when there is a node at either end and an antinode at its centre.

  b If the rope in **a** is 4.0 m in length, calculate the wavelength of the waves on the rope for the pattern you have drawn.

2 The stationary wave pattern shown in Figure 6 is set up on a rope of length 3.0 m.

O   3.0 m   C

A B

Figure 6

  a Calculate the wavelength of these waves.

  b State the phase difference between the particle vibrating at O and the particle vibrating at **i** A, **ii** B, **iii** C.

3 State two differences between a stationary wave and a progressive wave in terms of the vibrations of the particles.

4 Microwaves from a transmitter are reflected back to the transmitter using a flat metal plate. A detector is moved along the line between the transmitter and the metal plate. The detector signal is zero at positions 15 mm apart.

  a Explain why the signal is zero at certain positions.

  b Calculate the wavelength of the microwaves.

12.6 More about stationary waves on strings

Learning objectives:

- What boundary condition must be satisfied at both ends of the string?

- What is the simplest possible stationary wave pattern that can be formed?

- How do the frequencies of the overtones compare with the fundamental frequency?

Specification reference: 3.2.3

🔬 💡 ℹ️ Stationary waves on a vibrating string

A controlled arrangement for producing stationary waves is shown in Figure 1. A string or wire is tied at one end to a mechanical vibrator connected to a frequency generator. The other end of the string passes over a pulley and supports a weight, which keeps the tension in the string constant. As the frequency of the generator is increased from a very low value, different stationary wave patterns are seen on the string. In every case, the length of string between the pulley and the vibrator has a node at either end. The boundary conditions for a stationary wave on a string are that there must be a node at each end of the string.

- The **fundamental pattern of vibration** is seen at the lowest possible frequency. This has an antinode at the middle as well as a node at either end. Because the length L of the vibrating section of the string is between adjacent nodes and the distance between adjacent nodes is $\frac{1}{2}\lambda$ the wavelength of the waves that form this pattern, the fundamental wavelength, $\lambda_0 = 2L$.

  Therefore, the fundamental frequency $f_0 = \frac{c}{\lambda_0} = \frac{c}{2L}$, where c is the speed of the progressive waves on the wire.

- The next stationary wave pattern, the **first overtone**, is where there is a node at the middle, so the string is in two loops. The wavelength of the waves that form this pattern $\lambda_1 = L$ because each loop has a length of half-a-wavelength.

  Therefore, the frequency of the first overtone vibrations, $f_1 = \frac{c}{\lambda_1}$

  $$= \frac{c}{L} = 2f_0$$

- The next stationary wave pattern, the **second overtone**, is where there are nodes at a distance of $\frac{1}{3}L$ from either end and an antinode at the middle. The wavelength of the waves that form this pattern $\lambda_2 = \frac{2}{3}L$ because each loop has a length of half-a-wavelength.

  Therefore, the frequency of the second overtone vibrations, $f_2 = \frac{c}{\lambda_2}$

  $$= \frac{3c}{2L} = 3f_0$$

In general, stationary wave patterns occur at frequencies f_0, $2f_0$, $3f_0$, $4f_0$, etc., where f_0 is the frequency of the fundamental vibrations. This is the case in any vibrating linear system that has a node at either end.

Explanation of the stationary wave patterns on a vibrating string

In the arrangement shown in Figure 1, consider what happens to a wave sent out by the vibrator. The crest reverses its phase when it reflects at the fixed end and travels back along the string as a trough. When it reaches the vibrator, it reflects and reverses phase again, travelling away from the vibrator once more as a crest. If this crest is reinforced by a crest created by the vibrator, the amplitude of the wave is increased. This is how a stationary wave is formed. The key condition is that the time

string at maximum displacement

nearly a node — node

frequency generator — vibrator — pulley

weight

N = node   A = antinode
(dotted line shows string half a cycle earlier)

a *fundamental*

b *first overtone*

c *second overtone*

Figure 1 *Stationary waves on a string*

taken for a wave to travel along the string and back should be equal to the time taken for a whole number of cycles of the vibrator.

- The time taken for a wave to travel along the string and back, $t = 2L/c$, where c is the speed of the waves on the string.
- The time taken for the vibrator to pass through a whole number of cycles $= m/f$, where f is the frequency of the vibrator and m is a whole number.

Therefore the key condition may be expressed as $\dfrac{2L}{c} = \dfrac{m}{f}$

Rearranging this equation gives $f = \dfrac{mc}{2L} = mf_0$ and $\lambda = \dfrac{c}{f} = \dfrac{2L}{m}$

In other words,

- stationary waves are formed at frequencies f_0, $2f_0$, $3f_0$, etc.
- the length of the vibrating section of the string $L = \dfrac{m\lambda}{2}$ = a whole number of half wavelengths.

How science works

Making music

A guitar produces sound when its strings vibrate as a result of being plucked. In an electronic guitar, the vibrations of the string are detected by a microphone, which produces electrical waves. These are amplified and converted back to sound waves in a loudspeaker. In an acoustic guitar, the string vibrations make the guitar surfaces vibrate and send out sound waves.

When a stretched string or wire vibrates, its pattern of vibration is a mix of its fundamental mode of vibration and the overtones. The sound produced is the same mix of frequencies which change with time as the pattern of vibration changes. A **spectrum analyser** can be used to show how the intensity of a sound varies with frequency and with time. Combined with a **sound synthesiser**, the original sound can be altered by amplifying or suppressing different frequency ranges.

The **pitch** of a note corresponds to frequency, so the pitch of the note from a stretched string can be altered by changing the tension of the string or by altering its length.

- Raising the tension or shortening the length increases the pitch.
- Lowering the tension or increasing the length lowers the pitch.

By changing the length or altering the tension, a vibrating string or wire can be tuned to the same pitch as a vibrating tuning fork. However, the sound from a vibrating string includes the overtone frequencies as well as the fundamental frequency, whereas a tuning fork vibrates only at its fundamental frequency. The wire is tuned when its fundamental frequency is the same as the tuning fork frequency. A simple visual check is to balance a small piece of paper on the wire at its centre and place the base of the vibrating tuning fork on one end of the wire. If the wire is tuned to the tuning fork, it will vibrate in its fundamental mode and the piece of paper will fall off.

Figure 2 A sound synthesiser

Summary questions

1 A stretched wire of length 0.80 m vibrates in its fundamental mode at a frequency of 256 Hz. Calculate **a** the wavelength of the progressive waves on the wire, **b** the speed of the progressive waves on the wire.

2 The fundamental frequency of vibration of a stretched wire is inversely proportional to the length of the wire. For the wire in Q1 above, calculate the length of the wire to produce a frequency of **a** 512 Hz, **b** 384 Hz. Assume that the tension of the wire is not changed.

3 Describe how you would expect the note from a vibrating guitar string to change if the string is **a** shortened, **b** tightened.

4 The speed, c, of the progressive waves on a stretched wire varies with the tension T in the wire, in accordance with the equation $c = (T/\mu)^{1/2}$, where μ is the mass per unit length of the wire. Use this formula to explain why a nylon wire and a steel wire of the same length, diameter and tension produce notes of different pitch. State, with a reason, which wire would produce the higher pitch.

1   A student adjusted the tension of a stretched metal wire of length 820 mm so that when it vibrated, it emitted sound at the same frequency as a 256 Hz tuning fork.

Figure 1

She then altered the length L of the vibrating section of the wire as shown in **Figure 1**, until it emitted sound at the same frequency as a 512 Hz tuning fork. She repeated the test several times to obtain the following measurements for the length L:

425 mm,   407 mm,   396 mm,   415 mm,   402 mm

(a) (i)   Calculate the mean length L at 512 Hz.

(ii) Estimate the uncertainty in this length measurement.   *(2 marks)*

(b) The student thought the measurements showed that the frequency of sound f emitted by the wire is inversely proportional to the length L of the vibrating section.

(i)   Discuss whether or not the measurements support this hypothesis.

(ii) In order to test the hypothesis further, state what further measurements the student could make and show how these measurements should be used. Assume further calibrated tuning forks are available.   *(9 marks)*

2   An ultrasonic signal from a ship travels vertically downwards through the water. The wavelength of the waves is 5.3×10^{-2} m and the frequency of the waves is 29 kHz.

(a) Calculate the speed of the sound through the water.   *(3 marks)*

(b) The sound is reflected from the sea bed and is received back at the ship 0.23 s after it is transmitted. Calculate the depth of the water.   *(2 marks)*

AQA, 2007

3   (a) State the characteristic features of

(i) longitudinal waves,

(ii) transverse waves.   *(3 marks)*

(b) Daylight passes horizontally through a fixed polarising filter **P**. An observer views the light emerging through a second polarising filter **Q**, which may be rotated in a vertical plane about point **X** as shown in **Figure 2**.

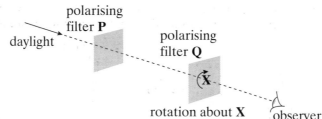

Figure 2

Describe what the observer would see as **Q** is rotated slowly through 360°.   *(2 marks)*

AQA, 2005

4   Polarisation is a property of one type of wave.

(a) There are two general classes of wave, longitudinal and transverse. Which class of wave can be polarised?   *(1 mark)*

(b) Give **one** example of the type of wave that can be polarised.   *(1 mark)*

(c) Explain why some waves can be polarised but others cannot.   *(3 marks)*

AQA, 2002

5 **Figure 3** shows three particles in a medium that is transmitting a sound wave. Particles **A** and **C** are separated by one wavelength and particle **B** is half way between them when no sound is being transmitted.

(a) Name the type of wave that is involved in the transmission of this sound. *(1 mark)*

(b) At one instant particle **A** is displaced to the point **A′** indicated by the tip of the arrow in **Figure 3**. Show on **Figure 3** the displacements of particles **B** and **C** at the same instant. Label the position **B′** and **C′**, respectively. *(2 marks)*

(c) Explain briefly how energy is transmitted in this sound wave. *(2 marks)*

Figure 3   AQA, 2005

6 **Figure 4** represents a stationary wave on a stretched string. The continuous line shows the position of the string at a particular instant when the displacement is a maximum. P and S are the fixed ends of the string. Q and R are the positions of the nodes. The speed of waves on the string is $200\,\mathrm{m\,s^{-1}}$.

Figure 4

(i) State the wavelength of the waves on the string.

(ii) Calculate the frequency of vibration.

(iii) Draw on a copy of the diagram the position of the string 3.0 ms later than the position shown. Explain how you arrive at your answer. *(5 marks)*

AQA, 2004

7 Short pulses of sound are reflected from the wall of a building 18 m away from the sound source. The reflected pulses return to the source after 0.11 s.

(a) Calculate the speed of sound. *(3 marks)*

(b) The sound source now emits a continuous tone at a constant frequency. An observer, walking at a constant speed from the source to the wall, hears a regular rise and fall in the intensity of the sound. Explain how the **minima** of intensity occur. *(3 marks)*

AQA, 2002

8 A microwave transmitter directs waves towards a metal plate, as shown in **Figure 5**. When a microwave detector is moved along a line normal to the transmitter and the plate it passes through a sequence of equally spaced maxima and minima of intensity.

Figure 5

(a) Explain how these maxima and minima are formed. *(4 marks)*

(b) The detector is placed at a position where the intensity is a minimum. When it is moved a distance of 144 mm it passes through nine maxima and reaches the ninth minimum from the starting point. Calculate:

(i) the wavelength of the microwaves,

(ii) the frequency of the microwave transmitter. *(3 marks)*

AQA, 2003

187

13 Optics

13.1 Refraction of light

Learning objectives:

■ What do we mean by rays?

■ What is Snell's law?

■ Does refraction differ for a light ray travelling from a transparent substance into air?

Specification reference: 3.2.3

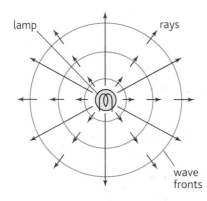

Figure 1 *Rays and waves*

Figure 2 *Investigating refraction*

Examiner's tip

Set your calculator mode to degrees when using Snell's law.

The wave theory of light can be used to explain reflection and refraction of light. However, when we consider the effect of lenses or mirrors on the path of light, we usually prefer to draw diagrams using light rays. Light rays represent the direction of travel of wavefronts.

Refraction is the change of direction that occurs when light passes non-normally across a boundary between two transparent substances. Figure 2 shows the change of direction of a light ray when it enters and when it leaves a rectangular glass block in air. The light ray bends:

■ towards the normal when it passes from air into glass,

■ away from the normal when it passes from glass into air.

No refraction takes place if the incident light ray is along the normal.

At a boundary between two transparent substances, the light ray bends:

■ towards the normal if it passes into a more refractive substance,

■ away from the normal if it passes into a less refractive substance.

■ Investigating the refraction of light by glass

Use a ray box to direct a light ray into a rectangular glass block at different angles of incidence at the midpoint P of one of the longer sides, as shown in Figure 2. Note that the angle of incidence is the angle between the incident light ray and the normal at the point of incidence.

For each angle of incidence at P, mark the point Q where the light ray leaves the block. The angle of refraction is the angle between the normal at P and the line PQ. Measurements of the angles of incidence and refraction for different incident rays show that:

■ the angle of refraction, r, at P is always less than the angle of incidence, i,

■ the ratio of $\sin i/\sin r$ is the same for each light ray. This is known as Snell's law. The ratio is referred to as the **refractive index**, n, of glass.

For a light ray travelling from air into a transparent substance,

$$\text{the refractive index of the substance, } n = \frac{\sin i}{\sin r}$$

Notice that **partial reflection** also occurs when a light ray in air enters glass (or any other refractive substance).

*Worked example:*_____

A light ray is directed into a glass block of refractive index 1.5 at an angle of incidence of 40°. Calculate the angle of refraction of this light ray.

Solution

$i = 40°, n = 1.5$

Rearranging: $\dfrac{\sin i}{\sin r} = n$ gives $\sin r = \dfrac{\sin i}{n} = \dfrac{\sin 40}{1.5} = \dfrac{0.643}{1.5} = 0.429$

Therefore $r = 25°$

glass block

Figure 3 *Comparing 'glass to air' refraction with 'air to glass' refraction*

Comparing 'glass to air' refraction with 'air to glass' refraction

In Figure 3, notice that the angle of refraction of the light ray emerging from the block is the same as the angle of incidence of the light ray entering the block. This is because the two sides of the block at which refraction occurs are parallel to each other.

■ If i_1 and r_1 are the angles of incidence and refraction at the point where the light ray enters the block, then the refractive index of the glass $n = \sin i_1/\sin r_1$

■ If i_2 and r_2 are the angles of incidence and refraction at the point where the light ray leaves the block, then because $i_2 = r_1$ and $r_2 = i_1$, $\sin i_2/\sin r_2 = 1/n$

Refraction of a light ray by a prism

Figure 4 shows the path of a light ray through a glass prism. The light ray refracts towards the normal where it enters the glass prism then refracts away from the normal where it leaves the prism.

Figure 4 *Refraction by a glass prism*

Summary questions

1 **a** A light ray in air is directed into water from air. The refractive index of water is 1.33. Calculate the angle of refraction of the light ray in the water for an angle of incidence of **i** 20°, **ii** 40°, **iii** 60°.

b A light ray in water is directed at the water surface at an angle of incidence of 40°.

   i Calculate the angle of refraction of the light ray at this surface.

   ii Sketch the path of the light ray showing the normal and the angles of incidence and refraction.

2 A light ray is directed from air into a glass block of refractive index 1.5. Calculate:

a the angle of refraction at the point of incidence if the angle of incidence is **i** 30°, **ii** 60°,

b the angle of incidence if the angle of refraction at the point of incidence is **i** 35°, **ii** 40°.

3 A light ray in air was directed at the flat side of a semicircular glass block at an angle of incidence of 50°, as shown in Figure 6. The angle of refraction at the point of incidence was 30°.

a Calculate the refractive index of the glass.

b Calculate the angle of refraction if the angle of incidence was changed to 60°.

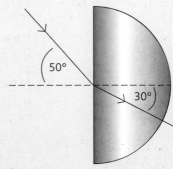

Figure 6

4 A light ray enters an equilateral glass prism of refractive index 1.55 at the midpoint of one side of the prism at an angle of incidence of 35°.

a Sketch this arrangement and show that the angle of refraction of the light ray in the glass is 22°.

b i Show that the angle of incidence where the light ray leaves the glass prism is 38°.

   ii Calculate the angle of refraction of the light ray where it leaves the prism.

13.2 More about refraction

Learning objectives:

- What happens to the speed of light waves when they enter a material such as water?

- How is refractive index related to the speed of light waves?

- Why does a glass prism split sunlight into the colours of a spectrum?

Specification reference: 3.2.3

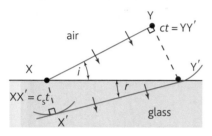

Figure 1 *Explaining refraction*

⚠ 💡 Explaining refraction

Refraction occurs because the speed of the light waves is different in each substance. The amount of refraction that takes place depends on the speed of the waves in each substance.

Consider a wavefront of a light wave when it passes across a straight boundary from a vacuum or air into a transparent substance, as shown in Figure 1. Suppose the wavefront moves from XY to X'Y' in time t, crossing the boundary between X and Y. In this time, the wavefront moves

- a distance ct at speed c in a vacuum from Y to Y'

- a distance $c_s t$ at speed c_s in the substance from X to X'.

Considering triangle XYY', since YY' is the direction of the wavefront in the vacuum and is therefore perpendicular to XY, then YY' = XY' $\sin i$, where i = angle YXY'.

$$\therefore ct = XY' \sin i$$

Considering triangle XX'Y', since XX' is the direction of the wavefront in the substance and is therefore perpendicular to X'Y', then XX' = XY' $\sin r$, where r = angle XY'X'.

$$\therefore c_s t = XY' \sin r$$

Combining these two equations therefore gives

$$\frac{\sin i}{\sin r} = \frac{c}{c_s}$$

Therefore the refractive index of the substance, $n_s = \dfrac{c}{c_s}$

This equation shows that the smaller the speed of light is in a substance, the greater is the refractive index of the substance.

Note:

The frequency f of the waves does not change when refraction occurs. As $c = \lambda f$ and $c_s = \lambda_s f$, where λ and λ_s are the wavelengths of the waves in a vacuum and in the substance respectively, then it follows that the refractive index of the substance,

$$n_s = \frac{c}{c_s} = \frac{\lambda}{\lambda_s}$$

Worked example: _____

The speed of light is $3.00 \times 10^8\,\mathrm{m\,s^{-1}}$ in a vacuum. A certain type of glass has a refractive index of 1.62. Calculate the speed of light in the glass.

Solution

Rearranging $n_s = \dfrac{c}{c_s}$ gives $c_s = \dfrac{c}{n_s} = \dfrac{3.0 \times 10^8}{1.62} = 1.85 \times 10^8\,\mathrm{m\,s^{-1}}$

Refraction at a boundary between two transparent substances

Consider a light ray crossing a boundary from a substance in which the speed of light is c_1 to a substance in which the speed of light is c_2. Using the same theory as on page 190 gives,

$$\frac{\sin i}{\sin r} = \frac{c_1}{c_2}$$

where i = the angle between the incident ray and the normal, r = the angle between the refracted ray and the normal.

This equation may be rearranged as $\dfrac{1}{c_1}\sin i = \dfrac{1}{c_2}\sin r$

Multiplying both sides of this equation by c, the speed of light in a vacuum, gives

$$\frac{c}{c_1}\sin i = \frac{c}{c_2}\sin r$$

Substituting n_1 for $\dfrac{c}{c_1}$ where n_1 is the refractive index of substance 1

and n_2 for $\dfrac{c}{c_2}$ where n_2 is the refractive index of substance 2 gives

$$n_1\sin i = n_2\sin r$$

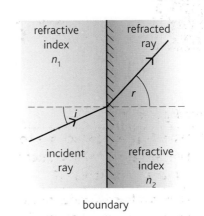

refractive index n_1 — refracted ray — incident ray — refractive index n_2 — boundary

Figure 2 *The 'n sin i' rule*

AQA **Examiner's tip**

Always use this equation in calculations if you know three of its four quantities.

Worked example:

A light ray crosses the boundary between water of refractive index 1.33 and glass of refractive index 1.50 at an angle of incidence of 40°. Calculate the angle of refraction of this light ray.

Solution

$n_1 = 1.33, n_2 = 1.50, i = 40°$

Using $n_1\sin i = n_2\sin r$ gives $1.33\sin 40 = 1.50\sin r$

$\therefore \sin r = \dfrac{1.33\sin 40}{1.5} = 0.57$

$r = 35°$

Note:

When a light ray passes from a vacuum into a transparent substance of refractive index n,

$$\frac{\sin i}{\sin r} = n$$

where i = the angle between the incident ray and the normal;
      r = the angle between the refracted ray and the normal.

The refractive index, n = $\dfrac{\text{the speed of light in a vacuum}}{\text{the speed of light in the transparent substance}}$

The speed of light in air at atmospheric pressure is 99.97% of the speed of light in a vacuum.

Therefore, the refractive index of air is 1.0003. For most purposes, the refractive index of air may be assumed to be 1.

AQA **Examiner's tip**

During refraction, the speed and wavelength both change but frequency stays constant.

Figure 3 *Dispersion of light*

■ The white light spectrum

We can use a prism to split a beam of white light from a filament lamp (or sunlight) into the colours of the spectrum by a glass prism, as shown in Figure 3. This happens because white light is composed of light with a continuous range of wavelengths, from red at about 650 nm to violet at about 350 nm. The glass prism refracts light by different amounts, depending on its wavelength. The shorter the wavelength in air, the greater the amount of refraction. So each colour in the white light beam is refracted by a different amount. This 'dispersive' effect occurs because the speed of light in glass depends on wavelength. Violet light travels more slowly than red light in glass so the refractive index of violet light is greater than the refractive index.

■ Summary questions

1 Water waves of frequency 4.0 Hz travelling at a speed of 0.16 m s⁻¹ travel across a boundary from deep to shallow water where the speed is 0.12 m s⁻¹.

    a Calculate the wavelength of these waves **i** in the deep water, **ii** in the shallow water.

    b The incident wavefronts cross the boundary at an angle of 25° to the boundary. Calculate the angle of the refracted wavefronts to the boundary.

2 **a** The speed of light in a vacuum is 3.00×10^8 m s⁻¹. Calculate the speed of light in **i** glass of refractive index 1.52, **ii** water. The refractive index of water = 1.33.

    b A light ray passes across a plane boundary from water into glass at an angle of incidence of 55°. Use the refractive index values from **a** to show that the angle of refraction of this light ray is 46°.

3 Calculate the angle of refraction for a light ray entering glass of refractive index 1.50 at an angle of incidence of 40° in:

    a air,

    b water of refractive index 1.33.

4 A white light ray is directed through the curved side of a semicircular glass block at the midpoint of the flat side, as shown in Figure 4. The angle of incidence of the light ray at the flat side is 30°.

The refractive index of the glass for red light is 1.52 and for blue light is 1.55.

    a Calculate the angle of refraction at the midpoint of **i** the red component, and **ii** the blue component of the light ray.

    b Hence show that the angle between the red and blue components of the refracted light ray is 1.3°.

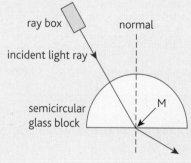

Figure 4

13.3 Total internal reflection

Learning objectives:

■ What are the conditions for total internal reflection?

■ How is the critical angle related to refractive index?

■ Why do diamonds sparkle?

Specification reference: 3.2.3

💡 **Figure 1** *Total internal reflection*

AQA **Examiner's tip**

Partial internal reflection always occurs at a boundary when the angle of incidence is less than or equal to the critical angle.

■ Investigating total internal reflection

When a light ray travels from glass into air, it refracts away from the normal. If the angle of incidence is increased to a certain value known as the **critical angle**, the light ray refracts along the boundary. Figure 1 shows this effect. If the angle of incidence is increased further, the light ray undergoes **total internal reflection** at the boundary, the same as if the boundary were replaced by a plane mirror.

In general, total internal reflection can only take place if:

1. the incident substance has a **larger refractive index** than the other substance,

2. the angle of incidence **exceeds the critical angle**.

At the critical angle i_c, the angle of refraction is 90° because the light ray emerges along the boundary. Therefore, $n_1 \sin i_c = n_2 \sin 90$ where n_1 is the refractive index of the incident substance and n_2 is the refractive index of the other substance. Since $\sin 90 = 1$, then

$$\sin i_c = \frac{n_2}{n_1}$$

Prove for yourself that the critical angle for the boundary between glass of refractive index 1.5 and air (refractive index = 1) is 42°. This means that if the angle of incidence of a light ray in the glass is greater than 42°, the light ray undergoes total internal reflection back into the glass at the boundary.

Why do diamonds sparkle when white light is directed at them?
When white light enters a diamond, it is split into the colours of the spectrum. Diamond has a very high refractive index of 2.417 so it separates the colours more than any other substance does. In addition, the high refractive index gives diamond a critical angle of 24.4°. So a light ray in a diamond may be totally internally reflected many times before it emerges, which means its colours spread out more and more. So the diamond sparkles with different colours.

🔲 How science works

Optical fibres

Optical fibres are used in medical endoscopes to see inside the body, and in communications to carry light signals. Figure 2 shows the path of a light ray along an optical fibre. The light ray is totally internally reflected each time it reaches the fibre boundary, even where the fibre bends, unless the radius of the bend is too small. At each point where the light ray reaches the boundary, the angle of incidence exceeds the critical angle of the fibre.

A communications optical fibre allows pulses of light that enter at one end, from a transmitter, to reach a receiver at the other end. Such fibres need to be highly transparent to minimise absorption of light. Each fibre consists of a core surrounded by a layer of cladding of lower refractive index.

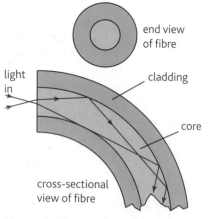

Figure 2 *Fibre optics*

■ Total internal reflection takes place at the core-cladding boundary. At any point where two fibres are in direct contact, light would cross from one fibre to the other if there were no cladding. Such crossover would mean that the signals would not be secure, as they would reach the wrong destination.

■ The core must be very narrow to prevent **multipath dispersion**. This occurs in a wide core because light travelling along the axis of the core travels a shorter distance per metre of fibre than light that repeatedly undergoes total internal reflection. A pulse of light sent along a wide core would become longer than it ought to be. If it was too long, it would merge with the next pulse.

Figure 3 *Multipath dispersion*

Note:

Pulse dispersion also occurs if white light is used instead of monochromatic light (light of a single wavelength or as small a range of wavelengths as possible). This **spectral dispersion** is because the speed of light in the glass depends on its wavelength. Violet light travels more slowly than red light. The difference in speed would cause white light pulses in optical fibres to become longer, as the violet component falls behind the faster red component of each pulse. So the light (or infrared radiation) used must be monochromatic to prevent pulse merging.

The medical endoscope contains two bundles of fibres. The endoscope is inserted into a body cavity, which is then illuminated using light sent through one of the fibre bundles. A lens over the end of the other fibre bundle is used to form an image of the body cavity on the end of the fibre bundle. The light that forms this image travels along the fibres to the other end of the fibre bundle where the image can be observed. This fibre bundle needs to be a **coherent** bundle, which means that the fibre ends at each end are in the same relative positions.

a *endoscope design*

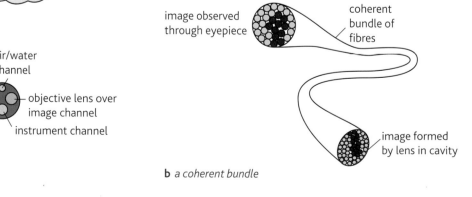

b *a coherent bundle*

Figure 4 *The endoscope*

Summary questions

1 **a** State two conditions for a light ray to undergo total internal reflection at a boundary between two transparent substances.

b Calculate the critical angle for **i** glass of refractive index 1.52 and air, **ii** water (refractive index = 1.33) and air.

2 **a** Show that the critical angle at a boundary between glass of refractive index 1.52 and water (refractive index =1.33) is 61°.

b Figure 5 shows the path of a light ray in water of refractive index 1.33 directed at an angle of incidence of 40° at a thick glass plate of refractive index 1.52. Calculate **i** the angle of refraction of the light ray at P, **ii** the angle of incidence of the light ray at Q.

Figure 5

c Sketch the path of the light ray beyond Q.

3 A window pane made of glass of refractive index 1.55 is covered on one side only with a transparent film of refractive index 1.40.

a Calculate the critical angle of the film–glass boundary,

b A light ray in air is directed at the film at an angle of incidence of 45° as shown in the diagram. Calculate **i** the angle of refraction in the film, **ii** the angle of refraction of the ray where it leaves the pane.

Figure 6

4 **a** In a medical endoscope, the fibre bundle used to view the image is coherent.

   i What is meant by a coherent fibre bundle?

   ii Explain why this fibre bundle needs to be coherent.

b i Why is an optical fibre used in communication composed of a core surrounded by a layer of cladding of lower refractive index ?

   ii Why is it necessary for the core of an optical communications fibre to be narrow?

13.4 Double slit interference

Learning objectives:

■ What is the general condition for the formation of a bright fringe?

■ Are Young's fringes equally spaced?

■ What factors could be (i) increased or (ii) decreased, to increase the fringe spacing?

Specification reference: 3.2.3

How science works

Young's double slits experiment

The wave nature of light was first suggested by Christian Huygens in the 17th century but it was rejected at the time in favour of Sir Isaac Newton's corpuscular theory of light. Newton considered that light was composed of tiny particles, which he referred to as corpuscles, and he was able to explain reflection and refraction using his theory. Huygens was also able to explain reflection and refraction using his wave theory. However, because of Newton's much stronger scientific reputation, Newton's theory of light remained unchallenged for over a century until 1803, when Thomas Young demonstrated interference of light.

Figure 1 *Thomas Young 1773–1829*

Figure 2 *Young's double slits experiment*

To observe interference of light, we can illuminate two closely spaced parallel slits (double slits) using a suitable light source, as described below. The two slits act as **coherent** sources of waves, which means that they emit light waves with a constant phase difference and the same frequency.

1 An arrangement like the one used by Thomas Young is shown in Figure 2. Young would have used a candle instead of a light bulb to illuminate a narrow single slit. The double slits arrangement is illuminated by light from the narrow single slit. Alternate bright and dark fringes, referred to as **Young's fringes**, can be seen on a white screen placed where the diffracted light from the double slits overlaps. The fringes are evenly spaced and parallel to the double slits.

Note:

If the single slit is too wide, each part of it produces a fringe pattern, which is displaced slightly from the pattern due to adjacent parts of the single slit. As a result, the dark fringes of the double slit pattern become narrower than the bright fringes, and contrast is lost between the dark and the bright fringes.

2 A laser beam from a low power laser could be used instead of the light bulb and the single slit. Figure 3 shows the arrangement. The fringes **must** be displayed on a screen, as a beam of laser light will damage the retina if it

laser beam
laser   double slits   screen

Figure 3 *Using a laser to demonstrate interference*

enters the eye. See Topic 13.5 for more information about laser light.

The fringes are formed due to **interference of light** from the two slits:

■ **Where a bright fringe is formed**, the light from one slit reinforces the light from the other slit. In other words, the light waves from each slit arrive in phase with each other.

■ **Where a dark fringe is formed**, the light from one slit cancels the light from the other slit. In other words, the light waves from the two slits arrive **180° out of phase**. See Topic 12.4 if necessary.

The distance from the centre of a bright fringe to the centre of the next bright fringe is called the fringe separation. This depends on the slit spacing s and the distance D from the slits to the screen, in accordance with the equation

$$\text{fringe separation, } w = \frac{\lambda D}{s}\text{, where } \lambda \text{ is the wavelength of light.}$$

The equation shows that the fringes become more widely spaced if:

■ the distance D from the slits to the screen is increased,

■ the wavelength λ of the light used is increased,

■ the slit spacing, s, is reduced. Note that the slit spacing is the distance between the centres of the slits.

⚠ The theory of the double slits equation

Consider the two slits S_1 and S_2 shown in Figure 4. At a point P on the screen where the fringes are observed, light emitted from S_1 arrives later than light from S_2 emitted at the same time. This is because the distance S_1P is greater than the distance S_2P. The difference between distances S_1P and S_2P is referred to as the **path difference**.

■ **For reinforcement at P, the path difference $S_1P - S_2P = m\lambda$**, where m = 0, 1, 2, etc.

Therefore, light emitted simultaneously from S_1 and S_2 arrives in phase at P if reinforcement occurs at P.

■ **For cancellation at P, the path difference $S_1P - S_2P = (m + \frac{1}{2})\lambda$,** where m = 0, 1, 2, etc.

Therefore, light emitted simultaneously from S_1 and S_2 arrives at P out of phase by 180° if cancellation occurs at P.

In Figure 4, a point Q along line S_1P has been marked such that $QP = S_2P$. Therefore, the path difference $S_1P - S_2P$ is represented by the distance S_1Q.

Warning!

Never look along a laser beam, even after reflection.

AQA Examiner's tip

Convert all distances into metres when substituting into the fringe spacing equation. The wavelength of visible light is usually quoted in nanometres (1 nm = 10^{-9} m).

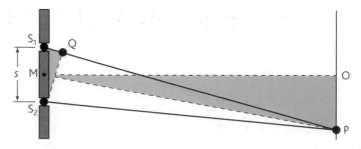

Figure 4 *The theory of the double slits experiment*

Consider triangles S_1S_2Q and MOP, where M is the midpoint between the two slits and O is the midpoint of the central bright fringe of the pattern. The two triangles are very nearly similar in shape, as angles $S_1\hat{S}_2Q$ and $P\hat{M}O$ are equal and the long sides of each triangle are of almost equal length. Therefore

$$\frac{S_1Q}{S_1S_2} = \frac{OP}{OM}$$

If P is the mth bright fringe from the centre (where $m = 0, 1, 2$, etc), then $S_1Q = m\lambda$ and $OP = mw$, where w is the distance between centres of adjacent bright fringes. Also, OM = distance D and S_1S_2 = slit spacing s.

Therefore,

$$\frac{m\lambda}{s} = \frac{mw}{D}$$

Rearranging this equation gives

$$\lambda = \frac{sw}{D}$$

or

$$w = \frac{\lambda D}{s}$$

By measuring the slit spacing, s, the fringe separation, w, and the slit-screen distance D, the wavelength λ of the light used can be calculated. The formula is valid only if the fringe separation, w, is much less than the distance D from the slits to the screen. This condition is to ensure that the triangles S_1S_2Q and MOP are very nearly similar in shape.

Notes:

1 To measure the fringe separation, w, measure across several fringes from the centre of a dark fringe to the centre of another dark fringe, because the centres of the dark fringes are easier to locate than the centres of the bright fringes. Obtain w by dividing your measurement by the number of fringes you measured across.

2 Light wavelengths are usually expressed in nanometres (nm) where $1\,\text{nm} = 10^{-9}\,\text{m}$.

Summary questions

1 In a double slits experiment using red light, a fringe pattern is observed on a screen at a fixed distance from the double slits. How would the fringe pattern change if:

   a the screen is moved closer to the slits,

   b one of the double slits is blocked completely?

2 The following measurements were made in a double slits experiment:

   Slit spacing, $s = 0.4\,\text{mm}$, fringe separation, $w = 1.1\,\text{mm}$, slit–screen distance $D = 0.80\,\text{m}$.

   Calculate the wavelength of light used.

3 In 2, the double slit arrangement was replaced by a pair of slits with a slit spacing of 0.5 mm. Calculate the fringe separation for the same slit–screen distance and wavelength.

4 The following measurements were made in a double slits experiment:

   Slit spacing, $s = 0.4\,\text{mm}$, fringe separation, $w = 1.1\,\text{mm}$, wavelength of light used = 590 nm. Calculate the distance from the slits to the screen.

13.5 More about interference

Learning objectives:

■ What are coherent sources?

■ Why are slits used, rather than two separate light sources, in Young's double slits experiment?

■ What are the roles of diffraction, and interference, when producing Young's fringes?

Specification reference: 3.2.3

vibrating beam

barriers

cancellations   cancellations

Figure 1 *Interference of water waves*

AQA Examiner's tip

It isn't necessary for two sources to be in phase for them to be coherent; a constant phase difference between them is sufficient.

a *in red light*

b *in blue light*

Figure 3 *The double slits fringe pattern*

Coherence

The double slits are described as **coherent sources** because they emit light waves with a constant phase difference, provided we illuminate the double slits with laser light, or light from a narrow single slit, if we are using non-laser light. Each wave crest or wave trough from the single slit always passes through one of the double slits a fixed time after it passes through the other slit. The double slits therefore emit wavefronts with a constant phase difference.

The double slits arrangement is like the ripple tank demonstration in Figure 1. Straight waves from the beam vibrating on the water surface diffract after passing through the two gaps in the barrier, and produce an interference pattern where the diffracted waves overlap. If one gap is closer to the beam than the other, each wavefront from the beam passes through the nearer gap first. However, the time interval between the same wavefront passing through the two gaps is always the same so the waves emerge from the gaps with a constant phase difference.

Light from two nearby lamp bulbs could not form an interference pattern because the two light sources emit light waves at random. The points of cancellation and reinforcement would change at random, so no interference pattern is possible.

Wavelength and colour

600 nm   500 nm   400 nm   300 nm
wavelength

Figure 2 *Wavelength and colour*

In the double slits experiment, the fringe separation depends on the colour of light used. White light is composed of a continuous spectrum of colours, corresponding to a continuous range of wavelengths from about 350 nm for violet light to about 650 nm for red light. Each colour of light has its own wavelength, as shown in Figure 2.

The fringe pattern photographs in Figure 3 show that the fringe separation is greater for red light than for blue light. This is because red light has a longer wavelength than blue light. The fringe spacing, w, depends on the wavelength λ of the light, according to the formula

$$w = \frac{\lambda D}{s}$$

as explained in Topic 13.4. Thus the longer the wavelength of the light used, the greater the fringe separation.

■ Light sources

Vapour lamps and discharge tubes produce light with a dominant colour. For example, the sodium vapour lamp produces a yellow/orange glow, which is due to light of wavelength 590 nm. Other wavelengths of light are also emitted from a sodium vapour lamp but the colour due to light of wavelength 590 nm is much more intense than any other colour. A sodium vapour lamp is in effect a monochromatic light source, because its spectrum is dominated by light of a certain colour.

Light from a filament lamp or from the Sun is composed of the colours of the spectrum and therefore covers a continuous range of wavelengths from about 350 nm to about 650 nm. If a beam of white light is directed at a colour filter, the light from the filter is a particular colour because it contains a much narrower range of wavelengths than white light does.

Light from a laser differs from non-laser light in two main ways:

■ **Laser light is highly monochromatic**, which means we can specify its wavelength to within a nanometre. The wavelength depends on the type of laser that produces it. For example, a helium-neon laser produces red light of wavelength 635 nm. Because a laser beam is almost perfectly parallel and monochromatic, a convex lens can focus it to a very fine spot. The beam power is then concentrated in a very small area. This is why a laser beam is very dangerous if it enters the eye. The eye lens would focus the beam on a tiny spot on the retina and the intense concentration of light at that spot would destroy the retina.

Never look along a laser beam, even after reflection.

■ **A laser is a convenient source of coherent light.** When we use a laser to demonstrate 'double slit' interference, we can illuminate the double slits directly. We do not need to make the light pass through a narrow single slit first as we do with light from a non-laser light source. This is because a laser is a source of coherent light. A light source emits light as a result of electrons inside its atoms moving to lower energy levels inside the atoms. Each such electron emits a photon, which is a 'packet' of electromagnetic waves of constant frequency. See Topic 1.3 for more about photons. Inside a laser, each emitted photon causes more photons to be emitted as it passes through the light-emitting substance. These 'stimulated' photons are in phase with the photon that caused them. As a result, the photons in a laser beam are in phase with each other. So the laser is a coherent source of light. In comparison, in a non-laser light source, the atoms emit photons at random so the photons in such a beam have random phase differences.

AQA Examiner's tip

For this AS specification, you need to know that a laser is a coherent source of light and a non-laser source is not a coherent source. Details of how a laser works are not required.

■ How science works

Laser light is used to read DVDs in computers and DVD players. The track of a DVD is very narrow and is encoded with 'pits' representing digital information. The 'pits' cause the intensity of the laser light reflected from the track to change. A detector converts the reflected light intensity into an electronic signal.

White light fringes

Figure 3 shows the fringe patterns observed with blue light and with red light. As explained above, the blue light fringes are closer together than the red light fringes. However, the central fringe of each pattern is in the same position on the screen. The fringe pattern produced by white light is shown in Figure 4. Each component colour of white light produces its own fringe pattern, each pattern centred on the screen at the same position. As a result:

The central fringe is white because every colour contributes at the centre of the pattern.

The inner fringes are tinged with blue on the inner side and red on the outer side. This is because the red fringes are more spaced out than the blue fringes and the two fringe patterns do not overlap exactly.

The outer fringes merge into an indistinct background of white light becoming fainter with increasing distance from the centre. This is because, where the fringes merge, different colours reinforce and therefore overlap.

Figure 4 *White light fringes*

Summary questions

1. **a** Sketch an arrangement that may be used to observe the fringe pattern when light from a narrow slit illuminated by a sodium vapour lamp is passed through a pair of double slits.

   b Describe the fringe pattern you would expect to observe in **a**.

2. In **1a**, describe how the fringe pattern would change if

   a one of the double slits is blocked,

   b the narrow single slit is replaced by a wider slit.

3. Double slit interference fringes are observed using light of wavelength 590 nm and a pair of double slits of slit spacing 0.50 mm. The fringes are observed on a screen at a distance of 0.90 m from the double slits. Calculate the fringe separation of these fringes.

4. Describe and explain the fringe pattern that would be observed in **3** if the light source were replaced by a white light source.

13.6 Diffraction

Specification reference: 3.2.3

Learning objectives:

- Why is diffraction of light important in the design of optical instruments?

- How does the single slit diffraction pattern compare with the pattern of Young's fringes?

- What is the effect of the single slit pattern on the brightness of Young's fringes?

Observing diffraction

Diffraction is the spreading of waves when they pass through a gap or by an edge. This general property of all waves is very important in the design of optical instruments, such as cameras, microscopes and telescopes. For example, when a telescope is used to observe planets, we can often see features that are not evident when observed directly. This is partly because less diffraction occurs when waves pass through a wide gap than through a narrow gap. Therefore, because a telescope is much wider than the eye pupil, much less diffraction occurs when using a telescope than when observing with the unaided eye.

Diffraction of water waves through a gap can be observed using a ripple tank, as explained in Topic 12.3. This arrangement shows that the diffracted waves spread out more if:

- the gap is made narrower, or
- the wavelength is made larger.

In addition, close examination of the diffracted waves should reveal that the each diffracted wavefront has breaks either side of the centre. These breaks are due to waves diffracted by adjacent sections on the gap being out of phase and cancelling each other out in certain directions.

Diffraction of light by a single slit can be demonstrated by directing a parallel beam of light at the slit. The diffracted light forms a pattern that can be observed on a white screen. The pattern shows a central fringe with further fringes either side of the central fringe, as shown in Figure 2. The intensity of the fringes is greatest at the centre of the central fringe. Figure 2 also shows the variation of the intensity of the diffracted light with the distance from the centre of the fringe pattern.

Hint

The central bright fringe of the single slit pattern is twice as wide as the others, and much brighter than them.

Figure 1

Figure 2 *Single slit diffraction*

Note:

- the central fringe is twice as wide as each of the outer fringes (measured from minimum to minimum intensity),
- the peak intensity of each fringe decreases with distance from the centre,
- each of the outer fringes is the same width,
- the outer fringes are much less intense than the central fringe.

More about single slit diffraction

If the single slit pattern is observed:

- using different sources of monochromatic light in turn, the observations show that the greater the wavelength, the wider the fringes,
- using an adjustable slit, the observations show that making the slit narrower makes the fringes wider.

It can be shown theoretically that the width W of the central fringe observed on a screen at distance D from the slit is given by

$$W = \frac{\text{the wavelength of the light } (\lambda)}{\text{the width of the single slit } (a)} \times 2D$$

Therefore, the width of each fringe is proportional to λ/a. For this reason, using blue light, the fringes are narrower than if red light had been used.

AQA Examiner's tip

The formula for W is not required in the Unit specification but it is helpful to remember that W is proportional to λ/a.

How science works

Microscopes and diffraction

Microscopes are often fitted with a blue filter as greater detail (better resolution) can be seen in microscope images observed with blue light than with white light. In an electron microscope, the resolution is increased when a higher voltage setting is used. This is because the higher the voltage, the greater the speed of the electrons in the microscope beam and therefore the smaller the de Broglie wavelength of the electrons (see Topic 3.6). Hence the electrons are diffracted less as they pass through the microscope's magnetic lenses.

Figure 3 *(a) An electron microscope in use (b) An electron microscope image*

Single slit diffraction and Young's fringes

In the double slits experiment in Topic 13.4, we saw that light passes through the two slits of the double slits arrangement and produces an interference pattern. However, if the slits are too wide and too far apart, no interference pattern is observed. This is because interference can only occur if the light from the two slits overlaps. For this to be the case:

- each slit must be narrow enough to make the light passing through it diffract sufficiently,
- the two slits must be close enough so the diffracted waves overlap on the screen.

In general, for monochromatic light of wavelength λ, incident on two slits of aperture width a at slit separation s (from centre to centre),

- the fringe spacing of the interference fringes, $w = \dfrac{\lambda D}{s}$

■ the width of the central diffraction fringe, $W = \dfrac{2\lambda D}{a}$, where D is the slit–screen distance.

Figure 4 shows the intensity variation with distance across the screen in terms of distance from the centre of the pattern. Using the expressions above, you should be able to see that only a few interference fringes will be observed in the central diffraction fringe if the slit separation s is small compared to the slit width a.

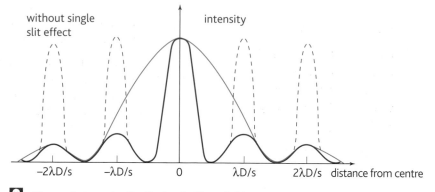

💡 **Figure 4** *Intensity distribution for Young's fringes*

Summary questions

1 Red light from a laser is directed normally at a slit that can be adjusted in width. The diffracted light from the slit forms a pattern of diffraction fringes on a white screen. Describe how the appearance of the fringes changes if the slit is made wider.

2 A narrow beam of white light is directed normally at a single slit. The diffracted light forms a pattern on a white screen.

  a A blue filter is placed in the path of the beam before it reaches the slit. The distance across five fringes including the central fringe is 18 mm. Calculate the width of the central fringe.

  b The blue filter is replaced by a red filter. Compare the red fringe pattern with the blue fringe pattern.

3 Figure 3 of Topic 13.5 shows the interference fringes observed in a Young's fringes experiment.

  a Explain why the fringes at the outer edges are dimmer than the fringes nearer the centre.

  b Describe how the appearance of the fringes would change if the slits were made wider without changing their centre-to-centre separation.

  c Sketch a graph to show how the intensity of the fringes varies with distance from the centre of the central fringe.

  d Explain why wider slits at the same spacing could produce fringes at the outer edges brighter than some of the fringes nearer the centre.

4 a Explain why an optical microscope image can be seen in more detail if it is observed using blue light instead of red light.

  b Explain why a radio telescope with a large reflecting dish gives more detailed images that one with a small dish.

13.7 The diffraction grating

Learning objectives:

- Why does a diffraction grating diffract monochromatic light in certain directions only?

- If a coarser grating is used, what is the effect on the number of diffracted beams produced and on the spread of each diffracted beam?

- How can we determine the grating spacing for any given grating, if it is not known?

Specification reference: 3.2.3

Testing a diffraction grating

A diffraction grating consists of a plate with many closely spaced parallel slits ruled on it. When a parallel beam of monochromatic light is directed normally at a diffraction grating, light is transmitted by the grating in certain directions only. This is because:

- the light passing through each slit is diffracted,

- the diffracted light waves from adjacent slits reinforce each other in certain directions only, including the incident light direction, and cancel out in all other directions.

Figure 1 shows one way to observe the effect of a diffraction grating on the incident light beam.

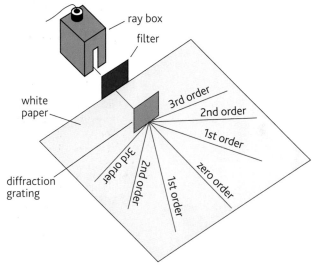

Figure 1 *The diffraction grating*

The central beam, referred to as the 'zero order beam', is in the same direction as the incident beam. The other transmitted beams are numbered outwards from the zero order beam. The angle of diffraction between each transmitted beam and the central beam increases if:

- light of a longer wavelength is used (e.g. by replacing a blue filter with a red filter),

- a grating with closer slits is used.

The diffraction grating equation

Consider a magnified view of part of a diffraction grating, as shown in Figure 2. Each slit diffracts the light waves that pass through it. Figure 2 shows a snapshot of the diffracted waves. As each diffracted wavefront emerges from a slit, it reinforces a wavefront from each of the adjacent slits. For example, in Figure 2, the wavefront emerging at P reinforces the wavefront emitted from Q one cycle earlier, which reinforces the wavefront emitted from R one cycle earlier, etc. The effect is to form a new wavefront PYZ which travels in a certain direction and contributes to the first order diffracted beam.

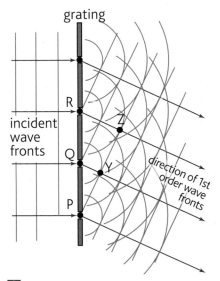

Figure 2 *Formation of the first order wavefront*

🔎 **Figure 3** *The nth order wavefront*

Figure 3 shows the formation of a wavefront of the nth order beam. The wavefront emerging from slit P reinforces a wavefront emitted n cycles earlier by the adjacent slit Q. This earlier wavefront therefore must have travelled a distance of n wavelengths from the slit. Thus the perpendicular distance QY from the slit to the wavefront is equal to $n\lambda$, where λ is the wavelength of the light waves.

Since the angle of diffraction of the beam, θ, is equal to the angle between the wavefront and the plane of the slits, it follows that $\sin\theta = QY/QP$, where QP is the grating spacing (i.e. the centre-to-centre distance d between adjacent slits).

Substituting d for QP and $n\lambda$ for QY therefore gives $\sin\theta = n\lambda/d$. Rearranging this equation gives the diffraction grating equation for the angle of diffraction of the nth order beam

$$d\sin\theta = n\lambda$$

Notes:

1   The number of slits per metre on the grating, $N = 1/d$ where d is the grating spacing.
2   For a given order and wavelength, the smaller the value of d, the greater the angle of diffraction. In other words, the larger the number of slits per metre, the bigger the angle of diffraction.
3   Fractions of a degree are usually expressed either as a decimal or in minutes (abbreviated ') where $1° = 60'$.
4   To find the maximum number of orders produced, substitute $\theta = 90°$ ($\sin\theta = 1$) in the grating equation and calculate n using $n = d/\lambda$.

The maximum number of orders is given by the value of d/λ rounded down to the nearest whole number.

How science works

Diffraction gratings in action

Diffraction gratings can be made by cutting parallel grooves very close together on a smooth glass plate. Each groove transmits some incident light and reflects or scatters some. So the grooves act as coherent emitters of waves just as if they were slits. However, the effective slit width needs to be much smaller than the grating spacing. This is so that the diffracted waves from each groove spread out widely. If they did not, the higher order beams would be much less intense than the lower order beams.

We can use a diffraction grating in a **spectrometer** to study the spectrum of light from any light source and to measure light wavelengths very accurately. A spectrometer is designed to measure angles to within 1 arc minute, which is a sixtieth of a degree. The angle of diffraction of a diffracted beam can be measured very accurately. The grating spacing of a diffraction grating can therefore be measured very accurately using light of a known wavelength. The grating can then be used to measure light of any wavelength.

Most industrial and research laboratories now use a **spectrum analyser**, which is an electronic spectrometer linked to a computer that gives a visual display of the variation of intensity with wavelength. The spectrometer shown in Figure 4a) would be used to check the calibration of the spectrum analyser. Knowledge of how a spectrometer or a spectrum analyser works or how they are used is not required in this specification.

Figure 4
(a) A spectrometer fitted with a diffraction grating (b) A spectrum analyser and display

Types of spectra

Continuous spectra

The spectrum of light from a filament lamp is a continuous spectrum of colour from deep violet at about 350 nm to deep red at about 650 nm, as shown in Figure 5. The most intense part of the spectrum depends on the temperature of the light source. The hotter the light source, the shorter the wavelength of the brightest part of the spectrum. By measuring the wavelength of the brightest part of a continuous spectrum, we can therefore measure the temperature of the light source.

Figure 5 *A continuous spectrum*

Line emission spectra

As explained in Topic 3.5, a glowing gas in a vapour lamp or a discharge tube emits light at specific wavelengths so its spectrum consists of narrow vertical lines of different colours as shown in Figure 6. The wavelengths of the lines are characteristic of the chemical element that produced the light. If a glowing gas contains more than one element, the elements in the gas can be identified by observing its line spectrum.

Figure 6 *A line emission spectrum*

Line absorption spectra

A line absorption spectrum is a continuous spectrum with narrow dark lines at certain wavelengths. For example, if the spectrum of light from a filament lamp is observed after passing it through a glowing gas, thin dark vertical lines are observed superimposed on the continuous spectrum, as shown in Figure 7. The pattern of the dark lines is due to the elements in the glowing gas. These elements absorb light of the same wavelengths they can emit at so the transmitted light is missing these wavelengths. The atoms of the glowing gas that absorb light then emit the light subsequently but not necessarily in the same direction as the transmitted light.

Figure 7 *A line absorption spectrum*

Summary questions

1 A laser beam of wavelength 630 nm is directed normally at a diffraction grating with 300 lines per millimetre. Calculate:

  a the angle of diffraction of each of the first two orders,

  b the number of diffracted orders produced.

2 Light directed normally at a diffraction grating contains wavelengths of 580 and 586 nm only. The grating has 600 lines per mm.

  a How many diffracted orders are observed in the transmitted light?

  b For the highest order, calculate the angle between the two diffracted beams.

3 Light of wavelength 430 nm is directed normally at a diffraction grating. The first order transmitted beams are at 28° to the zero order beam. Calculate:

  a the number of slits per millimetre on the grating,

  b the angle of diffraction for each of the other diffracted orders of the transmitted light.

4 A diffraction grating is designed with a slit width of 0.83 μm. When used in a spectrometer to view light of wavelength 430 nm, diffracted beams are observed at angles of 14° 55′ and 50° 40′ to the zero order beam.

  a Assuming the low-angle diffracted beam is the first order beam, calculate the number of lines per mm on the grating.

  b Explain why there is no diffracted beam between the two observed beams. What is the order number for the beam at 50° 40′?

(Reminder: 1 degree = 60 minutes.)

1 In a secure communications system, an optical fibre is used to transmit digital signals in the form of infrared pulses. The fibre has a thin core, which is surrounded by cladding that has a lower refractive index than the core.

(a) **Figure 1** shows a cross-section of a straight length of the fibre.

Figure 1

   (i) The core has a refractive index of 1.52 and the cladding has a refractive index of 1.35. Show that the critical angle at the core–cladding boundary is 62.6°.

   (ii) Sketch the path of a light ray in the core that is totally internally reflected when it reaches the core–cladding boundary. *(6 marks)*

(b) (i) Explain why the cladding is necessary.

   (ii) An optical fibre is used to transmit digital images from a security camera to a computer where the images are stored. A prominent notice near the camera informs people that the camera is in use. Discuss the benefits and drawbacks associated with making and storing images of people in this situation. *(7 marks)*

2 The diagram shows a cube of glass. A ray of light, incident at the centre of a face of the cube, at an angle of incidence θ, goes on to meet another face at an angle of incidence of 50°, as shown in **Figure 2**.

critical angle at the glass–air boundary = 45°

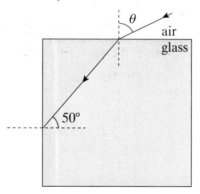

Figure 2

(a) Draw on the diagram the continuation of the path of the ray, showing it passing through the glass and out into the air. *(3 marks)*

(b) Show that the refractive index of the glass is 1.41. *(2 marks)*

(c) Calculate the angle of incidence, θ. *(3 marks)*

AQA, 2005

3 **Figure 3** shows a ray of monochromatic light, in the plane of the paper, incident on the end face of an optical fibre.

Figure 3

(a) (i) Draw on a copy of the diagram the complete path followed by the incident ray, showing it entering into the fibre and emerging from the fibre at the far end.

(ii) State any changes that occur in the speed of the ray as it follows this path from the source.

Calculations are not required. *(4 marks)*

(b) (i) Calculate the critical angle for the optical fibre at the air boundary. refractive index of the optical fibre glass = 1.57.

(ii) The optical fibre is now surrounded by cladding of refractive index 1.47. Calculate the critical angle at the core–cladding boundary.

(iii) State **one** advantage of cladding an optical fibre. *(6 marks)*

AQA, 2004

4 (a) State what is meant by *coherent sources* of light. *(2 marks)*

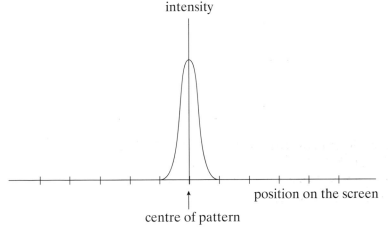

Figure 4

(b) Young's fringes are produced on the screen from the monochromatic source by the arrangement shown in **Figure 4**.

(i) Explain why slit S should be narrow.

(ii) Why do slits S_1 and S_2 act as coherent sources? *(4 marks)*

(c) The pattern on the screen may be represented as a graph of intensity against position on the screen. The central fringe is shown on the graph in **Figure 5**. Copy and complete this graph to represent the rest of the pattern by drawing on **Figure 5**. *(2 marks)*

intensity

position on the screen

centre of pattern

Figure 5

AQA, 2005

5 A diffraction grating has 940 lines per mm.

(a) Calculate the distance between adjacent lines on the grating. *(1 mark)*

(b) Monochromatic light is incident on the grating and a second-order spectral line is formed at an angle of 55° from the normal to the grating. Calculate the wavelength of the light. *(3 marks)*

AQA, 2006

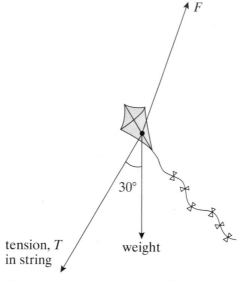
Unit 2 questions: Mechanics, materials and waves

1   **Figure 1** shows the forces acting on a stationary kite. The force F is the force that the air exerts on the kite.

F

$30°$

tension, T
in string

weight

Figure 1

(a) Show on the diagram how force F can be resolved into horizontal and vertical components.   *(1 mark)*

(b) The magnitude of the tension, T, is 25 N.
Calculate:
   (i) the horizontal component of the tension,
   (ii) the vertical component of the tension.   *(2 marks)*

(c) (i)   Calculate the magnitude of the vertical component of F when the weight of the kite is 2.5 N.
   (ii) State the magnitude of the horizontal component of F.
   (iii) Hence calculate the magnitude of F.   *(5 marks)*

AQA, 2002

2   A uniform heavy metal bar of weight 250 N is suspended by two vertical wires, supported at their upper ends from a horizontal surface, as shown.

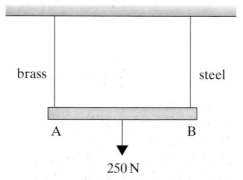

brass   steel

A   B

250 N

Figure 2

One wire is made of brass and the other of steel. The cross-sectional area of each wire is $2.5 \times 10^{-7}\,m^2$ and the unstretched length of each wire is 2.0 m.

the Young modulus for brass = 1.0×10^{11} Pa

the Young modulus for steel = 2.0×10^{11} Pa

   (i)   Calculate the extension of the steel wire, if the tension in it is 125 N

  (ii)   Estimate how much lower the end A will be than the end B.   *(5 marks)*

AQA, 2002

3   **Figure 3** shows the velocity–time graph for a vertically bouncing ball, which is released above the ground at A and strikes the floor at B. The effects of air resistance have been neglected.

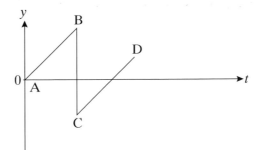

Figure 3

(a) (i)   What does the gradient of a velocity–time graph represent?

    (ii)   Explain why the gradient of the line CD is the same as line AB.

   (iii)   What does the area between the line AB and the time axis represent?

   (iv)   State why the velocity at C is negative.

    (v)   State why the speed at C is less than the speed at B.   *(5 marks)*

(b)   The ball has a mass of 0.15 kg and is dropped from an initial height of 1.2m. After impact the ball rebounds to a height of 0.75m.

     Calculate:

    (i)   the speed of the ball immediately before impact,

   (ii)   the speed of the ball immediately after impact.   *(4 marks)*

AQA, 2003

4   In a vehicle impact, a car ran into the back of a lorry. The car driver sustained serious injuries, which would have been much less had the car been fitted with a driver's air bag.

(a)   Explain why the effect of the impact on the driver would have been much less if an air bag had been fitted and had inflated in the crash.   *(4 marks)*

(b)   Calculate the deceleration of the car if it was travelling at a speed of 18 m s^{-1} when the impact occurred and was brought to rest in a distance of 2.5 m.   *(2 marks)*

AQA, 2004

5   **Figure 4** shows a spacecraft that initially moves at a constant velocity of 890 m s^{-1} towards **A**.

To change course, a sideways force is produced by firing thrusters. This increases the velocity towards **B** from 0 to 60 m s^{-1} in 25 s.

Figure 4   thrusters

(a)   The spacecraft has a mass of 5.5×10^4 kg. Calculate:

    (i)   the acceleration of the spacecraft towards **B**,

   (ii)   the force on the spacecraft produced by the thrusters.   *(3 marks)*

(b)   Calculate the magnitude of the resultant velocity after 25 s.   *(2 marks)*

(c)   Calculate the angle between the initial and final directions of travel.   *(1 mark)*

AQA, 2004

6 (a) Explain why a raindrop falling vertically through still air reaches a constant velocity. *(4 marks)*

(b) A raindrop falls at a constant vertical velocity of $1.8\,\text{m s}^{-1}$ in still air. The mass of the raindrop is $7.2 \times 10^{-9}\,\text{kg}$.

Calculate:

(i) the kinetic energy of the raindrop,

(ii) the work done on the raindrop as it falls through a vertical distance of 4.5 m.

(4 marks)

(c) The raindrop in part (b) now falls through air in which a horizontal wind is blowing. If the velocity of the wind is $1.4\,\text{m s}^{-1}$, use a scale diagram or calculation to determine the magnitude and direction of the resultant velocity of the raindrop. *(3 marks)*

AQA, 2005

7 A wind turbine, as shown in **Figure 5**, has blades of length 22 m. When the wind speed is $15\,\text{m s}^{-1}$ its output power is 1.5 MW.

Figure 5

(i) The volume of air passing through the blades each second can be calculated by considering a cylinder of radius equal to the length of the blade. Show that $2.3 \times 10^4\,\text{m}^3$ of air passes through the blades each second.

(ii) Calculate the mass of air that passes through the blades each second.

density of air $= 1.2\,\text{kg m}^{-3}$

(iii) Calculate the kinetic energy of the air reaching the blades each second.

(iv) Assuming that the power output of the turbine is proportional to the kinetic energy of the air reaching the blades each second, discuss the effect on the power output if the wind speed decreased by half. *(7 marks)*

AQA, 2005

8 Tidal power could make a significant contribution to UK energy requirements. This question is about a tidal power station which traps sea water behind a tidal barrier at high tide and then releases the water through turbines 10.0 m below the high tide mark.

Figure 6

(i) Calculate the mass of sea water covering an area of $120\,\text{km}^2$ and depth 10.0 m.

density of sea water $= 1100\,\text{kg m}^{-3}$

(ii) Calculate the maximum loss of potential energy of the sea water in part (i) when it is released through the turbines.

(iii) The potential energy of the sea water released through the turbines, calculated in part (ii), is lost over a period of 6.0 hours. Estimate the average power output of the power station over this time period. Assume the power station efficiency is 40%. *(7 marks)*

AQA, 2003

9 A winch in a boatyard uses a 230 V electric motor to raise objects from a boat onto the quayside, as shown in **Figure 7**.

Figure 7

(a) The winch takes 22 s to raise an object of mass 160 kg through a height of 5.0 m. The motor current during this time is 14 A. Calculate the efficiency of the winch. *(3 marks)*

(b) (i) The steel cable that is used to raise the 160 kg object has a cross-sectional area of 1.8×10^{-4} m². Calculate the strain in the cable when it raises the object at constant speed.

the Young modulus for steel = 2.1×10^{11} Pa

(ii) The length of steel cable from the object to the winch is 14 m when the object is on the boat. Calculate the extension of the cable when it supports the object. *(5 marks)*

AQA, 2005

10 An aerial system consists of a horizontal copper wire of length 38 m supported between two masts, as shown in **Figure 8**. The wire transmits electromagnetic waves when an alternating potential is applied to it at one end.

Figure 8

(a) The wavelength of the radiation transmitted from the wire is twice the length of the copper wire. Calculate the frequency of the transmitted radiation. *(1 mark)*

(b) The ends of the copper wire are fixed to masts of height 12.0 m. The masts are held in a vertical position by cables, labelled **P** and **Q**, as shown in **Figure 8**.

(i) **P** has a length of 14.0 m and the tension in it is 110 N. Calculate the tension in the copper wire.

(ii) The copper wire has a diameter of 4.0 mm. Calculate the stress in the copper wire.

(iii) Discuss whether the wire is in danger of breaking if it is stretched further due to movement of the top of the masts in strong winds.

breaking stress of copper = 3.0×10^8 Pa *(7 marks)*

AQA, 2006

11   (a) **Figure 9** shows an arrangement used to investigate the properties of microwaves.

Figure 9

When the transmitter T was rotated through 90° about the straight line XY, the receiver signal decreased to zero. Explain why this happened and state the property of microwaves responsible for this effect.   *(3 marks)*

(b) A microwave oven produces microwaves of wavelength 0.12 m in air.

   (i) Calculate the frequency of these microwaves.

   (ii) In a certain oven, explain why food heated in a fixed position in this oven would be uncooked at certain points if stationary waves were allowed to form.   *(3 marks)*

AQA, 2004

12   **Figure 10** shows a cross-sectional view of the base of a glass tank containing water. A point monochromatic light source is in contact with the base and ray, R_1, from the source has been drawn up to the point where it emerges along the surface of the water.

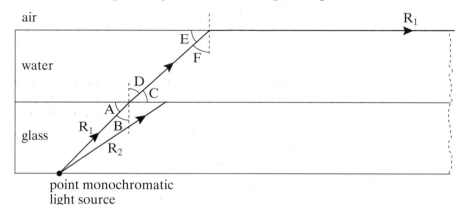

Figure 10

(a) (i) Which angle, A to F, is a critical angle?

   (ii) Explain how the path of R_1 demonstrates that the refractive index of glass is greater than the refractive index of water.   *(2 marks)*

(b) Using the following information

   A = 47.1°

   B = 42.9°

   C = E = 41.2°

   D = F = 48.8°

   calculate

   (i) the refractive index of water,

   (ii) the ratio, $\dfrac{\text{speed of light in water}}{\text{speed of light in glass}}$ *(5 marks)*

(c) Ray R_2 emerges from the source a few degrees away from ray R_1 as shown. Draw the continuation of ray R_2. Where possible show the ray being refracted.   *(2 marks)*

AQA, 2004

13 Red light from a laser is passed through a single narrow slit, as shown in **Figure 11**. A pattern of bright and dark regions can be observed on the screen which is placed several metres beyond the slit.

Figure 11   **Figure 12**

(a) The pattern on the screen may be represented as a graph of intensity against distance along the screen. The graph has been started in outline in **Figure 12**. The central bright region is already shown. Complete this graph to represent the rest of the pattern by drawing on **Figure 12**. *(4 marks)*

(b) State the effect on the pattern if each of the following changes is made separately.

   (i) The width of the narrow slit is reduced.

   (ii) With the original slit width, the intense red source is replaced with an intense source of green light. *(3 marks)*

AQA, 2002

14 (a) A student stands some distance away from a wall and claps her hands. She listens to the echoes produced by the sound reflected from the wall and adjusts her rate of clapping so that each clap coincides with the echo of the previous clap. A fellow student counts the number of times she claps in 20 s.

   (i) There were 47 claps in 20 s.

      Calculate the time between two successive claps.

   (ii) The speed of sound in air is 340 m s^{-1}.

      Calculate the distance of the student from the wall. *(3 marks)*

(b) The student goes on to carry out a diffraction experiment. She stands on one side of a fence that consists of evenly-spaced wooden strips. The fence behaves as a diffraction grating for sound waves. **Figure 13** shows the arrangement.

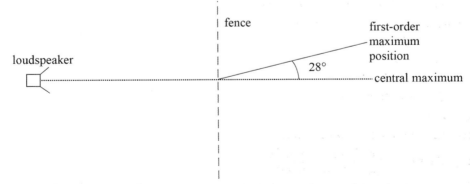

Figure 13

   (i) She uses a loudspeaker to send a sound wave of frequency 2.4 kHz towards the fence.

      Calculate the wavelength of this sound wave.

      speed of sound in air, $y = 340$ m s^{-1}

   (ii) A diffracted first-order maximum is observed at an angle of 28°. Calculate the spacing between adjacent wooden strips.

   (iii) Determine the highest order of maximum that could be heard. *(6 marks)*

AQA, 2006

Investigative and practical skills

Chapters in this unit

■ Moving on from GCSE

Practical work is an integral feature of your AS physics course as it helps you develop your understanding of important concepts and applications. It also teaches you how scientists work in practice. You will find out how important discoveries are made in the subject. You might even make important discoveries yourself. AS level practical skills build on the practical skills you have developed in your GCSE course. For example, you will need to build on your GCSE knowledge of dependent and independent variables, control variables, reliability and precision. In addition, you will be able to learn new skills, such as how to use measuring instruments (e.g. micrometers and oscilloscopes) and how to determine the accuracy of the measurements you make. Always remember that experiments and investigations are at the heart of how science works.

■ Assessment overview

During your course, you will carry out practical experiments and investigations to develop your skills and you will be assessed on how well you can:

- ■ **carry out practical work**
- ■ **analyse data from practical experiments and investigations**
- ■ **evaluate the results of practical experiments and investigations.**

Assessment of these skills will take place after you have carried out appropriate practical work as part of your course. There are two separate assessment schemes, T and X. Your teacher will decide which scheme you will be assessed on. The assessment is in two parts.

Scheme T The ISA/PSA scheme

1 **The investigative skills assignment (ISA)** consists of a practical task on a topic in the specification followed by a written test on your ability to analyse data and evaluate results. The written test will ask you about the results of your own task and about given results from a related practical investigation. The practical task and the written test are both set by AQA and are taken under supervision after you have studied the relevant topic. The ISA counts for 41 out of the 50 marks for the unit. More details are given about the ISA in Topic 15.1.

2 **The practical skills assessment (PSA)** will assess how well you can follow instructions and on how well you can make measurements. The assessment is made by your teacher towards the end of your course and is based on your practical work during the course, specifically your ability to follow instructions, your skill in using equipment and how well you can organise yourself and work safely in the laboratory. The PSA assessment counts for 9 out of the 50 marks for the unit. More details are given about the PSA in Topic 15.1.

Scheme X The AQA-marked scheme

This AQA-marked scheme is in three parts:

1 You are required to carry out 5 short practical exercises in normal class time on measuring tasks set by AQA. Your teacher will check that you have carried out each of these tasks satisfactorily. Some of the measuring skills in these tasks will be assessed in the AQA-set practical experiment in part 2.

2 and 3 These parts consist of practical experiments and a written test set and marked by AQA. You will need to obtain reliable and accurate results in the experiments (part 2) as you have to analyse and evaluate them in the written test (part 3). More details about scheme X are given in Topic 15.2.

The notes that follow apply equally well to either scheme as the skills you need are the same for both schemes. References in Chapter 14 to PSA or ISA features in scheme T apply equally well to the corresponding features in scheme X unless specifically stated.

14 Practical work in physics

14.1 Moving on from GCSE

In the laboratory

The experimental skills you will develop during your course are part of the 'tools of the trade' of every physicist. Data loggers and computers are commonplace in modern physics laboratories, but awareness on the part of the user of precision, reliability, errors and accuracy are just as important as when measurements are made with much simpler equipment. Let's consider in more detail what you need to be aware of when you are working in the physics laboratory.

Safety and organisation

Your teacher will give you a set of safety rules and should explain them to you. You must comply with them at all times. You must also use your common sense and organise yourself so that you work safely. For example, if you set up an experiment with pulleys and weights, you need to ensure they are stable and will not topple over.

Working with others

Most scientists work in teams, each person cooperating with other team members to achieve specific objectives. This is effective because, although each team member may have a designated part to play, the exchange of ideas within the team often gives greater insight and awareness as to how to achieve the objectives.

In your AS level practical activities, you will often work in a small group in which you need to cooperate with the others in the group so everyone understands the objectives of the practical activity and everyone participates in planning and carrying out the activity. Part of the PSA assessment is based on how effectively you contribute when you work with others. See the PSA assessment notes on pages 227–228.

Planning

At AS level, you may be asked to plan an experiment or investigation. The practical activities you carry out during your course should enable you to prepare a plan. Here are the key steps in drawing up a plan:

1 Decide in detail what you intend to investigate. Note the independent and dependent variables you intend to measure and note the variables that need to be controlled. The other variables need to be controlled to make sure they do not change. A **control variable** that can't be kept constant would cause **the dependent variable to alter.**

2 Select the equipment necessary for the measurements. Specify the range of any electrical meters you need.

3 List the key stages in the method you intend to follow and make some preliminary measurements to check your initial plans. Consider safety issues before you do any preliminary tests. If necessary, modify your plans as a result of your preliminary tests.

4 If the aim of your investigation is to test a hypothesis or theory or use the measurements to determine a physical quantity (e.g. resistivity), you need to know how to use the measurements you make.

Carrying out instructions and recording your measurements

In some investigations, you will be expected to follow instructions supplied to you either verbally or on a worksheet. You should be able to follow a sequence of instructions without guidance. Part of the PSA assessment is on how well you follow instructions. However, always remember safety first and, if the instructions are not clear, ask your teacher to clarify them.

When you record your measurements, tabulate them with a column for the independent variable and one or more columns for the dependent variable to allow for repeat readings and average values, if appropriate. The table should have a clear heading for each of the measured variables, with the unit shown after the heading, as below.

Single measurements of other variables (e.g. control variables) should be recorded together, immediately before or after the table. In addition, you should record the precision (i.e. the least detectable reading) of each measurement. This information is important when you come to analyse and evaluate your measurements.

Table 1 *Tabulating the measurements from an investigation of pd against current for a wire*

potential difference / V	current / A			average current / A
	1st set	2nd set	3rd set	

length of wire / m = _____
diameter of wire / mm = _____, _____, _____
average diameter of wire / mm = _____

14.2 Making careful measurements

Measurements and errors

Measurements play a key role in science, so they must be:

1 **reliable** – which means that a consistent value should be obtained each time the same measurement is repeated. An unreliable weighing machine in a shop would cause the customers to go elsewhere. In science, you can't go elsewhere so the measurements must be reliable. Each time a given measurement is repeated, it should give the same value within acceptable limits.

2 **valid** – which means the measurements are of the required data or can be used to give the required data. For example, a voltmeter connected across a variable resistor in series with a lamp and a battery would not measure the potential difference across the lamp.

Errors of measurement are important in finding out how accurate a measurement is. We need to consider errors in terms of differences from the mean value. Consider the example of measuring the diameter of a uniform wire using a micrometer. Suppose the following diameter readings are taken for different positions along the wire from one end to the other:

$$0.34\,\text{mm}, 0.33\,\text{mm}, 0.36\,\text{mm}, 0.33\,\text{mm}, 0.35\,\text{mm}.$$

- The **range** of the measurements is 0.03 mm. This is the difference between the lowest and the highest reading. We will see later we can use this to estimate the **uncertainty** or probable error of the measurement.

- The **mean value**, $<d>$, is 0.34 mm, calculated by adding the readings together and dividing by the number of readings. If the difference between each reading and $<d>$ changed regularly from one end of the wire to the other, it would be reasonable to conclude that the wire was non-uniform. Such differences are called **systematic errors**. If no such differences can be seen in the set of readings, in other words, there is no obvious pattern or bias or trend in the differences, the differences are said to be **random errors**.

What causes random errors? In the case of the wire, vibrations in the machine used to make the wire might have caused random variations in its diameter along its length. The experimenter might not use or read the micrometer correctly consistently. This shouldn't happen to a skilled experimenter.

The range of the diameter readings above is from 0.33 mm to 0.36 mm. The readings lie within 0.015 mm (i.e. half the range) of the mean value, which we will round up to 0.02 mm. The diameter can therefore be written as 0.34 ± 0.02 mm. The diameter is accurate to ± 0.02 mm. The uncertainty or probable error in the mean value of the diameter is therefore ± 0.02 mm.

Using instruments

Instruments used in the physics laboratory range from the very basic (e.g. a millimetre scale) to the highly-sophisticated (e.g. a multichannel data recorder). Whatever type of instrument you use, you need to know what the following terms mean.

Figure 1 *Physics instruments*

Zero error

Does the instrument read zero when it is supposed to? If not, the zero reading must be taken into account when measuring the gap width otherwise there will be a systematic error in the measurements.

Uncertainty

The uncertainty in the mean value of a measurement is half the range, expressed as a ± value (e.g. $I = 2.6 \pm 0.2\,A$). If the readings are the same, the instrument precision should be used as the uncertainty. At A level, probable error is used as an alternative term for uncertainty.

Accuracy

An **accurate** measurement is one that has been obtained using accurately-calibrated instruments correctly and where there are no systematic errors. **Accuracy** is a measure of confidence in a measurement and is usually expressed as the uncertainty in the measurement.

Precision

The **precision** of a measurement is the degree of exactness of the measurement. The precision of an instrument is the smallest non-zero reading that can be measured using the instrument.

■ If the reading of an instrument fluctuates when it is being taken, take several readings and calculate the mean value and range of the measurements. The precision of the measurement is then given by the uncertainty of the readings (i.e. half the range of the readings).

■ If the reading is constant, estimate the precision of a measurement directly from the instrument (or use the stated precision from the instrument specification).

Precise readings are not necessarily accurate readings, because systematic errors could make precise readings all lower or all higher than they ought to be.

Linearity

This is a design feature of many instruments; it means the reading is directly proportional to the magnitude of the variable that causes the reading to change. For example, if the scale of a moving coil meter is linear, the reading of the pointer against the scale should be proportional to the current.

A lens may be used to read a scale with greater precision. Provided the pointer is thin compared to a scale division, using a lens enables the scale to be read to within 0.2 of a division. In Figure 2, the scale can be read to $\pm 0.02\,A$ (= 0.2 of a scale division × 0.1 A).

Measurement errors are caused in analogue instruments if the pointer on the scale is not observed correctly. The observer must be directly in front of the pointer when the reading is made. Figure 3 shows how a plane mirror is used for this purpose. The image of the pointer must be directly behind the pointer to ensure the observer views the scale directly in front of the pointer.

Instrument range

Multirange instruments such as multimeters have a 'range' dial that needs to be set according to the maximum reading to be measured. For example, if the dial can be set at $0-0.10\,A$, $0-1.00\,A$ or $0-10.0\,A$, you would use the $0-1.00\,A$ range to measure the current through a 0.25 A torchbulb as the $0-0.10\,A$ range is too low and the $0-1.00\,A$ range is more sensitive than the $0-10.0\,A$ range.

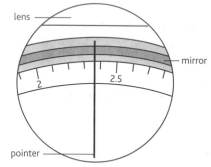

Figure 2 *Magnifying a scale*

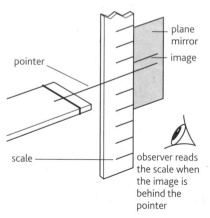

Figure 3 *Reading a scale*

Figure 4 *A multimeter*

14.3 Everyday physics instruments

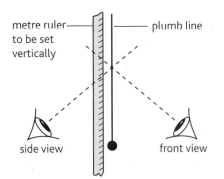

Figure 1 *Finding the vertical*

metre ruler to be set vertically — plumb line

side view — front view

If the metre ruler appears parallel to the plumb line from the front and the side, the ruler must be vertical.

Rulers and scales

Metre rulers are often used as vertical or horizontal scales in mechanics experiments.

To set a metre ruler in a vertical position:

- use a set square perpendicular to the ruler and the bench, if the bench is known to be horizontal, or
- use a plumb line (a small weight on a string) to see if the ruler is vertical. You need to observe the ruler next to the plumb line from two perpendicular directions. If the ruler appears parallel to the plumb line from both directions, then it must be vertical.

To ensure a metre ruler is horizontal, use a set square to align the metre ruler perpendicular to a vertical metre ruler.

Micrometers and verniers

gap — stem — barrel — knob

mm

Figure 2 *Using a micrometer*

Micrometers give readings to within 0.01 mm. A **digital** micrometer gives a read-out equal to the width of the micrometer gap. An **analogue** micrometer has a barrel on a screw thread with a pitch of 0.5 mm. For such a micrometer:

- the edge of the barrel is marked in 50 equal intervals so each interval corresponds to changing the gap of the micrometer by 0.5/50 mm = 0.01 mm
- the stem of the micrometer is marked with a linear scale graduated in 0.5 mm marks
- the reading of a micrometer is where the linear scale intersects the scale on the barrel.

Figure 2 shows a reading of 4.06 mm. Note that the edge of the barrel is between the 4.0 and 4.5 mm marks on the linear scale. The linear scale intersects the 6th mark after the zero mark on the barrel scale. The reading is therefore 4.00 mm from the linear scale + 0.06 mm from the barrel scale.

To use a micrometer correctly:

1. Check its zero reading and note the zero error if there is one.
2. Open the gap (by turning the barrel if analogue) then close the gap on the object to be measured. Turn the knob until it slips. Don't overtighten the barrel.
3. Take the reading and note the measurement after allowing if necessary for the zero error.
4. Note that the precision of the measurement is ±0.010 mm because the precision of the reading and the zero reading are both ±0.005 mm. So the difference between the two readings (i.e. the measurement) has a precision of 0.010 mm.

Vernier callipers are used for measurements of distances up to 100 mm or more. Readings can be made to within 0.1 mm. The sliding scale of an analogue vernier has ten equal intervals covering a distance of exactly 9 mm so each interval of this scale is 0.1 mm less than a 1 mm interval. To make a reading:

1 The zero mark on the sliding scale is used to read the main scale to the nearest millimetre. This reading is rounded down to the nearest millimetre.

2 The mark on the sliding scale closest to a mark on the millimetre scale is located and its number noted. Multiplying this number by 0.1 mm gives the distance to be added on to the rounded-down reading.

mm scale

sliding scale

The 0 of the sliding scale gives 3.9 cm and the 5th mark coincides with a mm mark

4   5

0   10

sliding scale

Figure 3 *Using a vernier*

Figure 3 shows the idea. The zero mark on the sliding scale is between 39 and 40 mm on the mm scale. So the rounded-down reading is 39 mm. The 5th mark after the zero on the sliding scale is nearest to a mark on the millimetre scale. So the extra distance to be added on to 39 mm is 0.5 mm (= 5 × 0.1 mm). Therefore, the reading is 39.5 mm.

■ Timers

Stopwatches used for interval timings are subject to human error because reaction time, about 0.2 s, is variable for any individual. With practice, the delays when starting and stopping a stopwatch can be reduced. Even so, the precision of a single timing is unlikely to be better than 0.1 s. Digital stopwatches usually have read-out displays with a resolution of 0.01 s but human variability makes such precision unrealistic and the precision of a single timing is the same as an analogue stopwatch.

Timing oscillations requires timing for as many cycles as possible. The timing should be repeated several times to give an average (mean) value. Any timing that is significantly different to the other values is probably due to miscounting the number of oscillations so that timing should be rejected. For accurate timings, a fiducial mark is essential. The mark should be lined up with the centre of the oscillations so it provides a reference position to count the number of cycles as the object swings past it each cycle.

Electronic timers use automatic switches or 'gates' to start and stop the timer. However, just as with a digital stopwatch, a timing should be repeated, if possible several times, to give an average value. Light gates may be connected via an interface unit to a microcomputer. Interrupt signals from the light gates are timed by the microcomputer's internal clock. A software program is used to provide a set of instructions to the microcomputer.

Balances

A balance is used to measure the weight of an object. Spring balances are usually less precise than lever balances. Both types of balance are usually much less precise than an electronic top-pan balance. The scale or read-out of a balance may be calibrated for convenience in kilograms or grams. The accuracy of an electronic top-pan balance can easily be tested using accurately known masses.

14.4 Analysis and evaluation

Data processing

For a single reading, the precision of the measuring instrument determines the precision of the reading. A micrometer with a precision of 0.01 mm gives readings that each have a precision of 0.01 mm.

For several readings, the number of significant figures of the mean value should be the same as the precision of each reading. For example, consider the following measurements of the diameter of a wire: 0.34 mm, 0.33 mm, 0.36 mm, 0.33 mm, 0.35 mm. The mean value of the diameter readings works out at 0.342 mm but the third significant figure cannot be justified, as the precision of each reading is 0.01 mm. Therefore the mean value is rounded down to 0.34 mm.

Note:

The uncertainty in the mean value is ± 0.02 mm (i.e. half the range) as explained in Topic 14.2.

Using error estimates

How confident can you be in your measurements and any results or conclusions you draw from your measurements? If you work out what each uncertainty is, as a percentage of the measurement (the percentage uncertainty), you can then see which measurement is least accurate. You can then think about how that measurement could be made more accurately.

Worked example:

The mass and diameter of a ball bearing were measured and the uncertainty of each measurement was estimated.

The mass, m, of a ball bearing = $4.85 \times 10^{-3} \pm 0.02 \times 10^{-3}$ kg

The diameter, d, of the ball bearing = $1.05 \times 10^{-2} \pm 0.01 \times 10^{-2}$ m

Calculate and compare the percentage uncertainty of these two measurements.

Solution

The percentage uncertainty of the mass $m = \dfrac{0.02}{4.85} \times 100\% = 0.4\%$

The percentage uncertainty of the diameter $d = \dfrac{0.01}{1.05} \times 100\% = 1.0\%$

The diameter measurement is therefore more than twice as inaccurate as the mass measurement.

More about errors

1 When two measurements are added or subtracted, the uncertainty of the result is the sum of the uncertainties of the measurements. For example, the mass of a beaker is measured when it is empty and then when it contains water:

■ the mass of an empty beaker = 65.1 ± 0.1 g

■ the mass of the beaker and water = 125.6 ± 0.1 g

Percentage uncertainty

To work out the percentage uncertainty of *A*, you could:

■ Calculate the area of cross-section for *d* = 0.34 – 0.01 mm = 0.33 mm.

This should give an answer of 8.55 × 10⁻⁸ m².

■ Calculate the area of cross-section for *d* = 0.34 + 0.01 mm = 0.35 mm.

This should give an answer of 9.62 × 10⁻⁸ m².

Therefore, the area lies between 8.55 × 10 m² and 9.62 × 10⁻⁸ m².

In other words, the area is (9.08 ± 0.53) × 10⁻⁸ m²

(as 9.08 – 0.53 = 8.55 and 9.08 + 0.53 = 9.62).

The percentage uncertainty of *A* is $\frac{0.53}{9.08}$ × 100% = 5.8%.

This is twice the percentage uncertainty of *d*.

It can be shown as a general rule that for a measurement *x*, the percentage uncertainty in *x*ⁿ is *n* times the percentage uncertainty in *x*.

then the mass of the water could be as much as

$(125.6 + 0.1) - (65.1 - 0.1)\,g = 60.7\,g$, or as little as

$(125.6 - 0.1) - (65.1 + 0.1)\,g = 60.3\,g$.

The mass of water is therefore $60.5 \pm 0.2\,g$.

2 When a measurement in a calculation is raised to a power *n*, the percentage uncertainty is increased *n* times. For example, suppose you need to calculate the area *A* of cross-section of a wire that has a diameter of 0.34 + 0.01 mm. You will need to use the formula $A = \pi d^2/4$. The calculation should give an answer of $9.08 \times 10^{-8}\,m^2$. The percentage uncertainty of *d* is $\frac{0.01}{0.34} \times 100\% = 2.9\%$. So the percentage uncertainty of *A* is 5.8% (= 2 × 2.9%). The consequence of this rule is that in any calculation where a quantity is raised to a higher power, the uncertainty of that quantity becomes much more significant.

■ Graphs and errors

Straight line graphs are important because they are used to establish the relationship between two physical quantities. For example, as explained in Topic 8.4, consider a set of measurements of the distance fallen by an object released from rest and the time it takes. A graph of distance fallen against (time)² should be a straight line through the origin. If the line is straight, the theoretical equation $s = \frac{1}{2}gt^2$ (where *s* is the distance fallen, and *t* is the time taken) is confirmed. The value of *g* can be calculated as the gradient of the graph is equal to $\frac{1}{2}g$. If the straight line does not pass through the origin, there is a systematic error in the distance measurement. Even so, the gradient is still $\frac{1}{2}g$.

A best-fit test

Suppose you have obtained your own measurements for an experiment and you use them to plot a graph that is predicted to be a straight line. The plotted points are unlikely to be exactly straight in line with each other. The next stage is to draw a straight line of best fit so that the points are on average as close as possible to the line. Some problems may occur at this stage:

1 There might be a point much further than any other point from the line of best fit. The point is referred to as an **anomaly**. Methods for dealing with an anomalous point are as follows:

■ If possible, the measurements for that point should be repeated and used to replace the anomalous point, if the repeated measurement is much nearer the line.

■ If the repeated measurement confirms the anomaly, there could be a fault in the equipment or the way it is used. For example, in an electrical experiment, it could be caused by a change of the range of a meter to make that measurement. If no fault is found, make more measurements near the anomaly to see if these measurements lead towards the anomaly. If they do, it is no longer an anomaly and the measurements are valid.

■ If a repeat measurement is not possible, the anomalous point should be ignored and a comment made in your report (or on the graph) about it.

2 The points might seem to curve away from the straight line of best fit. The uncertainty of each measurement can be used to give a small range or error bar for each measurement. Figure 1 shows the idea. The straight line of best fit should pass through all the error bars. If it doesn't, the following notes might be helpful. You could use the error

V / volts

Figure 1 *Error bars*

bars to draw a straight line of maximum gradient and a straight line of minimum gradient.

■ The points lie along a straight line over most of the range but curve away more further along the line. This would indicate that a straight line relationship between the plotted quantities is valid only over the range of measurements which produced the straight part of the line.

■ Only two or three points might seem to lie on a straight line. In this case, it cannot be concluded that there is a linear relationship between the plotted quantities. You might need to plot further graphs to find out if a different type of graph would give a straight line relationship. A data analysis software package on a computer could be used to test different possible relationships (or at A2 a log graph could be plotted).

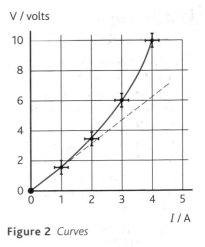

Figure 2 *Curves*

Evaluating your results

You should be able to form a conclusion from the results of an investigation. This might be a final calculation of a physical quantity or property (e.g. resistivity) or a statement of the relationship established between two variables. As explained earlier, the degree of accuracy of the measurements could be used as a guide to the number of significant figures in a 'final result' conclusion. Mathematical links established or verified between quantities should be stated in a 'relationship' conclusion.

You always need to evaluate the conclusion(s) of an experiment or investigation to establish its validity. This evaluation could start with a discussion of the strength of the experimental evidence used to draw the conclusions:

■ Discuss the reliability of the data and suggest improvements, where appropriate, that would improve the reliability. You may need to consider the effect of the control variables, if the experimental evidence is not as reliable as it should be.

■ Discuss the methods taken (or proposed) to eliminate or reduce any random or systematic errors. Describe the steps taken to deal with anomalous results.

■ Evaluate the accuracy of the results by considering the percentage uncertainties in the measurements. These can be compared to identify the most significant sources of error in the measurements, which can then lead to a discussion of how to reduce the most significant sources of error.

■ Propose improvements to the strategy or experimental procedures, referring to the above discussion on validity as justification for the proposals.

■ Suggest further experimental work, based on the strength of the conclusions. Strong conclusions could lead to a prediction and how to test it.

15.1 The ISA/PSA scheme (scheme T)

Investigative skills assignments

Two AS level physics ISAs are set by AQA each year. You will be assessed using one of these ISAs if you are being assessed through the ISA/PSA scheme. Previous ISAs must not be used for assessment purposes although they may be used in preparation for one of the two authorised ISAs. The ISA counts for 41 marks out of the 50 mark total for Unit 3.

The ISA is carried out under supervision and is in two stages.

Stage 1 The practical task

The practical task requires you to carry out practical work using an AQA task sheet, which outlines the investigation. The task sheet may be prescriptive, giving precise instructions, or it may be more open-ended. Your teacher will tell you in advance when you will carry out the ISA. Also, a few weeks before the ISA task, your teacher will tell you the general topic area of the ISA.

The task is carried out in the laboratory in a timetabled lesson (or lessons) under supervision, and should take no more than about an hour. The task will require you to make measurements and present them in a table of your own design. You will be asked to process the measurement data and to use the data to draw a graph. Your teacher is not allowed to instruct candidates on the presentation of the data, or the choice or presentation of the graph. You are not allowed to take work away from the ISA session and all completed work must be handed to your teacher who will assess the work, using AQA marking guidelines. Your teacher is not allowed to write any marks or comments on your work, as it will be returned to you for use in the written test. The practical task counts for 10 of the 41 marks on the ISA. You will not be allowed to redraft or repeat an ISA.

The practical task itself is an individual task which you will carry out in the laboratory under exam conditions. You will be provided with a complete set of practical equipment necessary for the practical task. This equipment should include familiar items that you have used before (e.g. clamps, stands, metre ruler, stopwatch etc.) but it might include an item or materials specific to the task (e.g. a sealed electrical box). The task sheet will tell you how to use the equipment and what measurements to make. Read it carefully to make sure you set up and use the equipment correctly. If you think an item of equipment is not working, ask your teacher to check it.

Stage 2 The written test

You will take the written test in a timetabled lesson under supervision, as soon as possible after completion of the practical task. The test is a 1 hour written paper set by AQA, and counts for 31 of the 41 ISA marks. Lines to write your answer are provided after each part-question. Your teacher will mark your written test, using AQA marking guidelines. In the exam room, just before the test begins, you will be provided with the test paper and your completed material from the practical task. The test is in two parts:

a   Section A will consist of a number of general questions about the practical task. For example, you might be asked about the control variables in the task or about the precision of your measurements. You will probably not be required to plot a graph here as you will have already done this in the practical task.

b   Section B will provide a further set of data on the practical task or a closely related task. The questions in this part will ask about methodology, analysis and evaluation of the data. You may be asked in your evaluation to suggest improvements or to discuss further work that could be done, for example to test a prediction.

The allocation of marks to each question will be shown on the written paper. The balance of marks between the two sections will vary according to the ISA and will generally be about one third on section A and two thirds on section B. A sample ISA giving you a clear idea of the style and format of the questions should be available from your teacher.

Table 1 *ISA marks*

component	skill area	mark
Stage 1 Practical task	Make measurements	
	Tabulate and process data	
	Plot a graph	10
Stage 2 Written test		
section A	Evaluate own measurements	
section B	Analyse given data on a related task	
	Evaluate related task	31

The practical skills assessment

The skills in the PSA are assessed in practical activities that you will do throughout your course. The practical activities will give you opportunities to demonstrate your practical skills. You will be given some instructions when you carry out these activities and you will need to make decisions for yourself about how you organise yourself and how you use the equipment. You will be assessed on your ability to:

- demonstrate safe and skilful practical techniques and processes
- select appropriate methods
- make measurements precisely and accurately
- make and record reliable and valid observations and measurements
- work with others in experimental activities.

The paragraphs below show how your PSA mark is determined. The three strands are each worth up to 3 marks, giving a total of 9 marks. Your teacher will assess the level you reach by the end of the course in each strand.

Following instructions and group work

- 3 marks are awarded if you are able to follow instructions on complex tasks[2] without guidance and can work with others making some contribution. **If not, see next.**

How science works

Measuring

Standard laboratory apparatus you will use to make measurements might include:

- basic apparatus (metre rule, set square, protractors, stopclock or stopwatch)
- electrical meters (analogue or digital)
- the micrometer, vernier callipers,
- a top-pan electronic balance, measuring cylinders
- thermometers, newtonmeters.

■ 2 marks are awarded if you are able to follow instructions in standard procedures[1] without guidance and can work with others making some contribution. **If not, see below.**

■ 1 mark is awarded if you are able to follow follow instructions in standard procedures[1] but sometimes need guidance. **If not**, no marks are awarded.

Selection and use of equipment

■ 3 marks are awarded if you can select and use standard laboratory equipment with appropriate precision[4] and recognise when it is appropriate to repeat measurements. **If not, see below.**

■ 2 marks are awarded if you can use standard laboratory equipment selecting the appropriate range[3]. **If not, see below.**

■ 1 mark is awarded if you are able to use standard laboratory equipment with some guidance as to the appropriate instrument / range[3]. **If not**, no marks are awarded.

Safety and organisation

■ 3 marks are awarded if you can work safely without supervision or guidance (will have effectively carried out own risk assessment[5]). **If not, see below.**

■ 2 marks are awarded if you can work in an organised manner with due regard for safety with only occasional guidance or reminders. **If not, see below.**

■ 1 mark is awarded if you can work in a safe and organised manner following guidance provided but need reminders. **If not**, no marks are awarded.

Notes:

1 Standard procedures above refer to setting up and using standard laboratory apparatus. For example, the setting up and use of a circuit to measure the resistance of a component would be a standard procedure.

2 Complex tasks refer to tasks which are not necessarily straightforward and which may involve several stages, where equipment needs to be rearranged at one or more stages. For example, the investigation of the heating effect of an electric current is a complex task, because the same heater would be used with different currents to heat the same amount of substance for the same length of time.

3 Appropriate instrument/range means choosing the most suitable instrument and range for a particular measurement task. See Topic 14.2.

4 Precision – see Topic 14.2.

5 Risk assessment: Before you carry out a practical task, you should eliminate (if possible) or minimise any health and safety hazards. A risk assessment requires you to think about the possible hazards in an activity and plan to eliminate or minimise them.

15.2 The AQA-marked scheme (scheme X)

Part 1

This part is carried out under supervision in the laboratory during normal class time. You will be required to work individually and carry out 5 short practical exercises. The exercises for each year are set by AQA at the start of the year and each one may be carried out at any stage during the year during or after coverage of the relevant topic . Your teacher will tell you in advance when you are to do them. You will not be expected to spend more than 3 hours of laboratory time in completing these exercises. The exercises will be typical of the normal practical work that would be expected to be covered as part of any AS course.

In carrying out these exercises, you could be asked to use ammeters, voltmeters, vernier callipers, a micrometer, a stopwatch or stopclock, a thermometer, a newtonmeter and an electronic balance as well sophisticated apparatus such as the oscilloscope. In using these instruments, you will be expected to follow instructions and work safely. In addition, you will be asked to make and record accurate measurements and assess the reliability and accuracy of your results.

At the end of each exercise, your results and observations are to be given to the teacher for verification purposes and may be returned to you for use during the remainder of the course. A sample set of Part 1 exercises are listed below

The practical skills developed during Part 1 will be assessed through the AQA-set practical experiments in Part 2.

Sample set of Part 1 exercises for AS level

	Exercise	Measuring equipment used
1	Measurement to produce the *IV* characteristic curve of a component	ammeter, voltmeter
2	Measuring the terminal velocity of a ball falling in oil	stopwatch, metre ruler, set square
3	Measurement of the density of a cylinder	vernier callipers, micrometer screw gauge, electronic balance
4	Measurement of the refractive index of a liquid	protractor, millimetre ruler
5	Using a potential divider with a thermistor as a temperature sensor	thermometer , voltmeter

■ Part 2

In this part, you carry out a short practical task and a longer practical task based on physics from Unit 1 and/or from Unit 2. The practical tasks to be carried out will be AQA set and marked. Once completed, you will not be able to attempt Part 2 again. The measurements and results from these experiments will be analysed and evaluated in Part 3, an AQA-set and marked written paper, thus testing relevant skills developed in the Part 1 exercises. However, you can not carry forward written work from Part 1 to Part 2.

Examples of some Part 2 practical experiments for AS level are listed below.

1 Investigation of the relationship between the terminal velocity of a sphere falling in oil and its radius (use of stopwatch, metre rule, set square, micrometer, thermometer).

2 Investigation of the variation of the resistance of a thermistor with temperature (use of an ammeter, a voltmeter, a thermometer, an electronic balance).

3 Investigation of the forces acting on an object in equilibrium (use of metre rule, set square, protractor, electronic balance).

Your teacher will tell you in advance when you are to carry out Part 2. This will be near the end of the course between March and the end of May. Because Part 2 is a skills test like the 'on the road' part of the driving test, it can be used to test other students at other times.

You have to work individually and be supervised throughout. You will be provided with a task sheet with sufficient information and instructions to enable you to obtain reliable measurements which you have to record, process and discuss. In carrying out the tasks, you will be expected to:

■ manipulate apparatus skilfully and safely,

■ make reliable and accurate measurements,

■ identify anomalous measurements,

■ minimise or take account of the effects of random and any systematic error,

■ tabulate the results in a well organised and systematic way, taking account of the expected conventions,

■ process data,

■ graph, or chart, these data as appropriate.

At the end of the experiment, you have to hand in all your written work (i.e. table of results, calculations, graph, and discussion of errors). This will be returned to you for use in Part 3.

■ Part 3

This is an AQA-set and marked written paper of duration of 1 hour 15 minutes. Your teacher will arrange when you are to take this test, preferably as soon as possible after Part 2. Before you commence the test, your written work from Part 2 will be returned to you. At the end of the test, all your written work from Parts 2 and 3 will be collected by your teacher who will send it to AQA for marking together with verification forms for Part 1.

Some of the questions in the paper will require you to:

■ use your Part 2 results and graph to carry out further analysis in order to arrive at a conclusion,

■ assess the overall accuracy of the outcome of the experiment.

In addition, you may be asked to:

■ carry out error calculations on the data from Part 2,

■ describe procedures used to overcome uncertainties involved in Part 2,

■ comment on the reliability of the evidence or procedures used during Part 2,

■ discuss all/some of the measurement techniques developed in Part 1,

■ make predictions about alternative outcomes

■ discuss ways of extending the range or reliability of the evidence produced during Part 2.

The work produced by the candidates in Parts 2 and 3 will sent to AQA for marking together with candidate Part 1 verification forms.

16.1 Data handling

This chapter covers the mathematical skills you will require for your whole AS Physics A course.

Table 1 *SI base units*

physical quantity	unit
mass	kilogram (kg)
length	metre (m)
time	second (s)
electric current	ampere (A)
temperature	kelvin (K)

Scientific units

Scientists use a single system of units to avoid unnecessary effort and time converting between different units of the same quantity. This system, the **Système International** (or **SI system**) is based on a defined unit for certain physical quantities including those listed in Table 1. Units of all other quantities are derived from the SI base units.

The following examples show how the units of all other physical quantities are derived from the base units.

- The unit of area is the square metre (m^2).
- The unit of volume is the cubic metre (m^3).
- The unit of density is the kilogram per cubic metre ($kg\,m^{-3}$).
- The unit of speed is the metre per second ($m\,s^{-1}$).

More about using a calculator

1 **'Exp'** (or 'EE' on some calculators) is the calculator button you press to key in a **power of ten**. To key in a number in standard form (e.g. 3.0×10^8), the steps are as follows:

- Step 1 Key in the number between 1 and 10 (e.g. 3.0).
- Step 2 Press the calculator button marked 'Exp' (or 'EE' on some calculators).
- Step 3 Key in the power of ten (e.g. 8).

If the display reads '3.0 08' this should be read as 3.0×10^8 (not 3.0^8 which means 3.0 multiplied by itself 8 times). If the power of ten is a negative number (e.g. 10^{-8} not 10^8), press the calculator button marked '+/–' after step 3 (or before, if you are using a graphic calculator) to change the sign of the power of ten.

2 **'Inv'** is the button you press if you want the calculator to give the value of the inverse of a function. For example, if you want to find out the angle, which has a sine of 0.5, you key in 0.5 on the display then press ' inv' then 'sin' to obtain the answer of 30°. Some calculators have a 'second function' or 'shift' button that you press instead of the 'inv' button.

3 **'log'** (or 'lg') is the button you press to find out what a number is as a power of ten. For example, press 'log' then key in 100 and the display will show 2, because $100 = 10^2$. Logarithmic scales have equal intervals for each power of ten.

4 **To raise any number to any power**, use the ^ button or y^x button (or x^y on some calculators). For example, if you want to work out

power of ten

number displayed = 6.62×10^{-34}

Figure 1 *Displaying powers of ten*

n	$\log n$
10^4	4
10^3	3
10^2	2
10	1
1	0

Figure 2 *A logarithmic scale*

the value of 2^8, key in 2 onto the display then y^x (or ^), then 8, and press =. The display should then show 256 as the decimal value of 2^8.

The y^x button can be used to find roots. For example, given the equation $T^4 = 5200$, you can find T by keying in 5200 onto the display, then pressing the y^x button, followed by $(1 \div 4)$ which will give the answer 8.49.

Significant figures

A calculator display shows a large number of digits. When you use a calculator, you should always round up or round down the final answer of a calculation to the same number of significant figures as the data given. Sometimes, a numerical answer to one part of a question has to be used in a subsequent calculation, in which case, the numerical answer to the first part should be carried forward without rounding it up or down. For example, if you need to calculate the value of $d \sin 65°$, where $d = 1.64$, the calculator will show $9.063077870 \times 10^{-1}$ for the sine of 65°. Multiplying this answer by 1.64 then gives 1.486344771, which should then be rounded off to 1.49 so it has the same number of significant figures as 1.64 (i.e. to 3 significant figures).

Worked example: _____

Calculate the cube root of 2.9×10^6.

Solution

Step 1 Key in 2.9×10^6 as explained earlier

Step 2 Press the y^x button

Step 3 Key in $(1 \div 3)$

Step 4 Press =

The display should show '1.426 02' so the answer is 142.6

Summary questions

Write your answers to each of the following questions in standard form, where appropriate, and to the same number of significant figures as the data.

1 Copy and complete the following conversions.

a i $500\,mm = \_\_\_\_m$,

ii $3.2\,m = \_\_\_\_cm$,

iii $9560\,cm = \_\_\_\_m$,

b i $0.45\,kg = \_\_\_\_g$,

ii $1997\,g = \_\_\_\_kg$,

iii $54\,000\,kg = \_\_\_\_g$,

c i $20\,cm^2 = \_\_\_\_m^2$,

ii $55\,mm^2 = \_\_\_\_m^2$,

iii $0.050\,cm^2 = \_\_\_\_m^2$

2 a Write the following values in standard form.

i 150 million km in metres, ii 365 days in seconds, iii 630 nm in metres, iv 25.7 µg in kilograms, v 150 m in millimetres, vi 1.245 µm in metres,

b Write the following values with a prefix instead of in standard form.

i $3.5 \times 10^4\,m = \_\_\_\_km$,

ii $6.5 \times 10^{-7}\,m = \_\_\_\_nm$,

iii $3.4 \times 10^6\,g = \_\_\_\_kg$,

iv $8.7 \times 10^8\,W = \_\_\_\_MW = \_\_\_\_GW$

3 a Use the equation 'average speed = distance/time' to calculate the average speed in $m\,s^{-1}$ of:

i   a vehicle that travels a distance of 9000 m in 450 s,

ii   a vehicle that travels a distance of 144 km in 2 h,

iii   a particle that travels a distance of 0.30 nm in a time of 2.0×10^{-18} s,

iv   the Earth on its orbit of radius 1.5×10^{11} m, given the time taken per orbit is 365.25 days.

b Use the equation

$$\text{Resistance} = \frac{\text{potential difference}}{\text{current}}$$

to calculate the resistance of a component for the following values of current I and pd V.

i $V = 15\,V$, $I = 2.5\,mA$,

ii $V = 80\,mV$, $I = 16\,mA$,

iii $V = 5.2\,kV$, $I = 3.0\,mA$,

iv $V = 250\,V$, $I = 0.51\,µA$,

v $V = 160\,mV$, $I = 53\,mA$.

4 a Calculate each of the following: i 6.7^3 ii $(5.3 \times 10^4)^2$ iii $(2.1 \times 10^{-6})^4$ iv $(0.035)^2$ v $(4.2 \times 10^8)^{1/2}$ vi $(3.8 \times 10^{-5})^{1/4}$

b Calculate each of the following:

i $\dfrac{2.4^2}{3.5 \times 10^3}$

ii $\dfrac{3.6 \times 10^{-3}}{6.2 \times 10^2}$

iii $\dfrac{8.1 \times 10^4 + 6.5 \times 10^3}{5.3 \times 10^4}$

iv $7.2 \times 10^{-3} + \dfrac{6.2 \times 10^4}{2.6 \times 10^6}$

16.2 Trigonometry

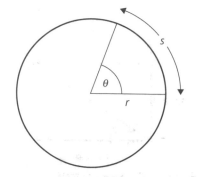

Figure 1 *Arcs and segments*

Angles and arcs

■ Angles are measured in degrees or radians. The scale for conversion is $360° = 2\pi$ radians. The symbol for the radian is rad, so $1\,\text{rad} = 360/2\pi = 57.3°$ (to 3 significant figures).

■ The circumference of a circle of radius $r = 2\pi r$. So the circumference can be written as the angle in radians (2π) round the circle $\times\, r$.

■ For a segment of a circle, the length of the arc of the segment is in proportion to the angle θ which the arc makes to the centre of the circle. This is shown in Figure 1. Because the arc length is $2\pi r$ (the circumference) for an angle of $360°$ ($= 2\pi$ radians), then

$$\frac{\text{arc length, } s}{2\pi r} = \frac{\theta \text{ in degrees}}{360°}$$

Triangles and trigonometry

Area rule

As shown in Figure 2,

$$\text{the area of any triangle } = \tfrac{1}{2} \times \text{its height} \times \text{its base.}$$

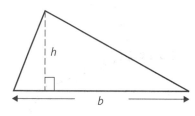

$\text{Area} = \tfrac{1}{2}hb$

Figure 2 *The area of a triangle*

Trigonometry calculations using a calculator

A scientific calculator has a button you can press to use either degrees or radians. Make sure you know how to switch your calculator from one of these two modes to the other. Many marks have been lost in examinations as a result of forgetting to use the correct mode. For example,

■ $\sin 30° = 0.50$, whereas $\sin 30 \text{ rad} = -0.99$

■ $\text{inv} \sin 0.17$ in degree mode $= 9.79°$, whereas $\text{inv} \sin 0.17$ in rad mode $= 0.171$

Also, watch out when you calculate the sine, cosine or tangent of the product of a number and an angle. For example, $\sin(2 \times 30°)$ comes out as 1.05 if you forget the brackets, instead of the correct answer of 0.867. The reason for the error is that, unless you insert the brackets, the calculator is programmed to work out $\sin 2°$ then multiply the answer by 30.

Trigonometry functions

Consider again the definitions of the sine, cosine and tangent of an angle, as applied to the right-angled triangle in Figure 3.

$\sin\theta = \dfrac{o}{h}$ where $o =$ the length of the side opposite angle θ

                         $h =$ the length of the hypotenuse

$\cos\theta = \dfrac{a}{h}$ $a =$ the length of the side adjacent to angle θ

$\tan\theta = \dfrac{o}{a}$

Figure 3 *A right-angled triangle*

Pythagoras' theorem and trigonometry

Pythagoras' theorem states that for any right-angled triangle, the square of the hypotenuse = the sum of the squares of the other two sides.

Applying Pythagoras' theorem to the right-angled triangle in Figure 3 gives

$$h^2 = o^2 + a^2$$

Since $o = h\sin\theta$ and $a = h\cos\theta$, then the above equation may be written

$$h^2 = h^2\sin^2\theta + h^2\cos^2\theta$$

Cancelling h^2 therefore gives the following useful link between $\sin\theta$ and $\cos\theta$,

$$1 = \sin^2\theta + \cos^2\theta$$

Figure 4 *Resolving a vector*

▉ Vector rules

Resolving a vector

As explained in Topic 7.1, any vector can be resolved into two perpendicular components in the same plane as the vector, as shown by Figure 4. The force vector F is resolved into a horizontal component $F\cos\theta$ and a vertical component $F\sin\theta$, where θ is the angle between the line of action of the force and the horizontal line.

Adding two perpendicular vectors

Figure 5 shows two perpendicular forces F_1 and F_2 acting on a point object X. The combined effect of these two forces, the resultant force, is given by the vector triangle in Figure 5. This is a right-angled triangle, where the resultant force is represented by the hypotenuse.

■ Applying Pythagoras' theorem to the triangle gives $F^2 = F_1^2 + F_2^2$, where F is the magnitude of the resultant force.
   Therefore $F = (F_1^2 + F_2^2)^{1/2}$

■ Applying the trigonometry formula $\tan\theta = o/a$, the angle between the resultant force and force F_1 is given by $\tan\theta = F_2/F_1$

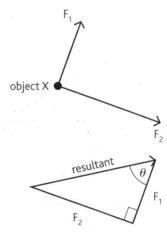

Figure 5 *Adding two perpendicular vectors*

Summary questions

1 a Calculate the circumference of a circle of radius 0.250 m.

b Calculate the length of the arc of a circle of radius 0.250 m for the following angles between the arc and the centre of the circle: i 360°, ii 240°, iii 60°

2 For the right-angled triangle XYZ in Figure 6, calculate:

a angle YXZ (= θ) if XY = 80 mm and

   i   XZ = 30 mm,
   ii XZ = 60 mm.
   iii YZ = 30 mm
   iv YZ = 70 mm

Figure 6

b XZ if i XY = 20 cm and θ = 30°, ii XY = 22 m and θ = 45°, iii YZ = 18 mm and θ = 75°, iv YZ = 47 cm and θ = 25°

3 a A right-angled triangle XYZ has a hypoteneuse XY of length 55 mm and side XZ of length 25 mm. Calculate the length of the other side.

b An aircraft travels a distance of 30 km due north from an airport P to an airport Q. It then travels due east for a distance of 18 km to an airport R. Calculate i the distance from P to R, ii the angle QPR.

4 a Calculate the horizontal component A and the vertical component B of:

   i   a 6.0 N force at 40° to the vertical,
   ii a 10.0 N force at 20° to the vertical,
   iii a 7.5 N force at 50° to the horizontal.

b Calculate the magnitude and direction of the resultant of a 2.0 N force acting due north and a 3.5 N force acting due east

16.3 More about algebra

Signs and symbols

If you used symbols in your GCSE course, you might have met the use of s for distance and I for current. Maybe you wondered why we don't use d for distance instead of s or C for current instead of I. The answer is that physics discoveries have taken place in many countries. The first person to discover the key ideas about speed was Galileo, the great Italian scientist, so he used the words 'scale' from his own language for distance and therefore assigned the symbol s to distance. Important discoveries about electricity were made by Ampère, the great French scientist, and he wrote about the intensity of an electric current, so he used the symbol I for electric current. The symbols we now use are used in all countries in association with the **SI system of units**.

Table 1 *Symbols for some physical quantities*

physical quantity	symbol	unit	unit symbol
distance	s	metre	m
speed or velocity	v	metre per second	m s^{-1}
acceleration	a	metre per second per second	m s^{-2}
mass	m	kilogram	kg
force	F	newton	N
energy or work	E	joule	J
power	P	watt	W
density	ρ	kilogram per cubic metre	kg m^{-3}
current	I	ampere	A
potential difference or voltage	V	volt	V
resistance	R	ohm	Ω

Signs you need to recognise

- Inequality signs are often used in physics. You need to be able to recognise the meaning of the signs in Table 2. For example, the inequality $I \geq 3\,\text{A}$ means that the current is greater or equal to 3 A. This is the same as saying that the current is not less than 3 A.

- The approximation sign is used where an estimate or an order-of-magnitude calculation is made, rather than a precise calculation. For an order-of-magnitude calculation, the final value is written with one significant figure only, or even rounded up or down to the nearest power of ten. Order-of-magnitude calculations are useful as a quick check after using a calculator. For example, if you are asked to calculate the density of a 1.0 kg metal cylinder of height 0.100 m and diameter 0.071 m, you ought to obtain a value of $2530\,\text{kg m}^{-3}$ using a calculator. Now let's check the value quickly:

Volume $= \pi(\text{radius})^2 \times \text{height}$
$= 3 \times (0.04)^2 \times 0.1 = 48 \times 10^{-5}\,\text{m}^3$

Density $= \text{mass/volume}$
$= 1.0/50 \times 10^{-5} = 2000\,\text{kg m}^{-3}$

This confirms our 'precise' calculation.

- Proportionality is represented by the $\propto$ sign. A simple example of its use in physics is for Hooke's law; the tension in a spring is directly proportional to its extension.

$$\text{Tension } T \propto \text{ extension } \Delta L$$

By introducing a constant of proportionality k, the link above can be made into an equation:

$$T = k\Delta L$$

where k is defined as the spring constant. See Topic 11.2. With any proportionality relationship, if one of the variables is increased by a given factor (e.g. $\times 3$), the other variable is increased by the same factor. So in the above example, if T is trebled, then extension ΔL is also trebled. A graph of tension T on the y-axis against extension ΔL on the x-axis would give a straight line through the origin.

Table 2 *Signs*

sign	meaning	sign	meaning	sign	meaning
$>$	greater than	$>>$	much greater than	$<x^2>$	mean square value
$<$	less than	$<<$	much less than	$\propto$	is proportional to
$\geq$	greater than or equal to	$\approx$	approximately equals	Δ	change of
$\leq$	less than or equal to	$<x>$	mean value	$\sqrt{}$	square root

More about equations and formulae

Rearranging an equation with several terms

The equation $v = u + at$ is an example of an equation with two terms on the right-hand side. These terms are u and at. To make t the subject of the equation,

1 Isolate the term containing t on one side by subtracting u from both sides to give $v - u = at$

2 Isolate t by dividing both sides of the equation $v - u = at$ by a to give

$$\frac{(v - u)}{a} = \frac{at}{a} = t$$

Note that a cancels out in the expression $\frac{at}{a}$

3 The rearranged equation may now be written

$$t = \frac{(v - u)}{a}$$

Rearranging an equation containing powers

Suppose a quantity is raised to a power in a term in an equation, and that quantity is to be made the subject of the equation. For example, consider the equation $V = \frac{4}{3}\pi r^3$ where r is to be made the subject of the equation.

1 Isolate r^3 from the other factors in the equation, by dividing both sides by 4π, then multiplying both sides by 3 to give $\frac{3V}{4\pi} = r^3$

2 Take the cube root of both sides to give $\left(\frac{3V}{4\pi}\right)^{\frac{1}{3}} = r$

3 Rewrite the equation with r on the left-hand side if necessary.

More about powers

1 Powers add for identical quantities when two terms are multiplied together. For example, if $y = ax^n$ and $z = bx^m$, then $yz = ax^m bx^n = abx^{m+n}$

2 An equation of the form $y = \frac{k}{z^n}$ may be written in the form $y = kz^{-n}$.

3 The nth root of an expression is written as the power $1/n$. For example, the square root of x is $x^{1/2}$. Therefore, rearranging $y = x^n$ to make x the subject gives $x = y^{1/n}$.

Summary questions

1 Complete each of the following statements:

   a If $x > 5$, then $1/x <$

   b If $4 < x < 10$, then _____ $< 1/x <$

   c If x is positive and $x^2 > 100$ then $1/x$ _____.

2 a Make t the subject of each of the following equations:

   i $v = u + at$, ii $s = \frac{1}{2}at^2$, iii $y = k(t - t_o)$, iv $F = \frac{mv}{t}$

   b Solve each of the following equations:

   i $2z + 6 = 10$, ii $2(z + 6) = 10$, iii $\frac{2}{z - 4} = 8$,

   iv $\frac{4}{z^2} = 36$

3 a Make x the subject of each of the following equations:

   i $y = 2x^{1/2}$, ii $2y = x^{-1/2}$, iii $yx^{1/3} = 1$, iv $y = \frac{k}{x^2}$

   b Solve each of the following equations:

   i $x^{-1/2} = 2$, ii $3x^2 = 24$, iii $\frac{8}{x^2} = 32$, iv $2(x^{1/2} + 4) = 12$

4 Use the data given with each equation below to calculate:

   a the volume V of a wire of radius $r = 0.34\,\text{mm}$ and length $L = 0.840\,\text{m}$, using the equation $V = \pi r^2 L$,

   b the radius r of a sphere of volume $V = 1.00 \times 10^{-6}\,\text{m}^3$, using the formula $V = \frac{4}{3}\pi r^3$,

   c the time period T of a simple pendulum of length $L = 1.50\,\text{m}$, using the formula $T = 2\pi(L/g)^{0.5}$, where $g = 9.8\,\text{m s}^{-2}$,

   d the speed v of an object of mass $m = 0.20\,\text{kg}$ and kinetic energy $E_k = 28\,\text{J}$, using the formula $E_k = \frac{1}{2}mv^2$.

16.4 Straight line graphs

Figure 1 *Straight line graph*

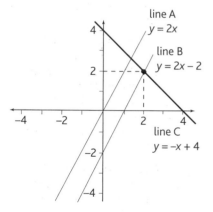

Figure 2 $y = mx + c$

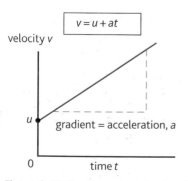

Figure 3 *Straight line graphs*

line A
$y = 2x$

line B
$y = 2x - 2$

line C
$y = -x + 4$

$$v = u + at$$

velocity v

u

gradient = acceleration, a

0   time t

Figure 4 *Motion at constant acceleration*

The general equation for a straight line graph

Links between two physical quantities can be established most easily by plotting a graph. One of the physical quantities is represented by the vertical scale (the 'ordinate', often called the y-axis) and the other quantity by the horizontal scale (the 'abscissa', often called the x-axis). The coordinates of a point on a graph are the x- and y-values, usually written (x, y) of the point.

The simplest link between two physical variables is where the plotted points define a straight line. For example, Figure 1 shows the link between the tension in a spring and the extension of the spring; the gradient of the line is constant and the line passes through the origin. Any situation where the y-variable is directly proportional to the x-variable gives a straight line through the origin. For Figure 1, the gradient of the line is the spring constant k. The relationship between the tension T and the extension ΔL may therefore be written as $T = k\Delta L$.

The general equation for a straight line graph is usually written in the form

$y = mx + c,$ where m = the gradient of the line, and c = the y-intercept.

- The gradient m can be measured by marking two points P and Q far apart on the line. The triangle PQR, as shown in Figure 2, is then used to find the gradient. If (x_p, y_p) and (x_Q, y_Q) represent the x- and y-coordinates of points P and Q respectively, then

$$\text{gradient } m = \frac{y_p - y_Q}{x_p - x_Q}$$

- The y-intercept, c, is the point at $x = 0$ where the line crosses the y-axis. To find the y-intercept of a line on a graph that does not show $x = 0$, measure the gradient as above, then use the coordinates of any point on the line with the equation $y = mx + c$ to calculate c. For example, rearranging $y = mx + c$ gives $c = y - mx$. Therefore, using the coordinates of point Q in Figure 2, the y-intercept $c = y_Q - mx_Q$.

Examples of straight line graphs

- Line A: $c = 0$ so the line passes through the origin. Its equation is $y = 2x$

- Line B: $m > 0$ so the line has a positive gradient; its equation is $y = 2x - 2$

- Line C: $m < 0$ so the line has a negative gradient; its equation is $y = -x + 4$

Straight line graphs and physics equations

You need to be able to work out gradients and intercepts for equations you meet in physics that generate straight line graphs. Some further examples in addition to Figure 1 are described below.

1 **The velocity v of an object moving at constant acceleration a at time t** is given by the equation $v = u + at$, where u is its velocity at time $t = 0$. Figure 4 shows the corresponding graph of velocity v on the y-axis against time t on the x-axis.

Rearranging the equation as $v = at + u$ and comparing this with $y = mx + c$ shows that

■ the gradient m = acceleration a

■ the y-intercept, c = the initial velocity u.

2 **The pd, V, across the terminals of a battery of emf ε and internal resistance r varies with current in accordance with the equation $V = \varepsilon - Ir$** (see Topic 5.3). Figure 5 shows the corresponding graph of pd, V, on the y-axis against current I on the x-axis.

Rearranging the equation as $V = -rI + \varepsilon$ and comparing this with $y = mx + c$ shows that

■ the gradient $m = -r$

■ the y-intercept, $c = \varepsilon$ so the intercept on the y-axis gives the emf ε of the battery.

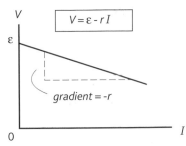

Figure 5 *Pd v current for a battery*

3 **The maximum kinetic energy E_{Kmax} of a photoelectron** emitted from a metal surface of work function ϕ varies with frequency f of the incident radiation, in accordance with the equation $E_{\text{Kmax}} = hf - \phi$.

Figure 6 shows the corresponding graph of E_{Kmax} on the y-axis against f on the x-axis.

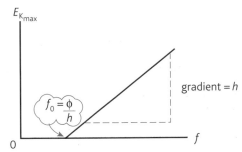

Figure 6 *Photoelectric emission*

Comparing the equation $E_{\text{Kmax}} = hf - \phi$ with $y = mx + c$ shows that

■ the gradient $m = h$

■ the y-intercept, $c = -\phi$

Note that the x-intercept is where $y = 0$ on the line. Let the coordinates of the x-intercept be $(x_0, 0)$. Therefore $mx_0 + c = 0$ so $x_0 = -c/m$. Applied to Figure 6, the x-intercept is therefore ϕ/h. Since the x-intercept is the threshold frequency f_0, then $f_0 = \phi/h$.

Simultaneous equations

In physics, simultaneous equations can be solved graphically by plotting the line for each equation. The solution of the equations is given by the coordinates of the points where the lines meet. For example, lines B and C in Figure 3 meet at the point $(2, 2)$ so $x = 2$, $y = 2$ are the only values of x and y that fit both equations.

Solving simultaneous equations doesn't require graph plotting if the equations can be arranged to fit one of the variables. Start by rearranging to make y the subject of each equation, if necessary. Considering the example above:

Line B: $y = 2x - 2$

Line C: $y = -x + 4$

At the point where they meet, their coordinates are the same, so solving $2x - 2 = -x + 4$ gives the x-coordinate. Rearranging this equation gives $3x = 6$ so $x = 2$.

Since $y = 2x - 2$, then $y = (2 \times 2) - 2 = 2$

1 For each of the following equations that represent straight line graphs, write down **i** the gradient, **ii** the y-intercept, **iii** the x-intercept:

a $y = 3x - 3$ **b** $y = -4x + 8$

c $y + x = 5$ **d** $2y + 3x = 6$

2 **a** A straight line on a graph has a gradient $m = 2$ and passes through the point $(2, -4)$. Work out **i** the equation for this line, **ii** its y-intercept.

b The velocity v (in $m\,s^{-1}$) of an object varies with time t (in s) in accordance with the equation $v = 5 + 3t$. Determine **i** the acceleration of the object, **ii** the initial velocity of the object.

3 **a** Plot the equations $y = x + 3$ and $y = -2x + 6$ over the range from $x = -3$ to $x = +3$. Write down the coordinates of the point P where the two lines cross.

b Write down the equation for the line OP, where O is the origin of the graph.

4 Solve the following pairs of simultaneous equations after making y the subject of each equation, if necessary:

a $y = 2x - 4$, $y = -x + 2$

b $y = 3x - 4$, $x + y = 8$

c $2x + 3y = 4$, $x + 2y = 2$

16.5 More on graphs

Figure 1 s against t

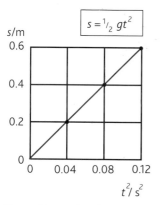

Figure 2 s against t^2

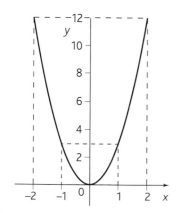

Figure 3 $y = 3x^2$

Curves and equations

Graphs with curves occur in physics in two ways.

1 In practical work, where one physical variable is plotted against another and the plotted points do not lie along a straight line. For example, a graph of p.d. on the y-axis against current on the x-axis for a filament lamp is a curve that passes through the origin.

2 In theory work, where an equation containing two physical variables is not in the form of the equation for a straight line $(y = mx + c)$. For example, for an object released from rest, a graph of distance fallen, s, on the y-axis against time, t, on the x-axis is a curve, because $s = \frac{1}{2}gt^2$. Figure 1 shows this equation represented on a graph.

Knowledge of the general equations for some common curves is an essential part of physics. When a curve is produced as a result of plotting a set of measurements in a practical experiment, few conclusions can be drawn as the exact shape of a curve is difficult to test. In comparison, if the measurements produce a straight line, it can then be concluded that the two physical variables plotted on the axes are related by an equation of the form $y = mx + c$.

If a set of measurements produces a curve rather than a straight line, knowledge of the theory could enable the measurements to be processed in order to give a straight line graph, which would then be a confirmation of the theory. For example, the distance and time measurements that produced the curve in Figure 1 could be plotted as distance fallen, s, on the y-axis against t^2 on the x-axis (where t is the time taken). Figure 2 shows the idea.

If a graph of s against t^2 gives a straight line, this would confirm that the relationship between s and t is of the form $s = kt^2$, where k is a constant. Because theory gives $s = \frac{1}{2}gt^2$, it can then be concluded that the theory applies to this set of measurements and that $k = \frac{1}{2}g$.

From curves to straight lines

Parabolic curves

These curves describe the flight paths of projectiles or other objects acted on by a constant force that is not in the same direction as the initial velocity of the object. In addition, parabolic curves occur where the energy of an object depends on some physical variable.

The general equation for a parabola is $y = kx^2$. Figure 3 shows the shape of the parabola $y = 3x^2$. Equations of the form $y = kx^2$ pass through the origin and they are symmetrical about the y-axis. This is because equal positive and negative values of x always give the same y-value.

The flight path for a projectile projected horizontally at speed U has coordinates $x = Ut$, $y = \frac{1}{2}gt^2$, where $x =$ horizontal distance travelled, $y =$ vertical distance fallen and t is the time from initial projection. See Topics 8.7 and 8.8.

Combining these equations gives the flight path equation $y = \frac{gx^2}{2u^2}$

which is the same as the parabola equation $y = kx^2$ where $\frac{g}{2u^2}$ is represented by k in the equation.

A set of measurements plotted as a graph of vertical distance fallen, y, against horizontal distance travelled, x, would be a parabolic curve as shown in Figure 3. However, a graph of y against x^2 should give a straight line (of gradient k) through the origin, because $y = kx^2$

Inverse curves

An inverse relationship between two variables x and y is of the form $y = \frac{k}{x}$, where k is a constant. The variable y is said to be inversely proportional to variable x. If x is doubled, y is halved. If x is increased tenfold, y decreases to a tenth.

Figure 5 shows the curve for $y = \frac{10}{x}$

The curve tends towards either axis but never actually meets the axes. The correct mathematical word for 'tending towards but never meeting' is 'asymptotic'. Consider the following example.

The resistance R of a wire of constant length L varies with the wire's area of cross-section, A, in accordance with the equation $R = \frac{\rho L}{A}$, where ρ is the resistivity of the wire. See Topic 4.3.

Therefore, R is inversely proportional to A. A graph of R (on the vertical axis) against A would therefore be a curve like Figure 5. However, a graph of R (on the vertical axis) against $1/A$ is a straight line through the origin. The gradient of this straight line is ρL.

Figure 4 y against x^2

Figure 5 $y = \frac{10}{x}$

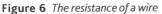

R against $\frac{1}{A}$

Figure 6 The resistance of a wire

Summary questions

1 The potential energy, E_p, stored in a stretched spring varies with the extension ΔL of the spring, in accordance with the equation $E_p = \frac{1}{2}k\,\Delta L^2$. Sketch a graph of E_p against **a** ΔL, **b** ΔL^2.

2 The energy E_{ph} of a photon varies with its wavelength λ in accordance with the equation $E_{ph} = hc/\lambda$, where h is the Planck constant and c is the speed of light. Sketch a graph of E_{ph} against **a** λ, **b** $1/\lambda$

3 The current I through a wire of resistivity ρ varies with the length L, area of cross-section A and pd V, in accordance with the equation $I = \frac{VA}{\rho L}$

    a Sketch a graph of I against **i** V, **ii** L, **iii** $1/L$.

    b Explain how you would determine the resistivity from the graph of I against **i** V, **ii** $1/L$.

4 An object released from rest falls at constant acceleration a and passes through a horizontal beam at speed u. The distance it falls in time t after passing through the light beam is given by the equation $s = ut + \frac{1}{2}at^2$

    a Show that $\frac{s}{t} = u + \frac{1}{2}at$

    b i Sketch a graph of s/t on the vertical axis against t on the horizontal axis.

      ii Explain how u and a can be determined from the graph.

16.6 Graphs, gradients and areas

Gradients

1 The gradient of a straight line = $\Delta y/\Delta x$, where Δy is the change of the quantity plotted on the y-axis and Δx is the change of the quantity plotted on the x-axis. As shown in Figure 1, the gradient of a straight line is obtained by drawing as large a gradient triangle as possible, and measuring the height Δy and the base Δx of this triangle, using the scale on each axis.

Note: As a rule, when you plot a straight line graph, always choose a scale for each axis that covers at least half the length of each axis. This will enable you to draw the line of best fit as accurately as possible, as explained in 14.4. The measurement of the gradient of the line will therefore be more accurate. If the y-intercept is required and it cannot be read directly from the graph, it can be calculated by substituting the value of the gradient and the coordinates of a point on the line into the equation $y = mx + c$

2 The gradient at a point on a curve = the gradient of the tangent to the curve at that point.

Figure 1 *Constant gradient*

Figure 2 *Tangents and curve*

The tangent to the curve at a point is a straight line that touches the curve at that point, without cutting across it. To see why, mark any two points on a curve and join them by a straight line. The gradient of the line is $\Delta y/\Delta x$, where Δy is the vertical separation of the two points and Δx is the horizontal separation. Now repeat with one of the points closer to the other; the straight line is now closer in direction to the curve. If the points are very close, the straight line between them is almost along the curve. The gradient of the line is then virtually the same as the gradient of the curve at that position. See Figure 2. In other words, the gradient of the straight line $\Delta y/\Delta x$ becomes equal to the gradient of the curve as $\Delta x \longrightarrow 0$. The curve gradient is written as $\dfrac{dy}{dx}$ where $\dfrac{d}{dx}$ means 'rate of change'.

The gradient of the tangent is a straight line and is obtained as explained above. Drawing the tangent to a curve requires practice. This skill is often needed in practical work. The **normal** at the point where the tangent touches the curve is the straight line perpendicular to the tangent at that point. An accurate technique for drawing the normal to a curve using a plane mirror is shown in Figure 3. At the point where the normal intersects the curve, the curve and its mirror image should join smoothly without an abrupt change of gradient where they join. After positioning the mirror surface correctly, the normal can then be drawn, and then used to draw the tangent to the curve.

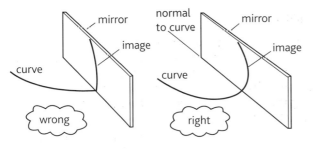

Figure 3 *Drawing the normal to a curve*

Turning points

A turning point on a curve is where the gradient of the curve is zero. This happens where a curve reaches a peak with a fall either side (i.e. a maximum) or where it reaches a trough with a rise either side (i.e. a minimum). Where the gradient represents a physical quantity, a turning point is where that physical quantity is zero. Figure 4 shows an example of a curve with a turning point. This is a graph of the vertical height against time for a projectile that reaches a maximum height, then descends as it travels horizontally. The gradient represents the vertical component of velocity. At maximum height, the gradient of the curve is zero, so the vertical component of velocity is zero at that point.

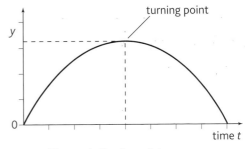

Figure 4 *Turning points*

Note:

If the equation of a curve is known, the gradient can be determined by the process of **differentiation**. This mathematical process is not needed for AS level physics. The essential feature of the process is that, for a function of the form $y = kx^n$, the gradient (written as dy/dx) $= nkx^{n-1}$

For example, if $y = \frac{1}{2}gt^2$, then $\dfrac{dy}{dt} = gt$

▪ Areas and graphs

The area under a line on a graph can give useful information if the product of the y-variable and the x-variable represents another physical variable. For example, consider Figure 5(a), which is a graph of the tension in a spring against its extension. Since 'tension × extension' is 'force × distance' which equals work done, then the area under the line represents the work done to stretch the spring.

Figure 5b) shows a tension against extension graph for a rubber band. Unlike (a), the area under the curve is not a triangle, but it still represents work done, in this case the work done to stretch the rubber band. See Topic 11.4.

The product of the y-variable and the x-variable must represent a physical variable with a physical meaning if the area is to be of use. A graph of mass against volume for different sizes of the same material gives a straight line through the origin. The mass is directly proportional to the volume, and the gradient gives the density. But the area under the line

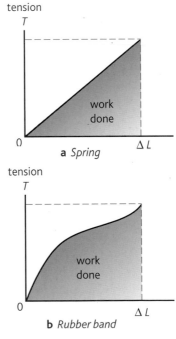

Figure 5 *Tension v extension*

has no physical significance since mass × volume does not represent a physical variable.

Note that even where the area does represent a physical variable, it may not have any physical meaning. For example, for a graph of pd against current, the product of pd and current represents power, but this physical quantity has no meaning in this situation.

More examples of curves where the area is useful include:

■ velocity against time where the area between the line and the time axis represents displacement

■ acceleration against time where the area between the line and the time axis represents change of velocity

■ power against time where the area between the curve and the time axis represents energy

■ potential difference against charge where the area between the curve and the charge axis represents energy

Summary questions

1 a Sketch a velocity against time graph (with time on the x-axis) to represent the equation $v = u + at$, where v is the velocity at time t.

   b What feature of the graph represents i the acceleration, ii the displacement?

2 a Sketch a graph of current (on the y-axis) against pd (on the x-axis) to show how the current through an ohmic conductor varies with pd.

   b How can the resistance of the conductor be determined from the graph?

3 An electric motor is supplied with energy at a constant rate.

   a Sketch a graph to show how the energy supplied to the motor increases with time.

   b Explain how the power supplied to the motor can be determined from the graph.

4 A steel ball bearing was released in a tube of oil and fell to the bottom of the tube.

   a Sketch graphs to show how i the velocity, ii the acceleration of the ball changed with time from the instant of release to the point of impact at the bottom of the tube.

   b What is represented on graph a i by i the gradient, ii the area under the line?

   c What is represented on graph a ii by the area under the line?

For reference

Useful data for AS Physics (Specification A)

■ Data

Fundamental constants and values

quantity	symbol	value	units
speed of light in vacuo	c	3.00×10^8	$m\,s^{-1}$
charge of electron	e	-1.60×10^{-19}	C
the Planck constant	h	6.63×10^{-34}	Js
the Avogadro constant	N_A	$6.02 \times 10^{+23}$	mol^{-1}
molar gas constant	R	8.31	$J\,K^{-1}mol^{-1}$
the Boltzmann constant	k	1.38×10^{-23}	$J\,K^{-1}$
electron rest mass	m_e	9.11×10^{-31}	kg
electron charge/mass ratio	e/m_e	1.76×10^{11}	$C\,kg^{-1}$
proton rest mass	m_p	$1.67(3) \times 10^{-27}$	kg
proton charge/mass ratio	e/m_p	9.58×10^7	$C\,kg^{-1}$
neutron rest mass	m_n	$1.67(5) \times 10^{-27}$	kg
gravitational field strength	g	9.81	$N\,kg^{-1}$
acceleration due to gravity	g	9.81	$m\,s^{-2}$
atomic mass unit	u	1.661×10^{-27}	kg

■ AS formulae

Particle physics

Fundamental particles

class	name	symbol	rest energy / MeV
photon	photon	γ	0
lepton	neutrino	ν_e	0
		ν_μ	0
	electron	$e^\pm$	0.510999
	muon	$\mu^\pm$	105.659
mesons	π meson	$\pi^\pm$	139.576
		π^0	134.972
	K meson	$K^\pm$	493.821
		K^0	497.762
baryons	proton	p	938.257
	neutron	n	939.551

Properties of quarks
Antiparticles have opposite signs

type	charge	baryon number	strangeness
u	$+\frac{2}{3}e$	$+\frac{1}{3}$	0
d	$-\frac{1}{3}e$	$+\frac{1}{3}$	0
s	$-\frac{1}{3}e$	$+\frac{1}{3}$	-1

Properties of leptons

lepton	lepton number
particles: $e^-, \nu_e; \mu^-, \nu_\mu; \tau^-, \nu_\tau$	+1
antiparticles: $e^+, \overline{\nu}_e; \mu^+, \overline{\nu}_\mu; \tau^+, \overline{\nu}_\tau$	-1

Geometrical equations

arc length $= r\theta$

circumference of circle $= 2\pi r$

area of circle $= \pi r^2$

surface area of cylinder $= 2\pi rh$

volume of cylinder $= \pi r^2 h$

area of sphere $= 4\pi r^2$

volume of sphere $= \frac{4}{3}\pi r^3$

Photons and energy levels

photon energy	$E = hf = \dfrac{hc}{\lambda}$
photoelectricity	$hf = \phi + E_{Kmax}$
energy levels	$hf = E_1 - E_2$
de Broglie wavelength	$\lambda = \dfrac{h}{p} = \dfrac{h}{mv}$

Electricity

current and pd	$I = \dfrac{\Delta Q}{\Delta t}$
	$V = \dfrac{W}{Q}$
	$R = \dfrac{V}{I}$
emf	$\varepsilon = \dfrac{E}{Q}$
	$\varepsilon = IR + Ir$
resistors in series	$R = R_1 + R_2 + R_3 + \ldots$
resistors in parallel	$\dfrac{1}{R} = \dfrac{1}{R_1} + \dfrac{1}{R_2} + \dfrac{1}{R_3} + \ldots$
resistivity	$\rho = \dfrac{RA}{L}$
power	$P = VI = I^2 R = \dfrac{V^2}{R}$
alternating current	$I_{rms} = \dfrac{I_0}{\sqrt{2}}$
	$V_{rms} = \dfrac{V_0}{\sqrt{2}}$

Mechanics

Moments	moment $= Fd$
velocity and acceleration	$v = \dfrac{\Delta s}{\Delta t}$
	$a = \dfrac{\Delta v}{\Delta t}$
equations of motion	$v = u + at$
	$s = \dfrac{(u + v)t}{2}$
	$v^2 = u^2 + 2as$
	$s = ut + \frac{1}{2}at^2$
force	$F = ma$
work, energy and power	$W = Fs\cos\theta$
	$E_K = \frac{1}{2}mv^2$
	$\Delta E_p = mg\,\Delta h$
	$P = \dfrac{\Delta W}{\Delta t} \quad P = Fv$
Efficiency of a machine	$= \dfrac{\text{useful output power}}{\text{input power}}$

Materials

density	$\rho = \dfrac{m}{V}$
Hooke's law	$F = k\Delta L$
Young modulus	$= \dfrac{\text{tensile stress}}{\text{tensile strain}} = \dfrac{FL}{A\,\Delta L}$
energy stored	$E = \frac{1}{2}k\,\Delta L^2 = \frac{1}{2}F\,\Delta L$

Waves

wave speed	$c = f\lambda$
period	$T = \dfrac{1}{f}$
fringe spacing	$w = \dfrac{\lambda D}{s}$
diffraction grating	$d\sin\theta = n\lambda$
refractive index of a substance s,	$n_s = \dfrac{c}{c_s}$

For two different substances of refractive indices n_1 and n_2,

law of refraction	$n_1\sin\theta_1 = n_2\sin\theta_2$
critical angle	$\sin\theta_c = \dfrac{n_2}{n_1} \quad$ for $n_1 > n_2$

Glossary

A

acceleration: change of velocity per unit time.

acceleration of free fall: acceleration of an object acted on only by the force of gravity.

accuracy: a measurement that is obtained, using accurately-calibrated instruments correctly, is said to be accurate.

accuracy: the degree of confidence in a measurement is usually quoted as the *uncertainty*.

alpha radiation: particles that each consist of two protons and two neutrons.

amplitude: maximum displacement of a vibrating particle; for a transverse wave, it is the distance from the middle to the peak of the wave.

annihilation: when a particle and its antiparticle meet, they destroy each other and become radiation.

antibaryon: a hadron consisting of three antiquarks.

antimatter: *antiparticles* that each have the same rest mass and, if charged, have equal and opposite charge to the corresponding particle. See *annihilation* and *pair production*.

antimuon: antiparticle of the muon; see *muon*.

antineutrino: the antiparticle of the *neutrino*.

antinode: fixed point in a stationary wave pattern where the amplitude is a maximum.

antiparticle: There is an antiparticle for every type of particle. A particle and its corresponding antiparticle have equal rest mass and, if charged, equal and opposite charge.

antiquark: antiparticle of a quark.

atomic number Z: the number of protons in the nucleus of an atom.

B

baryon: a hadron consisting of three quarks.

base units: the units that define the SI system (e.g. the metre, the kilogram, the second, the ampere).

beta radiation: β^- particles are fast moving electrons emitted by unstable neutron-rich nuclei; β^+ particles are fast moving *positrons* emitted by unstable proton-rich nuclei.

braking distance: the distance travelled by a vehicle in the time taken to stop it.

breaking stress: see *ultimate tensile stress*.

brittle: snaps without stretching or bending when subject to stress.

C

centre of mass: the centre of mass of a body is the point through which a single force on the body has no turning effect.

charge carriers: charged particles that move through a substance when a pd is applied across it.

circuit rule for current (Kirchhoff's 1st Law): 1. The current passing through two or more components in series is the same through each component.
2. At a junction, the total current in = the total current out.

circuit rules for pd (Kirchhoff's 2nd Law): 1. For two or more components in series, the total pd across all the components is equal to the sum of the pd's across each component.
2. The sum of the emf's round a complete loop in a circuit = the sum of the pd's round the loop.

coherent: two sources of waves are coherent if they emit waves with a constant phase difference.

conservation rules: conservation of energy, charge, *baryon number* and *lepton numbers* applies to all particle interactions. Conservation of *strangeness* applies to strong interactions only.

couple: pair of equal and opposite forces acting on a body but not along the same line.

critical angle: the angle of incidence of a light ray must exceed the critical angle for *total internal reflection* to occur.

critical temperature of a superconducting material: temperature at and below which its resistivity is zero.

cycle: interval for a vibrating particle (or a wave) from a certain displacement and velocity to the next time the particle (or the next particle) that has the same displacement and velocity.

D

de Broglie hypothesis: matter particles have a wave-like nature characterised by the de Broglie wavelength.

de Broglie wavelength: the wavelength of a matter particle = h/p, where p is the momentum of the particle.

de-excitation: process in which an atom loses energy by photon emission, as a result of an electron inside an atom moving from an outer shell to an inner shell.

density of a substance: mass per unit volume of the substance

diffraction: spreading of waves on passing through a gap or near an edge.

diffraction grating: a plate with many closely-ruled parallel slits on it.

dispersion: splitting of a beam of white light by a glass prism into colours.

displacement: distance in a given direction.

drag force: the force of fluid resistance on an object moving through the fluid.

ductile: stretches easily without breaking.

E

efficiency: the ratio of useful energy transferred (or the useful work done) by a machine or device to the energy supplied to it.

effort: the force applied to a machine to make it move.

elastic limit: point beyond which a wire is permanently stretched.

elasticity: property of a solid that enables it to regain its shape after it has been deformed or distorted.

electrolysis: process of electrical conduction in a solution or molten compound: due to ions moving to the oppositely charged electrode.

electrolyte: a solution or molten compound that conducts electricity.

electromagnetic radiation: see *electromagnetic wave*.

electromagnetic wave: an electric and magnetic wavepacket or *photon* that can travel through free space.

electromotive force (emf): the amount of electrical energy per unit charge produced inside a source of electrical energy.

electron capture: process in which an inner-shell electron of an atom is captured by the nucleus.

electron volt: amount of energy equal to 1.6×10^{-19} J defined as the work done when an electron is moved through a pd of 1 V.

endoscope: optical fibre device used to see inside cavities.

energy: the capacity to do work; see *work*.

energy levels: the energy of an electron in an electron shell of an atom.

equilibrium: state of an object when at rest or in uniform motion.

error bar: representation of an uncertainty on a graph.

error of measurement: uncertainty of a measurement.

excitation: process in which an atom absorbs energy without becoming ionized as a result of an electron inside an atom moving from an inner shell to an outer shell.

F

Feynman diagram: representation of the interaction between two particles or antiparticles or the decay of a particle or antiparticle.

fluorescence: glow of light from a substance exposed to ultraviolet radiation; the atoms de-excite in stages and emit visible photons in the process.

force: any interaction that can change the velocity of an object.

free-body force diagram: a diagram of an object showing only the forces acting on the object.

frequency: the number of cycles of a wave that pass a point per second.

friction: force opposing the motion of a surface that moves or tries to move across another surface.

fundamental mode of vibration: pattern of stationary waves on a string when it vibrates at its fundamental (i.e. lowest possible) frequency.

G

gamma radiation: high-energy photons emitted by unstable nuclei.

gravitational field strength: force of gravity per unit mass on a small object.

ground state: lowest energy state of an atom.

H

hadron: particles and antiparticles that can interact through the strong interaction.

Hooke's law: the extension of a spring is proportional to the force needed to extend it.

I

inertia: resistance of an object to change of its motion.

interference: formation of points of cancellation and reinforcement where two coherent waves pass through each other.

internal resistance: resistance inside a source of electrical energy; the loss of pd per unit current in the source when current passes through it.

ion: a charged atom.

ionisation: process of creating ions.

isotopes of an element: atoms of an element with different numbers of neutrons and the same number of protons.

K

kaon (or K meson): a *meson* that consists of a *strange quark* or *antiquark* and another quark or antiquark.

kinetic energy: the energy of an object due to its motion.

L

laser: device that produces a parallel coherent beam of monochromatic light.

lepton: electrons, muons, neutrinos and their antiparticles are classified as leptons because they cannot interact through the strong interaction. They interact through the weak interaction and, in the case of electrons and positrons, through the electromagnetic interaction.

lepton number: a lepton number is assigned to every lepton and antilepton, on the basis that the total lepton number for each branch of the lepton family is always conserved.

light-dependent resistor: resistor which is designed to have a resistance that changes with light intensity.

limit of proportionality: the limit beyond which, when a wire or a spring is stretched, its extension is no longer proportional to the force that stretches it.

linear: two quantities are said to have a linear relationship if the change of one quantity is proportional to the change of the other.

load: the force to be overcome by a machine when it shifts or raises an object.

longitudinal waves: waves with a direction of vibration parallel to the direction of propagation of the waves.

M

mass number: see *nucleon number*

mass: measure of the inertia or resistance to change of motion of an object.

matter waves: the wave-like behaviour of particles of matter.

meson: a hadron consisting of a quark and an antiquark.

moment of a force about a point: force × perpendicular distance from the line of action of the force to the point.

momentum: mass × velocity.

motive force: the force that drives a vehicle.

multipath dispersion: the lengthening of a light pulse as it travels along an optical fibre, due to rays that repeatedly undergo total internal reflection having to travel a longer distance than rays that undergo less total internal reflection.

muon: a *lepton* which is negatively charged and has a greater rest mass than the electron.

N

negative temperature coefficient: the resistance of a semiconductor decreases when its temperature is increased.

neutrino: uncharged *lepton* with a very low rest mass compared with the electron.

neutrino types (or 'branches'): there are 3 types of neutrinos, the electron neutrino, the muon neutrino and the tau neutrino. This specfication only requires knowledge of the electron neutrino and the muon neutrino branches (and their antiparticles) of the lepton 'family'.

Newton's 1st law: an object remains at rest or in uniform motion unless acted on by a resultant force.

Newton's 2nd law for constant mass: resultant force = mass × acceleration.

node: fixed point in a stationary wave pattern where the amplitude is zero.

nucleon: a neutron or proton in the nucleus.

nucleon number A: the number of neutrons and protons in a nucleus; also referred to as *mass number*.

nuclide: a type of nucleus with a particular number of protons and neutrons.

O

Ohm's Law: The pd across a metallic conductor is proportional to the current, provided the physical conditions do not change.

optical fibre: a thin flexible transparent fibre used to carry light pulses from one end to the other.

P

pair production: when a gamma photon changes into a particle and an antiparticle.

pascal: unit of pressure or stress equal to $1 \, \mathrm{N \, m^{-2}}$.

path difference: the difference in distances from two coherent sources to an interference fringe.

period of a wave: time for one complete cycle of a wave to pass a point.

phase difference: the fraction of a cycle between the vibrations of two vibrating particles, measured either in radians or degrees.

photoelectricity: emission of electrons from a metal surface when the surface is illuminated by light of frequency greater than a minimum value known as the *threshold frequency*.

photon: packet or 'quantum' of electromagnetic waves.

pion (or π meson): a *meson* that consists of an up or down *quark* and an up or down *antiquark*.

plane-polarised waves: transverse waves that vibrate in one plane only.

plastic deformation: deformation of a solid beyond its elastic limit.

positive temperature coefficient: the resistance of a metal increases when its temperature is increased.

positron: *antiparticle* of the electron.

potential difference: work done or energy transfer per unit charge between two points when charge moves from one point to the other.

potential divider: two or more resistors in series connected to a source of pd.

potential energy: the energy of an object due to its position.

power: rate of transfer of energy.

precision of a measurement: the degree of exactness of a measurement, usually expressed as the uncertainty of the readings used to obtain a measurement.

precision of an instrument: the smallest non-zero reading that can be measured, also sometimes referred to as the instrument sensitivity or resolution.

pressure: force per unit area acting on a surface perpendicular to the surface.

principle of conservation of energy: energy cannot be created or destroyed.

principle of moments: for an object in equilibrium, the sum of the clockwise moments about any point = the sum of the anticlockwise moments about that point.

probable error: estimate of the *uncertainty* of a measurement.

progressive waves: waves which travel through a substance or through space if electromagnetic.

projectile: a projected object in motion acted on only by the force of gravity.

Q

quark: protons and neutrons and other hadrons consist of quarks. There are six types of quarks, the up quark, the down quark, the strange quark, the charmed quark, the top quark and the bottom quark. This specification only requires knowledge of the up, down and strange quarks and their antiquarks.

quark model (or standard model): a quark can join with an antiquark to form a *meson* or with two other quarks to form a *baryon*. An antiquark can join with two other antiquarks to form an *antibaryon*.

R

radian: measure of an angle defined such that 2π radians = $360°$.

random error: error of measurement due to readings that vary randomly with no recognisable pattern or trend or bias.

range of a set of a readings: the range of a set of readings of the same measurement is the difference between the minimum and the maximum reading.

range of an instrument: the difference between the minimum and the maximum reading that can be obtained using the instrument.

refraction: change of direction of a wave when it crosses a boundary where its speed changes.

refractive index: speed of light in free space / speed of light in the substance.

resistance: pd/current.

resistivity: resistance per unit length × area of cross-section.

rest energy: energy due to rest mass m_0, equal to $m_0 c^2$, where c is the speed of light in free space.

root mean square value of an alternating current or pd: the value of direct current that would give the same heating effect as the alternating current in the same resistor; rms current (or pd) = $1/\sqrt{2} \times$ peak current (or pd).

S

scalar: a physical quantity with magnitude only.

semiconductor: a substance in which the number of charge carriers increases when the temperature is raised.

sensitivity of an instrument: the output reading per unit input quantity.

SI system: the scientific system of units.

specific charge: charge/mass value of a charged particle.

spectrometer: instrument used to measure light wavelengths very accurately.

speed: change of distance per unit time.

stationary waves: wave pattern with nodes and antinodes formed when two or more progressive waves of the same frequency and amplitude pass through each other.

stiffness constant: the force per unit extension needed to extend a wire or a spring.

stopping distance: thinking distance + braking distance.

strain: extension per unit length of a solid when deformed.

strangeness number: A strangeness number is assigned to every particle and antiparticle on the basis that strangeness is always conserved in the strong interaction, but not in a weak interaction or a decay involving a strange quark or antiquark.

stress: force per unit area of cross-section in a solid perpendicular to the cross-section.

strong interaction: interaction between two hadrons.

strong nuclear force: attractive force between nucleons that holds the nucleons in the nucleus.

superconductor: a material that has zero electrical resistance.

superposition: the effect of two waves adding together when they meet.

systematic error: error of measurement due to readings that systematically differ from the true reading and follow a pattern or trend or bias.

T

terminal speed: the maximum speed reached by an object when the drag force on it is equal and opposite to the force causing the motion of the object.

thermistor: resistor which is designed to have a resistance that changes with temperature.

thinking distance: the distance travelled by a vehicle in the time it takes the driver to react.

threshold frequency: minimum frequency of light that can cause *photoelectric emission*.

torque of a couple: force × perpendicular distance between the lines of action of the forces.

total internal reflection: A light ray travelling in a substance is totally internally reflected at a boundary with a substance of lower refractive index, if the angle of incidence is greater than a certain value known as the *critical angle*.

transverse waves: waves with a direction of vibration perpendicular to the direction of propagation of the waves.

types of light spectra:
continuous spectrum
– continuous range of colours corresponding to a continuous range of wavelengths,
line emission spectrum
– characteristic coloured vertical lines, each corresponding to a certain wavelength,
line absorption spectrum
– dark vertical lines against a continuous range of colours, each line corresponding to a certain wavelength.

U

ultimate tensile stress: tensile stress needed to break a solid material.

uncertainty: half the range of the readings or, if the readings are the same, the instrument precision.

useful energy: energy transferred to where it is wanted when it is wanted.

V

vector: a physical quantity with magnitude and direction.

velocity: change of displacement per unit time.

virtual photon: carrier of the electromagnetic force; a photon exchanged between two charged particles when they interact.

W

W boson: carrier of the weak nuclear force; W bosons have non-zero rest mass and may be positive or negative.

wave particle duality: matter particles have a wave-like nature as well as a particle-like nature; photons have a particle-like nature as well as a wave-like nature.

wavefronts: lines of constant phase (e.g. wavecrests).

wavelength: the least distance between two adjacent vibrating particles with the same displacement and velocity at the same time (e.g. distance between two adjacent wave peaks).

weak interaction: interaction between two leptons.

weak nuclear force: force responsible for beta decay.

weight: the force of gravity acting on an object.

work: force × distance moved in the direction of the force.

work function of a metal: minimum amount of energy needed by an electron to escape from a metal surface.

Y

Y-gain (or Y-sensitivity) of an oscilloscope: pd per division.

yield point: point at which the stress in a wire suddenly drops when the wire is subjected to increasing strain.

Young's fringes: parallel bright and dark fringes observed when light from a narrow slit passes through two closely spaced slits.

Young modulus: stress/strain (assuming the limit of propotionality has not been exceeded).

Answers to summary questions

1.1

1 **a** i 6p, 6n   ii 8p, 8n   iii 92p, 143n
      iv 11p, 13n   v 29p, 34n

   b i $^{235}_{92}$U   ii $^{12}_{6}$C and $^{16}_{8}$O

2 **a** neutron   **b** electron   **c** neutron

3 **a** $+3.2 \times 10^{-19}$ C   **b** 63   **c** 3.04×10^{6} C kg^{-1}

4 **a** 2.67×10^{-26} kg   **b** 8 neutrons and 10 electrons

1.2

1 **a** electrostatic force   **b** strong nuclear force

   c strong nuclear force   **d** electrostatic force

2 **a** $^{225}_{88}$Ra, $^{4}_{2}\alpha$ **b** $^{65}_{29}$Cu, $^{0}_{-1}\beta$

3 **a** Each beta emission increases the proton number by 1 and the alpha emission decreases it by 2, so the number of protons at the end is unchanged, which means the final nuclide is a bismuth nucleus.

   b i 209   ii 82p, 127n

4 **a** A hypothesis is an untested idea or theory.

   b i It is uncharged; it hardly interacts with matter.

      ii The sun, a nuclear reactor, a beta-emitting isotope

1.3

1 **b** i 5.1×10^{14} Hz   ii 1.5×10^{6} Hz

3 **a** 7.0×10^{14} Hz   **b** 4.6×10^{-19} J

4 **a** 4.7×10^{14} Hz, 3.1×10^{-19} J   **b** 4.8×10^{15}

1.4

1 **a** 939 MeV (5 sf values for c, e and h give 938.26 MeV)

2 The rest energy of an electron and a positron is less than 2 MeV but not for a proton–antiproton pair, so pair production can happen for an electron and positron.

3 **a** 0.511 MeV   **b** i 1.180 MeV

4 **a** A proton in the nucleus changes into a neutron, and a positron and a neutrino are created and emitted from the nucleus.

   b No photon is involved in positron emission; no neutrino is emitted in pair production.

1.5

1 See 1.5 Fig 1

2 See 1.5 Fig 4

3 **a** See 1.5 Fig 3   **b** 0.001 fm, 10^{-27} s

4 **a** The W-boson is charged and the photon is uncharged; the W boson has a non-zero rest mass and the photon has zero rest mass; the W boson is the exchange particle of the weak nuclear force whereas the virtual photon is the exchange particle of the electromagnetic force.

   b In Fig 4b), a W$^+$ boson interacts with a neutrino, which turns into a β^- particle. In Fig 5, the W$^+$ boson decays into a β^- particle and a neutrino.

2.1

1 **a** the electron, the muon, the π^+ meson, the K^0 meson, the proton, the neutron

   b the K^0 meson, the neutron

2 **a** weak   **b** weak   **c** strong

3 **a** A muon   **b** They both decay; the π meson has a greater rest mass than a muon.

4 **a** i They decay into π mesons, muons and antineutrinos and antimuons and neutrinos.

      ii They decay into muons and antineutrinos and antimuons and neutrinos.

   b electrons, neutrinos and antineutrinos

2.2

1 **a** i A particle that experiences the strong interaction

      ii A particle that does not experience the strong interaction

   b i lepton   ii a baryon   iii a meson

2 **a** Both carry negative charge; the muon does not interact through the strong nuclear force, the π^- meson does (or they have different rest masses).

   b Both carry positive charge; the K meson has more rest mass (or is strange).

   c Both are uncharged; a neutron is a baryon whereas a K^0 meson is a meson (or they have different rest masses and strangeness).

3 **a** lepton   **b** baryons, mesons,   **c** mesons

4 **a** $\pi^- \pi^+ \pi^+$ **b** 74 MeV

2.3

1 **a** Both are negatively charged and do not interact through the strong nuclear force; they have different rest masses.

   b Both are uncharged and do not interact through the strong nuclear force; the electron neutrino does not interact with the muon and the muon neutrino does not interact with the electron.

2 **a** **i** A strong interaction **ii** a weak interaction

   iii a weak interaction

   b **i** $\mu^- \longrightarrow e^+ + \nu_e + \bar{\nu}_\mu$ **ii** 105.5 MeV

3 **a** **i** 0 **ii** +1 **iii** +1 **iv** 0

   b **i** +1 **ii** −1 **iii** −1 **iv** −1

4 **a** No, charge is not conserved. **b** Yes

   c No, the (electron) lepton number is not conserved.

   d No, neither the electron lepton number nor the muon lepton number is conserved.

2.4

1 **a** meson = quark + antiquark, baryon = 3 quarks

   b proton = uud, neutron = udd

2 **a** any corresponding quark–antiquark **b** $\overline{u}\overline{u}\overline{d}$

   c $s\overline{u}$, **d** sud

3 **a** See Figure 3 **b** a u quark in a proton changes to a d quark and emits a W⁺ boson, which decays into a positron and a neutrino.

4 **a** dds has a charge of −1 (= 3 × −⅓) and a strangeness of −1 due to the s quark

   b $d\overline{u} + uud \longrightarrow u\overline{s} + sdd$; an up antiquark and an up quark annihilate each other and create a strange quark and a strange antiquark, which form a meson, consisting of an up quark and a strange antiquark, and a baryon, consisting of a strange quark and two down quarks.

2.5

1 **a** **ii** baryon number

   c **ii** proton = uud, neutron = udd

   ii $uud + uud \longrightarrow uud + udd + u\overline{d}$

2 **a** **i** +⅓ **ii** −1 **iii** 0 **b** **i** +1 **ii** −1 **iii** 0

3 **a** sss

   b **i** charge = 0, strangeness = −2

   ii the weak interaction

   iii $sss \longrightarrow ssu + d\overline{u}$; an s quark changes to a d quark and a $u\overline{u}$ pair is created.

4 **a** the weak interaction **ii** no

   b **i** The charge on the RH = the charge on the LH side = −1; to conserve charge for 3 *charged* π mesons, two must be negative and one must be positive.

   ii $K^- \longrightarrow \pi^+ + \pi^- + \pi^-$

   c **ii** $K^+ \longrightarrow \pi^+ + \pi^0$ **ii** $u\overline{s} \longrightarrow u\overline{d} + u\overline{u}$; an $\overline{s}$ antiquark decays into a $\overline{d}$ antiquark and a quark-same antiquark pair are created, for example an up quark and antiquark pair.

3.1

2 **a** **i** 6.7×10^{14} Hz, 4.4×10^{-19} J

   ii 2.0×10^{14} Hz, 1.3×10^{-19} J

3 **a** 1.7×10^{14} Hz **b** 2.7×10^{-19} J

4 **a** 3.1×10^{-19} J **b** 1.6×10^{-19} J **c** 2.5×10^{14} Hz

3.2

2 **a** 1.6×10^{12}

3 **a** 3.4×10^{-19} J **b** 1.5×10^{15} **c** 2.5×10^{12}

4 **a** **i** 4.0×10^{14} Hz **ii** 2.7×10^{-19} J,

   b 2.7×10^{-19} J

3.3

Similarity; energy is absorbed by the atom;
Difference; an electron stays in the atom when excitation occurs but leaves the atom when ionisation occurs.

2 **a** 1.66×10^{-18} J, **b** 1.6 eV

3 **a** less **b** more, gains, lost

4 **a** An electron inside the atom moves to an outer shell.

3.4

1 **a** 9.0 eV

   b There are 3 energy levels below the 5.7 eV level. There are 3 possible transitions to the ground state, 2 to the first excited state and 1 to the second excited state. The energy changes for these transitions are all different. Hence there are 6 possible photon energies.

2 **a** The energy of an electron in the atom increases in excitation and decreases in de-excitation. Excitation can occur through photon absorption or electron collision. De-excitation only occurs through photon emission.

   b **i** There are two excited levels at 1.8 eV and 4.6 eV above the ground state;

   ii photon energies 1.8 eV, 2.8 eV and 4.6 eV.

3 **a** The intermediate level could be at 0.6 eV or at 3.2 eV. The diagram shows one of these alternatives.

b An electron in the atom absorbs the 3.8 eV photon and moves to an outer shell. It moves to an inner shell and emits a 3.2 eV photon. An electron moves from this shell to the ground state, emitting a 0.6 eV photon.

4 When the electricity supply is switched off, excitation by collision of the gas atoms in the tube ceases because the supply of electrons to the tube is cut off. Therefore the mercury atoms no longer emit ultraviolet radiation and so the coating atoms can no longer emit light.

3.5

1 A line spectrum consists of discrete coloured lines whereas a continuous spectrum has a continuous spread of colours. A line spectrum is due to photons of certain energies only, whereas a continuous spectrum is due to a continuous spread of photon energies.

2 **a** 1.28×10^{-19} J   **b** 1.55×10^{-6} m

3 **a** 3.21×10^{-19} J   **b** 2.0 eV

4 The energy levels of the atoms of an element are unique to those atoms. The photons emitted by them have energies equal to the energy differences between the levels. Therefore the photon energies are characteristic of the atoms and can be used to identify the element.

3.6

3 **a** 3.6×10^{-11} m   **b** 2.0×10^{-14} m

4 **a** 1.3×10^{-27} kg m s^{-1}, 1.5×10^3 m s^{-1}

   b 1.3×10^{-27} kg m s^{-1}, 0.78 m s^{-1}

4.1

1 **a i** 3.5 C **ii** 210 C   **b i** 3.0 A **ii** 0.15 A

2 **a** 3.8×10^{15} **b** 1.9×10^{22}

3 **a** 72 mC   **b** 4.5×10^{17}

4 **a** 800 C   **b i** 1600 s **ii** 8000 s

4.2

1 **a** 29 kJ   **b** 720 J

2 **a** 2.0 A   **b** 22 kJ

3 **a i** 48 kJ **ii** 3.5 A   **b** 5 A

4 **a** 12 kJ   **b** 4.5 W   **c** 2700 s

4.3

1 **a** 6.0 Ω, 10 V, 0.125 mA, 160 Ω . 2.5 mA   **b** 7.5 Ω

2 31 Ω

3 0.11 mΩ

4 **a** 1.8×10^{-6} Ω m **b** 33 mm

4.4

1 **a** 0.25 A, 12 Ω

   b The filament would become brighter and hotter until it melts and breaks as a result.

2 **a** 0.03 mA   **b** 0.38 mA

3 **a**

   b The diode would then be 'reverse-biased' so the current in the circuit would be negligible.

4 **a** 30.4 Ω   **b** 46°C

5.1

1 **a** 1.0 A, 4.0 A   **b** 5.0 A   **c** 30 W

2 **b i** 2.0 V   **ii** 0.20 A

3 **b i** 4.0 V   **ii** 2.0 V   **iii** 10 Ω

4 **a** 3.6 V   **b** 30 Ω

5.2

1 **a** 16 Ω   **b** 3.0 Ω   **c** 4 Ω

2 **a** 2 Ω   **b** 6 Ω   **c** 1.0 A   **d** 4.0 W

3 **a** 3.6 Ω   **b** 0.83 A

   c 2 Ω: 0.5 W, 4 Ω: 1.0 W, 9 Ω: 1.0 W   **d** 2.5 W

4 **a** 14.4 W   **b** 2.4 Ω

5.3

1 **a** 6.0 Ω   **b** 2.0 A   **c** 3.0 V   **d** 9.0 V

2 **a** 0.5 A   **b** 1.25 V   **c** 0.63 W   **d** 0.13 W

3 **a** 2.0 Ω   **b** 1.5 V

4 **a** 12 V, 2 Ω

5.4

1 **a** 12.0 Ω   **b** 0.25 A

   c 4 Ω: 0.25 A, 1.0 V, 24 Ω: 0.08 A, 2.0 V; 12 Ω: 0.17 A, 2.0 V

2 **a** 20.0 Ω   **b** 1.05 A   **c** 1.05 A, 15.8 V

3 **a i** 2.0 W **ii** 2.0 W   **b i** 2.0 W **ii** 8.0 W

4 **a** Q: 0.6 V, 0.06 mA; P: 2.4 V, 0.48 mA; X: 0.6 V, 0.42 mA; Y: 2.4 V, 0

   b P: 0.6 V, 0.12 mA ; Q: 2.4 V, 0.24 mA; X: 2.4 V, 0; Y: 0.6 V, 0.12 mA

5.5

1 **a** $1\,k\Omega : 0.75\,V; 5.0\,k\Omega : 3.75\,V$

   b $1\,k\Omega : 1.3\,V; 5.0\,k\Omega : 3.2\,V$

2 The brightness of the light bulb increases gradually from zero to maximum brightness.

3 **a** **i** 0.5 A   **ii** $8.0\,\Omega : 4.0\,V; 4.0\,\Omega : 2.0\,V$

   b **i** 3.0 V,   **ii** 4.0 V

4 **a** **i** 2.8 V   **iii** $6.4\,k\Omega$

6.1

1 **a** 5 ms   **b** 0.071 A

2 **a** **i** 2.12 A **ii** 8.49 V   **b** (i) 36 W **ii** 18 W

3 **a** **i** 4.35 A **ii** 6.15 A **iii** 2.0 kW

   b The fuse melts only if the rms current exceeds 5 A. The rms current in this case is less than 5 A so the fuse does not melt.

4 **a** **i** 4.0 A   **ii** 5.66 A   **iii** 17.0 V

   b **i** $V_{rms} = I_{rms}R = 4.0 \times 0.5 = 2.0\,V$ **ii** 19.8 V

6.2

1 **a** **i** $5.0\,V\,cm^{-1}$ **ii** 2.4 cm   **b** **i** 1.63 V **ii** 1.15 V

2 **a** 22 ms   **b** 45.5 Hz

3 **a** 12.5 V, 8.8 V   **b** 10 ms, 100 Hz

4 **a** A straight horizontal line 2.0 cm above the centre line would be seen.

   The waveform seen on the screen has a peak height above the centre of 2.83 cm and 1.5 cycles would appear on the screen.

7.1

1 **a** 3.7 N at 33° to 3.1 N   **b** 17.1 N at 21° to 16 N

   c 1.4 N at 45° to 3 N and 1 N

2 **a** 14.0 N in the same direction   **b** 6.0 N in the direction of the 10 N force   **c** 10.8 N at 22° to the 10 N force

3 6.1 kN vertically up, 2.2 kN horizontal

4 **a** 268 N   **b** 225 N

7.2

1 **a** 7.3 N   **b** 7.3 N at 31.5° to the vertical

2 **b** **i** 2.7 N   **ii** 4.7 N

3 **a** 139 N   **b** 95 N

4 **a** 73°   **b** 6.8 N

7.3

1 300 N

2 **b** 6.2 N

3 0.27 m

4 6.75 N

7.4

1 0.51 N at 100 mm mark, 0.69 N at the 800 mm mark

2 **a** 122 N at 1.0 m end and 108 N at the other end, both vertically upwards

   b 122 N at 1.0 m end and 108 N at the other end, both vertically downwards

3 620 kN, 640 kN

4 **a** 100 N, 50 N   **b** 150 N

7.5

1 The centre of mass is higher if the upper shelves are filled instead of the lower shelves. If tilted, it will topple over at a smaller angle with the upper shelves full, than if they were empty.

2 89 N

3 **a** 48°   **b** Yes, they will raise the overall centre of mass so it will topple on a less steep slope.

4 On a horizontal road, the moment due to the vehicle weight about the wheels on one side is the total weight × half the width of the wheelbase. If the side winds create a greater moment, the lorry will tilt, then topple. The greater the lorry weight, the greater the moment the side winds need to overcome, to make the lorry tilt. If the road is sloped sideways, the side winds do not need to be as strong, as the moment, due to the vehicle's weight, is less than on a flat road, because the perpendicular distance from the line of action of the weight to the wheels is less on a sloped road.

7.6

1 **a** 50 N   **b** 250 N

2 **a** 1800 N m   **b** 1800 N

3 **a** 6.0 kN   **b** 10.8 kN

4 1.5 N in the cord at 40° to the beam, 1.9 N in the other cord

7.7

1 **a** 15 N   **b** 3.0 N   **c** 10.8 N

2 7 N

3 **a** 6.8 N   **b** 52°

4 18.0 N

5 **a** 16.9 kN   **b** 16.9 kN

6 **a** 6.2 N   **b** 12.2 N

7 Move it further 50 mm away from the pivot.

8 **a** 6.8 N   **b** 9.8 N

9 **a** 2200 N   **b** 3100 N

10 **b** 950 N at X, 750 N at Y

11   **a** 2820 kN   **b** 1660 kN and 1540 kN (to 3sf)

12   **a** 8.0 N and 16.0 N **b** 38 N and 76 N

13   **b** 11 kN, 11 kN

14   **b** 28.4 N

8.1

1   **a** 80 km h^{-1} **b** 22 m s^{-1}

2   **a** 2.5 × 10^4 km h^{-1} **b** 7.0 × 10^3 m s^{-1}

3   **a** 45 000 m   **b** 28.3 m s^{-1}

4   **b** **i** 4.0 km

      ii 30 m s^{-1} then 25 m s^{-1} in the opposite direction

8.2

1   **a** 1.5 m s^{-2} **b** −2.5 m s^{-2}

2   **a** 0.45 m s^{-2} **b** 7.9 m s^{-1}

3   **b** 0.60 m s^{-2}, 0, −0.40 m s^{-2}

8.3

1   **a** 2.0 m s^{-2} **b** 221 m

2   **a** 43 s   **b** −0.93 m s^{-2}

3   **a** **i** 0.2 m s^{-2} **ii** 90 m

      b **i** −0.75 m s^{-2} **ii** 8.0 s

      d 3.0 m s^{-1}

4   **a** 5.0 m s^{-2} **b** 7.5 m   **c** 18 m   **d** 6.4 m s^{-1}

8.4

1   **a** 4.0 m   **b** 8.8 m s^{-1}

2   **a** 3.2 s   **b** 31 m s^{-1}

3   **a** **i** 3.9 s   **ii** 38 m s^{-1}

4   **a** 1.6 m s^{-2} **b** 3.6 m s^{-1} **c** 0.64 m

8.5

1   **a** **i** 83 s   **ii** 127 s

2   **a** 600 s

3   **a** velocity / m s^{-1}

4   **a** **i** 0.61 s **ii** 5.9 m s^{-1} **iii** 0.43 s **iv** 4.2 m s^{-1}

8.6

1   **a** **i** 52 s   **ii** 0.49 m s^{-2}

      b **i** 406 m   **ii** −1.04 m s^{-2}

2   **a** 15 m   **b** −0.13 m s^{-2}

      c 0.67 m s^{-1} downwards, 13.4 m from the start

3   **a** **i** 80 m   **ii** 8.0 m s^{-1}

      b **i** 65 s   **ii** −0.12 m s^{-2}

4   **a** **i** 180 m s^{-1} **ii** 2.7 km

      b 4.4 km

      c 290 m s^{-1}

8.7

1   **a** 32 m s^{-1} **b** 2.8 s   **c** 39 m

2   **a** 3.0 s   **b** 49 m

      c 34 m s^{-1} (at 62° to the horizontal)

3   **a** 0.20 s   **b** 11.7 m s^{-1}

4   **a** 354 m   **b** **i** 1020 m **ii** 1020 m   **c** 146 m s^{-1}

8.8

1   **a** 470 mm **b** 3.0 m s^{-2} **c** 2.7 m s^{-1}

2   **a** 2.02 s   **b** 50.5 m

3   **a** 21.5 m s^{-1} **b** 35.7 m   **c** 34.1 m s^{-1}

4   **a** 3.5 m s^{-1}, 3.0 m s^{-1} **b** **i** 150 m **ii** 20 m

9.1

1   **a** 0.24 m s^{-2} **b** 190 N   **c** 0.024

2   **a** 2.4 m s^{-2} **b** 12 000 N

3   **a** 360 N   **b** 23 s

4   **a** −1.3 × 10^5 m s^{-2} **b**   260 N

9.2

1   **a** 5400 N   **b** 7700 N

2   **a** 60 N   **b** 270 N

3   **a** 11.8 kN   **b** 11.8 kN   **c** 12.3 kN   **d** 12.3 kN

4   **a** 1.0 m s^{-2} **b** 12.5 N

9.3

1   **a** **i** 0.04 m s^{-1} **ii** 1.5 N

3   **a** 0.14 m s^{-2} **b** 520 m

9.4

1   **a** **i** 7.2 m   **ii** 33.7 m   **b** 4.1 m

2   **a** 6.75 m s^{-2} **b** 6750 N

4   **b** 76 m

9.5
1 a 2.0 g   b 24 kN
2 a 80 ms   b 375 kN
3 a 7.5 m s^{-2} b 6750 N
4 b i 6.4 g   ii 4250 N

10.1
1 a 200 J   b 4.5 J
2 a 48 J   b 24 J   c 0
3 a 1000 J   b 600 J   c 400 J
4 a 2.4 N   b 0.12 J

10.2
1 a 9.0 J   b 9.0 J   c 1.8 m
2 a i 2.9 J   ii 2.4 J   b 0.59 J
3 a 15.7 kJ   b 5.8 kJ
     c 9.9 kJ   d 20 N
4 a 590 kJ   b 2.4 kJ   c 470 kJ   d 122 kJ   e 1.6 kN

10.3
1 a 1.1 kJ   b 62.5 J s^{-1}
2 500 MW
3 a 156 MJ   b 140 MJ   c 12 MW
4 122 m

10.4
1 a 450 J s^{-1} b 1800 J s^{-1}
2 a 480 J   b 50 J   c 10%
3 a 570 MJ s^{-1} b 6.2 × 10^5 kg
4 a 600 s   b 3.7 MJ   c 8%

10.5
1 1.0 × 10^7 m^2
2 4 MW
3 125 m^3 s^{-1}
4 a 6.3 × 10^{11} kg   b 430 MW

11.1
1 a 8.0 × 10^{-4} m^3 b 3.1 × 10^3 kg m^{-3}
2 a 6.3 kg   b 2.0 × 10^{-3} m^3 c 3.1 × 10^3 kg m^{-3}
3 a 9.6 × 10^{-6} m^3 b 7.5 × 10^{-2} kg
4 a i 0.29 kg   ii 0.12 kg   b 2.3 × 10^3 kg m^{-3}

11.2
1 a 0.40 m   b 12.5 N
2 a 20 N   b 100 mm   c 200 N m^{-1}
3 a 40 N   b 200 mm
4 a 12.3 N m^{-1} b 8.8 × 10^{-2} J   c 2.2 N

11.3
1 1.0 × 10^9 Pa
2 1.3 × 10^{11} Pa
3 a 9.4 × 10^8 Pa   b 1.1 × 10^{-2} m

11.4
1 a 3.3 × 10^6 Pa   b 2.8 × 10^{-4} m   c 0.21 J
2 a 2.3 mm   b 1.7 × 10^{-2} J
3 a 470 kN   b 47 J
4 a 10.0 J   b 4.2 J

12.2
1 a 0.10 m   b 1.9 × 10^{-2} m
2 a 10 GHz   b 5.0 × 10^{14} Hz
3 1.0 V, 1.0 kHz
4 a i   amplitude = 8 mm, wavelength = 47 mm
     ii 180°   iii 270°
    b +8 mm

12.5
1 b 8.0 m
2 a 2.0 m   b i 180°   ii 225°   iii 0
4 b 30 mm

12.6
1 a 1.6 m   b 410 m s^{-1}
2 a 0.4 m   b 0.53 m

13.1
1 a i 14.9°   ii 28.9°   iii 40.6°
    b i 58.7°   ii See diagram below

2 a i 19.5°   ii 35.2°   b i 59.4°   ii 74.6°
3 a 1.53   b 34.5°
4 b 72.6°

13.2
1 a i 0.040 m   ii 0.030 m,   b 18.5°
2 a 1.97 × 10^8 m s^{-1} b 2.26 × 10^8 m s^{-1}
3 a 25.4°   b 35°
4 a red 49.5°   b blue 50.8°

13.3

1   b   i   41°   ii   49°
2   b   i   34°   ii   34°
3   a   65°   b   i   30°   ii   45°

13.4

2   550 nm
3   0.9 mm
4   0.75 m

13.5

3   1.1 mm

13.6

2   a   6 mm

13.7

1   a   10.9°, 22.2°   b   5
2   a   2   b   0.58 (= 35')
3   a   1090   b   69.9°
4   a   599 mm^{-1} b   3

16.1

1   a   i   0.500 m   ii   320 cm   iii   95.6 m
    b   i   450 g   ii   1.997 kg   iii 5.4×10^7 g
    c   i 2.0×10^{-3} m^2 ii 5.5×10^{-5} m^2
      iii 5.0×10^{-6} m^2

2   a   i 1.50×10^{11} m   ii 3.15×10^7 s
      iii 6.3×10^{-7} m   iv 2.57×10^{-8} kg
      v 1.50×10^5 mm   vi 1.245×10^{-6} m
    b   i   35 km   ii   650 nm   iii 3.4×10^3 kg
      iv   870 MW (= 0.87 GW)

3   a   i   20 m s^{-1} ii   20 m s^{-1} iii 1.5×10^8 m s^{-1}
      iv 3.0×10^4 m s^{-1}
    b   i 6.0×10^3 Ω   ii   5.0 Ω   iii 1.7×10^6 Ω
      iv 4.9×10^8 Ω   v   3.0 Ω

4   a   i   301   ii 2.8×10^9 iii 1.9×10^{-23}
      iv 1.2×10^{-3} v 2.0×10^4 vi 7.9×10^{-2}
    b   i 1.6×10^{-3} ii 5.8×10^{-6}
      iii   1.7   iv 3.1×10^{-2}

16.2

1   a   1.57 m   b   i   1.57 m   ii   1.05 m   iii   0.26 m
2   a   i   68°   ii   41°   iii   22°   iv   61°
    b   i   17 cm   ii   16 m (15.6 m to 3sf)   iii   4.8 mm
      iv   101 cm
3   a   49 mm   b   i   35 km   ii   31°
4   a   i   3.9 N, 4.6 N   ii   3.4 N, 9.4 N   iii   4.8 N, 5.7 N
    b   4.0 N, 30° to 3.5 N

16.3

1   a   0.2   b   0.1, 0.25   c   < 0.1
2   b   i   2   ii   −1   iii   4.25   iv   ⅓
3   b   i   0.25   ii   ± 2.8   iii   ± 0.5   iv   4
4   a 3.1×10^{-7} m^3
    b 6.2×10^{-3} m
    c   2.5 s
    d   17 m s^{-1}

16.4

1   a   i   3   ii   −3   iii   1
    b   i   −4   ii   8   iii   2
    c   i   −1   ii   5   iii   5
    d   i   −1.5   ii   3   iii   2
2   a   i $y = 2x − 8$ ii   −8
    b   i   3 m s^{-2} ii   5 m s^{-1}
3   a   (1, 4)   b $y = 4x$
4   a $x = 2, y = 0$ b $x = 3, y = 5$ c $x = 2, y = 0$

16.5

3   b   i   use gradient $= \dfrac{A}{\rho L}$ ii   use gradient $= \dfrac{VA}{\rho}$
4   b   ii $u = y$-intercept, ½a = gradient

16.6

1   b   i   gradient   ii   area under line
2   b   Resistance $= \dfrac{1}{\text{gradient}}$
3   b   The power is constant and is represented by the gradient of the line.
4   b   i   acceleration   ii   distance fallen   c   velocity

Index

Acknowledgements

Photograph Acknowledgements

The authors and publisher are grateful to the following for permission to reproduce photographs and other copyright material in this book.

Alamy/Mary Evans Picture Library: p 10 (bottom); **Alamy/ Sciencephotos:** 206 (top); **Ann Ronan Picture Library:** p 196; **Corel 487 (NT):** p 114; **Corel 671 (NT):** pp 4, 154; **Digital Vision 6 (NT)/ Photodisc 54:** p 10 (middle left); **Digital Vision 6 (NT)/Photodisc 31:** p 68; **Digital Vision 6 (NT):** p 124; **Digital Vision 6 (NT)/Ingram Real Vol 2:** p 141; **Digital Vision 1 (NT):** p 157; **Digital Vision 6 (NT)/ Photodisc 54:** p 159 (right); **Digital Vision 6 (NT)/Photodisc 4:** p 176; **Digital Vision 6 (NT)/Eyewire DTE:** p 179 (middle right); **Digital Vision (NT)/Stockbyte 36:** p 182; **Education Development Centre:** p 178 (bottom); **Education Development Centre:** p 178 (top), p 179, p 181; **Education Development Centre/Matjar Bancina:** p 49 (right); **Imperial College, Department of Physics:** pp 39 (right), 207 (middle); **iStock:** p 49 (left & right); **Illustrated London News:** p 32; **iStockphoto/Nick Schlax:** p89; **Jim Breithaupt:** pp 199 (left), 201; **Kodansha Publishers Ltd:** p 126; **Martyn Chillmaid:** p 48; **NASA, ESA, and The Hubble Heritage Team (STScI/AURA):** p3; **Science Photo Library/Philippe Plailly:** p 4; **Science Photo Library/Rosenfeld Images Ltd:** p 9; **Science Photo Library/Carl Anderson:** p 12; **Science Photo Library/Prf. G. Piragino:** p 18; **Science Photo Library/Andrew Lambert Photography:** p 19 (top); **Science Photo Library/Peter Menzel:** p 19 (middle); **Science Photo Library/David Parker:** p 21; **Science Photo Library/Cern:** p 22; **Science Photo Library/NASA / ESA / STSCI / R.Williams, HDF Team:** p 27; **Science Photo Library/David Parker:** 39 (left); **Science Photo Library/Hank Morgan:** p 43; **Science Photo Library/David parker:** p 112; **Science Photo Library:** p 119; **Science Photo Library/Keith Kent:** p 138; **Science Photo Library/TRL Ltd:** p 143 (top), p 143 (bottom); **Science Photo Library/Y Derome:** p 158; **Science Photo Library/Martin Bond:** p 159 (left); **Science Photo Library/Hank Morgan:** p 185; **Science Photo Library/David Parker:** p 192; **Science Photo Library/Mauro Fermariello:** p 203 (top); **Science Photo Library/Steve Gschmeissner:** p 203 (bottom); **Science Photo Library/Seti Institute:** p 206 (bottom); **Science Photo Library/Andrew Lambert Photography:** p216; **Science Photo Library/Sheila Terry:** p 217; **Science Photo Library/Sheila Terry:** p 219 (top); **Science Photo Library/Cristina Pedrazzini:** p 219 (bottom); **Science Photo Library/Andrew Lambert Photography:** p 220.

Every effort has been made to trace and contact all copyright holders and we apologise if any have been overlooked. The publisher will be pleased to make the necessary arrangements at the first opportunity.

I would like to thank my family for their support in the preparation of this book, particularly my wife, Marie, for secretarial support and cheerful encouragement. I am also grateful to the publishing team at Nelson Thornes, in particular Eleanor O'Byrne and Carol Usher who initiated the project and to Sharon Thorn who coordinated the production of the book. I am grateful to Ian Holt and Patrick Organ for their contributions and advice and I wish also to thank AQA for their support.

Jim Breithaupt